Jonathan Edwards's Philosophy of History

Jonathan Edwards's Philosophy of History

THE REENCHANTMENT OF THE WORLD IN THE AGE OF ENLIGHTENMENT

Avihu Zakai

PRINCETON UNIVERSITY PRESS   PRINCETON AND OXFORD

Copyright © 2003 by Princeton University Press

Published by Princeton University Press, 41 William Street,
Princeton, New Jersey 08540
In the United Kingdom: Princeton University Press,
3 Market Place, Woodstock, Oxfordshire OX20 1SY

Library of Congress Cataloging-in-Publication Data

Zakai, Avihu.
Jonathan Edwards's philosophy of history : the reenchantment of the world in the Age of
Enlightenment / Avihu Zakai.
p. cm.
Includes bibliographical references and index.
ISBN 0-691-09654-6 (alk. paper)
1. Edwards, Jonathan, 1703–1758—Contributions in history of philosophy. 2. History—
Philosophy. 3. Enlightenment. I. Title.
B873 .Z35 2003
231.7'6'092—dc21   2002031742

British Library Cataloging-in-Publication Data is available

This book has been composed in Sabon and Centaur
Printed on acid-free paper. ∞

www.pupress.princeton.edu

Printed in the United States of America

10 9 8 7 6 5 4 3 2 1

To Yehoshua Arieli ————————————————————

AND TO THE CENTER OF THEOLOGICAL INQUIRY IN PRINCETON

WHERE MOST OF THE BOOK WAS WRITTEN

Contents

AW   *Apocalyptic Writings*, ed. Stephen Stein, vol. 5 of *The Works of Jonathan Edwards*

EccW   *Ecclesiastical Writings*, ed. David Hall, vol. 12 of *The Works of Jonathan Edwards*

EW   *Ethical Writings*, ed. Paul Ramsey, vol. 8 of *The Works of Jonathan Edwards*

FW   *Freedom of the Will*, ed. Paul Ramsey, vol. 1 of the *Works of Jonathan Edwards*

GA   *The Great Awakening*, ed. C. C. Goen, vol. 4 of *The Works of Jonathan Edwards*

HWR   *A History of the Work of Redemption*, ed. John F. Wilson, vol. 9 of *The Works of Jonathan Edwards*

JEAE   *Jonathan Edwards and the American Experience*, ed. Nathan O. Hatch and Harry S. Stout (New York: Oxford University Press, 1988)

LPW   *Letters and Personal Writings*, ed. George S. Claghorn, vol. 16 of *The Works of Jonathan Edwards*

MIS   *The 'Miscellanies': Entry Nos. a–z, aa–zz, 1–500*, ed. Thomas A. Schafer, vol. 13 of *The Works of Jonathan Edwards*

MISA   *The 'Miscellanies': Entry Nos. 501–832*, ed. Ava Chamberlain, vol. 18 of *The Works of Jonathan Edwards*

MISC   *The Miscellanies*, typescript on disk. Works of Jonathan Edwards Office, Yale Divinity School, New Haven, Connecticut

NOS   *Notes on Scriptures*, ed. Stephen J. Stein, vol. 15 of *The Works of Jonathan Edwards*

OS   *Original Sin*, ed. Clyde A. Holbrook, vol. 3 of *The Works of Jonathan Edwards*

RA   *Religious Affections*, ed. John E. Smith, vol. 2 of *The Works of Jonathan Edwards*

SDK   *Sermons and Discourses, 1720–1723*, ed. Wilson H. Kimnach, vol. 10 of *The Works of Jonathan Edwards*

SDL   *Sermons and Discourses, 1734–1738*, ed. M. X. Lesser, vol. 19 of *The Works of Jonathan Edwards*

SDM   *Sermons and Discourses, 1723–1729*, ed. Kenneth P. Minkema, vol. 14 of *The Works of Jonathan Edwards*

SDV   *Sermons and Discourses, 1730–1733*, ed. Mark Valeri, vol. 17 of *The Works of Jonathan Edwards*

SJE   *The Sermons of Jonathan Edwards: A Reader*, ed. Wilson H.
        Kimnach et al. (New Haven: Yale University Press, 1999)

SPW   *Scientific and Philosophical Writings*, ed., Wallace E. Anderson,
        vol. 6 of *The Works of Jonathan Edwards*

TW   *Typological Writings*, ed. Wallace E. Anderson and Mason I.
        Lowance, Jr., vol. 11 of *The Works of Jonathan Edwards*

RECENT YEARS have seen a flow of fresh and stimulating scholarly works devoted to the thought, influence, and relevance of Jonathan Edwards, whom Perry Miller called 'the greatest philosopher-theologian yet to grace the American scene.' Edwards is now widely recognized as America's most important theologian, and he is no less celebrated as a prominent philosopher, ethicist, and moralist. Given such prominence in the life of the mind in America, it is not surprising that many studies have attempted to assess Edwards's impact on his own time, his influence on later generations, and the legacy he bequeathed to Protestant religious culture in America. Edwards's theology and philosophy are still a matter of great scholarly interest today, and recent studies have dealt with almost every aspect of his thought. Strangely enough, however, so far there has been no serious attempt to explore Edwards's philosophy of history and to analyze the content and form of his distinct mode of historical thought.

The present study examines Edwards's sense of time and vision of history. It analyzes the development of Edwards's historical consciousness and the ideological context of his philosophy of salvation history. This dimension in Edwards's intellectual life demands serious attention. Without it much of his philosophy and theology would be unintelligible, and the significance he accorded to his actions, as well as the ultimate sacred historical meaning he attached to his own time, as evidenced by his decisive role in initiating, advancing, and promoting the Great Awakening, would remain uncomprehended. Edwards was the American Augustine, not least because like the church father he formulated a singular philosophy of history that exercised great influence on subsequent Christian generations and greatly conditioned their historical consciousness. In Edwards's case, his evangelical historiography had an abiding importance for American Protestant culture. His *History of the Work of Redemption* was the most popular manual of Calvinist theology in the nineteenth century. One of the main reasons for the great success of this work was that Edwards placed revival at the center of salvation history, habituating American Protestants to see religious awakening as the essence of providential history and the main manifestation of divine agency in worldly time. This evangelical theodicy of history signified that the heart of history is the revival, through which the Spirit of God consistently advances the work of redemption. So defined, these awakenings are the exclusive domain of God's will and power, and hence beyond the reach of human agency. Conceiving the locus of history in this way, Edwards made the phenomenon of revival the crucial element in the drama of salvation and redemption.

This philosophy of salvation history helped to create the revival tradition in America. For antebellum evangelists, Edwards's theological teleology of history provided the main source for understanding human history as a dramatic narrative propelled by a divine design and covenant of redemption. Such ideas caused later generations to see revivals as the main mark of divine redemptive activity in history, and hence to attach millennial and eschatological significance of the greatest proportion to awakening. In this sense Edwards influenced nineteenth-century evangelists' understanding of the coming of the kingdom. His philosophy of history was installed at the center of the predominant Protestant culture of America, and his theme of God's redemption of the world became the central meaning and significance of that culture.

The premise of the present study is that analysis of Edwards's historical thought will first of all recognize that the mental universe of this New England divine transcended his local setting in Northampton and the narrow intellectual life of provincial New England. More specifically, it was Edwards's reaction to the metaphysical and theological implications of Enlightenment historical narratives, which increasingly tended to set aside theistic considerations in the realms of morals and history, which led in part to the development of his redemptive mode of historical thought— the doctrine that the process of history depends entirely and exclusively on God's redemptive activity as manifested in a series of revivals throughout time, and not on autonomous human power. I attempt therefore to discuss the ideological origins of Edwards's historical thought in the broader context of the threat faced by the Christian theological teleology of history in the early modern period, with the emergence of a secular conception of history and the modern legitimacy of historical time. In contrast to the growing Enlightenment emphasis on human agency in determining the course of history, Edwards strove to return to God his preeminence within the order of time. Against the de-Christianization of history and the de-divination of the historical process, as evidenced in various Enlightenment historical accounts, Edwards looked for the reenthronement of God as the author and Lord of history, the reenchantment of the historical world.

Edwards fully understood the serious challenges posed by Enlightenment ideas to religious faith and experience. He was alarmed by the conception of history as a self-contained and independent domain, free from subordination to God and not affected by his ever-watchful eyes. With great dismay he observed that Enlightenment historical narratives not only deprived the realm of history of teleological ends and theological purposes, but stipulated that history did not manifest the presence of God's redemptive activity. In response, he constructed his own theological teleology of history, which celebrates God's glory and sovereignty in determining and regulating its course. By providing an alternative view of the meaning of history that would lead eventually to the reenchantment of the historical world, Edwards intended to demonstrate the infinite power of God's sovereignty in the order of time. Hence, against the Enlightenment notion of *historia humana*, Edwards declared that history is a space of sacred time designated by God from eternity for the execution of his work of redemption. In response to endeavors to liberate history from its traditional subservience to theology, Edwards contended that the entire historical process is inextricable from God's redemptive activity, and vice versa. Rather than conceiving history as the direct result of human action, and hence as a manifestation of immanent human progress, as Enlightenment historians believed, Edwards constructed it from the perspective of God and the manifestations of his redemptive activity in creation in the form of revivals and awakenings.

In such a theological and teleological context, history is designed by divine providence as a special sacred dimension of time meant solely for the accomplishment of the plan of redemption, and it should therefore be understood from the perspective of its maker and author. History is a sacred space of time destined from eternity for God's self-glorification— the display of the Deity's excellence in creation—as evidenced in his work of redemption; hence human beings' existence as well as their history is dependent on God. Edwards wished to demonstrate that the fate of human beings cannot be separated from divine action in time. Earthly, mundane events are intelligible only by reference to God's work of redemption. This theology of salvation history to a large extent determined Edwards's actions during the Great Awakening, and it is on the basis of this historical interpretation that he is considered the father of the great colonial revival of the 1740s and the putative father of American postmillennialism in general.

In order to present the content and form of Edwards's philosophy of history, I examine it within the wider ideological and theological context of his thought. I try in this book to convey something of the course and quality of Edwards's life of the mind, or to present an intellectual biography within which his philosophy of history may be best understood. Not only did he live in an age of rapid and dramatic intellectual changes that characterized early modern European history, such as produced the scientific revolution, the Enlightenment, deism, new theories of ethics and mortals, and so forth, but he self-consciously took upon himself a mission of their refutation, setting him apart from other Protestant evangelists. The historian of early modern European intellectual history and of early American history may trace through Edwards's many theological and ideological controversies the process that was to turn him into one of the most acute critics of the scientific culture of his time and the new concepts of ethics and modes of historical thought engendered by the Enlightenment.

This perspective naturally demanded that I concentrate on specific aspects of Edwards's universe of thought. I have not dealt systematically, for example, with his theology but have tried to explore it mainly in relation to his philosophy of history. Many excellent studies of Edwards have appeared in recent years, and what I have failed to address here others have treated with much skill and ability.

One of the many pleasures involved in research and writing is the opportunity to meet with scholars, to enhance relationships with old friends and to make new ones. While working on this study, I have incurred many debts and obligations to friends and colleagues and to various institutions and foundations. The writing actually began during my stay at the Center of Theological Inquiry (CTI). In this stimulating intellectual environment, the "garden of Eden," as the fellows usually describe this citadel of learning, first under the leadership of Dan Hardy, and later William Lazarat, and currently Wallace Allston, I met a group of scholars who inspired my own work and made an essential contribution to it in terms of shaping its final content and form. Among them, especially, James Buckley, David Dawson, Don Browning, Timothy McDermott, Gerald McDermott, George Lindbeck, John Coleman, George Hunsinger, Torrance Kirby, Sang Hyun Lee, Robert Jenson, Victor Nuovo, Peter Ochs, Peter Scott, Mark Reasoner, Anthony Ugolnik, Max Stackhouse, and Michael Welker. I owe special thanks to Gerald McDermott, a great Edwardsean scholar, who not only enthusiastically introduced me to Edwards's universe of thought and shared important insights with me, but showed me the real meaning of Christian charity in various and mysterious ways. Kenneth Minkema, executive editor of *The Works of Jonathan Edwards* at Yale, proved, as so many other Edwardsean scholars have found, indispensable in terms of locating sources pertaining to Edwards's life and thought. Without his expertise, this study would have suffered from many errors and shortcomings. At Princeton University Press, I owe special thanks to my editors Thomas LeBien and Fred Appel, and to Maura Roessner, editorial assistant, and Anne Reifsnyder, production editor. They never ceased to believe in the worth of this project and followed it closely until its final production.

Several colleagues and friends read the whole or part of my work and offered comments and criticism. Among them, James Buckley, Gerald McDermott, Peter Scott, David Weinstein, Timothy McDermott, Yehoshua Arieli, Shira Wolosky, Ayval Ramati, Menahem Blondheim, Michael

Heyd, Michael Kramer, Michael Zuckerman, Torrance Kirby, George Lindbeck, Louis Dupré, and Neil Kamil. I am particularly grateful to John F.
Wilson. His suggestions and criticism helped sharpen the argument in a
legion of ways. I owe special thanks to Jack P. Greene and Walter Nugent
for their long and constant support regarding this book.

Numerous librarians gave me constant assistance and spared no time or
effort in locating books and manuscripts; Regina Gruzman at the Hebrew
University Library, Mount Scopus; Hanna Caine-Braunschvig at the Van
Leer Institute, Jerusalem; Bill Harris at Luce Library, and Kate Skrebu-
tenas at Speer Library (Princeton Theological Seminary) went out of their
way in helping me track down sources, books, and articles. Special thanks
are due to the staff at the Center of Theological Inquiry while I was resident there: Kate Le Van, Maureen Montgomery, and Linda Sheldon. Finally, I am most grateful to my editor for many years, Mira Frankel Reich,
and my devoted assistant Shira Gvir.

Over the years several institutions have provided me with generous fi-
nancial support, enabling me to pursue my study of Edwards: an American Research Fellowship from the United States-Israel Educational Foundation (Fulbright Grant); a research grant from the Israel Science
Foundation, the Israel Academy of Sciences and Humanities; a research
grant from the Center of Theological Inquiry, Princeton; a fellowship
from the Center for Theology and the Natural Sciences, Berkeley, California; and a fellowship from the Templeton Foundation.

Part of chapter 2 appeared as "The Conversion of Jonathan Edwards,"
in the *Journal of Presbyterian History* 76, no. 1 (Summer 1998): 1–12,
and part of chapter 3 as "Jonathan Edwards and the Language of Nature:
The Re-Enchantment of the World in the Age of Scientific Reasoning," in
the *Journal of Religious History* 26, no. 1 (February 2002): 15–41 (both
in somewhat different versions). I am grateful to the editors of these jour-
nals for permission to use this material here.

Jonathan Edwards's Philosophy of History

Introduction_____

The American Augustine

The history of the development of man's consciousness of history involves a large aspect of the whole evolution of his experience. It is a
major part of his attempt to adjust himself to the world in which
his life is set.
 (Herbert Butterfield, *The Origins of History*, 1981)

[The Enlightenment mind] refuses to recognize an absolutely supernatural or an absolutely super-historical sphere. . . . History bears
the torch for the Enlightenment; [because it was liberated] from the
bonds of scripture dogmatically interpreted and the orthodoxy of
the preceding centuries.
 (Ernst Cassirer, *The Philosophy of the Enlightenment*, 1955)

[Edwards's philosophy of history] makes him stand out against his
eighteenth-century Enlightenment background more sharply than
his other writings. Herein may lie his most impressive originality.
 (Sydney E. Ahlstrom, "Theology in America," 1961)

THE PREMISE of this study is that a careful examination of the content
and form of Jonathan Edwards's philosophy of history is warranted and
in some respects long overdue. Edwards's reputation rests above all on
the insights he advanced in his many theological and philosophical writings. In contrast to this extensive corpus of works, on only one occasion
did he seriously undertake the writing of a full-scale historical narrative,
entitled *A History of the Work of Redemption*—a series of thirty sermons
preached before his Northampton congregation during the spring and
summer of 1739.[1] This work constituted the fullest and most systematic
exposition of his philosophy of salvation history, although he continued
to grapple with the issue of divine agency in history in the many *Miscellanies* he wrote from 1739 until his death. Yet, as I shall argue, behind the
composition of this narrative stood many years of struggle to define properly the relationship between the order of grace and the order of time,

---

[1] Jonathan Edwards, *A History of the Work of Redemption*, in *HWR*. The best exposition of Edwards's redemption discourse can be found in John F. Wilson's introduction to
the above volume. Throughout this study, as the reader will recognize, I owe a great debt to

redemption and history, or between divine agency and the course of history. Viewed in the context of the growth of Edwards's historical consciousness, the narrative of history presented in the 1739 sermons reflects the maturing of his historical thought, which constituted an essential dimension of his life of the mind. Without it much of Edwards's universe of thought is unintelligible and the significance he attached to the historical moment in which he lived would be difficult to grasp.

A knowledge of Edwards's historical thought is necessary to an interpretation of the meaning he gave to his actions, the prominence he accorded revivals within salvation history, and the decisive role he assigned to awakenings in the course of sacred providential history. Here lies Edwards's importance in inaugurating the revival tradition in American history.[2] Indeed, "no one person was more responsible than Edwards" in shaping the character of the New England revival of 1740–43.[3] This applies not only to his actions during this revival, but also, and most important, to the historical interpretation he offered for the eighteenth-century Protestant evangelical awakening in Europe in general and the Great Awakening in particular, envisioning them as a singular moment in sacred, salvation history. It is the argument of this study that an examination of Edwards's philosophy of history, or his distinct redemptive mode of historical thought—the doctrine that the process of history depends exclusively on God's redemptive activity in time and not on human power and autonomy—is necessary not only to the discussion of his sense of time and his vision of history as they appear in the *History of the Work of Redemption*, but also to an understanding of the significance he conferred upon the Great Awakening of 1740–43 within salvation history, and of his zeal in defending it against every adversary.

A distinct mode of historical thought pervaded Edwards's life of the mind, and was chiefly responsible for the content and form of his historical consciousness, or his "space of experience" and "horizon of expectation."[4] Nowhere is this argument more supported than in the historical

---

Professor Wilson, who brilliantly positions Edwards's historical thought within the overall context of his philosophical theology.

[2] For the place of Edwards's *History of the Work of Redemption* in the history of religion and culture in America, see Wilson, introduction, in *HWR*, pp. 79–100; and, more recently, Joseph A. Conforti, *Jonathan Edwards, Religious Tradition, & American Culture* (Chapel Hill: University of North Carolina Press, 1995). See also the various essays in *Edwards in Our Time: Jonathan Edwards and the Shaping of American Religion*, ed. Sang Hyun Lee and Allan C. Guelzo (Grand Rapids: Eerdmans, 1999).

[3] Sydney E. Ahlstrom, "Theology in America: A Historical Survey," in *The Shaping of American Religion*, ed. James W. Smith et al., 2 vols. (Princeton: Princeton University Press, 1961), I, p. 246.

[4] Reinhart Koselleck, " 'Space of Experience' and 'Horizon of Expectations': Two Historical Categories," in *Futures Past: On the Semantics of Historical Time* (Cambridge, Mass.: MIT Press, 1985), pp. 267–88.

justification he offered for the Great Awakening. Behind his defense of that event, which so radically transformed religious life and experience in eighteenth-century New England, stood a well-defined and coherent philosophy of history, an evangelical historiography, which informed his actions and was responsible for the historical meaning he conferred on them. The works he wrote during that awakening, such as *Sinners in the Hands of an Angry God* (1741), *The Distinguishing Marks of a Work of the Spirit of God* (1741), and *Some Thoughts Concerning the Present Revival of Religion in New England* (1742), can only be appreciated as deeply animated by a special sense of time and vision of history. Further, Edwards's understanding of his own role in the revival, and the high expectations he developed of it, were strongly informed by a singular historical vision, enabling him to define the Great Awakening, being an integral part of the great eighteenth-century Protestant evangelical awakening, as a decisive moment in sacred providential history, thus rescuing it from dismissal as a provincial event pertaining only to the religious history of colonial New England. On the basis of this historical understanding he was able in his thinking to transform the New England revival and other contemporary revivals in Europe into crucial acts in the drama of the history of salvation and redemption. Since the Great Awakening inaugurated the revival tradition in America, it is all the more important to understand the historical meaning assigned to it by one of its most ardent champions.

The purpose of the present study is to enhance the understanding of Edwards's ideology of history by establishing some contexts within which it may be best studied and analyzed. It will provide a series of contextualizations, an exploration of his intellectual life in a succession of settings through which the *History of the Work of Redemption* may be best studied and understood. The historical narrative will be analyzed first within the slow and gradual growth of Edwards's historical consciousness before he came to compose this work. Such an investigation is necessary in order to follow the development of his ideology of history and of his unique redemptive mode of historical thought. Further, I place Edwards's philosophy of history in the wider context of sacred ecclesiastical history, as a Christian mode of historical thought. Edwards was an heir of Christian theological teleology of history, salvation history, although he transformed it radically in order to proclaim God as the author and Lord of history.

An account of Edwards's philosophy of history demands reference to the rise of new modes of historical thought in the early modern period. It was, in part, in response to the emergence of new historical explanations that Edwards constructed his own narrative and in reaction to them that he formulated his redemptive interpretation of history. The allusion, more specifically, is to the Enlightenment historical narratives that led increasingly to the exclusion of theistic considerations from the realm of history.[5] Response to this constituted, among other things, an important dimension of Edwards's *History of the Work of Redemption*.

Much of Edwards's intellectual development can be characterized, in his own words, as a long struggle "against most of the prevailing errors of the present day," which tended to "the utter subverting of the gospel of Christ."[6] During his time, he believed, "every evangelical doctrine is run down," and many "bold attempts are made" against "Christ, and the religion he taught."[7] Many themes in his philosophical and theological enterprise were developed in response to the decline of Christian thought and belief in face of the rise of new modes of thought in early modern history, among them, new scientific explanations of the essential nature of reality, the novel theories of ethics and morals, and the Enlightenment historical narratives. Edwards's universe of thought thus clearly transcended his local setting and the narrow intellectual and religious life of provincial New England. Such was the case, for example, with his response to the new scientific thought and imagination coming out of Europe, traditionally referred to as the scientific revolution,[8] as is evident in his various scientific and philosophical writings.[9] In these works on natural philosophy he reacted against certain metaphysical and theological principles that often accompanied the scientific revolution, leading to the growing detachment of God from his creation and contributing to the disenchantment of the world. This was also the case with the response in Edwards's ethical writings[10] to new theories in ethics and morals, such as the British school of moral sense, whose proponents, the philosophers Francis Hutcheson (1694–1746), David Hume (1711–76), and others, rejected the traditional view that morality is based on the will of God,

---

[5] The development of the various Enlightenment narratives of history is discussed, among others, in Karen O'Brien, *Narratives of Enlightenment: Cosmopolitan History from Voltaire to Gibbon* (Cambridge: Cambridge Universtiy Press, 1997); Philip Hicks, *Neoclassical History and English Culture: From Clarendon to Hume* (London: Macmillan, 1996); and J.G.A. Pocock, *Barbarism and Religion: The Enlightenments of Edward Gibbon, 1737–1764* (Cambridge: Cambridge University Press, 1999); idem, *Barbarism and Religion: Narratives of Civil Government* (Cambridge: Cambridge University Press, 1999).

[6] Edwards, "Letter to the Trustees of the College of New Jersey," 1757, in *LPW*, p. 727.

[7] Edwards, "To the Reverend Thomas Foxcroft," February 11, 1757, in *LPW*, p. 695.

[8] In recent years historians have begun to question the very concept of *the* scientific revolution, and even altogether "to undermine one of our most hallowed explanatory frameworks, that of the Scientific Revolution." See B.J.T. Dobbs, "Newton as Final Cause and First Mover," in *Rethinking the Scientific Revolution*, ed. Margaret J. Osler (Cambridge: Cambridge University Press, 2000), p. 25.

[9] Edwards's various works on natural philosophy appeared in *Scientific and Philosophical Writings*, in *SPW*.

[10] Edwards, *Ethical Writings*, in *EW*.

and maintained that morality depends on human nature, or that virtue should be considered natural to human beings, and hence that morals come naturally to man.[11] The same can be said about Edwards's lifelong battle against deism and Arminianism.[12]

Edwards's philosophy of history should be understood as well in light of his reaction to intellectual developments in the early modern European period. His *History of the Work of Redemption* was composed within a specific context, which witnessed the gradual exclusion of religious thought and belief from history, the physical world, and the realm of morals. More specifically, the formulation of Edwards's redemptive mode of historical thought may be seen, in part, as a response to the Enlightenment narratives of history, which rejected the Christian sense of time and vision of history and thus posed a threat to traditional theological teleology of history. Against the growing de-Christianization of the world of history and the de-divination of the historical process, as evidenced in the various Enlightenment narratives of history, Edwards's quest was for the reenthronement of God as the sole author and Lord of history.

Edwards's reaction to the rise of new modes of historical thought in early modern history may be understood in light of the grave ramifications the Enlightenment project posed for traditional Christian thought and belief, especially in regard to the realm of history. Generally speaking, the Enlightenment "was the revolution of man's autonomous potentialities over against heteronomous powers which were no longer convincing."[13] This is evident in the new attitude toward history and the growing importance attached to human autonomy and freedom in determining its course. The Enlightenment mind "refuse[d] to recognize an absolutely supernatural or an absolutely super-historical sphere," and attempted to

---

[11] Knud Haakonssen, *Natural Law and Moral Philosophy: From Grotius to the Scottish Enlightenment* (Cambridge: Cambridge University Press, 1996), p. 66. See also Norman Fiering, *Jonathan Edwards's Moral Thought and Its British Context* (Chapel Hill: University of North Carolina Press, 1981).

[12] Edwards's lifelong struggle against deism is described most recently in Gerald R. McDermott, *Jonathan Edwards Confronts the Gods: Christian Theology, Enlightenment Religion, and Non-Christian Faiths* (New York: Oxford University Press, 2000); and Ava Chamberlain, introduction, in *MISA*, especially pp. 24–34. For Edwards's battle against Arminianism, see Perry Miller, *Jonathan Edwards* (Amherst: University of Massachusetts Press, 1981 [1949]); and C. C. Goen, introduction, in *GA*, pp. 4–19. A study that views Edwards's theology as an apology for the Christian faith and a response to the Enlightenment is Michael J. McClymond, *Encounters with God: An Approach to the Theology of Jonathan Edwards* (New York: Oxford University Press, 1998). For Edwards and the philosophy of the Enlightenment, see Leon Chai, *Jonathan Edwards and the Limits of Enlightenment Philosophy* (New York: Oxford University Press, 1998).

[13] Paul Tillich, *A History of Christian Thought: From Its Judaic and Hellenistic Origins to Existentialism*, ed. Carl E. Braaten (New York: Simon and Schuster, 1968), p. 323.

free historical thought "from the bonds of scripture dogmatically interpreted and the orthodoxy of the preceding centuries."[14] Instead of ordering the structure of history on the dimension of "sacred time,"[15] or the operation of divine providence, Enlightenment historical narratives were based on secular, "historical time."[16] Hume, Voltaire, Bolingbroke, and Gibbon, to name only a few, attempted to "liberate history writing from its subservience to theology" and to free it from the theological view that conceived "the course of human history as the realization of a divine plan."[17] Instead of seeing the historical process as contingent on a metaphysical reality beyond and above it, Enlightenment historians attached the highest importance to human beings' actions and deeds in determining the progress of history. This process of "de-divination of the world" meant that traditional Christian symbols were "no longer revelatory of the immersion of the finite world in the transcendent."[18] No longer considered as the narrative of a God-given providential plan or as revealing the teleological scheme of time, the historical realm was defined more and more as a space of time intended for the realization of the possibilities and abilities inherent in the nature of human beings. "For the men of the Enlightenment the idea of world-history was particularly congenial. It fitted in with their notion of progress, their view of mankind, advancing steadily from primitive barbarism to reason and virtue and civilization."[19] In place of the religious vision of history as the drama, or tragedy, of salvation and redemption, which would materialize only *beyond* history, historical thought during the Enlightenment developed the concept of "progress," or the notion of an immanent human advance based on the belief that utopian visions regarding human freedom and happiness could be fulfilled *within* history. *Historia humana*,[20] or the annals of human history, gradually replaced salvation history in the European mind.

For religious thought and practice, such a transformation regarding the historical realm carried profound consequences. "In much the same way that the world became the object of scientific inquiry in the sixteenth and

[14] Ernst Cassirer, *The Philosophy of the Enlightenment* (Boston: Beacon, 1962), p. 199.

[15] J.G.A. Pocock, "Modes of Action and their Pasts in Tudor and Stuart England," in *National Consciousness, History and Political Culture in Early Modern Europe*, ed. Orest Ranum (Baltimore: Johns Hopkins University Press, 1975), pp. 98–117.

[16] Reinhart Koselleck, "Modernity and the Planes of Historicity," in *Futures Past: On the Semantic of Historical Time* (Cambridge, Mass.: MIT Press, 1985), p. 5.

[17] Peter Gay, *The Enlightenment: The Science of Freedom* (New York: Norton, 1977), pp. 372–73.

[18] Eric Voegelin, *From Enlightenment to Revolution*, ed. John H. Hallowell (Durham, N.C.: Duke University Press, 1975), p. 21.

[19] G. Barraclough, "Universal History" (1962), as quoted in Sidney Pollard, *The Idea of Progress* (Harmondsworth: Penguin, 1971), p. 33.

[20] Koselleck, "Modernity and the Planes of Historicity," p. 10.

seventeenth centuries through a process of desacralisation, so too, religious practices" were "demystified by the imposition of *natural laws*. As the physical world ceased to be a theatre in which the drama of creation was constantly re-directed by divine intervention, human expressions of religious faith came increasingly to be seen as outcomes of natural processes rather than the work of God or of Satan and his legions."[21] Once considered the sole source and locus for human life, experience, and expectations, religious thought and belief were increasingly pushed out of the realm of nature and history. The "history of religion since the seventeenth century can be seen as the driving-back of faith from history, from the physical world, and from the realm of morals." Thus, "religion, withdrawing from its claim to give objective truth about the nature of reality in all its aspects, ends by seeking to stimulate certain sorts of inner feeling in those who care for that sort of thing."[22] Having based their historical narratives on the secular, historical time dimension, in contrast to Christian sacred time, or the time dimension of grace, Enlightenment historians refused to assign divine agency an exclusive role in determining the passing of time. They thus arrived at the de-Christianization of history.

Since Edwards knew of and was familiar with the main arguments of Enlightenment historians, an analysis of the content and form of his ideology of history cannot be based only on the immediate context of his life in Northampton. The best presentation of such a limited approach is that of Perry Miller, who said that the *History of the Work of Redemption* "definitely embodies Edwards's time and place; it is the history of Northampton writ large. It is a cosmic realization of the communal revival" of 1734–35 in that town.[23] Apart, however, from the problem of finding too clear and easy a causal relationship between text and social context,[24] this is indeed a strange assertion from one of the staunchest advocates of intellectual history and the autonomy of the history of ideas,[25] who once

[21] Peter Harrison, *"Religion" and the Religions in the English Enlightenment* (Cambridge: Cambridge University Press, 1990), p. 5.

[22] Keith Ward, *Religion & Revelation: A Theology of Revelation in the World's Religions* (Oxford: Oxford University Press, 1994), p. 284.

[23] Miller, *Jonathan Edwards*, p. 315. The same approach can be found in Alan Heimert, *Religion and the American Mind from the Great Awakening to the Revolution* (Cambridge, Mass.: Harvard University Press, 1996), pp. 98–99.

[24] Quentin Skinner has warned historians not to jump to the conclusion that it suffices to study a given text by simply examining the social context in which it was composed. See Skinner, "Meaning and Understanding in the History of Ideas," *History and Theory* 7 (1969): 3–53.

[25] On Perry Miller's overall approach to American history, see Avihu Zakai, "Epiphany at Matadi: Perry Miller's *Orthodoxy in Massachusetts* and the Meaning of American History," *Reviews in American History* 4 (December 1985): 627–41; and "Perry Miller," in *The Dictionary of Historians* (Oxford: Basil Blackwell, 1988), pp. 279–81.

claimed "I have difficulty imagining that anyone can be a historian without realizing that history itself is part of the life of the mind."[26] I argue to the contrary that Edwards's theological and teleological interpretation of universal history transcended his local setting in provincial New England. It ought to be viewed, among other things, in the wider context of his response to the challenge of Enlightenment historical narratives, and his ambition to refute the growing disenchantment of the world.

Edwards owned and read many works by Enlightenment historians,[27] among them Pierre Bayle's *Historical and Critical Dictionary* (1702), Samuel Pufendorf's *An Introduction to the History of the Principal Kingdoms and States of Europe* (1702), Henry St. John, Lord Bolingbroke's *Remarks on the History of England* (1731) and *Letters on the Study and Use of History* (1752), Gilbert Burnet's *History of his Own Time* (1724–34), John Oldmixions's *Critical History of England* (1724), Paul de Rapin-Thoyras's *Histoire d'Angleterre* (1721–31), and David Hume's *Essays Moral, Political and Literary* (1742), which included "Of the Study of History." In these works Edwards discovered, to his great dismay, that divine agency was no longer considered intrinsic to history. In fact, these writers found religion a great obstacle to the development of human institutions, the advance of civil society, and the fostering of reason and freedom, which became the hallmark of the Enlightenment project. "The 'Enlightenment narrative' " was "both a historiography of state and a historiography of society";[28] its proponents were skeptical of the "chronology of Christian universal history." Instead, they endeavored "to modify or transform their readers' sense of national self-awareness through the writing of narrative history."[29]

Acquaintance with the varieties of Enlightenment historical narrative enabled Edwards to assess its threat to the Christian theory of history. For example, in the *Historical and Critical Dictionary*, Pierre Bayle, the French philosopher who was also a pioneer of disinterested, critical history, "carries out the 'Copernican Revolution' in the realm of historical science." Instead of assuming that all historical facts are based on the authority of the Bible, and that the validity of the scriptures in turn rests on that of the church, whose authority rests on tradition, Bayle "no longer bases history on some dogmatically given objective content which he finds in the Bible or in the doctrine of the Church." His influential *Dictionary*

---

[26] Perry Miller, preface, *Errand Into the Wilderness* (Cambridge, Mass.: Harvard University Press, 1976), p. ix.

[27] See Edwards, "Catalogue of Reading," typescript on disk, Works of Jonathan Edwards Office, Yale Divinity School, New Haven, Conn.

[28] Pocock, *Barbarism and Religion: Narratives of Civil Government*, pp. 2–8.

[29] O'Brien, *Narratives of Enlightenment*, pp. 10, 1.

was not a mere treasure of knowledge but directly challenged traditional religious historical interpretation. "His sharp and unsparing analytical mind freed history once and for all from the bonds of creed and placed it on an independent footing."[30] This is evident, for example, in the entry on "David," where Bayle declared: "It is perfectly permissible for a private person like myself to judge facts contained in Scripture when they are not expressly qualified by the Holy Ghost."[31]

Likewise, Edwards owned Samuel Pufendorf's *An Introduction to the History of the Principal Kingdoms and States of Europe*, where the German historian and the founder of modern natural law praised the value of universal history, that is, of Europe, for the political education of the ruling elite. He emphasized the need "to understand modern history," or the history of the modern "nations" of Europe as well as their various forms of government.[32] The uses of studying history are thus primarily political and social, and much less theological and religious. The same can be said about David Hume, who in his essay "Of the Study of History" claimed that history's main use is to reveal the progress of "human society" from "its infancy . . . towards arts and sciences" and to present "all human race, from the beginning of time" in order to improve human "knowledge" and "wisdom."[33] *Historia humana*, the annals of human institutions, laws, manners, nations, and so on, in contrast to the sacred, became the enterprise of the Enlightenment. Constructed primarily as the narrative of human action, it refused to accept the religious and theological interpretation of history. The course of history was not conceived as dealing primarily with the narrative of God's action in time, to which the deeds of human beings were at best ancillary and might be irrelevant; rather, historical explication was based more and more on human action and conduct. Thus, Hume wrote that the chief use of "history" is "to discover the constant and universal principles of human nature, by showing men in all varieties of circumstances and situations," enabling us to "become acquainted with the regular spring of human action and behavior."[34] Likewise, William Warburton, bishop of Gloucester (1698–1779), argued that "the knowledge of human nature" is "the noblest qualifica-

---

[30] Cassirer, *The Philosophy of the Enlightenment*, pp. 207–8.

[31] Pierre Bayle, "David," in *Historical and Critical Dictionary*, trans. Richard H. Popkin (Indianapolis: Bobbs-Merrill, 1965), pp. 62–63.

[32] Samuel Pufendorf, *An Introduction to the History of the Principal Kingdoms and States of Europe* (1702), in *Versions of History: From Antiquity to the Enlightenment*, ed. Donald R. Kelley (New Haven: Yale University Press, 1991), pp. 435–38.

[33] David Hume, *Essays, Moral, Political and Literary*, 2 vols. (London: Longmans, 1882), II, pp. 388–91.

[34] David Hume, "History as Guide," in *The Portable Enlightenment Reader*, ed. Isaac Kramnick (New York: Penguin, 1995), p. 359.

tions for the historian."[35] In contrast, therefore, to sacred history, whose primary task was to exhibit the actions of divine agency in the world, or to reveal the divine plan determining human life and existence and of which world history is simply a product, the Enlightenment narrative emphasized human freedom and autonomy in the shaping of history. It dealt mainly with civil society, irrespective of the theological and religious consequences.

The writing of civil history, of civil government and society, instead of the sacred history of God's providence and the annals of the church, was the focus of the Enlightenment historical narrative. This can be seen, for example, in *Remarks on the History of England* by Henry St. John, first Viscount Bolingbroke. In this work, published in weekly installments in 1730–31, Bolingbroke deals almost exclusively with human institutions, or "the spirit which created and has constantly preserved or retrieved, the original freedom of the British and Saxon constitutions."[36] Further, in Ephraim Chambers's *Cyclopaedia; or an Universal Dictionary of Arts and Sciences* (1728), another book Edwards owned,[37] the English forerunner of the French *Encyclopédie* made the distinction between *"History"* in general and "Sacred *history*." The first deals with the *"history of nature"* as well as "the *history of actions* . . . either of a single person, a nation, or several persons and nations," and the second "lays before us the mysteries and ceremonies of religion, visions or appearances of the Deity, etc. miracles, and other supernatural things, whereof God alone is the author." Chambers added a third category, *"Civil history,"* which deals with "peoples, states, republics, communities, cities, etc."[38] This division clearly displays the growing erosion in the Christian narrative of history.

The development of civil history is further evident in many works dealing with English history. Edwards owned and read many of them and could find there that the divine agency was no longer considered intrinsic to history. Bishop Gilbert Burnet's *History of his Own Time* "recorded the triumph, in 1688–9, and precarious survival, during the reign of Anne, of Whig and Protestant ideals." Edwards possessed also John Oldmixions's radical Whig *Critical History of England*, which was "centrally preoccupied with the country's constitution, right and liberties." The

[35] William Warburton, as cited in Hicks, *Neoclassical History and English Culture*, p. 142.
[36] Lord Bolingbroke, "Remarks on the History of England," in *Lord Bolingbroke: Historical Writings*, ed. Isaac Kramnick (Chicago: University of Chicago Press, 1972), p. 177.
[37] Edwards, "To Unknown Correspondent," 1746, in *LPW*, p. 202. See also Edwards, "Unpublished Letter on Assurance and Participation in the Divine Nature," in *EW*, p. 639.
[38] Ephraim Chambers, *Cyclopaedia; or an Universal Dictionary of Arts and Sciences* (1728), in *Versions of History*, ed. Donald R. Kelley, p. 441.

same can be said about the most popular historical work to appear in England at the time, Paul de Rapin-Thoyras's *Histoire d'Angleterre*; it "provided the Whig with a secular and scholarly account of the origins of the nation's mixed and liberal constitution." Because of the enormous popularity of the work during the first half of the eighteenth century, Rapin's history played an important role "in the political education of the nation," thus helping forge England's "national self-awareness in this period."[39]

More serious, though, for traditional religious thought and belief were the Enlightenment historians' denunciations of the Christian interpretation of history. Hume argued, for example, that religion "has contributed to render CHRISTENDOM the scene of religious wars and divisions. Religions," and this includes Christianity, "arise in ages totally ignorant and barbarous" and "consist mostly of traditional tales and fictions." Such negative views do not refer only to the past. On the contrary, in "modern times, parties of religion are more furious and enraged than the most cruel factions that ever arose from interest and ambition."[40] Hume denounced ecclesiastical historians' interpretation of history: "The Monks, who were the only annalists" during the medieval period, "lived remote from public affairs, considered the civil transactions as entirely subordinate to the ecclesiastical, and besides partaking of the ignorance and barbarity . . . were strongly infected with credulity, with the love of wonder, and with propensity to imposture; vices almost inseparable from their profession, and manner of life."[41] These unfavorable characterizations of Christianity and of ecclesiastical historians obviously left no room for accepting the traditional Christian interpretation of history. Instead they emphasized its destructive role in terms of the growth of civil society in Europe and the development of European civilization in general.

Also serious as regards the traditional Christian narrative of history was the threat to the authority of the Bible itself as a historical source, and the attack on its inability to portray adequately the "history" of the "first ages." This was the major assault levied by Bolingbroke on ecclesiastical history in the *Letters on the Study and Use of History*. The "historical part" of the "Old Testament," wrote Bolingbroke, "must be reputed insufficient" to the study of history "by every candid and impartial man" since the Jews had been "slaves to the Egyptians, Assyrians, Medes, and Persians." Not only is the Bible an insufficient and unreliable source, but

---

[39] O'Brien, *Narratives of Enlightenment*, pp. 14–18; Hicks, *Neoclassical History and English Culture*, pp. 126–30, 146–50.

[40] David Hume, "Of Parties in General" (1741), in *David Hume: Essays Moral, Political and Literary*, ed. Eugene F. Miller, pp. 62–63.

[41] Hume, *The History of England from the Invasion of Julius Caesar to the Revolution in 1688*, 6 vols. (Indianapolis: Liberty Classics, 1983), I, p. 25.

"history has been purposely and systematically falsified in all ages" by church historians. Moreover, "ecclesiastical authority has led the way in this corruption" of history "in all ages." In the pagan world, for example, how "monstrous were the absurdities that the priesthood imposed on the ignorance and superstition of mankind." Since "the foundations of Judaism and Christianity" were not built on truth, but on "voluntary and involuntary errors," it is no wonder that "numberless fables have been invented [by ecclesiastical historians] to raise, to embellish, and to support" faith. Instead of providing historical truths, the Christian interpretation of history has led to the "abuse of history": "Deliberate, systematical lying has been practised and encouraged from age to age" by church historians, "and among all the pious frauds that have been employed to maintain a reverence and zeal for their religion in the minds of men, this abuse of history has been the principal and most successful." Sadly, noted Bolingbroke, this "lying spirit has gone from ecclesiastical to other historians."[42]

Edwards was fully aware of these trends in European historical thought. Continually acquiring new books from England, and always closely following intellectual developments within the European republic of letters, he was by no means a novice in the thinking of Enlightenment historians. In their works he discovered a growing trend to play down the role of religion in history, and he saw that the de-Christianization of history was leading to its de-divination. In formulating his historical narrative, Edwards sought to show how inextricable religious faith and experience are from history. William James expressed a somewhat similar view, with which Edwards would certainly have concurred, when he said: "Religion, occupying herself with personal destinies and thus in contact with the only absolute realities which we know, must necessarily play an eternal part in human history."[43] To Edwards this meant, among others, that the realm of history cannot be understood without taking account of divine agency and redemptive activity.

One should understand the development of Edwards's historical thought, and his goal in composing the *History of the Work of Redemption*, as well as its particular content and form, within this broad ideological context. Reacting against Enlightenment historical narratives, he asked: "Shall we prize a history that gives us a clear account of some great earthly prince or mighty warrior, as of Alexander the Great or Julius Caesar; or the duke of Marlborough, and shall we not prize the history

---

[42] Bolingbroke, "Letters on the Study and Use of History," in *Lord Bolingbroke: Historical Writings*, ed. Isaac Kramnick, pp. 35–36, 51, 53–55.

[43] William James, *The Varieties of Religious Experience* (New York: Penguin, 1984), p. 503.

that God has given us of the glorious kingdom of his son, Jesus Christ, the prince and savior of the world."[44] This belief stood behind Edwards's historical project, and constituted, among other things, such as biblical and apocalyptic interpretation, the heart of his narrative of history as it appeared in the *History of the Work of Redemption*.

Early in his life Edwards conceived the doctrine of "God's absolute sovereignty,"[45] and coined the term God's "work of redemption,"[46] and ever afterward he wrestled with the meaning of divine agency in time, redemption, and history. Striving to understand the mystery of divine activity in creation, and attempting to unveil God's "grand scheme" in history, he sought to reveal the "historical order" by which the Deity executes its plan in history through "the great work and successive dispensations of the infinitely wise God in time."[47] During his long search to understand the nature and meaning of divine agency in the order of history, he came to the conclusion that revivals, being "special seasons of mercy"[48] or grace, constitute a unique dimension of sacred time, or epochs of time, *kairos*, in history. Through the effusion of the Spirit, God orders major and decisive turning points in salvation history in terms of fulfilled or realized time. These constitute the main stages in sacred providential history, and only through these can history, its goal and destiny, be properly understood.

Paul Tillich made a distinction between *chronos*—"quantitative time," or "clock time, time which is measured"—and *kairos*—"the qualitative time of the occasion, the right time," such as "the right time for the coming of Christ"—and made special use of it in his philosophy of history.[49] *Kairos* is a special time or epoch in salvation history in which the eternal judges and transforms the temporal.[50] Before Tillich, however, Edwards had already proposed this concept and made it the cornerstone of his philosophy of history. Edwards's historical narrative deals primarily with the "rise and continued progress of the dispensation of grace towards fallen mankind,"[51] or the outpouring of the Spirit of God as "dispensa-

[44] Edwards, *History of the Work of Redemption*, p. 291.

[45] Edwards, *Personal Narrative*, in *LPW*, p. 792.

[46] Edwards, *Miscellany* no. 38 (c. 1723), p. 221.

[47] Edwards, "Letter to the Trustees of the College of New Jersey," in *LPW*, pp. 727–28.

[48] Edwards, *History of the Work of Redemption*, pp. 511, 143.

[49] Tillich, *A History of Christian Thought*, p. 1.

[50] Compare Tillich's distinction with the more secular approach of Walter Benjamin: "History is the subject of a structure whose site is not homogenous, empty time, but time filled by the presence of the now." See Benjamin, "Theses on the Philosophy of History," in *Illuminations: Essays and Reflections*, ed. Hannah Arendt (New York: Schocken, 1969), p. 261. In Edwards's case, historical events acquired their meaning and significance from a meta-historical structure.

[51] Edwards, *History of the Work of Redemption*, p. 285.

tions of providence" and, correspondingly, with its immediate historical manifestations in the form of decisive periods, or epochs, of awakenings as they appear in "special seasons of mercy"[52] throughout history. This was Edwards's response to the Enlightenment fashioning of new modes of secular, historical thought.

Within this broad context of early modern history I seek to locate, in part, the origins of Edwards's theology of history. Accordingly, I portray him not so much as an "American theologian," or as "America's Theologian,"[53] a trend dominant in modern historiography, but as an important early modern theologian and philosopher who took upon himself the task of responding to the growing disenchantment of the historical world. The present study, then, takes into account not only the narrow setting of Edwards's life in provincial New England, but also examines his historical thought in the wider intellectual context of his defense of the Christian ideology of history in a world approaching the gradual separation of God and his creation and in an age becoming increasingly hostile to Christ and his church.

Seen in this context, in the line of Christian theologians I can find no better comparison with Edwards's historical endeavor than St. Augustine.[54] A case can be made that Edwards's ideology resembles that of Eusebius Pamphili (c. 260–c. 340), the father of ecclesiastical history, especially as regards the use of divine dispensation to describe divine activity in the realm of history. Yet the profound difference in the historical context within which each work was composed obviously influenced the nature of their historical narrative and their interpretation of salvation history, and thus makes such a comparison untenable.[55] Eusebius's history

---

[52] Ibid., pp. 511, 143.

[53] Robert W. Jenson, *America's Theologian: A Recommendation of Jonathan Edwards* (New York: Oxford University Press, 1988).

[54] This comparison, although less explicitly made, was suggested by H. Richard Niebuhr in the preface to his classic *The Kingdom of God in America*, where he declared his hope that his own study of the kingdom of God in America would serve as "a stepping stone" to the work of some "American Augustine who will write a *City of God* that will trace the story of the eternal city in its relation to modern civilization instead of to ancient Rome, or of Jonathan Edwards *redivivus* who will bring down to our own time the *History of the Work of Redemption*." See H. Richard Niebuhr, *The Kingdom of God in America* (New York: Harper & Brothers, 1959 [1937]), p. xvi. See also H. Richard Niebuhr, "The Anachronism of Jonathan Edwards," *Christian Century* (May 1, 1996), pp. 480–85. This address was originally delivered in Northampton, Mass., on March 9, 1958, to commemorate the bicentennial of the death of Jonathan Edwards.

[55] Eusebius's aim in his *History of the Church* (*Ecclesiastical History*) was, in part, to show "the dispensation" of Christ throughout history. See Eusebius, *History of the Church from Christ to Constantine* (New York: Dorset, 1965), pp. 32–33. Eusebius wrote his *History* at the time of Constantine's conversion to Christianity and the rise of the church to prominence in the world, and thus he displays an optimistic belief that the triumph of Chris-

reflects the triumph of Christianity after the conversion of Constantine, while Augustine and Edwards wrote their apologetics in a world exhibiting antagonism toward Christian faith and belief. Both rejected Eusebius's imperial theology of history—the belief that the emperor, or a godly prince, is providentially ordained to protect the church and ensure its triumph in the world—and tried to explain the fate of God's people within a world marked by hostility to Christ and his church.

Yet, the comparison between the Doctor of the Church and the New England theologian does not stop here, because for both the composition of their historical work constituted only part of their overall theological and philosophical enterprise. Thus, like Augustine, who assumed the mission of defending traditional Christian belief during the early Christian period, Edwards, as I argue throughout this study, took upon himself the mission of protecting religious faith in a world becoming more and more alienated from God and his word. Augustine's *City of God* and Edwards's *History of the Work of Redemption*, then, may be regarded as an integral part of their apology for the Christian church. Augustine's and Edwards's life of the mind is characterized by a lifelong struggle against all sorts of opposition within the church itself, and a striving to expose the poverty of its enemies without. After his conversion, Augustine began to write against, among others, the Manichaens, Donatists, and Pelagiants. Later, after the fall of Rome, he composed the *City of God* to defend Christianity from the serious charge that this faith was responsible for the terrible disaster that had befallen the empire.[56] Likewise, Edwards fought not only against "Socinianism and Arianism and Quakerism and Arminianism,"[57] but devotedly attempted to counter the challenges that Christian life was experiencing with the flourishing of new theories in ethics, science, and history.

Further, although both lived on the periphery of their respective empires and far from the foci of contemporary learning and culture, Augustine in Hippo Regius in North Africa and Edwards in Northampton, New England, each found it necessary to react specifically to the threats against Christianity that arose in the centers of their worlds. Augustine wrote the

---

tianity will be realized in the process of history, and that the progress of history bears witness to the gradual yet inevitable triumph of the church throughout the world. Augustine's and Edwards's historical contexts were very different. On the difference between Eusebius's and Augustine's historical contexts, see Avihu Zakai and Anya Mali, "Time, History and Eschatology: Ecclesiastical History from Eusebius to Augustine," *Journal of Religious History* 17 (December 1993): 393–417.

[56] Peter Brown, *Augustine of Hippo: A Biography* (Berkeley: University of California Press, 1969); R. A. Markus, *Saeculum: History and Society in the Theology of St. Augustine* (Cambridge: Cambridge University Press, 1988).

[57] Edwards, *History of the Work of Redemption*, p. 467.

City of God in response to the fall of Rome—a city that had been free from fear of attack for over 800 years—brought about by Alaric and the Goths in 410. Similarly, but less dramatically, Edwards wrote his major historical work, *A History of the Work of Redemption*, after the collapse of the "little revival" of 1734–35 in Northampton, aiming to prove, in part, against the Enlightenment notion of *historia humana*, that history is a space of sacred time designated from eternity by God for the execution of his work of redemption. In response to attempts to liberate history from its traditional subservience to theology, Edwards claimed that the entire historical process was inextricable from God's redemptive activity and vice versa. Thus, as Augustine's thought transcends his life in North Africa, so with Edwards; his universe of thought as well as the main thrust of his philosophical and ideological endeavor transcended his life in British colonial America. Far from the centers of learning in England, he attempted to rescue the foundations of the Christian theological teleology of history from the menace of the Enlightenment concept of secular time. His aim was to exalt "the history" of God's "glorious kingdom" in the world.[58] Both Augustine's and Edwards's goals were to preserve Christian faith and belief in a hostile world.

I begin the discussion of the formation of Edwards's historical philosophy with a brief overview of his intellectual development. This may help to place his narrative of history within the general context of his universe of thought and within the main philosophical and theological issues he treated during his lifetime. Chapter 1 therefore offers a short intellectual biography in order to establish the background for the formation of Edwards's redemptive mode of historical thought. Simply put, Edwards's life of the mind can be described as evolving along three main stages: during the 1720s, following his conversion, he formulated his natural philosophy in order to provide an alternative to the dominant mechanical philosophy view of the essential nature of reality; during the 1730s, he developed the premises of his philosophy of salvation history, whose full and systematic exposition appeared in the *History of the Work of Redemption*; finally, during the 1750s, after his expulsion from his parish and living in exile at Stockbridge, Edwards immersed himself in the task of responding to the Enlightenment debate on moral philosophy. In these three spheres, he tried to explain the meaning of divine agency in time and the Deity's redemptive work for fallen humanity. Thus, in discussing Edwards's philosophy of history, I found it necessary to deal as well with his explorations in the realms of science and ethics, since these issues were closely intertwined in his mind with the dimension of history.

[58] Ibid., p. 291.

The account of Edwards's life of the mind, as I write in chapter 2, must start at the moment of his conversion, a profound spiritual experience that determined the agenda for much of his future theological and philosophical work. Many features of his thought, in both form and content, can be traced directly to this signal moment when the whole of his religious identity was transformed. Ultimately, this spiritual experience led Edwards to reconstruct, among other things, the external world of nature and the realm of history, the "order of nature" and the "order of time,"[59] as well as the realm of ethics and morals, in accordance with the theological convictions he acquired during his conversion. In all these spheres he sought to reenchant the world in order to manifest God's unshaken absolute sovereignty in creation.

The genesis of Edwards's theology of nature, his interpretation of the essential nature of reality, as I argue in chapter 3, was founded upon his conversion experience. His long subsequent engagement with fundamental issues of natural philosophy, as in the long series of scientific and philosophical writings[60] composed during the early 1720s, was embarked upon in order to redefine the phenomena of nature in light of this experience. Edwards's theology of nature therefore constituted a radical departure from mechanical philosophy—the doctrine that all natural phenomena can be explained in terms of the mechanics of matter and motion alone—which became the predominant mode of thought during the scientific revolution. One of his main goals in interpreting the world of nature was to ascertain God's relation to his creation, to define the relationship between the order of grace and the order of nature, and to get a clear "knowledge of the manner of God's exerting himself" with respect "of his operations concerning Matter and Bodies."[61] For he firmly believed, following his conversion, that "the corporal world is to no advantage but to the spiritual," hence "to find out the reasons of things in natural philosophy is only to find out the proportion of God's acting."[62]

Constructing the created order upon such theological and teleological premises illustrates the dialectic in Edwards's thought between God's utter transcendence and divine immanence, and the tension between his simultaneous distance from and immediate presence in the world. The created order's ontological status is seen as inferior and subordinate to the divine reality beyond and above it. This notion lay behind Edwards's assertion that God is intimately present in creation, a contention neces-

---

[59] Edwards, *Freedom of the Will*, 1754, in *FW*, p. 177; *Miscellany* no. 704 (c. 1736), in *MISA*, p. 314.

[60] Edwards's work on natural philosophy appears in *Scientific and Philosophical Writings*, in *SPW*.

[61] Edwards, *Diary*, February 12, 1725, in *LPW*, p. 787.

[62] Edwards, *The Mind*, 34 (1724), in *SPW*, pp. 353–55.

sary to his claim that the divine agency is not alienated from history and hence that redemptive activity is inextricable from the historical process. The formation of Edwards's philosophy of history, especially with regard to his unique mode of historical thought—the doctrine that the process of history depends exclusively on God's redemptive activity in time, as appears in the close connection between the effusion of the Spirit and its manifestation in the form of revival—is thus inextricable from his construction of the world of nature.

One of Edwards's main goals in constructing his historical narrative, *A History of the Work of Redemption*, was to combat the growing separation between the order of grace and the order of time, redemption and history. In chapter 4, I discuss the ideological context of Edwards's historical thought in light of the threat faced by the Christian theological teleology of history in the early modern period, with the emergence of a secular conception of history and the modern "legitimacy" of historical time.[63] This is followed by an analysis of Edwards's philosophy of salvation history, which locates the formation of his redemptive mode of historical thought within the larger context of Christian ecclesiastical history.

What is most remarkable about Edwards's ideology of history, however, is his radical departure from the traditional ecclesiastical history, which constituted the dominant mode of historical thought from the rise of Christianity during the fourth century until "the secularization of theological teleology of history" announced by the Enlightenment of the eighteenth.[64] This mode of thought regards the Christian church as the locus of history, and thus deals chiefly with the events affecting this body in the world. This is how, for example, Eusebius, the father of church history, defined sacred, providential history. Edwards, however, attempted to write a history as it lies in the mind of omniscient God, a history based on God's redemptive activity in the form of revivals and awakenings. Eusebius's primary concern was to describe "the many important events recorded in the story of the Church," as well as the many vicissitudes this body endured.[65] Edwards's narrative deals primarily with the content and form of divine activity, the power of the Spirit, and its historical manifestations in the form of conversion and revival. Eusebius wrote his history from the point of view of the church's affairs in the world. Edwards wrote his from the perspective of God and his redemptive activity. Hence, the first dwelt at length upon the persecutions and sufferings of God's people

[63] The legitimacy of historical time is discussed in Hans Blumenberg, *The Legitimacy of the Modern Age* (Cambridge, Mass.: MIT Press, 1987).

[64] Rudolf Bultmann, *History and Eschatology* (Edinburgh: The University Press, 1957), p. 65.

[65] Eusebius, *The History of the Church from Christ to Constantine*, p. 31.

in the world, while the later emphasized almost exclusively the rise and decline of revivals and awakenings throughout history. In contrast to Eusebius, therefore, Edwards's history is not ecclesiastical history per se. It is a history of God's work of redemption.

Similarly, Edwards's narrative of salvation history differs from Augustine's *City of God*. While Augustine saw the course of history as predominantly characterized by a perpetual and uncompromising struggle between the earthly city and the City of God, the world and the church, Edwards does not base his view upon such a dichotomy. Given his central premise of the universal character of God's redemptive activity, his narrative of history deals with the universal power of the Spirit as evidenced in revivals and awakenings. Augustine distinguished between redemption and history—divine providence is concerned with salvation, not with history[66]—while to Edwards they are inextricable—there is no history without redemption and no redemption without history.

Edwards's historical narrative also differs from the Protestant and Puritan apocalyptic tradition in England, which developed during the sixteenth century around the doctrine that the struggle against the Church of Rome constituted the hallmark of salvation history. Since Edwards's historical thought was written from the point of view of God's mind and is based on the universal character of redemptive activity, he could not accept that divine agency might be limited to any particular national or geographical center. Hence his strong belief that the aim of divine dispensation during the Great Awakening was to reveal the "day of God's mighty power and glorious grace to *the world of mankind*" (emphasis added).[67] Edwards's narrative therefore differed, for example, from John Foxe's *Acts and Monuments*, which represented the whole span of English history as based upon the Church of Rome's persecution of the true church, the Church of England. Edwards, in other words, does not deal primarily with the persecution and suffering of God's martyrs, early Christian or others.

Finally, Edwards's historical vision is very different from earlier New England Puritan narratives, which may explain the transformation he caused in the concept of the Puritan "errand into the wilderness" in America.[68] In contrast to his forerunners, who sought to explain the mean-

---

[66] Markus, *Saeculum*, pp. 20–21; P. Brown, "Saint Augustine," in *Trends in Medieval Political Thought*, ed. B. Smalley (Oxford: Oxford University Press, 1965), p. 11; Zakai and Mali, "Time, History and Eschatology," pp. 393–417.

[67] Edwards, "To the Rev. George Whitefield," February 12, 1739–40, in *LPW*, p. 80.

[68] For an exposition of the Puritan "errand," see Miller, "Errand Into the Wilderness," in *Errand Into the Wilderness*, pp. 1–15; and Avihu Zakai, *Exile and Kingdom: History and Apocalypse in the Puritan Migration to America* (Cambridge: Cambridge University Press, 1992).

ing of their migration to America by propounding an unbridgeable gulf between the Old World and the New, thus cutting the history of New England off from England, Edwards's history is not based on such eschatological expectations and apocalyptic visions. He did not believe the millennium would take place in New England, but rather "prophesied that the millennium would be global; hence" the attempt to ascribe to his thought "every form of tribalist nationalism is inherently misconceived."[69] Instead of refurbishing his predecessors' perception of New England's particularistic role in salvation history, Edwards described its fate as inseparable from that of the Old World. The power of the Spirit knows no boundaries, and God's redemptive activity cannot be limited to a specific geographical space. Hence he consistently examined the New England revival of 1740–43 in light of the general context of the "outpouring of the Spirit of God" in "Germany"[70] and "the hopeful state of reviving religion in England."[71] He understood the Great Awakening as inseparable from the revivals characterizing the Protestant evangelical movement in early-eighteenth-century Europe, such as the "remarkable reviving of religion" in "Saxony,"[72] or God's "glorious work" in the revival in Kilsyth, Scotland (1740).[73] Defined as the work of the Spirit, the history of revival becomes a universal history.

For many years Edwards endeavored to develop a coherent philosophy of history that would enable him to establish the proper relationship between divine agency and the process of history. In chapter 5, I offer an analysis of the formation of Edwards's historical thought, and how he developed his views in accordance with the changing historical and ideological context in which he found himself, starting with his early adoption in 1723 of the term God's "work of redemption,"[74] and following the relationship he found between redemption and history until the composition of the *History of the Work of Redemption* in 1739. In these earlier formulations of his theology of history, he strove to define "God's end in making and governing the world,"[75] to decipher God's "great design' " in the order of time, and to understand the Deity's ultimate aim in the "affairs of redemption."[76] He spent many years searching for a feasible

[69] Gerald R. McDermott, *One Holy & Happy Society: The Public Theology of Jonathan Edwards* (University Park: Pennsylvania State University Press, 1992), pp. 6, 50–63.

[70] Edwards, *Much in Deeds of Charity*, 1741, in *SJE*, p. 210.

[71] Edwards, "To Sec. Josiah Willard," June 1, 1740, in *LPW*, p. 83.

[72] Edwards, *Much in Deeds of Charity*, p. 210; *Some Thoughts Concerning the Present Revival of Religion in New England*, 1742, in *GA*, p. 528.

[73] Edwards, "To the Rev. James Rose," May 12, 1743, in *LPW*, p. 108.

[74] Edwards, *Miscellany* no. 38 (c. 1723), p. 221.

[75] Edwards, *Miscellany* no. 547 (c. 1731), in *MISA*, pp. 93–94.

[76] Edwards, "To the Trustees of the College of New Jersey," p. 728; Edwards, *God Glorified in the Work of Redemption*, July 8, 1731, in *SJE*, p. 78.

historical phenomenon on the basis of which he could assert God's redemptive activity, and show the power of the "wheels of providence,"[77]
or "the chariots of his salvation,"[78] in history, looking for the most appropriate agent by which to demonstrate the "design that God is pursuing,
and [the] scheme that he is Carrying on, in the various changes and revolutions that from age to age happen in the world."[79]

Edwards toiled throughout the 1730s to define the meaning of God's
work of redemption, an effort that resulted in his laying down the main
premises of his philosophy of salvation history. In 1736, he came to the
conclusion that the work of redemption constituted the "great end and
drift of all God's works."[80] This led to his attempt to explain the work of
redemption as part of the fabric of the entire creation, and to claim that
it constituted the essential dynamism behind the teleology of sacred order
inherent in the structure of the universe: "The work of redemption may
be looked upon as the great end and drift of all Gods works & dispensations from the beginning & even the end of the work of creation it self."[81]
The affairs of redemption, he came to think, dealt with the cause and
destiny, nature and meaning, of creation.

The fullest and most systematic exposition of this philosophy of salvation history is contained in the thirty sermons on the *History of the Work
of Redemption*. As I argue in chapter 6, the construction of the historical
narrative in these sermons may be seen, in part, in the larger context of
the early Enlightenment. Instead of conceiving history as the direct result
of human action, and as a manifestation of immanent human progress,
as Enlightenment historians believed, Edwards constructed it from the
perspective of God and the manifestations of his redemptive activity in
creation. In such a theological and teleological context, history is designed
by divine providence as a special dimension of time meant solely for the
accomplishment of the plan of redemption, and therefore it should be
understood exclusively from the perspective of its maker and author. History, then, is a sacred space of time destined from eternity for God's self-
glorification—the display of the Deity's excellence in creation—as evidenced in his work of redemption; hence human beings' existence as well
as their history is totally dependent on God.

To show that the course of history is inextricable from God's work of
redemption, and hence that the fate of human beings cannot be separated
from divine action in time, Edwards proposed that the effusion of the

[77] Edwards, *Notes on Scriptures*, 389 (1739), in *NOS*, p. 373.
[78] Edwards, "To the Rev. Joseph Bellamy," January 21, 1741–12, in *LPW*, p. 99.
[79] Edwards, *Miscellany* no. 547 (c. 1731), p. 93.
[80] Edwards, *Miscellany* no. 702 (c. 1736), p. 284.
[81] Ibid.

Spirit of God as manifested in the form of revivals and awakenings was
the ultimate mark of the divine agency in history. Throughout history
God's work of redemption determines the condition of human life, as is
manifested in a long series of outpourings of the Spirit, and their immediate effects in revivals and awakenings. "God advances his work of redemption" most of all "through successive effusions of his Spirit."[82]
Hence, the *History of the Work of Redemption* deals primarily with the
"rise and continued progress of the dispensation of grace towards fallen
mankind";[83] it is based on the effusion of the Spirit in the form of "dispensations of providence" as manifested in periods of revivals, or "special
seasons of mercy."[84] In sum, "from the fall of man to this day wherein we
live the Work of Redemption in its effects has mainly been carried on by
remarkable pourings out of the Spirit of God . . . [and] the way in which
the greatest things have been done toward carrying on this work has always been by remarkable pourings out of the Spirit at special seasons of
mercy."[85] History is the "theater" of God, because his transcendent ends
determine the drama of human history upon earth. Yet history is not
merely the "theater of God's judgments," for God continuously and progressively exhibits in history, through his word and work, the divine plan
of redemption for fallen humanity.

The premises of such a philosophy of history, as I argue in chapter 7,
constituted the main source of Edwards's apocalyptic and eschatological
interpretation of the Great Awakening in 1740–43 and of his defense of
this New England revival. Basing himself on his redemptive mode of historical thought, he plainly saw the magnitude and significance of this event
in the overall progress of salvation history, becoming its most ardent
champion in New England and the British world as a whole. If Edwards
made himself the leader of that moment of *kairos* which inaugurated the
revival tradition in America, not the least reason for this was his attributing to it a vital role within providential history. The revival demanded its
own historian, a person who could expound its meaning in the broadest
sense and provide it with the fullest historical and theological justification.
This figure was Edwards. His historical interpretation of the revival placed
it in the wider context of salvation history, thus infusing this specific New
England historical moment with a glorious meaning in sacred history. By
showing the continuity between this provincial event and similar awakenings in the Old World, Edwards made the Great Awakening an inseparable
part of the general, universal history of God's work of redemption.

[82] Stephen Stein, introduction, in *AW*, p. 22.
[83] Edwards, *History of the Work of Redemption*, p. 285.
[84] Ibid., pp. 511, 143.
[85] Ibid., p. 143.

Without a knowledge of Edwards's historical thought, some of his most important works pertaining to the Great Awakening, among them *Sinners in the Hands of an Angry God*, *The Distinguishing Marks of a Work of the Spirit of God*, and *Some Thoughts Concerning the Revival*, might remain obscure. In these writings he developed his singular apocalypse and eschatology of the Great Awakening, deeming revival the culmination of salvation history. Moreover, the Great Awakening was not to be judged as a mere provincial event leading only to the conversion of some fallen American colonists. On the contrary, together with other revivals taking place in the Protestant world, such as in Scotland and Germany, it illuminated the general scheme of God's historical work of redemption. On the basis of this theological teleology of history, Edwards interpreted the New England revival as an integral part of the general Protestant evangelical awakening in the early eighteenth century, claiming it heralded "the commencement of that last and greatest outpouring of the Spirit of God, that is to be in the latter ages of the world."[86] Believing the power of the Spirit is universal and not related to any particularistic center in history, he saw in the Great Awakening a proof of that "glorious work of God, so often foretold in Scripture, which in the progress and issue of it, shall renew the *world of mankind*" (emphasis added).[87] From the Deity's point of view, which it was Edwards's aim to expound, history is a grand theater in which God reveals his redemptive plan, and revivals, such as the Great Awakening, illustrate the historical necessity, or indeed inevitability, of the progress of God's historical scheme of redemption.

Edwards's main achievement in the field of historical thought was the development of a singular evangelical historiography according to which revivals and awakenings constitute the heart and core of the historical process. This philosophy of salvation exercised an enormous influence in New England and America in general. The publication of Edwards's *History of the Work of Redemption* in the 1770s "helped to fuel the transference of religious convictions into the political realm," a transference that was noticeable during the American Revolution and later crucial to the "revival of interest in eschatology" and the millennium "that occurred in the 1790s."[88] Later this book went through a "process of canonization during the Second Great Awakening, 1800–30, and added to [Edwards's] stature as the preeminent authority on revivalism."[89] Further, as H. Rich-

---

[86] Edwards, *The Distinguishing Marks of a Work of the Spirit of God*, in *GA*, p. 230.

[87] Edwards, *Some Thoughts*, p. 353.

[88] Wilson, introduction, in *HWR*, pp. 92–93. See also Ruth Bloch, *Visionary Republic: Millennial Themes in American Thought, 1756–1800* (New York: Cambridge University Press, 1985); and Donald Weber, *Rhetoric and History in Revolutionary New England* (New York: Oxford University Press, 1988).

[89] Conforti, *Jonathan Edwards, Religious Tradition & American Culture*, pp. 47–49.

ard Niebuhr held, Edwards's philosophy of salvation history influenced nineteenth-century evangelists' understanding of "the coming of the kingdom," leading them to believe that "the divine sovereignty was the fruition not only of divine goodness but of human badness in conflict with that unconquerable goodness."[90] Edwards's theology of history was thus installed at the center of the story of the predominant Protestant culture of America.

Since the issue of divine agency in time concerns not only history but ethics and morals as well, a realm where the Deity constantly advances the work of redemption in terms of the establishment of true virtue, in chapter 8 I analyze Edwards's moral thought in the wider context of his reaction to the Enlightenment project in ethics, and the debate on moral philosophy, as can be seen in his *Freedom of the Will* (1754), *The Nature of True Virtue* (1755), and *Original Sin* (1758). He conducted this enterprise throughout the 1750s, in the final decade of his life, while living in isolation at Stockbridge. Taken as a whole, these works represent Edwards's aim to demonstrate "God's Moral Government of the world,"[91] and to show that the Deity is the sole source of ethics and morals; "nothing is of the nature of true virtue . . . in which God is not the first & the last."[92] Accordingly, he denounced "that grand objection, in which the modern writers have so much gloried, and so long triumphed, with so great a degree of insult towards the most excellent divines and, in effect, against the gospel of Jesus Christ, viz. that the Calvinistic notions of God's moral government are contrary to the common sense of mankind."[93] In his ethical writings, more specifically, Edwards rejected "that notion of virtue maintained by My Lord Shaftesbury, [Francis] Hutcheson, and [George] Turnbull; which seems to be most in vogue at this day," and according to which "all mankind are naturally disposed to virtue, and are without any native depravity."[94]

Finally, in the epilogue I try briefly to assess Edwards's contribution to Protestant culture in America, arguing that his reaction to scientific, historical, and moral thought in early modern history contributed much to the creation of a distinct Protestant culture in America with a lasting influence on American history. In terms of the formation of American identity, Edwards's thought shows that the development of an American culture during the eighteenth century did not depend on a simple and linear transference of ideas from the core culture in Britain, nor on an

---

[90] Niebuhr, *The Kingdom of God in America*, p. 138.

[91] Edwards, *Miscellany* no. 864 (c. 1740).

[92] Edwards, *Miscellany* no. 1208.

[93] Edwards, "To The Reverend John Erskine," July 7, 1752, in *LPW*, p. 491.

[94] Edwards, "To the Reverend Thomas Foxcroft," February 11, 1757, in *LPW*, p. 696.

easy accommodation of them in America. Rather, in some matters it was the rejection of certain well-established European intellectual traditions in the early modern period that helped the formation of a well-defined Protestant cultural space in America.

Examination of Edwards's life of the mind in this context of the philosophical and theological controversies taking place in early modern history, as well as of his contribution to the creation of a distinct Protestant culture in America, may suggest that the comparison between him and Augustine is not too far-fetched. The wide range of his works and the varieties of themes he dealt with, as well as the solutions he offered for Christian life and thought in his time, justify, I would argue, the conferring upon him of the title of the "American Augustine." The similarities between the Doctor of the Church and the New England theologian are revealing in terms of the depth of their religious experience and the wide range of controversies they engaged in. Both Augustine and Edwards underwent a profound conversion experience, which radically transformed their lives and inscribed in their souls a profound experience of God; this event established their sense of God and launched them on a journey to defend the Christian church from its adversaries within and without. One of the many justifications for studying Augustine, according to Gerald Bonner, lies "in the depth of his experience of God, and in his extraordinary flair of communicating that experience to others. This is what sets Augustine apart from the other Fathers of the Church."[95] The same can be said about Edwards. It was the vision of God's absolute sovereignty in the order of creation—"God's absolute sovereignty and justice," he wrote, "is what my mind seems to rest assured of, as much as of any thing that I see with my eyes"[96]—that he tried to make known to the world around him throughout his life and writings. The experience of conversion thus transformed Augustine's and Edwards's lives into a struggle against the many errors of their respective times.

Moreover, because they both lived in an age where Christian thought and belief were under attack from many directions, both developed a deep sense of Christian exile and pilgrimage in the world. After the sack of Rome in 410, Augustine preached to his fellow Christians in Carthage: "Citizens of Jerusalem, O God's own people, O Body of Christ, O high-born race of foreigners on earth—you do not belong here, you belong

---

[95] Gerald Bonner, *St. Augustine of Hippo: Life and Controversies* (London: SCM, 1963), pp. 9–10. See also T. Kermit Scott, *Augustine: His Thought in Context* (New York: Paulist, 1995); and Carol Harrison, *Augustine: Christian Truth and Fractured Humanity* (Oxford: Oxford University Press, 2000).

[96] Edwards, *Personal Narrative*, p. 792.

somewhere else."[97] And Edwards, preaching to his congregation in Northampton during the 1730s, echoed Augustine almost word for word when
he said:

> This world is not our abiding place. Our continuance here is but very short.
> Man's days on earth, are as a shadow. . . . It was never designed by God that
> this world should be our home. . . . The future world was designed to be our
> settled and everlasting abode. There it was intended that we should be fixed;
> and there alone is a lasting habitation, and a lasting inheritance.[98]

"We are pilgrims and strangers here" on earth, said Edwards in another
sermon, "and are principally designed for a future world. We continue in
this present state but a short time; but we are to be in that future state to
all eternity."[99]

Yet this sense of exilic displacement and pilgrimage did not lead to
alienation from the world, since for both Augustine and Edwards the
saeculum is a place of trial for God's people in their long journey to their
last abode; hence the sense of exile in the world did not hinder either of
them from composing a profound apology for the Christian church. As
the Doctor of the Church formulated out of his many controversies an
interpretation of Christian belief that exercised a lasting influence on the
history of Christianity, so the New England theologian constructed out
of his many struggles against various strains of early modern thought an
interpretation that had an important influence on Protestant life and culture in America. Both engaged in a grand intellectual effort of constructing a defense of Christian thought and belief. Such an enterprise in
the end amounted to a reconstruction of the human condition, which later
generations found meaningful for the problems they faced in their own
historical moment.

[97] Brown, *Augustine of Hippo*, pp. 313–14.
[98] Edwards, *The Christian Pilgrim*, in *Jonathan Edwards: Representative Selections*, ed.
Clarence H. Faust and Thomas H. Johnson (New York: American Book Company, 1935),
p. 130.
[99] Edwards, *Sermon 1*, in *The Works of Jonathan Edwards*, 2 vols. (Edinburgh: Banner
of Truth Trust, 1995 [1834]), II, p. 820.

Edwards's Life of the Mind

One

A Short Intellectual Biography

My heart hath been . . . against most of the prevailing errors of the
present day, which I cannot with any patience see maintained (to
the utter subverting of the gospel of Christ) with so high a hand,
and so long continued a triumph, with so little control, when it appears so evident to me, that there is truly no foundation for any of
this glorying and insult.
(Jonathan Edwards, "To the Trustees of the College
of New Jersey," October 19, 1757)

JONATHAN EDWARDS (1703–58) was perhaps the outstanding American
theologian and certainly the ablest American philosopher to write before
the great period of Charles S. Peirce (1839–1914), William James (1842–
1910), Josiah Royce (1855–1916), John Dewey (1859–1952), and George
Santayana (1863–1952). Judged over two centuries, Edwards stands out
as one of America's great original minds, "one of the very few whose
depiction of reality has known enduring attraction."[1] He is considered as
the "foundation stone in the history of American philosophy";[2] and the

---

[1] Nathan O. Hatch and Harry S. Stout, introduction, in *JEAE*, p. 3. For constructing
Edwards's life of the mind, I have consulted the following works: *Biographical Sketches of
the Graduate of Yale College, 1701–1745* (New York: Henry Holt, 1885); Alexander
Leitch, *A Princeton Companion* (Princeton: Princeton University Press, 1919); Baird Tip-
son, "New England Puritanism," in *Encyclopedia of American Religious Experience: Studies of Traditions and Movements*, ed. C. H. Lippy et al., 3 vols. (New York: Charles Scribner's Sons, 1988), I, pp. 467–80; William K. B. Stoever, "The Calvinist Theological Tradition
in America," in *Encyclopedia of American Religious Experience*, II, pp. 1039–56; Stephen
A. Marini, "The Great Awakening," in *Encyclopedia of American Religious Experience*, II,
pp. 775–98, and Stuart C. Henry, "Revivalism," in *Encyclopedia of American Religious
Experience*, II, pp. 799–812. I used as well Wallace E. Anderson, introduction, in *SPW*, pp.
1–136; Thomas A. Schafer, introduction, in *MIS*, pp. 1–113; Kenneth P. Minkema, introduction, in *SDM*, pp. 1–46; C. C. Goen, introduction, in *GA*, pp. 1–83; Paul Ramsey, introduction, in *FW*, pp. 1–118; Mark Valeri, introduction, in *SDV*, pp. 3–45; Clyde A. Holbrook,
introduction, in *OS*, pp. 1–85; Stephen J. Stein, introduction, in *AW*, pp. 1–54; John E.
Smith, introduction, in *RA*, pp. 2–43; M. X. Lesser, introduction, in *SDL*, pp. 3–37; Paul
Ramsey, introduction, in *EW*, pp. 1–104; and Wilson H. Kimnach, introduction, in *SDK*,
pp. 1–36.
[2] Bruce Kuklick, "Jonathan Edwards and American Philosophy," in *JEAE*, p. 246.

unique theology and philosophy he formulated "entitled him to the rank of the greatest American theologian and the greatest American philosopher before the Civil War."[3]

Early Life, Education, and Works

Edwards was born in the east parish of Windsor, now the town of South Windsor, Connecticut, on October 5, 1703, the only son in a family of eleven children. His parents were the Rev. Timothy Edwards (1669–1758) and Esther Stoddard Edwards (1672–1771), daughter of the Rev. Solomon Stoddard (1643–1729) of Northampton, Massachusetts. In his youth Edwards was nurtured and instructed in Reformed theology and the practice of Puritan piety. Prepared for college at his father's tutoring school, in 1716, at the age of thirteen he was admitted to the Collegiate College (renamed Yale College in 1718). The course of study included classical and biblical languages, logic, and natural philosophy. With the modernization of the curriculum at Yale during 1717–18,[4] Edwards encountered the philosophy of "Mr. Locke and Sir Isaac Newton."[5] He became acquainted with the ideas of the scientific revolution and the early Enlightenment, which tended to diminish divine sovereignty with respect to creation, providence, and redemption and "to enhance human independence, producing by degrees an estimate of humankind more morally capable and of God more benevolent."[6] For the rest of his life, dialogue with these intellectual movements was an inseparable part of his philosophical and theological enterprise. Edwards was awarded his B.A. degree in September 1720 and was chosen to deliver the valedictory oration in that year. After graduating, he continued to reside at the college for two more years, pursuing theological studies.

During the summer of 1721, when he was seventeen years old and working toward his M.A. degree, Edwards experienced a religious conversion that shook his life and reshaped his whole experience and existence. As he later described this experience, "the appearance of every thing was altered; there seemed to be, as it were, a calm, sweet cast, or

---

[3] Elizabeth Flower and Murray G. Murphey, *A History of Philosophy in America*, 2 vols. (New York: Capricorn, 1977), I, p. 137.

[4] Wallace E. Anderson, introduction, in *SPW*, p. 15; Flower and Murphey, *A History of Philosophy in America*, I, pp. 81–83.

[5] Anderson, introduction, p. 15.

[6] William K. B. Stoever, "The Calvinist Tradition in America," in *Encyclopedia of American Religious Experience: Studies of Traditions and Movements*, ed. Charles H. Lippy and Peter W. Williams, 3 vols., II, p. 1044.

appearance of divine glory, in almost every thing." Many features of Edwards's thought can be traced to this signal existential moment. Among these are his *theologia gloriae*—the theology that celebrates God's majestic glory and sovereignty as evident in the coherence and beauty, order, and harmony of God's creation—and the uncompromising notion of "God's absolute sovereignty";[7] the construction of a theology of nature, or typology, interpreting the physical world as a representation or a "shadow" of the spiritual, whereby "natural things were ordered for types of spiritual things";[8] and his idealistic phenomenalism—the thesis that physical objects exist only in the mind, or cannot exist unless they are perceived. It should be noted, however, that for Edwards the "created world abides as a system of the permanently fixed general laws or tendencies that God has established and according to which he causes actual existence (actual ideas) in time and space."[9] After his conversion, an impressive outpouring of writings ensued in which Edwards tried to convert the whole world around him and reconstruct it according to his newly acquired religious convictions and theological persuasions. In 1722, he began his seventy *Resolutions*, or guidelines for self-examination and monitoring of his motives and actions; his *Diary*, a long series of scientific and philosophical essays on natural philosophy; and *Miscellanies*, an enormous body of private writings that reflect Edwards's spiritual and intellectual biography. Shortly thereafter, he started *Notes on the Apocalypse* (1723) and *Notes on Scripture* (1724).

Edwards's works on natural philosophy, among them most notably *Of Being* (1722), *Of Atoms* (1722), and *The Mind* (1724), signified the genesis of his theology of nature, that is, his endeavor to redefine the phenomena of nature in light of his spiritual experience and to provide proof for his participation in the transatlantic republic of letters. Aiming to show God's existence in his sovereign majesty and glory within the created world, he attacked the dominant mechanical philosophy—the doctrine that all natural phenomena can be explained in terms of the mechanics of matter and motion alone—claiming "there is no such thing as mechanism, if that word" meant that "bodies act each upon other, purely and properly by themselves,"[10] because "the very being, and the manner of being, and the whole of bodies depends immediately on the divine power."[11] He appropriated the atomic doctrine of mechanical philosophy

---

[7] Edwards, *Personal Narrative*, in *LPW*, pp. 792–94.

[8] Edwards, *Images of Divine Things*, in *TW*, pp. 53, 62.

[9] Sang Hyun Lee, *The Philosophical Theology of Jonathan Edwards* (Princeton: Princeton University Press, 1988), p. 63.

[10] Edwards, *Of Atoms*, in *SPW*, p. 216.

[11] Edwards, *Things to be considered an[d] Written fully about*, in *SPW*, p. 235.

but Christianized it, arguing that God's infinite power is responsible for holding the "atoms together"[12] and that every "atom in the universe is managed by Christ so as to be most to the advantage of the Christian."[13] Likewise, he rejected the mechanistic understanding of the concept of natural laws because these laws, setting up a mediating sphere between God and his creation, restricted God's infinite power and limited the divine immanence within the phenomena of the world: what "we call the laws of nature" are only "the stated methods of God's acting with respect to bodies."[14] He therefore denounced mechanical philosophers who argued that God "himself in common with his creatures" is "subject in his acting to the same laws with inferiour being," thus dethroning God from his place as "the head of the universe" and "the foundation & first spring of all."[15]

Edwards's theology of nature signified a serious and systematic attempt to provide a plausible alternative to new modes of thought emerging in early modern Europe that threatened traditional Christian thought and belief and led increasingly to the disenchantment of the world. His goal was the reenchantment of the world by demonstrating the infinite power of God's absolute sovereignty in both the "order of nature" and the "order of time."[16] Edwards's interpretation of the essential nature of reality therefore constituted a radical departure from the prevailing mechanical philosophy. Believing "the corporeal world is to no advantage but to the spiritual," he argued that "to find out the reasons of things in natural philosophy is only to find out the proportion of God's acting."[17] In this enterprise of the reenchantment of the world, Edwards was not alone, as can be seen in the close affinities between his thought and other anti-Newtonians at that time, such as George Berkeley (1685–1753) and William Blake (1757–1827).

Edwards was not only a prominent American intellectual. He was also an early modern philosopher who developed a singular natural philosophy, a view regarding the essential nature of reality which entitles him to a distinguished place among early modern philosophers who reacted against the metaphysical and theological implications of the scientific revolution. Along with Pierre Gassendi (1592–1655), Giordano Bruno (1548–

[12] Edwards, *Of Atoms*, p. 214.

[13] Edwards, *Miscellany ff*, in *MIS*, p. 184.

[14] Edwards, *Of Atoms*, p. 216.

[15] Edwards, *Miscellany* no. 1263, in *The Miscellanies*, typescript on disk, Works of Jonathan Edwards Office, Yale Divinity School, New Haven, Conn.

[16] Edwards, *Miscellany* no. 704, in *MISA*, p. 314; *Freedom of the Will*, 1754, in *FW*, p. 177.

[17] Edwards, *The Mind*, in *SPW*, pp. 353–55.

1600), Nicolas Malebranche (1638–1715), Gottfried Wilhelm Leibniz (1646–1716), and George Berkeley, to name only a few, Edwards formulated his philosophy of nature in reaction against materialism and the mechanical philosophy of nature that had become the predominant mode of scientific thought and imagination during the scientific revolution.

In this venture of the reenchantment of the world, Edwards was not alone. His attempt to understand the constitution of the natural world and to ascertain God's relation to his physical creation bears close affinities with the thought of several early modern philosophers. By the end of the seventeenth century, atomism as a mechanical philosophy was the conservative view in England. Such a doctrine may lead to the claim that motion is an inherent property of matter, and hence that a Godless universe can exist and subsist. Edwards rejected such contentions and strove to modify the atomic doctrine by maintaining God's absolute sovereignty through the agency of atoms: "it is God himself, or the immediate exercise of his power, that keeps the parts of atoms" or bodies "together."[18] Such a view resembles that of Giordano Bruno, whose writings Edwards read while at Yale, and according to whom God becomes the source of all change in nature, as well as the source of its existence via the agency of the atom.[19] Both Bruno and Edwards used the atomic doctrine to enhance nature's dependence on God's will and power. Edwards's views on atomism are also close to the ideas of the philosopher and mathematician Pierre Gassendi, whose works Edwards read as well, who attempted to Christianize the classical atomist doctrine of Epicurus and Lucretius by arguing that God directs the atoms.[20] Edwards's thought also had close affinity with that of the philosopher and theologian Nicolas Malebranche, especially in regards to the theory of occasionalism—the doctrine that finite created beings have no causal efficacy and that only God is a true causal agent.[21] Natural causes provide only the occasion for the operation of the one and only real cause, which is God, or a "universal Being."[22] The theory of

[18] Edwards, *Of Atoms*, p. 214.

[19] Giordano Bruno, *Cause, Principle, and Unity: Five Dialogues by Giordano Bruno*, trans. Jack Lindsay (Westport, Conn.: Greenwood, 1962); and Paul H. Michel, *The Cosmology of Giordano Bruno*, trans. R.E.W. Madison (Ithaca: Cornell University Press, 1973), pp. 147–49.

[20] Edwards read Gassendi's *Institutio Astronomica* (London, 1653), and Gassendi's attack on Descartes in the *Disquisitio metaphysica anti-Cartesianas* [*Metaphysical Colloquy, or Doubts and Rebuttals concerning the Metaphysics of René Descartes*] (1644), during his senior year at Yale. See Anderson, introduction, pp. 12–13, 21–22.

[21] Nicolas Malebranche, *Dialogues on Metaphysics and on Religion*, trans. Morris Ginsberg (London: George Allen & Unwin, 1923).

[22] Malebranche, *The Search after the Truth*, trans. and ed. Thomas M. Lennon et al. (Cambridge: Cambridge University Press, 1997), pp. 241, 618.

occasionalism had an influence on Edwards's thought: it "was the vehicle most available to Edwards for shattering belief in the autonomy of nature, a mechanistic universe, and the independence of second causes." In such a system of reasoning, "the harmony and regularity of natural physical laws" are "essentially an expression of God's love of order."[23]

Edwards's response to mechanical philosophy should also be considered in the wider context of the reaction to Newtonian science by men like Leibniz, Berkeley, and others, who were reluctant to distance God from the phenomena of nature, or to detach the order of grace from the order of nature, as Newton's universal active principles appeared to do. Edwards and Leibniz were united in their negative reaction to mechanism: against the mechanistic interpretation, Leibniz argued that "all order and all physical rules" in the natural world "arise *not* from purely material determination," as "certain men among the moderns," or mechanical philosophers believe, "but from the contemplation of indivisible substances, and especially of God." Hence, "matter and motion are not so much substances or things as they are the phenomena of percipient beings."[24] Edwards likewise denounced "mechanism," claiming bodies cannot "act each upon other, purely and properly by themselves,"[25] because the very being of material bodies "depends immediately on the divine power."[26] In their efforts to refute materialism, Berkeley and Edwards both developed independently an extreme idealism, the view that physical objects exist only in the mind or cannot exist unless they are perceived. Berkeley denounced matter altogether and claimed that no sensible qualities exist "without the mind."[27] He developed his own non-material, theocentric universe, whose *esse* was *percipi*, in which human "spirits" were conceived as conversing directly with the mind of God. Edwards's idealistic phenomenalism similarly stipulated that physical objects exist only in the mind or cannot exist unless they are perceived: "the world, i.e. the material universe, exists nowhere but in the mind." And given "all existence is mental," therefore "the existence of all exterior things is ideal." In sum, argued Edwards, "the substance of all bodies is the infinitely exact and precise and perfectly stable idea in God's mind."[28]

---

[23] Norman Fiering, "The Rationalist Foundations of Edwards's Metaphysics," in *JEAE*, p. 80.

[24] Gottfried Wilhelm Leibniz, *Philosophical Papers and Letters* (1706), as quoted in Christopher Kaiser, *Creation and the History of Science* (London: Marshall Pickering, 1991), pp. 160–61.

[25] Edwards, *Of Atoms*, p. 216.

[26] Edwards, *Things to be considered*, in *SPW*, p. 235.

[27] George Berkeley, *A Treatise Concerning the Principles of Human Knowledge* (1710), as quoted in Kaiser, *Creation and the History of Science*, pp. 248–49.

[28] Edwards, *The Mind*, pp. 350–56.

Early Career and Studies

Life demanded more than intellectual activity, however, and Edwards was soon called to the ministry. In early August 1722, he accepted his first pastorate at a small English Presbyterian congregation in New York City, a position he held for eight months until the end of April 1723. Here, surrounded by warm Christian fellowship but in relative intellectual and ecclesiastical isolation, he began writing his *Miscellanies*, wide-ranging essays in which he outlined his apology for the Christian faith and articulated his response to deism,[29] Enlightenment ideas, and contemporary scientific culture. More than any of his other works, the *Miscellanies*, written over a period of more than thirty years and comprising over 1,400 entries, embody Edwards's spiritual and intellectual autobiography.

After his brief sojourn in New York, Edwards returned to his father's house on the last day of April 1723. Except for several journeys to Boston, Norwich, and other places, he stayed at home to complete the requirements for his master's degree and give himself energetically to his private studies. During that time he prepared his master's thesis on the nature of justification, entitled *A Sinner is not Justified in the Sight of God Except Through the Righteousness of Christ Obtained by Faith*.[30] This discourse dealt with the complex of doctrines on the nature and grounds of justification, in dispute between Calvinists and Arminians (the latter stressed confidence in human beings' ability to gain some purchase on the divine favor by human endeavor). The refutation of Arminianism occupied Edwards for the rest of his life. He delivered his thesis at the Yale commencement in September 1723 and received the M.A. degree. While living in New York, Edwards had been invited to serve the church of the newly settled town of Bolton, Connecticut. During the month of October 1723, he concluded the negotiations and, on November 11, signed the Bolton town book, agreeing to settle as a pastor. His second pastorate lasted until May 1724. This was an active and creative period in Edwards's intellectual life. Apart from regularly writing entries on natural philosophy, in which he continued to set forth his idealism, he commenced two new notebooks, one on the book of Revelation (*Notes on the Apocalypse*)[31] and the other on Scripture (*Notes on Scripture*,)[32] both of which he continued writing for the rest of his life.

[29] Edwards's response to deism is analyzed most recently in McDermott, *Jonathan Edwards Confronts the Gods*.

[30] Edwards, *A Sinner is not Justified in Sight of God Except Through the Righteousness of Christ Obtained by Faith*, in SDK, pp. 60–66.

[31] Edwards, *Notes on the Apocalypse*, in AW.

[32] Edwards, *Notes on Scripture*, in NOS.

On May 21, 1724, Edwards was elected to a tutorship at Yale College, and early the following month, he took up his duties there. He held this office for almost two years, until September 1726. Owing to the vacancy in the rectorship for the whole of this period, his position was one of special responsibilities. The appointment provided Edwards with a useful opportunity to keep abreast of the world of ideas and further develop his theological and philosophical interests. Through his renewed access to the college library, he became better acquainted with major authors in theology and philosophy, and the long list of book titles appearing in his *Catalogue*[33] of reading testifies to the wide range of his theological and philosophical interests at this time. During these twenty-eight months at Yale, he continued to pursue his studies and writings: he further elaborated the premises of his theology of nature by enlarging the scale of his treatise on natural philosophy and making considerable additions to the manuscript.

Edwards also began collecting materials for a work in mental philosophy, *The Mind*, where he formulated his idealistic phenomenalism, according to which the material universe exists nowhere "but in the mind"; and since "all material existence is only idea," the "world therefore is an ideal one."[34] His main intention in *The Mind*, many of whose essays were written in response to Locke's empiricism, was to show that the essence of reality is a matter of the relationship between God and the created order. The principle underlying his theological teleology, the order of being inherent in the structure of the universe, was the concept of excellency. Edwards defined this concept as the "consent of being to being, or being's consent to entity," which in turn defined the relationship within the hierarchy of spirits according to their consent to the supreme being, God. "So far as a thing consents to being in general," Edwards wrote, "so far it consents to him," hence "the more perfect created spirits are, the nearer do they come to their creator in this regard." Since "the more the consent is, and the more extensive, the greater is the excellency," therefore in "the order of beings in the natural world, the more excellent and noble any being is, the more visible and immediate hand of God is there in bringing them into being," with "the most noble of all" the "soul of man."[35]

Judged by these scientific and philosophical writings, it was the mark of Edwards's brilliance that he fully understood the serious challenges posed by mechanical philosophy to traditional religious faith and experience. He was alarmed by the metaphysical and theological principles that often accompanied the scientific revolution, such as the mechanistic conception of the world of nature as a self-contained and independent reality

[33] Edwards, "Catalogue of Reading," typescript on disk, Works of Jonathan Edwards Office, Yale Divinity School, New Haven, Conn.

[34] Edwards, *The Mind*, pp. 350–56.

[35] Ibid., pp. 336–37; *Miscellany* no. 541, in *MISA*, p. 89.

of its own, or as a huge machine that runs by itself according to abstract, universal laws of nature, freed from subordination to God's dominion and not affected by his ever-watchful eyes. With great dismay Edwards saw that mechanical philosophy's notion of a homogeneous, uniform, and symmetrical, one-dimensional world of nature not only deprived the created order of any teleological ends and purposes, but stipulated that nature could no longer manifest the presence of God. In response, he constructed his own theology of nature, a typology interpreting the physical world as a representation or a "shadow" of the spiritual which celebrates God's glory and sovereignty as they are evidenced in the coherence and beauty, order and harmony, of world phenomena. Hence his claim that "the things of the world are ordered [and] designed to shadow forth spiritual things."[36] While attempting to provide an alternative view regarding the essence of reality, which would lead eventually to the reenchantment of the world, Edwards's goal was to demonstrate the infinite power of God's absolute sovereignty in both the order of nature and the order of time.

Northampton Pastorate

After two years, in September 1726, Edwards resigned his tutorship at Yale College to become the ministerial colleague of his grandfather, the Rev. Solomon Stoddard. Stoddard, then eighty-four, was in the fifty-fifth year of his pastorate in Northampton, Massachusetts. Edwards arrived at Northampton in October. The town invited him to settle as Stoddard's colleague in November and on February 15, 1727, he was ordained. On July 28, he was married to Sarah Pierpont (1713–58) of New Haven, daughter of the late Rev. James Pierpont (1660–1714), the first pastor in the town. They had three sons and eight daughters.

Probably in late September or early October 1728, Edwards commenced the writing of another notebook, *Images of Divine Things*, to which he continued to add new entries until 1756. This work contains his major statements on the exegetical discipline of typology. In contrast to traditional Christian typology—the exercise of matching biblical types such as prophetic figures, events, or circumstances in the Old Testament with their antitypes or fulfillment in the New—Edwards's typology comprehended not only Scripture but also nature and history. For him, types were to be found not only in the Old Testament. The phenomenal world also declared divine truths: "the works of nature are intended and contrived of God to signify and indigitate spiritual things," hence the "Book of Scripture is the interpreter of the book of nature," "declaring to us

---

[36] Edwards, *Images of Divine Things*, p. 53.

those spiritual mysteries that are indeed signified or typified in the constitution of the natural world."[37]

The death of his venerable grandfather on February 11, 1729, left Edwards in charge of one of New England's most prestigious parishes. Edwards, age twenty-six, became the sole pastor and assumed the whole round of duties belonging to the pastorate of a large congregation in the most important town in western Massachusetts. As a consequence, he gradually abandoned the treatises on natural philosophy and *The Mind*, as his time, efforts, and interests were more fully commanded by the concerns of his ministry and as new responsibilities directed his attention more and more to ecclesiastical affairs in his congregation. A lecture he gave in Boston in 1731, *God Glorified in the Work of Redemption*—a defense of the Calvinist doctrine of God's absolute sovereignty as the foundation of all right doctrine—became the first of his sermons to be published, and he soon gained a reputation as a defender of Reformed doctrines.[38] During this period he also became a leading member of the Hampshire Association, a local organization of clergymen, and played a significant role in 1735 in efforts to prevent Rev. Robert Breck's ordination in the church of Springfield because of his suspected Arminian sympathies.

Under Edwards's pastoral care, the Northampton congregation experienced during the winter of 1734–35 an extraordinary manifestation of religious zeal and awakening known as the "little revival." Edwards's accounts of the revival, especially *A Faithful Narrative of the Surprising Work of God* (1737),[39] circulated throughout the American colonies and in Great Britain, establishing him as a prominent leader in the Protestant evangelical awakening in both British America and Great Britain. After the fervor and ferment of the revival declined, and struggling to revive the days when Northampton was "a city set on a hill,"[40] Edwards preached a series of sermons in 1738, published in 1852 under the title *Charity and Its Fruits; Or, Christian Love as Manifested in Heart and Life*. There he attacked, in part, the British school of moral sense of Francis Hutcheson, David Hume, and others, who developed the rationalist idea of disinterested benevolence as the criterion for moral judgment. This ethical theory rejected the traditional, popular view that morality is based on the will of God, maintaining that morality depends on human nature. Hutcheson's moral theory is primarily concerned with qualities in persons, that is to say "virtue, which he considered to be natural to man." He developed the idea of a moral sense cognitivism, the notion that "man is naturally supplied with a special moral sense." In his moral theory, "morals, in the

---

[37] Ibid., pp. 66, 106.
[38] Edwards, *God Glorified in the Work of Redemption*, in *SJE*, pp. 66–82.
[39] Edwards, *A Faithful Narrative of the Surprising Work of God*, in *GA*, pp. 144–212.
[40] Ibid., p. 210.

sense of both sentiments and ideas, come naturally to man."[41] Against this theory, which excludes theistic considerations from the realms of ethics and morals, Edwards assessed moral matters ultimately by their "worth in the sight of God," and claimed that without "love to God there can be no true honor," or, conversely, that from "love to God springs love to man."[42] Gracious affections therefore stand above and beyond the natural affections of which all are capable, and true virtue, or divine love, stands above and beyond the disinterested benevolence that marks the ultimate achievement of natural man.

The "little revival" of the 1730s left an indelible mark on Edwards. He struggled to understand the nature of divine agency in the order of time, the essential relationship between redemptive activity and the course of history, attempting to decipher God's "great design"[43] in the "affairs of redemption" and "in the disposition of things in redemption."[44] The fruit of these efforts was a series of thirty sermons on the *History of the Work of Redemption*, preached to his congregation during the spring and summer of 1739, which constitute Edwards's most systematic exposition of salvation history. Against the Enlightenment denial of any theistic interpretation of the historical process, leading to the de-Christianization or even the secularization of history, Edwards viewed history as lying exclusively in the mind of omniscient God. He thus developed his singular redemptive mode of historical thought, the view that the course of history is based exclusively on God's redemptive activity, in part in response to Enlightenment narratives rejecting the Christian sense of time and vision of history.

Taking God as the sole author and Lord of history, Edwards argued that history has been constructed by divine providence as a special dimension of sacred, redemptive time designed solely for the accomplishment of God's work of redemption for fallen humanity: "the world itself seems to have been created in order" to effect that work of redemption, for the "work of creation was in order to God's works of providence."[45] Hence, it should be understood exclusively from the perspective of its maker and author. In this sacred, redemptive context, the "pourings out of the Spirit" and its historical manifestation in the form of revival and awakening constitute the ultimate mark of divine agency in the order of time: "from the fall of man to this day wherein we live the Work of Redemption in its

[41] Knud Haakonssen, *Natural Law and Moral Philosophy: From Grotius to the Scottish Enlightenment* (Cambridge: Cambridge University Press, 1996), p. 66.

[42] Edwards, *Charity and Its Fruits*, in *EW*, pp. 63, 137, 142.

[43] Edwards, *Miscellany* no. 547, in *MISA*, pp. 93–95.

[44] Edwards, *God Glorified in the Work of Redemption*, in *SJE*, p. 78.

[45] Edwards, *History of the Work of Redemption*, in *HWR*, p. 118. See also *Miscellany* no. 702, 1736, in *MISA*, p. 284, where that argument was defined in this way: "the work of creation in itself seems to be so done that it should shadow forth the work of redemption."

effects has mainly been carried on by remarkable pourings out of the Spirit of God" at "special seasons of mercy," or revivals.[46] From the Deity's point of view, which it was Edwards's aim to expound, history is a grand theater in which God reveals his redemptive plan, and revivals, such as the Great Awakening, illustrate the historical necessity, or indeed inevitability, of the progress of God's historical scheme of redemption. This was Edwards's specific contribution to evangelical historiography and his answer to Enlightenment historians, such as Henry St. John, Lord Bolingbroke (1678–1751), and Hume, who instead of seeing the historical process as contingent on a metaphysical reality beyond and above it, attached the highest importance to human beings' actions and deeds in determining the course of history.

Edwards's philosophy of salvation history exercised an enormous influence in New England and Protestant America in general. He is considered not only the father of the great colonial revival of the 1740s but also as "the putative father of American postmillennialism," the belief that the coming of Jesus would occur only after the millennium.[47] During the early nineteenth century, the *History of the Work of Redemption* was "the most popular manual of Calvinist theology." Indeed, for antebellum evangelists Edwards's philosophy of salvation history provided the main source for understanding history as a "grand narrative propelled by a divine 'design and covenant of redemption.' "[48] He laid the groundwork for the Second Great Awakening, influencing nineteenth-century evangelists' understanding of "the coming of the kingdom," and leading them to believe that "the divine sovereignty was the fruition not only of divine goodness but of human badness in conflict with that unconquerable goodness."[49] Further, Edwards's theology of history, emphasizing that "effort to progress toward the coming of the kingdom by self-discipline," not only led to the recognition of divine sovereignty within the realm of history but ushered in "a new awareness of the coming kingdom." Hence, through his and others' efforts during the Awakening "the coming of the kingdom" became "the dominant idea" in American Protestantism.[50] Edwards's theme of God's redemption of the world became "at once the core of the Christian movement in America and the central meaning and significance of the culture."[51]

[46] Edwards, *History of the Work of Redemption*, p. 143.
[47] James H. Moorhead, *World Without End: Mainstream American Protestant Visions of the Last Things, 1880–1925* (Bloomington: Indiana University Press, 1999), pp. 5–6.
[48] Conforti, *Jonathan Edwards, Religious Tradition & American Culture*, pp. 48–49.
[49] Niebuhr, *The Kingdom of God in America*, p. 138.
[50] Ibid., pp. 135–38.
[51] Wilson, introduction, in *HWR*, p. 95.

The Great Awakening

The religious situation in New England changed dramatically in 1740. In the fall of that year, George Whitefield (1714–71), the "Grand Itinerant," set all New England aflame. Whitefield's grand tour of the British colonies (1739–41) led to a pietistic revival known as the Great Awakening (1740–42), which engulfed much of British America and inaugurated the revival tradition in America. Edwards immediately assumed a prominent role in the movement that shattered the harmony of the established Congregational churches in New England. Hoping to advance the cause of the revival, to save its detractors from sealing their doom, and to move honest doubters to positive approval of what he regarded as the latter-day miracle, Edwards preached his now famous sermon, *Sinners in the Hands of an Angry God*, in July 1741 at Enfield, Massachusetts, evoking the terrifying image of the unconverted as a spider hanging by a single thread "over the pit of hell."[52] Zealously defending the revival in his commencement address at Yale in September 1741—*The Distinguishing Marks of a Work of the Spirit of God*—Edwards defined the marks of the Spirit of God's saving operations, and declared that the revival "is undoubtedly, in the general, from the Spirit of God." Warning those who opposed the revival that they were fighting against God and committing an unpardonable sin against the Holy Spirit, he placed the Awakening within the grand, sacred, redemptive context he had already developed in the *History of the Work of Redemption*, claiming that the present revival was clear evidence that "Christ is come down from heaven into this land, in a remarkable and wonderful work of his Spirit."[53]

During the revivals of the 1730s and 1740s, Edwards not only rapidly emerged as a leader in New England, but his various writings pertaining to the revivals were soon printed and widely circulated in Europe, securing him a prominent place in the transatlantic Protestant evangelical awakening of that period.[54] The Great Awakening in New England was an integral part of a series of revivals taking place in the Protestant world during the first half of the eighteenth century in England, Scotland, and Germany, encompassing Pietists in Germany, Methodists in England, and

[52] Edwards, *Sinners in the Hands of an Angry God*, in *SJE*, p. 55.
[53] Edwards, *The Distinguishing Marks of a Work of the Spirit of God*, in *GA*, pp. 260, 270.
[54] See W. R. Ward, *The Protestant Evangelical Awakening* (Cambridge: Cambridge University Press, 1992); Michael J. Crawford, *Seasons of Grace: Colonial New England's Revival Tradition in Its British Context* (New York: Oxford University Press, 1991); and Mark A. Noll et al., eds., *Evangelicalism: Comparative Studies of Popular Protestantism in North America, The British Isles, and Beyond, 1700–1990* (New York: Oxford University Press, 1994).

Reformed—Congregationalists and Presbyterians—in Scotland and colonial British America. Edwards quickly emerged as a leader in this transatlantic movement. Evidence can be found of the enthusiastic reception of his writings and their impact on many Protestant theologians in Europe. An English edition of his *A Faithful Narrative of the Surprising Work of God* (1737) appeared in London in 1737 and was immediately reprinted in Edinburgh in 1737 and 1738. Its influence was felt also in the Welsh revival. A Scottish edition of *The Distinguishing Marks of the Work of the Spirit of God* (1741) appeared in 1743, and the sermon *Sinners in the Hands of an Angry God*, delivered on July 1741, circulated in Glasgow in 1742, and was published there in 1745. In England Wesley eagerly read the *Faithful Narrative* in October 1738, and this work as well as other writings, such as *Distinguishing Marks* and *A Treatise Concerning Religious Affections* (1746), exercised an enormous influence on the English Methodist movement, the "Wesleyan Revival." Likewise, Edwards's *The Nature of True Virtue* (written in 1755, published in 1765) was regarded by orthodox Christians in England who opposed Enlightenment moral theories and strove to emphasize the superiority of Christian ethics, as "the most elaborate, acute, and rational account of this interesting subject."[55] Edwards's *A Faithful Narrative* appeared in 1738 in German, as did also his *Life of David Brainerd* (1749).

The emotional outbursts accompanying the Great Awakening became increasingly controversial, causing critics to question the legitimacy of the revivalists. By 1742, opponents of the revival, called "Old Lights" to distinguish them from the "New Lights" or those who were in favor of the revival, began launching their attack.[56] Chief among the critics was Charles Chauncy (1705–87) of Boston's First Church. This captain of the antirevival forces launched the first onslaught against the revival, denouncing overt enthusiasm and calling for a return to sane, rational religion in his sermon *Enthusiasm Described and Caution'd Against* (1742). In another work, *Seasonable Thoughts on the State of Religion in New England* (1743)—a compendium of horror stories about the worst emotional extravagances of the Awakening—Chauncy declared the accounts "about the SPIRIT's influence" are nothing but "a *notorious* Error."[57] Edwards quickly concentrated on defending the revival as a divine work against rationalists and conservatives alienated by its emotion and tumult, and against over-enthusiasts who celebrated both. Believing the revival to be a true work of the Spirit, he claimed: "If this ben't the work of God, I

---

[55] Isabel Rivers, *Reason, Grace, and Sentiment: A Study of the Language of Religion and Ethics in England 1660–1780*, vol. II: *Shaftesbury to Hume* (Cambridge: Cambridge University Press, 2000), p. 194.

[56] C. C. Goen, introduction, in *GA*, pp. 60–65.

[57] Chauncy, *Enthusiasm Described and Caution'd Against* (Boston, 1742); *Seasonable Thought on the State of Religion in New England* (Boston, 1743), p. 319.

have all my religion to learn over again, and know not what use to make of the Bible." Moreover, since "Christ gloriously triumphs at this day," New England should "give glory to him who thus rides forth in the chariots of his salvation."[58]

In his answer to Chauncy's attacks, *Some Thoughts Concerning the Present Revival of Religion in New England* (1742), his most ambitious work yet (378 pages), Edwards asserted that the rationalistic objections to the Awakening rested on a false philosophy that divorced "the affections of the soul" from the "will." Instead of the rationalist view of man, according to which the "passions" are sub-rational appetites to be held in check by the reason, a perspective requiring that religion should seek to enlighten the mind rather than raise the affections, Edwards adopted Locke's sensationalist psychology, arguing for the direct action of God upon the heart. Edwards's *Some Thoughts* is perhaps the clearest example of his interpretation of the Great Awakening in terms of God's work of redemption in history, according to the philosophy of history he had already formulated in the *History of the Work of Redemption*. In *Some Thoughts*, Edwards's "*heilsgeschichtliches* reading of human events in terms of historical progress toward a goal defined by the providence of God" reached its zenith.[59] In face of the extraordinary character of the revival, he believed "this work of God's Spirit" was "the dawning, or at least a prelude, of that glorious work of God" when he shall "renew the world of mankind"[60] Edwards not only defended the Awakening as the work of God's Spirit, but claimed that this revival, along with other Protestant awakenings, as in Saxony and Scotland,[61] was "the dawning, or forerunner of an happy state" of the "church on earth,"[62] which would precede the millennial age.

During the Awakening, and as a result of the growing controversy over "the nature and signs of the gracious operations of God's spirit," Edwards preached (probably in 1742) a long series of sermons that became the nucleus for his fullest statement on the evangelical nature of true religion, *A Treatise Concerning Religious Affections* (1746). Like his other tracts of the period, it provides a commentary upon and defense of revivalism. Rejecting the rationalistic objections to the revival, he held that the dynamic center of a willing acting self lies not in the intellect but in the disposition, or the "new sense of the heart." Striving to show how the presence of the divine Spirit could be discerned, and to define the soul's

---

[58] Edwards, "To the Reverend Joseph Bellamy," January 21, 1741/2, in *LPW*, pp. 97–98.

[59] Goen, introduction, p. 71.

[60] Edwards, *Some Thoughts Concerning the Present Revival of Religion in New England*, in *GA*, p. 353.

[61] Edwards, *Much in Deeds of Charity*, in *SJE*, p. 210; *Some Thoughts*, pp. 528, 309, 311; "To the Rev. James Rose," May 12, 1743, in *LPW*, p. 108.

[62] Edwards, *Some Thoughts*, pp. 296–97, 324.

relationship to God, his concern in this work was with the "nature and signs" of "gracious" affections, in contrast to things of the "mind," which "are not of a saving nature." He thus distinguished the life of the saints beyond anything that can be achieved by natural man. The central problem this tract examined is "the distinguishing qualifications of those that are in favour with God and entitled to his eternal reward." Edwards defined "true religion" as chiefly a matter of "holy affections" respecting divine things. He identified twelve "signs" that are "gracious" or "saving" and provided an exhaustive account of them.[63] Given that each sign served as a mark through which the presence of the divine Spirit could be known, each pointed to the activity of saving grace. As a whole these signs revealed the presence of the Spirit and were evidence of the working of the divine saving grace in the heart of the believer. Thus, against "the British Moral philosophers' movement toward a secularized understanding of the affections grounded in an innate 'moral sense,' Edwards grounded what he deemed to be specifically religious, that is, God-given 'gracious' affections, in a new 'spiritual sense.' "[64] Like other evangelists of his time, Edwards emphasized the personal, unmediated experience of new birth and argued that the regenerative process of "conversion by grace" is "immediate" and dependent upon God's word and Spirit.[65] God thus works a permanent qualitative change beyond anything of which natural faculties are capable; the mind is enlightened to apprehend God and the will becomes disposed to love and seek God for his own sake.

In the aftermath of the Awakening, Edwards sought new ways to foster religious life in his congregation and abroad, including a plan for a worldwide "concert of prayer." He published his reflections on the book of Revelation in the *Humble Attempt* (1747), in which he advanced the contention, already discussed in Scotland, that a union of praying Christians would "open the doors and windows of heaven" after the withdrawal of the Spirit. Edwards believed that the saints had good reason to unite in a concert of prayer, for it seemed evident to him that "the beginning of that glorious work of God's Spirit" which will culminate in "the glory of the latter-days, is not far off."[66] In 1749, as a sequel to his earlier writings relating to the Great Awakening, Edwards published *The Life of David Brainerd* (1718–47), the biography of a missionary to the Indians on the western border of Massachusetts. Here Edwards articulated the genuine spiritual life and the new birth in a man with abundant concrete evidence.

[63] Edwards, *Religious Affections*, in RA, pp. 84, 89, 118–19, 272.

[64] Ann Taves, *Fits, Trances & Visions: Experiencing Religion and Explaining Experience from Wesley to James* (Princeton: Princeton University Press, 1999), p. 38.

[65] Conrad Cherry, *The Theology of Jonathan Edwards: A Reappraisal* (Bloomington: Indiana University Press, 1990), p. 57.

[66] Edwards, *Humble Attempt*, in AW, pp. 446–47, 325, 421.

Closer to home, in the course of his pastoral duty at Northampton, Edwards thought it necessary to censure publicly a large number of his parishioners for indulging in immoral practices. He consequently incurred the displeasure of some of the most influential families in the town. Conflict developed over questions of ministerial authority. Edwards's announcement that he intended to discontinue his grandfather's practice of admitting to communion those in good standing unless they could provide evidence of a work of grace in their lives provoked an open rupture. The conflict spread into town politics and into relations with neighboring ministers, causing bitter factionalism. Edwards formally made his views known to the Standing Committee of the church in February 1749. Since Stoddard's system of open communion had been practiced for nearly half a century, it was inevitable that Edwards's attempts to reform it would give offense and that he would be removed from his duties. After several months of bitter strife, a council of ministers and laity recommended a separation between Edwards and his congregation, and Edwards's formal dismissal followed in mid-1750. A council called on June 22, 1750, voted by a bare majority to dismiss him. He preached his farewell sermon nine days later.

Life and Works at Stockbridge

After his removal, Edwards faced uncertain prospects. He supplied the vacant pulpit in Canaan, Connecticut, and contemplated settling there. At the same time, he received several offers, including one from Scotland. In December 1750, a proposal came to him from the congregation in Stockbridge in western Massachusetts to become its minister; at about the same time a proposal came from the Commissioners of the London Society for Propagating the Gospel in New England to become a missionary to the Housatonic Indians who lived in or near Stockbridge. In the first week of August 1751, Edwards moved with his family to Stockbridge. Life in this mission outpost, populated by a few whites and more than 250 Indian families, was very difficult, especially after the outbreak of the French and Indian War (1754–63). The conflict reached the village in 1754 when, after a raiding party of French and Indians killed several inhabitants, the town was temporarily turned into a garrison.

Edwards's success in Stockbridge was apparently small, but the place nonetheless afforded him comparative retirement for study and composition. Despite the hard conditions of the frontier settlement, these years were perhaps Edwards's most productive. Not only did he continue his pattern of study, but he also wrote several major treatises. Among them are well-known works such as *Freedom of the Will* (1754), which is considered his greatest literary achievement, *Concerning the End for Which*

God Created the World and *The Nature of True Virtue* (both published posthumously in 1765), and *Original Sin* (1758).

Edwards's theological standing in his own day rested significantly on his *Freedom of the Will*, which was both a staunch defense of Calvinism and an assertion of God's absolute sovereignty. His goal in this work, as he wrote in 1752, was to refute the claim by "modern writers" that "the Calvinistic notions of God's moral government are contrary to the common sense of mankind."[67] Accordingly, in this tract he attacked the Arminians' and deists' "grand article concerning *the freedom of the will requisite to moral agency*," the belief that absolute self-determinacy of will was necessary to human liberty and moral virtue. If the Arminian view was correct, he believed, God's providential and redemptive economy was contingent on the unpredictable actions of moral agents. Such a condition contradicts the doctrine of divine foreknowledge and the premise that God, as absolute governor of the universe, orders events according to his sovereign wisdom. Instead, Edwards argued that since "every event" in the physical as well as the moral world "must be ordered by God," the "liberty of moral agents does not consist in self-determining power." Human beings must do as they will, in accordance with their fallen nature, and they have liberty only in the sense that nothing prevents them from doing what they will in accordance with their nature. Because "nothing in the state or acts of the will of man is contingent" but "every event of this kind is necessary," God's foreknowledge eliminates the possibility of contingency in the world, for contingency is the antithesis of God's unlimited prescience. Given that "the power of volition" belonged only to "the man or the soul," there is no such thing as "freedom of the will." That freedom is incompatible with the individual's necessary willing of what he or she can will in accordance with a nature of self already determined.[68] In the end, Edwards "saw the whole spectrum of moral endeavour solely in terms of his notion of the visible saints whose character was already determined."[69] His *Freedom of the will*, as the title suggests, does affirm freedom. Edwards was not denying it but affirming it in order to vindicate God's justice in damning the non-elect.

Edwards's *Original Sin* played a part in the larger debates between the Enlightenment belief in the innate goodness of human beings and the emphasis placed by the Reformation on human depravity. Against the revolution that took place in the Western mind during the eighteenth century regarding human nature and potentialities, and the Enlightenment notion of human beings as fundamentally rational and benevolent, Ed-

---

[67] Edwards, "To The Reverend John Erskine," July 7, 1752, in *LPW*, p. 491.

[68] Edwards, *Freedom of the Will*, pp. 163, 431–33.

[69] John E. Smith, *Jonathan Edwards: Puritan, Preacher, Philosopher* (Notre Dame: University of Notre Dame Press, 1992), p. 78.

wards provided "a *general defense* of that great important doctrine" of original sin. This doctrine proclaimed both the depravity of the human heart and the imputation of Adam's first sin to his posterity: all Adam's posterity are "exposed, and justly so, to the sorrow of this life, to temporal death, and eternal ruin, unless saved by grace." The corruption of humankind, however, cannot be accounted for by considering the sin of each individual. It is essential to the human condition based on "the *arbitrary constitution of the Creator*" in creation.[70]

In *The Nature of True Virtue* (1755), Edwards responded more directly to contemporary "controversies and variety of opinions" about "the nature of true virtue."[71] More specifically, as Edwards wrote, it was "principally designed against that notion of virtue maintained by My Lord Shaftesbury, [Francis] Hutcheson, and [George] Turnbull," according to which "all mankind are naturally disposed to virtue, and are without any native depravity."[72] Accordingly, Edwards's goal in this work was to define the disposition that distinguished the godly. Elaborating his definition of excellency, he declared that true "virtue most essentially consists in benevolence to Being in general." True virtue is a kind of beauty. In moral beings, virtuous beauty pertains to a disposition of heart and exercise of will, namely, "that consent, propensity and union of heart to Being in general," or God, "which is immediately exercised in good will."[73] True virtue in creatures appears in the degree to which their love coincides with God's love of his creation and agrees with the end that he intended for it.

Taken as a whole, Edwards's ethical writings, such as *Charity and Its Fruits* (1738), *Concerning the End for which God Created the World* (1755), *The Nature of True Virtue* (1755), as well as *Original Sin* (1758), may be examined in light of his reaction against Enlightenment views of ethics and morals. Theories of morals emerged during the early eighteenth century which stood in opposition to traditional Christian teaching. Writers such as Francis Hutcheson and David Hume argued that it is possible to have knowledge of good and evil without, and prior to, knowledge of God. The main assumption behind this conception of ethics was the belief that human beings can know from within themselves, without relying on traditional sources of religious authority, what God intends and expects of them as moral creatures. Edwards read several works by Enlightenment moral theorists, such as Hutcheson's *An Inquiry into the Original of Our Ideas of Beauty and Virtue* (1725) and *An Essay on the Nature and Conduct of the Passions and Affections with Illustration on the Moral Sense* (1728), and Hume's *An Enquiry Concerning Human Understanding*

---

[70] Edwards, *Original Sin*, in *OS*, pp. 102, 395, 403.
[71] Edwards, *The Nature of True Virtue*, in *EW*, p. 539.
[72] Edwards, "To the Reverend Thomas Foxcroft," February 11, 1757, in *LPW*, p. 696.
[73] Edwards, *The Nature of True Virtue*, p. 540.

(1748), *A Treatise on Human Nature* (1739), and *Enquiry Concerning the Principles of Morals* (1751). Here he could see that the new theories of morals were leading to the detachment of the moral system from God. Edwards accordingly strongly attacked the Enlightenment view of ethics and morals, claiming it was "evident that true virtue must chiefly consist in love to God,"[74] and that "all true *virtue*" is based on "love of Being, and the qualities and acts which arise from it."[75]

Finally, in *Concerning the End for Which God Created the World*, Edwards continued to develop the notion that the whole creation is the overflowing of divine being. God's "internal glory" consists in his knowledge, resident in his understanding, and his holiness and happiness, seated in his will, which glory is "enlarged" by communication "*ad extra.*" The "great and last end" of all God's works is the manifestation of "the glory of God," as "the effulgence" of "light from a luminary," and in the "creature's knowing, esteeming, loving, and rejoicing," God's glory is both "acknowledged [and] returned."[76]

After six years at Stockbridge, in September 1757, five days after the death of Aaron Burr (1716–57), who was Edwards's son-in-law and president of the College of New Jersey (now Princeton University), Edwards received a letter from the trustees of the college inviting him to become its third president. Edwards was a popular choice, for he had been a friend of the college from its inception. His three sons graduated from Princeton, and for several years he kept in close touch with college affairs, attending commencement regularly and usually preaching on his visits. His response of October 19, 1757, was equivocal, listing many deficiencies that might disqualify him. The trustees, brushing these objections aside, pressed him to accept without delay. Accordingly, on January 8, 1758, he preached his farewell sermon to the Indians at Stockbridge. A few days later he left for Princeton, arriving on February 16. He was formally inducted into office on the same day. He preached in the college chapel and gave out questions in divinity to the senior class. These seniors spoke enthusiastically of the "light and instruction which Mr. Edwards communicated."[77] One week later, February 23, he was vaccinated against smallpox, and one month later, on March 22, as a result of the inoculation, he was dead. Edwards was buried in the President's Lot in Princeton cemetery beside his son-in-law, Aaron Burr.

---

[74] Edwards, *Concerning the End for which God Created the World*, in *EW*, p. 550.
[75] Edwards, *The Nature of True Virtue*, p. 548.
[76] Edwards, *Concerning the End for Which God Created the World*, pp. 527, 530–51.
[77] Leitch, *A Princeton Companion*, p. 153.

The Soul

Two

Young Man Edwards: Religious Conversion
and *Theologia Gloriae*

There is a history in all men's lives,
Figuring the nature of the times deceased;
The which observed, a man may prophesy,
With a near aim, of the main chance of things
As yet not come to life, which in their seeds
And weak beginnings lie intreasured.
   (Shakespeare, *Henry IV*, Part Two)

To the Protestant . . . life seems a pilgrim's progress which, whether
made solitarily or in company, proceeds through unpredictable contingencies and crises toward the destination beyond life and death
where all the trumpets blow. . . . The Protestant memory of the past
is not focused in one grand event when the true human community
was reconstituted by the Lord and when the church came into being
as representative and guardian of that community. The great event
was one of arrivals, departures, and promises of return.
   (H. Richard Niebuhr, "The Protestant Movement and
   Democracy in the United States," *The Shaping of American
   Religion*, 1961)

JONATHAN EDWARDS's theological and philosophical views matured
slowly and gradually over time, but underlying the development of his
intellectual world and universe of thought a single tremendous spiritual
experience may be found. During the summer of 1721, when he was seventeen years old and studying toward his M.A. degree at Yale College, a
religious conversion shook the entire life of young man Edwards and radically reshaped his whole experience and existence. Then, as Edwards described his existential and spiritual condition after the event of conversion,
the "appearance of every thing was altered; there seemed to be, as it were,
a calm, sweet cast, or appearance of divine glory, in almost every thing."[1]

---

[1] Edwards's description of his religious conversion can be read in his *Personal Narrative*,
in *LPW*, pp. 790–804. The quotation is on pp. 793–94. Edwards wrote the *Personal Narrative* a long time after the experience, probably by the middle of the 1730s, according to Alan

Edwards obviously regarded his experience as of monumental and life-changing importance. Strangely enough, however, few historians have found this event worth describing or analyzing, and even fewer have found this critical religious experience to bear any crucial consequences for his life and thought.[2] Nevertheless, many features of Edwards's thought, in both form and content, can be traced directly to this signal existential moment when the whole of his religious identity and experience was shaped. Among these are his *theologia gloriae*[3]—the theology that celebrates God's majestic glory and sovereignty as evident in the coherence and beauty, order and harmony, of his creation—and the notion of God's absolute sovereignty; his construction of a redemptive mode of historical thought in which conversion experience occupies a prominent role and is inextricable from God's work of salvation and redemption; as well as the central place he assigned to conversion, revival, and awakening in the overall history of the Christian church.

Heimert, *Religion and the American Mind: From the Great Awakening to the Revolution* (Cambridge, Mass.: Harvard University Press, 1966), p. 61, or by "1739 or 1740," according to Wilson Kimnach. See Kimnach, introduction, in *SDK*, p. 267. This view has been confirmed more recently by George S. Claghorn in his introduction, in *LPW*, pp. 747–50.

[2] Edwards's conversion has been described in many studies, yet so far no serious and comprehensive attempt has been made to analyze his morphology of conversion. For studies touching on Edwards's conversion, see Ola E. Winslow, *Jonathan Edwards, 1703–1758: A Biography* (New York: Macmillan, 1940), and idem, ed., *Jonathan Edwards: Basic Writings* (New York: New American Library, 1966); William S. Morris, *The Young Jonathan Edwards: A Reconstruction* (New York: Carlson, 1991); R. C. De Prospo, *Theism in the Discourse of Jonathan Edwards* (Newark: University of Delaware Press, 1985); Stephen R. Yarbrough and John C. Adams, *Delightful Conviction: Jonathan Edwards and the Rhetoric of Conversion* (Westport, Conn.: Greenwood, 1993); Harold P. Simonson, *Jonathan Edwards: Theologian of the Heart* (Macon: Mercer University Press, 1982); Anri Morimoto, *Jonathan Edwards and the Catholic Vision of Salvation* (University Park: University of Pennsylvania Press, 1995); Daniel B. Shea, *Spiritual Autobiographies in America* (Princeton: Princeton University Press, 1968); Iain H. Murray, *Jonathan Edwards: A New Biography* (Edinburgh: Banner of Truth Trust, 1987); Edward H. Davidson, "Sovereign God and Reasoning Man," in *Critical Essays on Jonathan Edwards*, ed. William J. Scheick (Boston: G. K. Hall, 1980), pp. 33–40; Richard L. Bushman, "Jonathan Edwards as Great Man: Identity, Conversion, and Leadership in the Great Awakening," in *Critical Essays on Jonathan Edwards*, ed. William J. Scheick, pp. 41–64; Conrad Cherry, "Conversion: Nature and Grace," in *Critical Essays on Jonathan Edwards*, ed. William J. Scheick, pp. 76–88. A discussion of Edwards's spiritual life during the time of his conversion can be found in Wilson Kimnach, introduction, in *SDK*, pp. 261–80.

[3] In the *Heidelberg Disputation* of 1518, Martin Luther describes the essence of true theology as theology of the cross (*theologia crucis*). The opposite of this is the theology of glory (*theologia gloriae*). According to Luther's *theologia crucis*, our knowledge of the being of God must be derived from the study of Christ in his humiliation and the sufferings he underwent on the cross. Luther opposed his *theologia crucis* to a *theologia gloriae*, which would maintain with the Scholastic theologians that a true knowledge of God could be obtained from the study of nature. See Paul Althaus, *The Theology of Martin Luther* (Philadelphia: Fortress, 1966), ch. 5: "The Theology of the Cross," pp. 25–34.

Constructing the Self: Edwards's Conversion Moment

In the existence of Jonathan Edwards, perhaps no event can be compared, in terms of intensity of religious life and spiritual experience, to his conversion. This moment transformed his existential condition in the world, radically shaped his religious consciousness, and determined the growth of his universe of thought; it led him to find his vocation in life, and not least, it provided him with the form and content for his lifelong theological and philosophical undertaking. Thus, as with the conversions of other religious figures in the history of Christianity, such as St. Paul, St. Augustine, and Martin Luther,[4] to name only a few, Edwards's conversion signified the greatest spiritual crisis of his life to that point, radically separating his intellectual and spiritual world from what had been before and ushering in a new sense of his existence. Eventually it launched him on a mission which came to transform all his experience, both private and public, and powerfully shape his theological and philosophical views.

The conversion moment was also crucial in terms of the construction of Edwards's religious identity and consciousness. For conversion, which signifies, among other things, the "total transformation of the person by the power of God,"[5] the "surrender" of the self and the "transformation of conscience," leads eventually to "the radical reorientation of one's entire life that occurs when God is allowed to move from the periphery to the center of one's being."[6] Hence, to say that "a man is 'converted' " means "that religious ideas, previously peripheral in his consciousness, now take a central place, and that religious aims form the habitual center of his energy."[7] Before his conversion, Edwards had had many objections to the religious culture of his time. More specifically, his mind "had been full of objections against the doctrine of God's sovereignty, in choosing

---

[4] The conversion of St. Paul is described in Acts 9:1–19; 22:5–16, and 26:12–18. The relation of St. Augustine's conversion appeared in *The Confessions of St. Augustine*, trans. Hal M. Helms (Orleans, Mass.: Paraclete, 1986), book VIII, section xxii. An analysis of Luther's conversion experience can be found in Erik H. Erikson's classic study *Young Man Luther: A Study in Psychoanalysis and History* (New York: W. W. Norton, 1958). Erikson's study, however, has been much criticized for its heavy-handed (presumptuous) and psychologizing (reductive) treatment of religious experience. For a general psychological and pragmatist approach to religious conversion, see William James's classic study, *Varieties of Religious Experience*. For good collection of conversion accounts spanning 2,000 years of Christian history, see Hugh T. Kerr and John M. Mulder, eds., *Famous Conversions: The Christian Experience* (Grand Rapids: Eerdmans, 1983).

[5] Lewis R. Rambo, *Understanding Religious Conversion* (New Haven: Yale University Press, 1993), p. xii.

[6] Walter Conn, *Christian Conversion: A Developmental Interpretation of Autonomy and Surrender* (New York: Paulist, 1986), pp. 30, 267.

[7] James, *Varieties of Religious Experience*, p. 196.

whom he would to eternal life, and rejecting whom he pleased." The Reformed dogma of election and predestination "appeared like a horrible doctrine" to him. After his conversion, however, "God's absolute sovereignty and justice, with respect to salvation and damnation," wrote Edwards, "is what my mind seems to rest assured of, as much as of any thing that I see with my eyes."[8]

This spiritual experience informed Edwards's theology of nature and led directly to his quest to reconstruct the whole material world after the model of his newly acquired religious vision. Before his conversion, Edwards had taken for granted the traditional understanding of the physical, material world, even devoting part of his time to an inquiry into natural phenomena. He wrote, for example, probably in 1720, *Of Insects*, a youthful essay on the "Ballooning" or "Flying spider," a meticulous description of natural phenomena almost devoid of any theological dimension.[9] After his conversion, however, armed with a new awareness of his religious identity, there arose in his soul a new sense of his existential condition within a divine universe, and a new vision of the natural world around him: "God's excellency, his wisdom, his purity and love, seemed to appear in every thing."[10]

After the conversion moment Edwards began slowly to construct a theology of science as part of his natural philosophy, according to which the material world of everyday life was only a manifestation of a divine universe, wonderfully made and harmonized according to God's will and design: " 'Tis certain that when God first created matter or the various chaoses of atoms . . . he designed the figures and shapes of every atom, and likewise their place." Consequently, "the least wrong step in a mote may, in eternity, subvert the order of the universe."[11] There is then "no such thing as mechanism, if that word is taken to be that whereby bodies act each upon other, purely and properly by themselves."[12]

The experience of conversion radically transformed the young man's existential condition; after this point everything seemed to have a singular part and role in a well-designed divine universe ruled directly by the sovereignty of God. The world of nature itself was an integral part of God's cosmic plan. As the young Edwards argued in 1723, "Every atom in the universe is managed by Christ so as to be most to the advantage of the

[8] Edwards, *Personal Narrative*, p. 792.

[9] Edwards, *Of Insects*, in *SPW*, pp. 154–62. Wallace E. Anderson dated this essay after Edwards came to New Haven in the summer of 1719, probably writing it in the autumn of 1720. See Anderson, introduction, in *SPW*, pp. 147–53.

[10] Edwards, *Personal Narrative*, p. 794.

[11] Edwards, *Things to be Considered an[d] Written fully about*, in *SPW*, pp. 265, 231. A similar contention can be found in modern chaos theory regarding the "butterfly effect."

[12] Edwards, *Of Atoms* (c. 1722), in *SPW*, p. 216.

Christian, every particle of air or every ray of the sun."[13] His conversion led Edwards to construct a remarkable cosmological conception regarding real being and true substance. Given that the material world is doomed to destruction in the final conflagration, only spirits and ideas constitute the real substances in God's universe, a divine universe extending from the eternity before the creation to the eternity that will follow the end of the world. For "the world exists only mentally."[14] Therefore, "those beings which have knowledge and consciousness are the only proper and real and substantial beings . . . [hence] spirits only are properly substance."[15] In this sense, the lives of human beings have only one purpose and significance: to acquire the knowledge of God, and to accept Christ's gospel of grace and salvation as the only means of rescuing them from their existential contingent condition in the world and of ensuring their participation in the blessing of eternity after life, or after the final conflagration. This cosmological vision of a divine universe, which sustained Edwards throughout his life and constituted the underlying theme of his whole theological and philosophical undertaking, can only be explained by the crucial effect of his conversion.

The conversion moment naturally influenced the development of Edwards's views concerning the place of the created world within God's overall plan of salvation and redemption. Thus, probably in the summer of 1723, he began to be seriously concerned with the "redemption motif," which, as John F. Wilson says, "was *a*, if not *the*, central focal point of his theological reflection."[16] The redemptive theme was eventually most fully expressed in Edwards's concept of the history of God's work of redemption; a sacred, providential history that constitutes a special dimension of time—in contrast to the dimension of eternity "before the world was created" and the dimension of eternity "after the end of the world"[17]—in which God's grand plan of the "Work of Redemption" is carried out from "the fall of man, the beginning, and the end of the world—the Day of Judgment—its end."[18] Situated between two long strings of eternity time—before the creation of the world and after its

---

[13] *Miscellany ff* (1723), in *MIS*, p. 184. For the dating of the *Miscellanies* entries, see Schafer, introduction, in *MIS*, especially "Table 2. The '*Miscellanies*' and Chronological Parallels: May 1719–August 1731," pp. 91–109.

[14] *Miscellany* no. 247 (c. 1726), p. 360.

[15] Edwards, *Of Being* (1722), in *SPW*, p. 207. For a discussion of Edwards's typology of nature, see Janice Knight, "Learning the Language of God: Jonathan Edwards and the Typology of Nature," *William and Mary Quarterly* 48 (1991): 531–51; and idem, *Orthodoxies in Massachusetts: Rereading American Puritanism* (Cambridge, Mass.: Harvard University Press, 1994).

[16] John F. Wilson, introduction, in *HWR*, pp. 14–15.

[17] Edwards, *History of the Work of Redemption*, p. 118.

[18] Ibid., p. 116.

end—the material, terrestrial world comprises only a small portion of God's universe; however, it constitutes the crucial space of time in God's work of redemption and the essential stage upon which the drama of human salvation and redemption takes place. "We are pilgrims and strangers here" on earth, Edwards preached to his congregation at Northampton, "and are principally designed for a future world. We continue in this present state but a short time; but we are to be in that future state to all eternity."[19]

The formation of Edwards's new religious identity led him to develop a vision regarding the advancement of the kingdom of Christ in the world. "My heart has been much on the advancement of Christ's kingdom in the world," he wrote shortly after his conversion, and "[my] mind has been much entertained and delighted with the scripture promises and prophecies, which relate to the future glorious advancement of Christ's kingdom upon earth."[20] Later, he developed these enthusiastic youthful beliefs into a remarkable theological system concerning God's grand design within time and history: "There is doubtless some design that God is pursuing, and scheme that he is carrying on, in the various changes and revolutions that from age to age happen in the world; there is some certain great design, to which providence subordinates all the successive changes that come to pass in the state of affairs of mankind."[21] An important part of Edwards's overall intellectual enterprise was indeed to elucidate in great detail his quest for the growth and success of the kingdom of God on earth.

The singularity of Edwards's conversion lay not only in the fact that it was a departure from the traditional New England Puritan "morphology of conversion,"[22] a fact that Edwards himself acknowledged, but that it inspired the formation of his *theologia gloriae*, the theology of God's majestic glory and sovereignty as evident in the harmony and order of the created world. "Edwards' theology was not dogma," wrote Perry Miller, "it was an indirect confession that for him . . . nature had become as compelling a way of God's speaking, if God speaks at all, as Scripture." Nature, for Edwards, "was not a disjointed series of phenomena; it was a living system of concepts, it was a complete, intelligible whole."[23] The

---

[19] Edwards, *Sermon 1*, in *The Works of Jonathan Edwards*, 2. vols. (Edinburgh: Banner of Truth Trust, 1995 [1834]), II, p. 820.

[20] Edwards, *Personal Narrative*, p. 800.

[21] Edwards, *Miscellany* no. 547 (c. 1731), in *MISA*, pp. 93–94.

[22] Patricia Caldwell, *The Puritan Conversion Narratives: The Beginnings of American Expression* (New York: Cambridge University Press, 1983), pp. 163–64; Morris, *The Young Jonathan Edwards*, p. 29; Yarbrough and Adams, *Delightful Conviction*, pp. 6–7.

[23] Perry Miller, introduction, in *Images or Shadows of Divine Things by Jonathan Edwards*, ed. Perry Miller (Westport, Conn.: Greenwood, 1977), p. 29.

conversion moment, then, was chiefly responsible for evoking in Edwards what H. Richard Niebuhr called the "sacramental sense of nature," according to which he saw "the whole creation as an emanation of the divine fullness."[24] Indeed, in his *theologia gloriae* Edwards attempted to overcome the separation of the orders of nature and grace, and thereby to resist the emergence of a graceless nature, or the detachment of grace from the natural world. This division between grace and nature which, according to Louis Dupré, began with late nominalism in the fourteenth century, and was greatly reinforced by the scientific revolution and the Enlightenment during the seventeenth and eighteenth centuries, was what Edwards tried to overcome in his theology of glory by endeavoring to infuse grace into nature and thus to rejoin nature, and hence history, to grace.[25]

In the *Heidelberg Disputations* of 1518, Martin Luther made the distinction between true theology (*theologia crucis*), and the theology of glory (*theologia gloriae*):

> That person does not deserve to be called a theologian who looks upon the invisible things of God as if it were clearly perceptible in those things which have actually happened. He deserves to be called a theologian, however, who comprehends the visible and manifest things of God seen through suffering and the cross.[26]

Luther described his own theology as a "theology of the cross," according to which the Christian's ultimate quest "is not the knowledge of God's invisible nature in his work but the knowledge of his back side visible through suffering."[27] In Luther's own words, "it is not sufficient for anyone, and it does him no good to recognize God in his glory and majesty, unless he recognizes him in humility and shame of the cross."[28] At the base of Luther's "theology of the cross was the proposition that 'God can be found only in suffering and the cross,' so that 'he who does not know

---

[24] Niebuhr, *The Kingdom of God in America*, p. 116.

[25] In a series of studies, Louis Dupré has analyzed the separation between the orders of grace and nature at the dawn of the modern age. See Dupré, *Passage to Modernity: An Essay in Hermeneutics of Nature and Culture* (New Haven: Yale University Press, 1993); "The Dissolution of the Union of Nature and Grace at the Dawn of the Modern Age," in *The Theology of Wolfhart Pannenberg*, ed. Carl E. Braaten and Philip Clayton (Minneapolis: Augsburg, 1988), pp. 95–121; and "Nature and Grace: Fateful Separation and Attempted Reunion," in *Catholicism and Secularization in America*, ed. David L. Schindler (Huntington, Ind.: Our Sunday Visitor Publishing Division, 1990), pp. 52–73.

[26] Martin Luther, Theses 19 and 20 of the *Heidelberg Disputation* (1518), quoted in Paul Althaus, *The Theology of Martin Luther* (Philadelphia: Fortress, 1966), p. 25.

[27] Althaus, *The Theology of Martin Luther*, p. 26.

[28] Ibid.

Christ does not know God hidden in suffering.' "[29] By emphasizing the
theology of the cross Luther opposed the theology of glory, which seeks
to know God from his works, or attempts "to know God directly in his
obviously divine power, wisdom and glory."[30]

Based upon these definitions, the distinctiveness of Edwards's theology
can be clearly seen as *theologia gloriae*, a theology that ultimately glorifies
God through his works. "For God to glorify himself is to discover himself
in his works," Edwards wrote, "or to communicate himself in his works,
which is all one."[31] Indeed, throughout his career, as a recent study shows,
"Jonathan Edwards celebrated the coherence and beauty of God's creation," consistently arguing that God "ceaselessly reveals himself alike
'by his *word* and *works*' and that the joy and duty of the Christian is to
observe and praise this sacred design."[32] The origins of Edwards's *theologia gloriae* may be seen in the unique morphology of his conversion. In
contrast to St. Augustine's and Luther's conversions, which were
grounded on Christocentric views, that of Edwards was based upon a
"God-entranced world view,"[33] and took place after reading 1 Timothy
1:17: *Now unto the King eternal, immortal, invisible, the only wise God,
be honour and glory for ever and ever. Amen.*

Conversion as an Existential Religious Experience

Throughout the history of Christianity, the conversion experience has
been seen as the most critical moment in the lives of leading figures in
Christianity. St. Paul's conversion on the road to Damascus, which domi-
nated Christian thinking about conversion in the New Testament, transformed his life and directed his missionary work among the Gentiles. St.
Augustine's conversion is vividly portrayed in his *Confessions*, where he
eloquently articulated the profound experience of interior transformation
that radically changed his life, making him one of the most important
figures among the fathers of the church and ensuring his prominent place
in Christian spirituality. The conversion of Martin Luther turned him
from a minor Augustinian hermit into the leader of the Protestant Reformation. Whereas among the Scholastics the moment of conversion had

---

[29] Jaroslav Pelikan, *The Christian Tradition: A History of the Development of Doctrine*,
5 vols. (Chicago: University of Chicago Press, 1971–89), vol. IV, *Reformation of Church
and Dogma (1300–1700)* (1984), pp. 155–56.

[30] Althaus, *The Theology of Martin Luther*, p. 27.

[31] *Miscellany* no. 247 (1727), p. 360.

[32] Knight, "Learning the Language of God," p. 531.

[33] John Piper, *The Supremacy of God in Preaching* (Grand Rapids: Baker Book House,
1990), p. 13.

lost its prominent role in Christian thought, Luther's experience came to signify the primacy of religious conversion in Protestantism.[34] Later, the role of conversion in Protestantism was further enhanced by Philip Spener and Pietism in Germany, John Wesley and Methodism in England, and of course Jonathan Edwards and the Great Awakening in America.

For decades, understanding of the conversion experience was influenced by William James's classic *Varieties of Religious Experience* (1902). Based upon his overall functionalist psychology and pragmatic views, James attempted to show that conversion is essentially a psychological process involving the unification of a sick and divided self:

> To be converted, to be regenerated, to receive grace, to experience religion, to gain an assurance, are so many phrases which denote the process, gradual or sudden, by which a self, hitherto divided, and consciously wrong inferior and unhappy, becomes unified and consciously right, superior and happy, in consequence of its firmer hold upon religious realities.[35]

More recently, however, several studies have considerably broadened James's narrow psychological and pragmatist definition of religious conversion, especially Christian conversion. Their perspectives shed light on the consequences of Jonathan Edwards's conversion for his life as a theologian and philosopher.

According to Walter Conn, "conversion radically redirects and transforms the concrete shape and orientation of personal subjectivity, the structure and content of one's conscience as character." In contrast to James's theory of a divided and sick self, he argued that conversion is based on the radical attempt to mediate between this world and the transcendent. This fundamental quest leads to "the person's radical drive for self-transcendence," that is, a yearning for transcendence in terms of "a self that is realized only in its active movement beyond itself."[36] More specifically, conversion involves "the radical reorientation of one's entire life that occurs when God is allowed to move from the periphery to the center of one's being," signifying the "total self-surrender" regarding the "illusion" of a human being having "absolute autonomy." Thus, "basic

---

[34] According to Patricia Caldwell, out of Luther's "two-stage theory of repentance came a 'morphology of conversion' which was, in effect, a model for all the later [Protestant and Puritan] ones." See Caldwell, *The Puritan Conversion Narratives*, p. 58.

[35] James, *The Varieties of Religious Experience*, p. 189. According to Louis Menand, "James regarded the investigation of religious experience as a branch of abnormal psychology." See Louis Menand, "William James & the Case of the Epileptic Patient," *The New York Review of Books* 45, no. 20 (December 17, 1998), p. 81. On William James and the philosophy of pragmatism, see James T. Kloppenberg, "Pragmatism: An Old Name for Some New Ways of Thinking?" *Journal of American History* 83 (June 1996): 100–138.

[36] Conn, *Christian Conversion*, pp. 31–33.

conversion," or "fundamental conversion," signifies "a transformation of the person's whole orientation" and constitutes "a radically new beginning" in one's life. In sum, Conn replaced James's inner sick and divided self by the powerful concept of "vertical conversion," that is, the total reconstruction of the self according to the radical quest for transcendence.[37]

More recently, Lewis R. Rambo has attempted to show that because conversion ultimately involves "religious factors," and not merely psychological issues, it should be defined "as a total transformation of the person by the power of God."[38] He called it a "process" because "conversion is very rarely an overnight, all-in-an-instant, wholesale transformation that is now and forever." Furthermore, the conversion phenomenon signifies "a universe of meaning," such as, for example, "a change of one's personal orientation toward life, from the haphazard of superstition to the providence of a deity," or toward "seeing all creation as a manifestation of God and beneficence," or toward "the belief that the rule of God is what fulfills human beings." In sum, conversion means "a radical shifting of gears that can take the spiritually lackadaisical to a new level of intensive concern, commitment, and involvement."[39]

As these comments show, religious conversion is a spiritual process in which the yearning for transcendence radically transforms one's self-identity, and hence one's whole personal life. By rejecting simple psychological explanations, these studies demonstrate the value of taking religious persuasion and belief into serious consideration when discussing religious phenomena, rather than judging them from the outside. For conversion is a profound experience capable of transforming a life and identity, leading to the formation of a new existential condition within the world, or a new mode of religious existence within a "divine universe." The conversion Jonathan Edwards experienced when he was seventeen years old radically transformed his whole condition, and from that moment his life was totally different from what it had been before.

Edwards's Experience of Conversion

There were many decisive moments and turning points in the life of Jonathan Edwards, most notably his appointment as a preacher at his grandfather's church in Northampton and his fruitful and dedicated work as a minister, which led eventually to the success of the "little revival" of

[37] Ibid., pp. 30–31.
[38] Rambo, *Understanding Religious Conversion*, pp. xi–xii.
[39] Ibid., pp. 1–2.

1734–35 in Northampton and the Great Awakening between 1740 and 1742 in New England, his expulsion from his church at Northampton, his removal to Stockbridge, and finally his appointment as the president of the College of New Jersey (later renamed Princeton University). Yet, for Edwards, as for other Protestants, life on earth constituted only a passage to the promise of eternal life. "To the Protestant . . . life seems a pilgrim's progress which, whether made solitarily or in company, proceeds through unpredictable contingencies and crises toward the destination beyond life and death where all the trumpets blow."[40] Public events, therefore, no matter how happy or gloomy, belonged only to the dimension of earthly life, and constituted only contingent and temporary moments in the overall drama of eternal salvation and redemption. In this context, the most critical event in Edwards's life was undoubtedly his religious conversion, which provided him with the goal he pursued throughout his life. Underlying his public life as well as his private and spiritual existence, was the vivid and continuous presence of the conversion experience, in which he dedicated his life to God and Christ.

Edwards spent almost ten years at New Haven, except for the eight-month sojourn of his pastorate at the New York City Presbyterian church. In 1716, at the age of thirteen, he began his studies at Yale College, leaving at the age of twenty-three in 1726. This period proved to be the most important one in the development of Edwards's theological and philosophical thought. During that time he produced most of his scientific writings, or works of natural philosophy, such as *Of Being*, *Of Atoms*, and *The Mind*, as well as various religious works such as the *Resolutions* and *Diary*, and began writing entries for his massive collection of *Miscellanies*, as well as for the *Notes on the Apocalypse* and the *Notes on Scripture*. Preceding these writings, however, was the critical religious experience of conversion.

It was during his time at Yale, as Edwards wrote later in his *Personal Narrative*, that he was "at times very uneasy, especially towards the latter part of my time at college; when it pleased God, to seize me with a pleurisy; in which he brought me nigh to the grave, and shook me over the pit of hell."[41] The attack of pleurisy took place in the winter of 1719–20, when Edwards was sixteen years old;[42] it marked the beginning of a spiritual process that eventually led to his conversion in 1721.[43] His sinful life, he thought, had brought him to the verge of death. He tried to renounce

---

[40] H. Richard Niebuhr, "The Protestant Movement and Democracy in the United States," in *The Shaping of American Religion*, ed. James W. Smith and A. Leland Jamison, p. 23.

[41] Edwards, *Personal Narrative*, p. 791.

[42] Morris, *The Young Jonathan Edwards*, p. 32.

[43] According to Iain H. Murray, Edwards's conversion took place "in May or June of 1721." See Murray, *Jonathan Edwards*, p. 35.

his former ways and obey the Lord's word. Shortly after his illness, however, he "fell again" into his "old ways of sin," which caused him to suffer many "great and violent inward struggles" in his soul. Time and again he tried to renounce his errant ways, but he constantly fell short of his promises and expectations. Thus, as he wrote, "after many conflicts with wicked inclinations, repeated resolutions, and bonds that I laid myself under by a kind of vows to God, I was brought wholly to break off all former wicked ways, and all ways of known outward sin; and to apply myself to seek salvation, and practise many religious duties." But even this determination eventually failed him and brought him instead to more "inward struggles and conflicts, and self reflections." Although, as he confessed, "seeking my salvation" was "the main business of my life," he soon doubted its sincerity: "it seems to me, I sought after a miserable manner; which has made me sometimes since to question whether ever it issued in that which was saving; being ready to doubt, whether such miserable seeking" after salvation would be successful.[44]

At this moment of agonized self-searching, Edwards recognized that something was wrong with his quest for salvation. Deep in his conscience he felt the need to change his attitude from a mere "seeking salvation" for his own personal benefit to a contemplation of Christ's place and role in the world. This was a critical point in Edwards's process of conversion: the transformation of a selfish interest in his own personal salvation to an awareness of Christ's glory. Consequently, as he wrote, "I was indeed brought to seek salvation in a manner that I never was before; I felt a spirit to part with all things in the world, for an interest in Christ" (ibid.). Edwards's initial turning to Christ in quest of genuine conversion, however, fell short of his high expectations. Not only did he fail to experience a genuine conversion, but his new and lively interest in Christ could not relieve his inner struggles and spiritual miseries: "My concern continued and prevailed," he wrote regarding his search for Christ, "with many exercising thoughts and inward struggles." Important, however, is the fact that at this early stage of Edwards's conversion process it "never seemed to be proper to express that concern" for Christ "by the name of terror" (ibid.).

Evidently, at this point in his painful spiritual journey, Edwards felt that his search would not be achieved through a terrified broken soul or an agonized spiritual crisis of great magnitude and proportion—common themes in traditional Puritan conversion narratives. Accordingly, his quest was not for his own salvation, but for the Deity's singular place in the world, or God's absolute sovereignty and justice within a divine uni-

---

[44] Edwards, *Personal Narrative*, p. 791. Subsequent pages appear parenthetically in the text.

verse; and, as it were, the assurance of conversion and salvation would come only after the construction of a singular place for God within the created world.

The discussion in Edwards's *Personal Narrative* changes sharply at this moment, and the personal voice, so often describing painful inner struggles and conflicts as in traditional Puritan conversion narratives, gives way to a glorious vision of God. Equally important is the confirmation of God's absolute sovereignty as the basis and trigger for the conversion experience. In a sense, Edwards's conversion process was to succeed only when he accepted without reservation the notion of God's absolute sovereignty. For years he had rejected this very idea: "From my childhood up, my mind had been full of objections against the doctrine of God's sovereignty, in choosing whom he would to eternal life, and rejecting whom he pleased; leaving them eternally to perish, and be everlastingly tormented in hell. It used to appear like a horrible doctrine to me." But now at last, during the process of conversion and through reasoning, Edwards finally "saw further" and his "reason apprehended the justice and reasonableness" regarding the "doctrine of God's sovereignty." He was "convinced, and fully satisfied, as to this sovereignty of God, and his justice in thus eternally disposing of men, according to his sovereign pleasure" (p. 792).

At this stage, however, Edwards's acknowledgment of the sovereignty of God, as he admitted, was without "any extraordinary influence of God's Spirit in it" (ibid.). His new awareness regarding God in majesty was "without any regard to his own personal condition. Objective, abstract general truth and not subjective, concrete, and particular revelation was his answer."[45] Soon, however, Edwards's awareness was transformed into a deeper understanding, and he finally grasped the idea of "God's absolute sovereignty and justice" with its religious ramifications:

> And there has been a wonderful alteration in my mind, in respect to the doctrine of God's sovereignty, from that day to this; so that I scarce ever have found so much as the rising of an objection against it, in the most absolute sense, in God's shewing mercy to whom he will shew mercy, and hardening whom he will. God's absolute sovereignty and justice, with respect to salvation and damnation, is what my mind seems to rest assured of, as much as of any thing that I see with my eyes.[46]

Over time, this awesome understanding of the doctrine of "God's absolute sovereignty" intensified; it brought Edwards not only a mere "conviction, but a delightful conviction." The doctrine," he wrote, "has very

---

[45] Morris, *The Young Jonathan Edwards*, p. 34.

[46] Edwards, *Personal Narrative*, p. 792. Subsequent pages appear parenthetically in the text.

often appeared exceeding pleasant, bright, and sweet. Absolute sovereignty is what I love to ascribe to God" (ibid.).

Edwards's "delightful conviction" soon received its fullest affirmation
in a scriptural passage. "The first instance that I remembered of that sort
of inward sweet delight in God and divine things that I have lived much
in since," wrote Edwards, "was on reading those words, 1 Tim. 1: 17.
*Now unto the King eternal, immortal, invisible, the only wise God, be
honour and glory for ever and ever. Amen*" (ibid.). These words greatly
enhanced Edwards's conversion experience; they transformed his "delightful conviction" into "that sort of inward, sweet delight in God and
divine things," and brought into his "soul . . . a sense of the glory of the
Divine Being; a new sense, quite different from any thing" he had "ever
experienced before" (ibid.). The influence of this passage on Edwards's
conversion was a decisive one:

> Never any words of Scripture seemed to me as these words did. I thought with
> myself, how excellent a Being that was: and how happy I should be, if I might
> enjoy that God, and be wrapt up to God in heaven, and be as it were swallowed
> up in him. (ibid.)

The conversion experience led Edwards to construe a most powerful
picture of God in his sovereign majesty and glory. This vision constituted
one of the most important motifs in his thought, as, for example, in his
best-known works: *God Glorified in the Work of Redemption* (1731), *A
History of the Work of Redemption* (1739), *Sinners in the Hands of an
Angry God* (1741), *Concerning the End for Which God Created the
World* (1755), and his *Miscellanies*.[47]

Yet, Edwards admitted that even at this level of his conversion, what
he really experienced was a rational apprehension of God in his sovereign
majesty, and he did not think there was "any thing spiritual, or of saving
nature in this."[48] Up to this point, the process was based upon "delightful
conviction" in the "doctrine of God's sovereignty" and glory, and this
belief was greatly enhanced through reading 1 Timothy. Only now, however, after his acknowledgment of the "glory of the Divine Being," did
Edwards began to develop new convictions concerning Christ and the
work of redemption. Thus, while the sense of God's glory deepened
within his soul, there arose in his heart new notions concerning Christ
and the way of salvation: "From about that time, I began to have a new
kind of apprehensions and ideas of Christ, and the works of redemption,
and the glorious way of salvation by him. An inward, sweet sense of these

---

[47] See, for example, the long discussions on conversion in *Miscellany* nos. 847, 849 (c.
1740).

[48] Edwards, *Personal Narrative*, p. 793. Subsequent pages appear parenthetically in the text.

things, at times, came into my heart; and my soul was led away in pleasant views and contemplations of them" (ibid.).

Here Edwards describes the nature of his conversion experience, from the first intellectual constitutive act of admitting and acknowledging God's glory and absolute sovereignty to the "ideas of Christ," and finally to Christ's "work of redemption, and the glorious salvation" by him (ibid.). Again, a passage from scripture was the ultimate inspiration for Edwards's new apprehensions of "the beauty and excellency" of Christ "and the lovely way of salvation by free grace in him." For, as he wrote,

> I found no books so delightful to me, as those that treated of these subjects. Those words Cant. ii, I, used to be abundantly with me, *I am the Rose of Sharon, and the Lily of the valleys*. These words seemed to me, sweetly to represent the loveliness and beauty of Jesus Christ. (ibid.)

At that stage, long meditation on Christ brought into the soul of the young man a strong spiritual sense of detachment from the material world. Sometimes he felt "a calm, sweet abstraction of soul from all the concerns of this world," and "sometimes a kind of vision, or fixed ideas and imaginations, of being alone in the mountains, or some solitary wilderness, far from all mankind, sweetly conversing with Christ, and wrapt and swallowed up in God" (ibid.). The spiritual experience of Christ had a crucial influence on Edwards's heart and soul. Awakened by visions of Christ, a remarkable process of internalization took place that supplanted mere reasoning and conviction. Now, for the first time in his conversion narrative, Edwards speaks of a spiritual experience that brought fire to his heart and fervor to his soul. "The sense I had of divine things, would often of a sudden kindle up, as it were, a sweet burning in my heart; an ardor of soul, that I know not how to express" (ibid.).

Edwards was finally on the verge of a complete conversion, on the edge of total self-transformation according to his new experience of the sovereign majesty of God and Christ's glorious work of salvation and redemption. Yet one critical act remained: the stamp of authority was required to certify that these spiritual experiences were indeed evidence of a genuine religious conversion. Thus, Edwards went home to tell his father, Timothy Edwards, the minister of the church at East Windsor, the whole of his spiritual odyssey. This was a critical moment for him. Without the approval of his father, his long and agonizing spiritual journey might prove invalid. As it was, however, the discussion with his father was most fruitful. Edwards wrote: "Not long after I first began to experience these things, I gave an account to my father of some things that had passed in my mind. I was pretty much affected by the discourse we had together" (ibid.).

With Timothy Edwards's final affirmation and approval of his son's spiritual journey, Jonathan Edwards's long process of conversion was completed. After the talk with his father, he took a short walk "in a solitary place" in his "father's pasture." Then, as he wrote, there

> came into my mind so sweet a sense of the glorious *majesty* and *grace* of God. . . . I seemed to see them both in sweet conjunction; majesty and meekness joined together; it was a sweet, and gentle, and holy majesty; and also majestic meekness; an awful sweetness; a high and great, and holy gentleness. (ibid.)

With this new sense of God and Christ, Edwards at last fully experienced the conversion moment: "The appearance of every thing was altered; there seemed to be, as it were, a calm, sweet cast, or appearance of divine glory, in almost every thing. God's excellency, his wisdom, his purity and love, seemed to appear in every thing" (pp.793–94).

The sense of the spiritual beauty of divine things, of God's excellence, wisdom, and love, signified that Edwards's process of conversion was complete; he had acquired a "full and constant sense of the absolute sovereignty of God, and delight in that sovereignty," and consequently "a sense of the glory of Christ, as a Mediator revealed in the gospel" (p. 803). No wonder, then, that from that time and throughout his life, "Edwards stressed the absolute importance of man's belief in God's sovereignty. It was the doctrine he made into a keystone of his own theology, and it was one that, when he became a minister, he drilled into his hearers as the primary necessity for their salvation."[49] Furthermore, the conversion experience profoundly influenced his conception of "practical" or "experimental" religion: "At the core" of Edwards's "religion of the heart is a sense of God's excellence and loveliness, or of the beauty and splendor of divine things."[50]

The Morphology of Edwards's Conversion

In order to understand the nature of Edwards's conversion event, it may be helpful to place it in the context of the conversion experiences of some prominent figures in the history of Christianity. What Edwards experienced was clearly not the great divine light and the mighty voice of God that Paul saw and heard on the road to Damascus, nor was it the painful,

[49] Davidson, "Sovereign God and Reasoning Man," p. 33.

[50] William Wainwright, "Jonathan Edwards and the Sense of the Heart," *Faith and Philosophy* 7 (January 1990): 43. See also Wainwright, *Reason and the Heart: A Prolegomenon to a Critique of Passional Reason* (Ithaca: Cornell University Press, 1995); and "Jonathan Edwards and the Language of God," *Journal of the American Academy of Religion* 48 (1980): 519–30.

soul-shattering experience of St. Augustine so vividly described in his *Confessions*, or the terrible lightning that struck Martin Luther on the road to Erfurt.[51] And Edwards did not experience the broken heart so common in cases of conversions analyzed in William James's *The Varieties of Religious Experience*.

The conversion of St. Paul took the form of a profound spiritual transformation accompanied by tremendous physical changes. The decisive event occurred on a mission to Damascus to arrest certain Christians and bring them back to Jerusalem for trial. Suddenly "there shone round about him a light from heaven," and he heard the voice of Christ asking him why he persecuted his followers. As he was lying on the ground "trembling and astonished," he was converted. The experience left its mark on his body, for he "was three days without sight, and neither did eat nor drink" (Acts. 9:1–19; 22:5–16; 26:12–18).

St. Augustine's conversion was marked by many years of soul-searching, inner struggle, and spiritual unhappiness. He underwent it in August 386, when he was almost thirty-three years old. He writes that shortly before this moment, deep spiritual misery had shaken all his body: "When my searching reflection had dredged up from the secret depth of my soul all my misery and piled it up in the sight of my heart, a mighty storm arose, bringing a great shower of tears." Then, immediately after reading a passage from Paul's epistles—*not in rioting and drunkenness, not in chambering and wantonness, not in strife and envying. But put ye on the Lord Jesus Christ, and make no provision for the flesh, to fulfil the lusts thereof* (Romans 13:13–14)—his conversion took place: "For instantly, at the end of this sentence, by a light, as it were, of serenity infused into my heart, all the darkness of doubt vanished away."[52]

---

[51] I have not attempted to draw a comparison between Edwards's and Calvin's conversions since historians are puzzled not only about the date of the latter but also about what it involved. For example, William J. Bouwsma argued that the "evidence for a 'conversion' " as a profound moment "in Calvin's life is negligible." Hence, "Calvin attached little or any significance to 'conversion' as a precise event in his many discussions of the Christian life and the way of salvation." See William J. Bouwsma, *John Calvin: A Sixteenth-Century Portrait* (New York: Oxford University Press, 1988), pp. 10–11. A relation of Calvin's conversion can be found in his *Commentary on the Psalms* (1557), where he says in a brief, tantalizing passage that he once had "a sudden conversion." See François Wendel, *Calvin: Origins and Development of His Religious Thought* (Grand Rapids: A Labyrinth Book, 1997 [1950]), pp. 37–45; and Kerr and Mulder, eds., *Famous Conversions*, pp. 24–28.

[52] *The Confessions of St. Augustine*, VIII, xxii, pp. 160–61. On Augustine's conversion, see J. G. Kristo, *Looking for God in Time and Memory: Psychology, Theology, and Spirituality in Augustine's Confessions* (Lanham, Md.: University Press of America, 1991); Colin Starnes, *Augustine's Conversion: A Guide to the Argument of Confessions I–IX* (Waterloo, Ontario: Wilfrid Laurier University Press, 1990); Peter Brown, *Augustine of Hippo: A Biography* (Berkeley: University of California Press, 1969); and Don Browning, "The Psychoanalytic Interpretation of St. Augustine's *Confessions*: An Assessment and New Probe," in *Psy-*

Martin Luther's conversion also took place after much pain and spiritual conflict, and it was accompanied by a decisive physical event. As Luther admitted, before his conversion in June 1505, he was "used to go around in sadness" and felt "oppressed."[53] Especially during the early summer of that year he "seems to have brooded over the question of death and the final judgment." At the end of June 1505, he returned to his life as a student in Erfurt. Then, only a few hours from his final destination, "he was surprised by a severe thunderstorm. A bolt of lightning struck the ground, and caused him to be seized by a severe, some say convulsive, state of terror" (p. 91). He felt, as he described later, as if he were "completely walled in by the painful fear of a sudden death." Instinctively, and before he knew it, he had called out: "Help me, St. Anne [his father's patron saint] . . . I want to become a monk." In July 1505, after much deliberation with his friends, he was ready to knock "on the door of the Augustinian Eremites in Erfurt" and ask for admission. This was granted immediately. And only then, "from behind the walls of the monastery did he write to his father" (pp. 91–92).

Luther's conversion "committed him to being *monos*, a professional monk," and the "promises of celibacy and obedience made at that time in his life can be said to have relieved him of burdens which he was not ready to assume" (p. 93). This was in contrast to the conversion of St. Paul—a non-Christian, mature man, and deputy prosecutor in the high priest's office, who afterward assumed a leading role in the spread of Christianity. Furthermore, both Luther and Paul experienced their conversions in the wilderness while undertaking a journey. Paul saw and heard the divine light and voice coming from without, while Luther experienced "the spiritual part of the experience" as "intra-psychic" (pp. 93–94).

In sum, St. Paul's conversion was marked by a light and voice from heaven, St. Augustine's by an inner light culmination of an inner storm, and Luther's by a terrible flash of lightning. Both Paul and Luther "were shaken by an attack involving both body and psyche"; they were in fact "thrown to the ground," and by this physical shock, they claimed, God had "changed their minds" (p. 94). Edwards's moment of conversion exhibits no such dramatic occurrences of supernatural power or natural violence. Whereas the conversions of Paul, Augustine, and Luther were in fact "instantaneous,"[54] that of Edwards was the "volitional type," according to which "the regenerative change is usually gradual, and consists

---

choanalysis and Religion, ed. Joseph H. Smith (Baltimore: Johns Hopkins University Press, 1990), pp. 134–59.

[53] Erikson, *Young Man Luther*, p. 96. Subsequent pages appear parenthetically in the text.

[54] James, *Varieties of Religious Experience*, p. 230.

in the building up, piece by piece, of a new set of moral and spiritual habits."[55] Moreover, while Augustine's and Luther's conversions were based upon a broken self converted through Christ's words, that of Edwards was grounded upon an acknowledgment of God in all his sovereign majesty and glory and resulted in a new vision of Christ.

Edwards's experience also differs from many seventeenth-century New England Puritan conversion narratives.[56] According to Patricia Caldwell, the model for Protestant conversion morphologies was Luther's "two stage theory of repentance." "First, under the work of the law, the sinner saw his sin and was sorry for it; only then, under grace, was he enabled to resolve to amend his life. That resolution was literally the turning point or conversion."[57] In Puritan New England during the seventeenth century, as described by Edmund S. Morgan, the morphology of conversion took the following form:

> First comes a feeble and false awakening to God's commands and a pride in keeping them pretty well, but also much backsliding. Disappointments and disasters lead to other fitful hearkenings to the word. Sooner or later true legal fear or conviction enables the individual to see his hopeless and helpless condition and to know that his own righteousness cannot save him, that Christ is his only hope. Thereafter comes the infusion of saving grace, sometimes but not always so precisely felt that the believer can state exactly when and where it came to him.[58]

But in Edwards's conversion "there had been no 'terror,' no willingness to be damned for the glory of God, no terrible humiliation of spirit, no all-absorbing convictions of sin, and no undue concentration on the state of his own soul." His conversion was—and this is of the greatest importance for his universe of thought—a profound spiritual transformation regarding God the Divine Being. "Objective content" in Edwards's conversion, "had predominated over subjective concern. The center had been God, and not his own soul."[59] Edwards himself admitted that his concern for salvation brought him "many exercising thoughts and inward struggles; but yet it never seemed to be proper to express that concern by the name of terror."[60] For what is absent from Edwards's conversion is "the experience of 'legal fear,' " or terror, which constituted "a key element in

---

[55] Ibid.

[56] Caldwell, *Puritan Conversion Narratives*, pp. 163–66; Yarbrough and Adams, *Delightful Conviction*, p. 7.

[57] Caldwell, *Puritan Conversion Narratives*, p. 58.

[58] Edmund S. Morgan, *Visible Saints: The History of a Puritan Idea* (Ithaca: Cornell University Press, 1963), p. 91.

[59] Morris, *The Young Jonathan Edwards*, p. 40.

[60] Edwards, *Personal Narrative*, p. 791.

most [Puritan] morphologies." Thus, rather than a radical "turning away *from* an old self toward God in fear of God's justice, Edwards experienced a turning *toward* God in appreciation of that justice."[61] Indeed, according to Ola E. Winslow, Edwards in his conversion moment

> experienced no conviction of sin, no sudden ecstasy of forgiveness. He could not tell the moment at which the new life had begun. He was merely brought . . . to 'new Dispositions' and a 'new Sense of Things'. For him the whole of his life was altered; the divine glory was everywhere; and with a finality of assurance he knew that religion was henceforth to be the main business of his life.[62]

Edwards himself felt keenly that his conversion was different from the established pattern spoken about by most orthodox Puritan divines:

> The reason why I, in the least, question my interest in God's love and favor, is, 1. Because I cannot speak so fully to my experience of the preparatory work, of which divines speak; 2. I do not remember that I experienced regeneration, exactly in those steps, in which divines say it is generally wrought.[63]

No wonder, then, that Edwards was sometimes much troubled about his spiritual state, because, as he wrote in his *Diary*, his conversion experience was different from the rich culture of the Puritan morphology of conversion in England and New England: "The chief thing, that now makes me in any measure to question my good estate, is my not having experienced conversion in those particular steps, wherein the people of New England, and anciently the Dissenters of Old England, used to experience it."[64] Obviously, therefore, he was much concerned about the nature of his conversion: "It seems to me, that whether I am now converted or not, I am so settled in the state I am in, that I shall go on in it all my life. But, however settled I may be, yet I will continue to pray to God, not to suffer me to be deceived about it, nor to sleep in an unsafe condition."[65]

At this point further comparison between Edwards's conversion and those of St. Augustine and Luther may throw light on the unique character of Edwards's conversion moment. The differences between Augustine and Edwards appear in the biblical passages each found as the stimulus for his long-sought conversion. Augustine's conversion was expressed through a Christocentric passage from Romans 13:13–14: *not in rioting and drunkenness, not in chambering and wantonness, not in strife and envying. But*

---

[61] Yarbrough and Adams, *Delightful Conviction*, p. 7.

[62] Winslow, *Jonathan Edwards*, p. 74.

[63] Edwards, *Diary* (1722), in *LPW*, p. 759. See also Sereno E. Dwight, "Memoirs of Jonathan Edwards," in *The Works of Jonathan Edwards*, 2 vols. (Edinburgh: Banner of Truth Trust, 1995 [1834]), I, p. 24.

[64] Edwards, *Diary*, as quoted in Caldwell, *Puritan Conversion Narratives*, p. 163.

[65] Edwards, *Diary*, p. 788.

put ye on the Lord Jesus Christ, and make no provision for the flesh, to fulfil the lusts thereof. Edwards's conversion, on the other hand, took place after reading a theocentric passage from 1 Timothy, 1:17: *Now unto the King eternal immortal, invisible, the only wise God, be honour and glory for ever and ever. Amen.* Prominent in Augustine is his Christology, the central role of Jesus Christ in his conversion, redemption, and salvation; what is most evident in Edwards is his vision of God's magnificent sovereignty and glory.

A comparison between Luther and Edwards, taking into account their cosmological views concerning time, history, and eternity, further illuminates the radical character of Edwards's experience.[66] The main difference between Luther and Edwards can be described in a variety of opposing conceptions that contributed to the development of their theologies, the *theologia crucis* and the *theologia gloriae*: self and mind, Christ and God, finite and infinite, Christocentric and theocentric. In Luther's conversion, as he wrote, the predominant mode was the quest for personal salvation: "Here I felt that I was altogether born again and had entered paradise itself through open gates."[67] In Edwards's experience the ultimate goal was "reconciliation with divine power."[68] Luther's conversion reveals his overwhelming concern with his own personal salvation, while Edwards's led to his concern with God's absolute sovereignty. Luther is Christocentric, assigning Jesus the chief role in the Christian drama of salvation and redemption, while Edwards is more theocentric, aiming to reconstruct the Deity's majestic role in the universe and unveil the coherence and beauty of God's creation. Hence Luther's conversion is more concerned with his inner soul and merciful role of Christ the savior, while Edwards's is based upon a theocentric vision of the glory of God, which later resulted in a new view of Christ. Luther deals with the finite human being, emphasizing sin and hence the role of Christ as the savior of souls. His quest was for personal salvation; he was not so much concerned with history or the cosmic vision of the universe of *theologia gloriae*. Edwards, on the other hand, absorbed in the infinity of God's sovereignty, was much more occupied with the history of redemption and salvation and the cause for which God created the world. Consequently, in contrast to Luther, who showed little interest in the cosmos, divine universe, and salvation history, the

---

[66] For my discussion of the differences between Luther's and Edwards's conversions, I owe much to Bishop Bill Lazareth of the Center of Theological Inquiry, Princeton, a Lutheran scholar who generously shared with me on several occasions his knowledge of Luther's theology and thought.

[67] The quotation from Luther is in Kerr and Mulder, introduction, in *Famous Conversions*, p. xvi.

[68] Bushman, "Jonathan Edwards as Great Man: Identity, Conversion, and Leadership in the Great Awakening," p. 54.

issue of the history of the work of redemption was an inextricable part of Edwards's theocentric thinking.

Finally, Edwards's conversion experience may also explain the difference between his and Calvin's theology of nature, especially in regard to nature's place and role within God's providential design. According to Calvin, "ever since the creation of the universe" God "brought forth those insignia whereby he shows his glory to us, whenever and wherever we cast our gaze."[69] In this sense, he argued, "the universe is for us a sort of mirror in which we can contemplate God, who is otherwise invisible."[70] And since God sustains "this infinite mass of heaven and earth by his Word . . . the praises of God's power form the testimonies of nature."[71] Believers "should contemplate him in his works" in "such a dazzling theater" of the heavens and the earth.[72] Indeed, as Louis Dupré shows, Calvin "leaves no doubt that the *ordo naturae* continues to manifest God's presence and guidance."[73] Moreover, it was also Calvin who warned that it is "harmful" to "involve God confusedly in the inferior course of his works," since "nature is rather the order prescribed by God."[74] In this context, the "entire order of nature, including the so-called natural law, has been imposed by divine decree. Henceforth only the positive divine law revealed in the Ten Commandments remains."[75] In sum, for Calvin "nature is no longer capable of serving as a reliable and sufficient guide on the journey through life," and, therefore, to "know what God has decreed nature must be studied in light of revelation." Nature therefore lost its independent and autonomous role in providential history. "All natural signs of God's greatness had been planted by divine decision for the salvation of the fallen world—they no longer are the intrinsic language of nature itself."[76]

In contrast, in Edwards's *theologia gloriae*, "nature had become as compelling a way of God's speaking" as "Scripture."[77] Thus, the order of nature, according to Edwards, became a primary source for God's communication:

---

[69] Calvin, *Institutes of the Christian Religion*, 2 vols., ed. J. T. McNeil and F. L. Battles (Philadelphia: Westminster, 1960), I, 5, 1.

[70] Ibid.

[71] Ibid., I, 5, 8.

[72] Ibid., I, 5, 8–9.

[73] Dupré, *Passage to Modernity*, pp. 209–10.

[74] Calvin, *Institutes of the Christian Religion*, I, 5, 5.

[75] Dupré, *Passage to Modernity*, p. 214.

[76] Ibid., p. 215.

[77] Miller, introduction, in *Images or Shadows of Divine Things by Jonathan Edwards*, pp. 28–29.

The manifestations God makes of himself in his works are the principal manifestations of his perfections and the declarations & teachings of his word are to lead to these. By Gods declaring & teaching that he is infinitely powerfull or wise, the creature believes that he is powerfull & wise as he teaches but in seeing his mighty & wise works the effects of his power & wisdom the creature not only hears & believes but sees his power & wisdom & so of his other perfections.[78]

Edwards's *theologia gloriae* therefore constituted the main source for his deification and divination of the world of nature. In other words, for Edwards "nature and human history are . . . legitimate sources of revelation, communicating God's purpose to his saints," because he believed in "the importance of nature as a vehicle for God's progressive communications," and that the Deity's "desire to communicate does not compromise God's majesty but instead fulfills it."[79] Thus, "the Son of God created the world for this very end, to communicate himself in an image of his own excellency."[80] Indeed, "he communicates himself properly only to spirits," because "they only are capable of being proper images of his excellency"; yet, at the same time, "he communicates a sort of shadow or glimpse of his excellencies to bodies," which are "but the shadows of beings, and not real beings."[81] We should understand "these shadows of divine things," he continues, "as the voice of God purposely by them teaching us these and those spiritual and divine things," or as a medium through which God is "speaking to us."[82] Accordingly, because the "natural things were ordered for types of spiritual things,"[83] God is working "throughout all nature,"[84] and this "to be on purpose to represent the dependence of our spiritual wellfare upon God's gracious influences and the effusions of His holy spirit."[85] In contrast therefore to Calvin, the world of nature in Edwards's

[78] Edwards, *Miscellany* no. 777, in *MISA*, pp. 427–28.
[79] Knight, "Learning the Language of God," pp. 536–37.
[80] Edwards, *Miscellany* no. 108 (c. 1724), p. 279.
[81] Ibid.
[82] Edwards, *Images of Divine Things*, 70 (1738), in *TW*, p. 74. For the dating of entries in *Images and Shadows of Divine Things*, see Thomas A. Schafer's "Table 2. The 'Miscellanies' and Chronological Parallels: May 1719–August 1731," in *MIS*, pp. 91–109; and Wallace E. Anderson, "Notes on the Manuscript of 'Images of Divine Things,' " in *TW*, pp. 34–47. On Edwards's typology and vocabulary of nature, see Miller, introduction, in *Images or Shadows of Divine Things by Jonathan Edwards*, pp. 1–41; Wallace E. Anderson, introduction, in *TW*, pp. 3–33; and Stephen H. Daniel, *The Philosophy of Jonathan Edwards: A Study in Divine Semiotics* (Bloomington: Indiana University Press, 1994), especially pp. 41–65.
[83] Edwards, *Images or Shadows of Divine Things*, 45 (1736), p. 62.
[84] Ibid., 8 (1728), p. 53.
[85] Ibid., 13 (1728), p. 54.

"theistic metaphysics"[86] became an important source of revelation. Indeed, "if it be thus fit that God should have a supreme regard to himself, then it is fit that this regard should appear, in those things by which he makes himself known, or by *word* and *works*; i.e. in what he says, and in what he does." Nature thus was accorded an important role in God's providence because God's "works should exhibit an image of himself their author, that it might brightly appear by his works what manner of being he is, and afford a proper representation of his divine excellencies, and especially his *moral* excellence."[87] Accordingly, as Perry Miller showed, Edwards made "an exaltation of nature to a level of authority co-equal with revelation."[88] Thus, through both the order of grace and the order of nature, God ceaselessly reveals himself, and by learning the "voice or language of God"[89] the saints may acquire knowledge of God's providential design "in the creating of the astonishing fabric of the universe which we behold."[90]

Conversion and the Development of Edwards's Theological and Philosophical Thought

The importance of Edwards's religious conversion is most evident in the development of his theological and philosophical views. Before his conversion Edwards wrote only one work, the monograph *Of Insects*, probably composed in the year 1720.[91] Immediately after his conversion in 1721, however, an outpouring of writings ensued; he penned his famous seventy *Resolutions* (c. 1722–23), began his *Diary* (1722) and a long series of scientific and philosophical writings (1722), and started the *Miscellanies* (1722), the earliest *Notes on the Apocalypse* (1723), and the first *Notes on Scripture* (1724). This body of work demonstrates the seriousness of Edwards's devotion to his spiritual life, and shows how powerfully the conversion experience influenced and informed his thought.

Edwards's seventy *Resolutions* were aimed at keeping and regulating his covenant with God and enhancing his religious life according to God's

[86] For the term "theistic metaphysics" as applied to Jonathan Edwards's philosophy and theology, see William J. Wainwright's study, *Reason and the Heart: A Prolegomenon to a Critique of Passional Reason*, pp. 35–40. A discussion of Edwards's theism in regard to nature can be found in De Prospo, *Theism in the Discourse of Jonathan Edwards*.

[87] Edwards, *Concerning the End for which God Created the World*, in *EW*, p. 422.

[88] Miller, introduction, in *Images or Shadows of Divine Things by Jonathan Edwards*, p. 28.

[89] Edwards, *Images or Shadows of Divine Things*, 57 (1737), p. 67; Knight, "Learning the Language of God," p. 531.

[90] Edwards, *Concerning the End for which God Created the World*, p. 419.

[91] Edwards, *Of Insects*, pp. 154–62.

word. The first thirty-four were written around 1722, and the last around 1723.[92] The *Resolutions* "show concern with inner values, chiefly religious, rather than with habits, manners, and various praiseworthy acts such as churchgoing, giving of alms, prayers at stated times, and keeping wide awake in meetings."[93] They throw light on the earnestness which the young man attached to his religious conversion, and the detailed, painstaking decisions he made in order to structure all the spheres of his life according to his covenant with God. Edwards dedicated himself to God:

> On January 12, 1723, I made a solemn dedication of myself to God, and wrote it down; giving up myself, and all that I had to God; to be for the future, in no respect, my own; to act as one that had no right to himself, in any respect. And solemnly vowed, to take God for my whole portion and felicity; looking on nothing else, as any part of my happiness, nor acting as if it were; and his law for the constant rule of my obedience: engaging to fight, with all my might, against the world, the flesh, and the devil, to the end of my life.[94]

Theocentric concerns—that is, issues dealing more with God's glory, the beginning of Edwards's *theologia gloriae*, and less with Christ and a *theologia crucis*—are most evident in these *Resolutions*. To be sure, at the beginning of the *Resolutions*, Edwards declared, "Being sensible that I am unable to do anything without God's help, I do humbly entreat him by his grace, to enable me to keep these Resolutions, so far as they are agreeable to his will, for Christ's sake."[95] But he went on to vow, "*I will do whatsoever* I think to be most to the glory of God," fully devoting his life "never *to do* any manner of thing, whether in soul or body . . . but what tends to the glory of God."[96] Like the conversion experience, Edwards's *Resolutions* are more or less devoid of images of brokenness and the agonized soul, illuminating instead his decision to dedicate his life to the glory of God.

Historians have described Edwards's *Diary*, begun late in the year 1722,[97] as "a colorless document, largely a supplement to his *Resolutions*, introspective and self-condemnatory. He does not record his readings,

[92] Edwards, *Resolutions* (1722–23), in *LPW*, pp. 753–59. See also Dwight, "Memoirs of Jonathan Edwards," pp. 20–22. For the dating of the "Resolutions," see George S. Claghorn's introduction, in *LPW*, pp. 741–45.

[93] Winslow, ed., *Jonathan Edwards: Basic Writings*, p. 68.

[94] Edwards, *Personal Narrative*, pp. 796–97.

[95] Edwards, *Resolutions*, p. 753.

[96] Ibid.

[97] According to Dwight, Edwards began to write his "Diary" on "Dec. 18, 1722." See Dwight, "Memoirs of Jonathan Edwards," I, p. 23. For the dating of Edwards's "Diary," see also Claghorn, introduction, p. 742.

interest in affairs or people, or his doings from day to day. Such things, no doubt, seemed to him of small moment."[98] However, seen in light of his conversion, worldly affairs evidently held little interest for Edwards. If the *Resolutions* were "instructions for life, maxims to be followed in all respects," then the *Diary* vividly "records Edwards' efforts to follow them," and thus "may tell us the most about Edwards as a person—at least as a young man."[99] The preservation of his conversion moment was his ultimate goal; therefore, the *Diary* "records chiefly self-blame and self-discipline to improve his listlessness in religious exercises."[100] The *Diary* contains many statements regarding God's glory: "The very thing I now want, to give me a clearer and more immediate view of the perfection and glory of God, as clear a knowledge of the manner of God's exerting himself, with respect to Spirits and Mind, as I have, of his operations concerning Matter and Bodies."[101] Here lies the beginning of Edwards's construction of the theology of nature as evidenced in his scientific and philosophical writings and his lifelong project of the *Miscellanies*.

In 1722, shortly after his conversion, Edwards began to compose his *Miscellanies*—an enormous body of theological writings that for "thirty five years" traced "the intellectual development and maturation" of his universe of thought and provide "valuable insights into his mind and spirit."[102] In the context of Edwards's conversion and his attempt to reconstruct the world according to his spiritual transformation, the *Miscellanies* "demonstrate how prolonged and deep was" Edwards's "commitment to develop a theology based upon the theme of the redemption of the world."[103] During the same period, while serving as a minister of the Presbyterian church in New York City (1722–23), Edwards "wrote his earliest comments on the Revelation."[104] As he admitted, after the experience of conversion he found the "greatest delight in the Holy Scriptures, of any book whatsoever," but developed a special interest in eschatology and apocalypse, "the advancement of Christ's kingdom in the world, and the glorious things that God would accomplish for his church in the latter days."[105] The outcome would be the *Notes on the Apocalypse*, consisting

---

[98] Faust and Johnson, "Notes," in *Jonathan Edwards: Representative Selections, With Introduction, Bibliography, and Notes,* ed. Clarence H. Faust and Thomas H. Johnson, p. 418.

[99] Claghorn, introduction, pp. 741–43.

[100] Winslow, ed., *Jonathan Edwards: Basic Writings,* p. 76.

[101] Edwards, *Diary* (1725), p. 787.

[102] Schafer, introduction, in *MIS,* p. 1.

[103] Wilson, introduction, in *HWR,* pp. 14–15.

[104] Stein, introduction, in *AW,* pp. 10, 77.

[105] Edwards, *Personal Narrative,* p. 797.

of his lengthy and detailed comments on the book of Revelation. Finally, during 1724, while serving as tutor at Yale College, Edwards began to write the first entries in his *Notes on Scripture*.[106]

Edwards's *Resolutions*, as well as the *Diary*, the *Miscellanies*, the *Notes on the Apocalypse*, and the *Notes on Scripture*, may be seen as the direct outcome of his religious conversion—the means the young man created and developed for maintaining the heat and fervor of his newly acquired religious identity and convictions. Above all, these writings portray his newly formed converted self and his determination to reconstruct every sphere of his life around the conversion experience. Consequently, he developed a *theologia gloriae* that provided meaning and significance for his experience of conversion. At about the same time he began in earnest to produce a wide range of works on natural philosophy—such as *Of Being* (1722), *Of Atoms* (1722), *The Mind* (1723), *Things to be Considered an[d] Written fully about* (1722–24)—which are usually described as his scientific and philosophical writings.[107] Traditionally, this body of work constitutes the proof for the close and essential association of Jonathan Edwards, the Enlightenment, and the scientific revolution. Yet, according to the best chronology of Edwards's writings for the years 1720–24, the great majority dealing with scientific issues were in fact composed after 1721—that is, following and not preceding his religious conversion.[108]

Only after the summer of 1721 did Edwards begin seriously to explore the premises of the scientific culture of his time, accommodating, for example, the Cambridge Platonist Henry More's refutation of Hobbes's materialism and the rejection of the Cartesian mechanistic system of matter and motion.[109] Thus, for example, he attempted to prove that "contrary to the opinion of Hobbes (that nothing is substance but matter), that no matter is substance but only God."[110] Such pronouncements, many of them in Edwards's scientific writings, should not be taken on purely scientific and philosophical terms but rather examined in the wider spiritual

[106] Stein, introduction, in *NOS*, p. 41.

[107] All these scientific works, and many others, are included in *SPW*.

[108] Schafer, introduction, pp. 91–109. Thus, according to Schafer, who based his calculation of the dates of Edwards's writings on Wallace E. Anderson, only a single scientific work, *Of Insects*, was written before 1721, the year of Edwards's conversion. The rest of the scientific and philosophical works were written after 1722, that is, after Edwards's conversion. For the dating of Edwards's various tracts on natural philosophy, see Anderson, "Note on 'Natural Philosophy,' " in *SPW*, pp. 173–91; and Thomas A. Schafer, "Table 2. The *'Miscellanies'* and Chronological Parallels: May 1719–August 1731," in *MIS*, pp. 91–109.

[109] Anderson, introduction, in *SPW*, pp. 54, 59.

[110] *Miscellany f* (1722), p. 166.

and religious context of his conversion and his quest to establish God's absolute sovereignty over the created, physical world.[111]

Moreover, comparison between Edwards's scientific writings before his conversion and those after it, such as "Natural Philosophy" and *The Mind*,[112] reveals a striking phenomenon. *Of Insects*, written before the conversion, is full of observations on the flying spider. Only at the very end, after portraying the spider's life and behavior in much detail, does Edwards express admiration "at the wisdom of the Creator" in the "Contrivance" of such insects.[113] After the conversion, however, Edwards argued for his newly acquired understanding of God's sovereignty. These later scientific writings show a different author from the one who wrote *Of Insects*. Now Edwards was engaging in a great theological and metaphysical debate with mechanical philosophers such as Hobbes and Descartes, trying to prove God in his sovereign majesty and glory within the created world. He declared, for example, that "the very being, and the manner of being, and the whole of bodies depends immediately on the divine power."[114] In this sense, indeed, Edwards's scientific writings should be seen as an integral part of the young man's effort to reconstruct a *theologia gloriae* in accordance with the religious convictions and persuasions he acquired with his conversion experience.

The tremendous influence of the conversion experience on Edwards's thought can be seen in the role he assigned to conversion in God's overall work of salvation and redemption. "We are dependent on the power of God to convert us, and give faith in Jesus Christ, and the new nature," Edwards declared in his sermon *God Glorified in the Work of Redemption* (1731). Conversion "is a work of creation," he claimed. "Yea, it is a more glorious work of power than mere creation, or raising a dead body to life, in that the effect attained is greater and more excellent." For that "holy and happy being, and spiritual life which is produced in the work of conversion, is a far greater and more glorious effect, than mere being and life."[115] The close association between conversion and redemption appears as well in *A Treatise Concerning Religious Affections* (1746), where Edwards argued that "conversion is often compared to opening the eyes of the blind, raising the dead, and a work of creation (wherein

---

[111] According to De Prospo, the "account of Edwards's conversion proves the steadfastness of Edwards's theism." See De Prospo, *Theism in the Discourse of Jonathan Edwards*, p. 183.

[112] Edwards, *Natural Philosophy and Related Papers*, in *SPW*, pp. 171–310; *The Mind*, in *SPW*, pp. 311–400.

[113] Edwards, *Of Insects*, p. 161.

[114] Edwards, *Things to be Considered*, p. 235.

[115] Edwards, *God Glorified in the Work of Redemption* (1731), in *SJW*, p. 72.

creatures are made entirely new), and becoming newborn children."[116] He returned to the theme later in this treatise:

> The Scripture representations of conversion do strongly imply and signify a change of nature: such as being born again; becoming new creatures; rising from the dead; being renewed in the spirit of the mind; dying in sin, and living to righteousness; putting off the old man, and putting on the new man; a being ingrafted into a new stock; a having divine seed implanted in the heart; a being made partakers of the divine nature, etc.[117]

The close and essential connection in Edwards's thought among conversion, revival, and the history of salvation and redemption is most evident in his *History of the Work of Redemption* (1739), in which he declared that "the work by which God wrought out redemption" is "carried on from the fall of man <to the end of the world> in two respects." The first is related primarily to individual, private souls, or "the effect wrought on the souls of the redeemed," and therefore deals with "converting souls, opening the blind eyes, and unstopping deaf [ears], and raising dead souls to life, and rescuing the miserable captured souls of men out of the hand of Satan."[118] The second aspect of the history of redemption is the outcome of the first, namely, the historical events relating to "the many successive works and dispensations of God" in history, with the ultimate goal "to reduce and subdue those enemies of God till they should all be put under God's feet."[119] Or again, "God's thus appearing gloriously above all evil and triumphing over all his enemies was one great thing that God intended by the Work of Redemption."[120] In both respects, however, the conversion of souls and God's triumph over his enemies, God's redemptive acts within history are aimed not at the restoration of humanity as a whole but only of the elect souls: "In doing this God's design was perfectly to restore all the ruins of the fall, so far as concerns the elect part of the world, by his son."[121]

Edwards's role in the revivals of the 1730s and 1740s cannot be separated from his conversion experience, because to a large extent the revivals, which he initiated and influenced, were for him a moment of religious conversion writ large. He conceived of the drama of salvation and redemption not only as an outward historical transformation taking place in the political and social realms, but also as an inward, spiritual transfor-

[116] Edwards, *Religious Affections*, in *RA*, p. 204.
[117] Ibid., p. 340.
[118] Edwards, *History of the Work of Redemption*, p. 120.
[119] Ibid., p. 123.
[120] Ibid., pp. 123–24.
[121] Ibid., p. 124.

mation within the believer's soul as manifested in historical religious revivals and awakenings. Consequently, in his *Some Thoughts Concerning
the Present Revival of Religion in New England* (1742), Edwards established a cosmic role for conversion in providential history: "I am bold to
say, that the work of God in the conversion of one soul, considered together with the source, foundation and purchase of it, and also the benefit,
end and eternal issue of it, is a more glorious work of God than the creation of the whole material universe: it is the most glorious of God's work,
as it above all others manifests the glory of God."[122]

Edwards's conversion was the source of his later concept of the *ordo
salutis*, or the morphology of conversion experience, during the revivals
of 1730s and 1740s. It led him to construct a prominent role for the
experience of conversion in the overall history of salvation and redemption.[123] Conversion denotes a special relationship between the orders of
grace and time, between redemption and history. "Conversion and the
rebirth to a new life change time and the experience of time," wrote Jürgen Moltmann, because "they make-present the ultimate in the penultimate, and the future of time in the midst of time." Conversion as the
private, spiritual experience of saving grace signifies God's indwelling in
time. In conversion saving grace mediates between the spiritual welfare
of the individual and the eschatological future of salvation, thus granting
that "the future is God's mode of being in history." Thus the "unity between the divine coming," in the form of saving grace, "and human conversion" indeed indicates sacred "fulfilled time."[124]

Scholars too often tend to explain Edwards's universe of thought in
terms of the contemporary culture in which they live. For example, there
have been attempts to describe Edwards's vision of history in terms of
modern historiography, or historicism, which tends to define everything
in historical terms, and on this basis to examine the failure of his historical
interpretation in colonial America.[125] But for Edwards history does not

---

[122] Edwards, *Some Thoughts*, p. 344. For Edwards's analysis of the morphology of conversion experience during the New England revivals of 1734–45 and 1740–43, see Michael
Jinkins, "The 'True Remedy': Jonathan Edwards' Soteriological Perspective as Observed in
his Revival Treatises," *Scottish Journal of Theology* 48 (1995): 185–209.

[123] For a recent interpretation of Edwards's understanding of the close relationship between conversion and revival, see Walter V. L. Eversley, "The Pastor as Revivalist," in *Edwards in Our Time: Jonathan Edwards and the Shaping of American Religion*, ed. Sang H.
Lee et al., pp. 113–30; and Helen P. Westra, "Divinity's Design: Edwards and the History
of the Work of Revival," in ibid.

[124] Jürgen Moltmann, *The Coming of God: Christian Eschatology* (Minneapolis: Fortress, 1996), pp. 22–24.

[125] Thus, for example, Perry Miller claimed: "Measured against modern scholarship, tex-
tual criticism, archeology, and comparative religion," Edwards's *History of the Work of
Redemption* "is an absurd book, where it is not pathetic." See Miller, *Jonathan Edwards*,

constitute evidence of faith and truth, because God existed before time and will exist after time. God created the world; hence, religious faith is not dependent on historical explanation, and revealed religion is not a construct of historical time. The same applies to sacred, providential history; for Edwards the whole course and progress of the history of God's work of redemption should not be shown exclusively in historical terms, for this redemptive work preceded the world and continues after it, and it gives meaning and significance to human history and experience upon the earth.

The conversion moment, therefore, is crucial to any understanding of the development of Edwards's universe of thought. The experience bestowed on him an awesome vision of God in his absolute sovereignty and glory, which constituted the content and form of his *theologia gloriae*. For, as Niebuhr wrote,

> What Edwards knew, what he believed in his heart and his mind, was that man was made to stand in the presence of eternal, unending absolute glory, to participate in the celebration of cosmic deliverance from everything putrid, destructive, defiling, to rejoice in the service of the stupendous artist who flung universes of stars on his canvas, sculptured the forms of angelic powers, etched with loving care miniature worlds within worlds.[126]

---

p. 310. Peter Gay said that when "we speak of Jonathan Edwards, we are bound to speak of tragedy," because he lived in an age when "Americans turned to new guides in the writing of history, discarding providence, and seeking the causes of events within the natural realm." See Gay, *A Loss of Mastery: Puritan Historians in Colonial America* (New York: Vintage, 1968), pp. 104, 116.

[126] Niebuhr, "The Anachronism of Jonathan Edwards" [1958], 480–85. The quotation is from page 483.

Space

Three

Theology in the Age of Scientific Reasoning: Edwards and the Reenchantment of the World

From one point of view, the history of religion since the seventeenth century can be seen as the driving-back of faith from history, from the physical world, and from the realm of morals. . . . So religion, withdrawing from its claim to give objective truth about the nature of reality in all its aspects, ends by seeking to stimulate certain sorts of inner feeling in those who care for that sort of thing.
   (Keith Ward, *Religion & Revelation*, 1994)

[The] whole universe (the soul of man excepted), [is] but a great Automaton, or self-moving engine, wherein all things are performed by the bare motion (or rest), the size, the shape, and the situation, or texture of the parts of the universal matter it consists of.
   (Robert Boyle, *The Excellency of Theology Compared with Natural Philosophy*, 1665)

There is no such thing as mechanism, if that word is taken to be that whereby bodies act each upon other, purely and properly by themselves.
   (Edwards, "Of Atoms," c. 1722)

To find out the reasons of things in natural philosophy is only to find out the proportion of God's acting."
   (Edwards, "The Mind," no. 34, c. 1725)

EDWARDS WAS ONE of America's great original minds, "one of those pure artists through whom the deepest urgencies of their ages and their country became articulated." He "was infinitely more than a theologian."[1] This is evident in Edwards's philosophical enterprise, which has led scholars to consider him the "foundation stone in the history of American philosophy."[2] The reference here is especially to the long series of scientific and philosophical writings[3] composed during the 1720s, where he attempted

---

[1] Miller, *Jonathan Edwards*, pp. xxx–xxxi.
[2] Kuklick, "Jonathan Edwards and American Philosophy," p. 246.
[3] Edwards, *Scientific and Philosophical Writings*, in *SPW*.

to define the essential nature of reality, or the dimension of the physical, material world. During that period, as he wrote in 1725, his goal was to ascertain God's relation to his creation, or to define the relationship between the orders of grace and nature: "The very thing" he demanded of himself was to get a clear "knowledge of the manner of God's exerting himself" with respect "of his operations concerning Matter and Bodies."[4] Ultimately, it is upon this inquiry into the dimension of the physical, material space within which human life is set that Edwards acquired his name as "the greatest American philosopher before the Civil War."[5]

For a long time Edwards was thought of as a preacher of revival and hellfire rather than as a theologian, and as a Calvinist theologian rather than as a philosopher of importance, and was accordingly dismissed. However, with the possible exception of Benjamin Franklin, Edwards was the most influential and widely read writer of colonial America. This New England divine was one of the rare people who recognized and faced the serious challenges posed to traditional Christian thought and belief by the emergence of new modes of thought in early modern history: the physical discoveries of Newton, the psychological observations of Locke, and the popular acceptance of the Enlightenment belief in "God more kind and man more worthy." Indeed, he was almost alone in the eighteenth century in rejecting the idea of universal moral sense and essential human goodness, "the psychological optimism of the Shaftesbury-Hutcheson gospel of the innate goodness of man."[6] Edwards, then, was more than a revivalist, more than a theologian. He was also a bold and independent philosopher. And nowhere is his force of mind more evident than in his reaction against the scientific culture and imagination of his time—mechanical philosophy, or the doctrine that all natural phenomena can be explained and understood by the mere mechanics of matter and motion—and, consequently, in his attempt to construct a plausible alternative to the mechanistic interpretation of the essential nature of reality, which would reconstitute the glory of God's absolute sovereignty, power, and will within creation.

Edwards began his undergraduate studies at Yale in 1716, and there he first became acquainted with the new scientific thought and imagination coming out of Europe, traditionally referred to as the scientific revolution.[7] With the modernization of the Yale curriculum during the year

[4] Edwards, *Diary*, February 12, 1725, in *LPW*, p. 787.
[5] Flower and Murphey, *A History of Philosophy in America*, I, p. 137.
[6] Fiering, *Jonathan Edwards's Moral Thought and Its British Context*, p. 148.
[7] In recent years historians have begun to question the very concept of *the* scientific revolution, and even altogether "to undermine one of our most hallowed explanatory frameworks, that of the Scientific Revolution." See B.J.T. Dobbs, "Newton as Final Cause and First Mover," in *Rethinking the Scientific Revolution*, ed. Margaret J. Osler, p. 25; and

1717–18,[8] he encountered the revolutionary ideas of scientific reasoning and the early Enlightenment. He read many works by mechanical philosophers, such as Boyle and Newton, and in these he discovered the new modes of scientific thought.[9] For the rest of his life, the dialogue with these early modern intellectual movements was part of his philosophical and theological enterprise. Indeed, one of the main marks of his life of the mind, as he himself defined it shortly before his death, was the constant struggle "against most of the prevailing errors of the present day," which he believed led "to the utter subverting of the gospel of Christ."[10]

The significance of Edwards's response to the metaphysical and theological principles that often accompanied mechanical philosophy should be seen in the wider intellectual context of colonial New England. He was almost alone in British America to take upon himself the mission of responding to the challenges posed to traditional religious faith and belief by the new culture of time and space. Indeed, among contemporaries he was alone in his "pursuit of reality," attempting to understand the "constitution of the natural world" and ascertain "God's relationship to his physical creation."[11] The new scientific theories reached New England as early as the middle of the seventeenth century. "The Copernican theory was known . . . as well as Kepler's work."[12] In the early years of the eighteenth century, Newton's and Locke's writings gradually found their way to New England and transformed the curriculum at Harvard and Yale. After reading Newton's *Opticks* (1704), Cotton Mather in his *Christian Philosopher* (1721) pronounced Newton "the *Perpetual Dictator* of the Learned World in the Principles of Natural Philosophy."[13]

No Puritan more clearly represents the temper of seventeenth-century New England curiosity about the phenomenal universe than Cotton Mather. He was an avid reader of the scientific literature of his day, and

---

Richard S. Westfall's rebuttal of Dobbs's thesis in his "The Scientific Revolution Reassessed," in *Rethinking the Scientific Revolution*, ed. Margaret J. Osler, pp. 41–55. See also Margaret J. Osler, "The Canonical Imperative: Rethinking the Scientific Revolution," in *Rethinking the Scientific Revolution*, ed. Margaret J. Osler, pp. 3–22; and H. Floris Cohen, *The Scientific Revolution: A Historiographical Inquiry* (Chicago: University of Chicago Press, 1994).

[8] Anderson, introduction, in *SPW*, p. 15; Flower and Murphey, *A History of Philosophy in America*, I, pp. 81–83.

[9] These included "the major scientific works of Robert Boyle," Newton, and many others, as well as various publications of the Royal Society. See Anderson, introduction, pp. 17–21. See also Edwards, "To Unknown Correspondent," 1746, in *LPW*, p. 202.

[10] Edwards, "To the Trustees of the College of New Jersey," p. 727.

[11] Wilson H. Kimnach, "Jonathan Edwards's Pursuit of Reality," in *JEAE*, pp. 102–4.

[12] Flower and Murphey, *A History of Philosophy in America*, I, p. 62.

[13] Cotton Mather, *The Christian Philosopher: A Collection of the Best Discoveries in Nature, with Religious Improvements* (London, 1721), p. 82.

familiar with the writings of mechanical philosophers like Descartes, Gassendi, and Boyle. Yet, with all Mather's formidable erudition, he never dared criticize or attempt to provide an alternative to the scientific thinking of his time. On the contrary; he declared that "corpusculatianism," or the view that attempts to account for the phenomena of nature, by the motion, figure, rest, position, and so on, of the minute particles of matter, "was the only right philosophy."[14] Indeed, Mather "readily accepted the new science," and for him "the Newtonian science was a splendid confirmation" of his Puritan convictions. He therefore used "natural theology as a means of showing that science supported Puritan religious beliefs, and his *Christian Philosopher* was the first such work written in America."[15] Unaware of the grave ramifications inherent in the premises of mechanical philosophy for the traditional Christian dialectic of God's transcendence and immanence, Mather did not realize that the new scientific interpretation was leading to the disenchantment of the world,[16] or to the growing separation between the order of grace and the order of nature,[17] between God and the world, and thus was incompatible with traditional Christian belief. This philosophical task was left to Jonathan Edwards.

Edwards fully grasped the serious threats mechanical philosophy posed to traditional religious modes of faith and experience. By the late seventeenth century, the "universe ha[d] become so mechanical, Fontenelle [Bernard Le Bovier de, 1657–1757] announced in 1686, that one might almost be ashamed of it."[18] The French writer, who heralds the age of the

---

[14] Kaiser, *Creation & the History of Science*, p. 205.

[15] Flower and Murphey, *A History of Philosophy in America*, I, pp. 75–76, 113.

[16] Max Weber argued that the origin of this process of the disenchantment of the world should be traced back to the Protestant Reformation, which brought about "the elimination of magic from the world." See Max Weber, *The Protestant Ethic and the Spirit of Capitalism* (London: Routledge, 1995 [1904]), p. 105. Modern studies today tend to see the beginning of the disenchantment of the world, or the separation of the order of grace and the order of nature, with the "nominalist revolution" of the fourteenth century. See Amos Funkenstein, *Theology and the Scientific Imagination from the Middle Ages to the Seventeenth Century* (Princeton: Princeton University Press, 1986), p. 27; Alexandre Koyré, *From the Closed World to the Infinite Universe* (New York: Harper Torchbooks, 1958), pp. 5–27; and Dupré, *Passage to Modernity*. See also Gordon Leff, *The Dissolution of the Medieval Outlook* (New York: Harper Torchbooks, 1976); and Avihu Zakai and Ayval Ramati, "The Metaphysical Foundations of Modern Scientific Imagination," in *Science and Religion Together*, ed. Robert L. Herrmann (Philadelphia: Templeton, 2001), pp. 41–51. Reprint: http://www.templeton.org/pdf/EHVG_Winners.pdf.

[17] For various theological attempts to define the separation between the order of grace and the order of nature along with its ramifications regarding the issue of modernity, see Dupré, *Passage to Modernity*; idem, "The Dissolution of the Union of Nature and Grace at the Dawn of the Modern Age," pp. 95–121; and idem, "Nature and Grace: Fateful Separation and Attempted Reunion," pp. 52–73.

[18] Fontenelle, as quoted in John H. Brooke, *Science and Religion: Some Historical Perspectives* (Cambridge: Cambridge University Press, 1991), pp. 117–18.

philosophes, only expressed the common view that with the mechaniza-tion of the world of nature becoming such an important feature of scien-tific thought, new questions arose which seriously challenged traditional Christian modes of thought and belief:

> What role could be left for God to play in a universe that ran like clockwork? Would one have to side with those who became known as 'deists,' who re-stricted that role to Christian conception of subsequent revelation? Would God's special providence, His watchful concern for the lives of individuals, not be jeopardized if all events were ultimately reducible to mechanical laws?[19]

In his scientific and philosophical writings, Edwards reacted against these metaphysical and theological consequences of the new scientific thought. He was alarmed by the basic postulate of mechanical philoso-phers that nature operates according to mere mechanical principles, or natural laws, formulated in mathematical terms, envisioning the world of nature as a huge machine that runs by itself according to abstract, univer-sal laws of nature, freed from subordination to God's dominion and not affected by his unceasing watchful eyes. With great dismay Edwards ob-served that mechanical philosophy's notion of a homogeneous, uniform, and symmetrical, one-dimensional world of nature not only deprived the created order of any teleological end and purpose, but stipulated that nature could no longer manifest the presence of God. Sadly he observed the mechanical philosophers' claim that the Almighty had created the world and then retired, releasing the realm of nature from its subordina-tion to God and establishing it as a "self-moving engine." In sum, Ed-wards reacted against the growing tendency to differentiate sharply be-tween nature and God. In response, he constructed his own theology of nature, or typology, interpreting the physical world as a representation or a "shadow" of the spiritual, which celebrates God's glory and sover-eignty as they are evidenced in the coherence and beauty, order and har-mony, of world phenomena. Against the scientific disenchantment of the world of nature, Edwards's quest was for its reenchantment.[20]

Edwards's reaction to mechanical philosophy therefore was obviously different from Mather's. He did not embrace the fundamental premises of mechanical science. Although he used some of its concepts, such as atomic doctrine, laws of nature, and so forth, he strove to discredit them. While undertaking to provide an alternative view regarding the essence of reality that would lead eventually to the reenchantment of the world, Edwards's goal was the demonstration of the infinite power of God's ab-

---

[19] Brooke, *Science and Religion*, pp. 117–18.
[20] For an excellent analysis of Edwards's "theocentric metaphysics," see Fiering, "The Rationalist Foundations of Edwards's Metaphysics," pp. 73–101.

solute sovereignty in both the "order of nature" and the "order of time."[21] For him, therefore, the challenge of the new scientific theories was "not atheism but the gradual elimination of God's special providence."[22] Edwards's interpretation of world phenomena thus constituted a radical departure from the prevailing mechanical philosophy. Believing "the corporeal world is to no advantage but to the spiritual," he claimed that "to find out the reasons of things in natural philosophy is only to find out the proportion of God's acting."[23] In this venture of the reenchantment of the world, Edwards was not alone in the British world, as can be seen in the close affinities between his thought and that of other anti-Newtonians of that time, such as George Berkeley and William Blake.[24] His natural theology may be studied as well in the context of the reaction by "many guardians of theological orthodoxy" in England against certain trends in contemporary natural philosophy, and their "theologically based suspicions of Newton's work."[25] The natural philosophy that Edwards developed entitles him to a distinguished place among other early modern philosophers who reacted against the metaphysical and theological implications of the new scientific ideas, such as Pierre Gassendi, Giordano Bruno, Nicolas Malebranche, and Gottfried Wilhelm Leibniz, to name only a few. Still, in his philosophical enterprise Edwards was clearly alone in New England, and here indeed lies his significance for the development of American philosophy.

As we saw in the previous chapter, the genesis of Edwards's construction of the theology of nature may be found in his conversion moment.

[21] Edwards, *Miscellany* no. 704 (c. 1736), in *MIS*, p. 314; Edwards, *Freedom of the Will*, 1754, p. 177.

[22] James Hoopes, "Jonathan Edwards's Religious Psychology," *Journal of American History* 69 (1983): 863.

[23] Edwards, *The Mind*, pp. 353–55.

[24] Edwards's criticism of mechanical philosophy may be considered in the wider context of British anti-Newtonians, such as Berkeley, Blake, and others, who were afraid of distancing God from the phenomena of nature, or of detaching the order of grace from the order of nature, as Newton's universal active principles appeared to do. Berkeley and Edwards developed their "idealism" independently, adopting the view that physical objects exist only in the mind or cannot exist until they are perceived. Both evidently ran the risk of emptying nature of any intrinsic structure and principles of its own. For a comparison of their views, see Kaiser, *Creation & the History of Science*, pp. 244–53; and Anderson, introduction, pp. 102–3.

[25] Michael Hunter, *Science and Society in Restoration England* (Cambridge: Cambridge University Press, 1981), p. 187; John Gascoigne, *Cambridge in the Age of the Enlightenment: Science, Religion and Politics from the Restoration to the French Revolution* (Cambridge: Cambridge University Press, 1989), p. 169; and "From Bentley to the Victorians: The Rise and Fall of British Newtonian Natural Theology," *Science in Context* 2 (1988): 219–56.

This momentous spiritual experience determined both the formation of his theology of nature and its distinct content and form, leading directly to his attempt to reconstruct the whole created order according to his newly acquired religious convictions and persuasions. Equipped with a strong awareness of his religious identity, as well as with a powerful sense of God's absolute sovereignty, Edwards developed an appreciation of his existential condition within a close-knit divine universe in which "God's excellency, his wisdom, his purity and love, seemed to appear in every thing."[26] Hence, his interpretation of the essential nature of reality constituted a serious and systematic attempt to provide a meaningful alternative to the new modes of thought in early modern Europe that countered traditional Christian thought and belief. The conversion experience dictated a program of work that required, in part, an interpretation of nature in harmony with his newly gained theological convictions. With such a mission in hand, Edwards found that the contemporary understanding of the essential nature of reality was incompatible with his religious persuasions. His aim, then, was to redefine natural phenomena in light of his spiritual experience in order to prove God's sovereign majesty within the created world. To this task Edwards devoted much time and thought in his scientific and philosophical writings during the 1720s.

In his works on natural philosophy, Edwards constructed a singular natural philosophy, or indeed theology of nature, according to which the material world of everyday life is only the manifestation of a divine universe, wonderfully made and harmonized according to God's will and design. Everything in the physical realm seemed to him to have a specific part and role in a well-designed, close-knit, divine universe ruled directly and immediately by God's absolute sovereignty: "And very much of the wisdom of God in the creation appears in his so ordering things natural, that they livelily represent things divine and spiritual."[27] Given the world of nature conceived as totally dependent upon God's power and will, it was obviously an integral part of the grand teleological and theological structure of order inherent in the universe and God's cosmic providential plan. As Edwards argued in 1723, "Every atom in the universe is managed by Christ so as to be most to the advantage of the Christian, every particle of air or every ray of the sun."[28]

Edwards developed his cosmological concept of real being and true substance in order, in part, to refute materialism. He rejected Hobbes's materialism, which held that the universe is a complete, autonomous, and self-sustaining system of unthinking bodies subject only to inherent, nec-

---

[26] Edwards, *Personal Narrative*, in *LPW*, p. 794.
[27] Edwards, *Miscellany* no. 119 (c. 1724), in *MIS*, p. 184.
[28] Edwards, *Miscellany ff* (c. 1723), in *MIS*, p. 184.

essary, and mathematically exact laws of mechanical causation, because it ruled out the divine and providential government of the world. Instead of "Hobbes' notion" that "all substance is matter,"[29] Edwards objected, "the world exists only mentally."[30] Therefore, "those beings which have knowledge and consciousness are the only proper and real and substantial beings . . . [hence] spirits only are properly substance."[31] In his reaction to materialism, Edwards formulated his own idealistic phenomenalism, the thesis that physical objects exist only in the mind or cannot exist unless they are perceived: "the world, i.e. the material universe, exists nowhere but in the mind," and given that "all material existence is only idea," the "world therefore is an ideal one."[32]

Edwards's conversion experience thus dictated a program of work that required an interpretation of nature in harmony with his profound new theological convictions. "The very thing I now want," he wrote in his "Diary" in 1725, is to get "a clearer and more immediate view of the perfections and glory of God," both in regard of "the manner of God's exerting himself, with respect to Spirits and Mind," and of the Deity's "operations concerning Matter and Bodies."[33] With this aim in mind he attacked mechanical philosophy, claiming in 1722 "there is no such thing as mechanism, if that word" meant that "bodies act each upon other, purely and properly by themselves,"[34] because "the very being, and the manner of being, and the whole of bodies depends immediately on the divine power."[35]

The Scientific Revolution's Disenchantment of the World

The mechanistic conception of nature was responsible for the emergence of a new culture of time and space that played a great part in the disenchantment of the world. As the "world became the object of scientific inquiry" during the sixteenth and seventeenth centuries "through a process of desacralisation," so too "religious practices" were "demystified by the imposition of *natural laws*." Consequently, "the physical world ceased to be a theatre in which the drama of creation was constantly redirected by divine intervention," and "human expressions of religious

[29] Edwards, *Things to be Considered an[d] Written fully about* (c. 1722–24), p. 235.
[30] Edwards, *Miscellany* no. 247 (c. 1726), in *MIS*, p. 360.
[31] Edwards, *Of Being*, in *SPW*, p. 207.
[32] Edwards, *The Mind*, in *SPW*, pp. 350–56.
[33] Edwards, *Diary*, February 12, 1725, in *LPW*, p. 787.
[34] Edwards, *Of Atoms*, in *SPW*, p. 216.
[35] Edwards, *Things to be Considered*, p. 235.

faith came increasingly to be seen as outcomes of natural processes rather than the work of God or of Satan and his legions."[36] In the face of this process of desacralization, the English churchman John Edwards complained in the 1690s that the new scientific theories were leading to the exclusion of religion considerations: "Learned Enquirers are apt to give Encouragement to Atheism by *an obstinate endeavouring to solve all the* Phenomena *in the world by mere Natural and Corporeal Causes,* and by their averseness to admit of the aid and concurrence of a Supernatural and Immaterial Principle for the production of them."[37] In a similar vein the non-juror George Hicks claimed: "It is their Newtonian philosophy which hath Made Not only so many Arians but Theists, and that Not only among the laity but I fear among the divines."[38] By the early eighteenth century, then, "many guardians of theological orthodoxy" found "the danger in mechanical philosophy," and "Newtonians like Samuel Clarke were pilloried for abetting the growth of heretical ideas."[39]

This disenchantment of the world radically influenced the relationship between reason and revelation, between the light of nature and God's word. From the early eighteenth century, "the concept of nature as an inherently active substance was developed explicitly in opposition to the Newtonian concept of nature." In contrast to "Newton's doctrine that all causal activity in nature was imposed by God's power and will," a new "theory of nature" emerged "in which activity was considered as immanent in the structure of nature"; hence, "nature was endowed with intrinsic active forces or powers."[40] According to the mechanistic interpretation, after the world was created God set it in motion and regulated it by laws of nature that may be formulated in mathematical terms, and these laws can be discerned by the light of nature and not solely through God's word.[41]

The mechanistic image of nature evidently has nothing to do with divine revelation, but rather everything with reason: "reason now becomes" the "first ground of all knowledge and the guideline of the determination

---

[36] Peter Harrison, *"Religion" and the Religions in the English Enlightenment* (Cambridge: Cambridge University Press, 1990), p. 5. See also Harrison, *The Bible, Protestantism, and the Rise of Natural Science* (Cambridge: Cambridge University Press, 1998).

[37] Hunter, *Science and Society in Restoration England,* p. 170.

[38] Gascoigne, *Cambridge in the Age of the Enlightenment,* p. 164.

[39] Hunter, *Science and Society in Restoration England,* p. 187.

[40] P. M. Heimann, "Voluntarism and Immanence: Conceptions of Nature in Eighteenth-Century Thought," *Journal of the History of Ideas* 39 (1978): 275–76.

[41] For a discussion of the shift in philosophical and theological perspectives regarding the concept of the laws of nature, see Francis Oakley, "Christian Theology and the Newtonian Science: The Rise of the Concept of the Laws of Nature," *Church History* 30 (1961): 433–57.

of the things."[42] Revelation, as the mechanical philosopher and the "great father figure of British natural philosophy in his time,"[43] Robert Boyle wrote, is "a foreign principle in this *philosophical enquiry*" of natural philosophy; therefore, the latter should be based only upon "the light of reason."[44] Up to the scientific revolution, "the authoritative truth was considered that of Church and faith. The means for the proper knowledge of beings were obtained by way of the interpretation of the sources of revelation, the write and the tradition of the Church."[45] Mechanical philosophy was founded upon rationalism, that is, the view that "nature operates according to mechanical principles, the regularity of which can be described in the form of natural laws, ideally formulated in mathematical terms."[46] This was indeed exactly what Newton attempted to accomplish in his *Philosophiae Naturalis Principia Mathematica* [*Mathematical Principles of Natural Philosophy*] (1687), writing that he offered "this work as the mathematical principle" of natural "philosophy, for the whole burden of philosophy seems to consist in this—from the phenomena of motion to investigate the forces of nature, and then from these forces to demonstrate the other phenomena."[47] Accordingly, Newton continued, "I wish we could derive the rest of the phenomena of Nature by the same kind of reasoning from mechanical principles."[48]

Knowledge of the mysteries of world phenomena was gradually divorced from divine revelation; instead, "an independent and original truth of nature" emerged. "This truth is revealed not in God's word but in his works; it is not based on the testimony of Scripture or traditions but is visible to us all the time. But it is understandable only to those who know nature's handwriting and can decipher her text."[49] Newton argued that a true understanding of the phenomena of nature is based upon "rational mechanics," or "reasoning from mechanical principles" of all "the

[42] Martin Heidegger, "Modern Science, Metaphysics, and Mathematics," in Heidegger, *Basic Writings*, ed. David F. Krell (New York: HarperCollins, 1993), p. 304.

[43] J. E. McGuire, "Boyle's Conception of Nature," *Journal of the History of Ideas* 33 (1972): 524.

[44] Robert Boyle, *A Free Enquiry into the Vulgarly Received Notion of Nature* (1686), in *Selected Philosophical Papers of Robert Boyle*, edited with an introduction, M. A. Stewart (Indianapolis: Hackett, 1991), p. 189.

[45] Heidegger, "Modern Science, Metaphysics, and Mathematics," p. 295.

[46] Brooke, *Science and Religion*, p. 119.

[47] Isaac Newton, "Newton's Preface to the First Edition" (1686), in *Sir Isaac Newton's Mathematical Principles of Natural Philosophy and His System of the World*, ed. Florian Cajori, 2 vols. (Berkeley: University of California Press, 1934), I, p. xvii.

[48] Newton, "Newton's Preface to the First Edition of the *Principia*," in *Newton's Philosophy of Nature: Selections from His Writings*, ed. H. S. Thayer (New York: Hafner, 1974), p. 9.

[49] Cassirer, *The Philosophy of the Enlightenment*, pp. 42–43.

phenomena of Nature" which are formulated according to "mathematical principles."[50] Contrary to revelation, in the realm of nature "the whole
plan of the universe lies before us in its undivided and inviolable unity,
evidently, waiting for the human mind to recognize and express it."[51]
Thus, if during the Middle Ages, "the normal use of natural reason was
obscured by blind faith in the absolute truth of Christian Revelation,"[52]
during the Age of Reason the supremacy and primacy of divine revelation
was attacked: "The role of reason was magnified, that of revelation was
depressed. The scriptures were subjected to intensive and often to unsympathetic scrutiny. Miracles were challenged. Prophecy was reassessed.
Christian thought faced a threat which might have stripped it of all its
uniqueness."[53]

Here lies the sources, in part, of the Enlightenment belief in human
autonomy. The Enlightenment, it should not be forgotten, was "the revolution of man's autonomous potentialities over against heteronomous
powers which were no longer convincing."[54] Among such powers was the
"authority of the Christian church and of its dogma and ultimately the
objective authority of Scripture and of transcendent revelation itself."[55] In
sum, with the new scientific ideas and the new modes of thought regarding
human beings' ability to understand the world of nature in which their
lives are placed, the power of religious faith and the belief in its providing
objective truths about the essential nature of reality underwent a crucial
transformation: "From one point of view, the history of religion since the
seventeenth century can be seen as the driving-back of faith from history,
from the physical world, and from the realm of morals." Thus "religion,
withdrawing from its claim to give objective truth about the nature of
reality in all its aspects, ends by seeking to stimulate certain sorts of inner
feeling in those who care for that sort of thing."[56] Edwards's entire philosophical and theological enterprise may be understood within this wider
ideological context, as an attempt to provide a plausible teleological and
theological alternative to the emergence of modes of thought that were
leading to the disenchantment of the world.

[50] Newton, "Newton's Preface to the First Edition," pp. xvii–xviii.

[51] Cassirer, *The Philosophy of the Enlightenment*, p. 43.

[52] Etienne Gilson, *Reason and Revelation in the Middle Ages* (New York: Scribner, 1938),
p. 4.

[53] Gerald R. Cragg, *The Church and the Age of Reason* (London: Penguin, 1990 [1960]),
pp. 12–13.

[54] Tillich, *A History of Christian Thought*, p. 323.

[55] Pelikan, *The Christian Tradition: A History of the Development of Doctrine*, vol. V,
Christian Doctrine and Modern Culture (since 1700), p. 60.

[56] Keith Ward, *Religion & Revelation* (Oxford: Clarendon, 1994), p. 284.

Atomic Doctrine

Edwards launched his criticism of the metaphysical and theological premises of the mechanical philosophy of nature with a discussion of atoms
because an atom is a *"minimum physicum,"*[57] that is, the smallest physical
particle in the universe; understanding it might lead to a better knowledge
of the mysteries of the material world. He began with the issue of the
atomic doctrine, for by the end of the seventeenth century "atomism as a
mechanical philosophy was, in England, the conservative view."[58] Indeed,
in his determination to establish God's sovereignty and activity in the
world, Edwards appropriated the prevailing atomic doctrine, given that
it was the available scientific language of his time, but he radically Christianized it in his desire to show how closely and intimately God's divine
activity controls and directs even the smallest particles of atoms in the
physical world. "All bodies whatsoever," he wrote, in accordance with
contemporary atomic doctrine, "must of absolute necessity be composed
of atoms, or bodies that are indiscerpible [sic], that can not be made less,
or whose parts cannot by any finite power whatsoever, be separated one
from another."[59] Edwards proposed, however, not only to define the "ontological status of bodies and their immediate dependence upon God's
power and will,"[60] but also to demonstrate the infinite power of divine
activity in controlling the world phenomena through the agency of the
very smallest physical particle of nature, and thus to show that it is "God
himself, or the immediate exercise of his power, which keeps the parts of
atoms" or bodies "together."[61] Believing in God's absolute sovereignty in
the moral and spiritual world, Edwards transposed this spiritual experience into the physical world, claiming that in the material world "all
body" or matter "is nothing but what immediately results from the exercise of divine power." Hence the ontological status of tangible, material
bodies is radically dependent on God, and "the constant exercise of the
infinite power of God is necessary to preserve bodies in being."[62] This
wider metaphysical and theological context also accounts for his radical
claim that every "atom in the universe is managed by Christ."[63]

[57] Edwards, *Of Atoms*, p. 212.
[58] Robert H. Kargon, *Atomism in England from Hariot to Newton* (Oxford: Clarendon,
1966), p. 133.
[59] Edwards, *Of Atoms*, p. 209.
[60] Anderson, introduction, p. 68.
[61] Edwards, *Of Atoms*, p. 214.
[62] Ibid., pp. 215, 214.
[63] Edwards, *Miscellany ff* (c. 1723), in *MIS*, p. 184.

The argument of God's immediate influence in controlling and regulating every atom, and hence the operation of all tangible, material bodies in the universe, enabled Edwards to reject mechanical philosophy's claim that natural phenomena can be explained by the mere mechanics of matter and its motion, or that, as the mechanical philosopher Robert Boyle wrote, "the phenomena of the world" are "physically produced by the mechanical affections of the part of matter, and what they operate upon one another according to mechanical laws."[64] Against this, Edwards argued that because atoms are totally and absolutely dependent on God's infinite power, the very framework of the material universe is evidence of God's omnipresence, omnipotence, and omniactivity: "the very being, and the manner of being, and the whole of bodies depends immediately on the divine power."[65] Since the being and existence of everything in creation stands under the constant, direct, and immediate absolute power and will of God, the whole world of nature is imbued with God's redemptive activity: " 'Tis exceeding evident in natural philosophy, that all the operations of the creatures are the immediate influence of the divine being."[66]

In *Original Sin* (1758), Edwards reiterated these views, claiming that "the existence of created substance" is "the effect of God's immediate power, in that moment, without any dependence on prior existence, as much as the first creation out of nothing."[67] The physical, material world was thus transformed from the mechanistic image of a huge machine, set going by a perfect watchmaker and regulated by mere natural laws, into a universe pervaded with divine activity, where God's infinite power is manifested in creating and sustaining the world anew at every moment through the agency of atoms.

Such an interpretation of the essential nature of reality contradicted certain metaphysical and theological implications that mechanical philosophers had drawn from the atomic doctrine. Hobbes argued that all "gross bodies are composed of small invisible subtle bodies" or atoms, "whose varieties of motion accounted for the various physical qualities to be found in nature." Because "motion cannot be understood to have any other cause besides motion," Hobbes continued, all natural phenomena have no "other cause than motion."[68] Edwards, however, asserted that "it is God himself," through "the immediate exercise of his power, that keeps the parts of atoms together" and preserves "bodies in being."

[64] Boyle, *About the Excellency and Grounds of the Mechanical Hypothesis* (1674), in *Selected Philosophical Papers of Robert Boyle*, p. 139.
[65] Edwards, *Things to be Considered*, p. 235.
[66] Edwards, *Miscellany* no. 178 (1725), in *MIS*, p. 327.
[67] Edwards, *Original Sin*, 1758, in *OS*, p. 402.
[68] Kargon, *Atomism in England from Hariot to Newton*, pp. 57, 59.

Hence "all body is nothing but what immediately results from the exercise of divine power in such a particular manner," and thus, ultimately, all "motion" of bodies "is from the immediate exercise of divine power."[69] Striving to proclaim divine activity in the world, Edwards argued that only "infinite power," or God himself, "keeps the parts of atoms together."[70] A similar view can be found in Newton's *Opticks* (1704), where he wrote concerning "Particles" of matter, or atoms, that "no ordinary Power" is able "to divide what God himself" made "in the first Creation."[71] The difference, however, is crucial; for Newton atoms were *made* in creation, while for Edwards God continues to keep, control, and continuously regulate the atoms "throughout all eternity."[72] Thus, Edwards can state that "the universe is created out of nothing every moment."[73]

Edwards's atom, or that smallest particle which is indivisible and "whose parts cannot by any finite power" be "separated one from another,"[74] served an important metaphysical and theological purpose: it is the agent by which God exercises his infinite power and the medium through which his immanence is realized within the order of creation. Edwards went further than Newton in asserting that the "nature of atoms" is "an infinite power," so that "all the nature of them that is not absolutely themselves must be God exerting his power upon them."[75] God not only created atoms during the moment of creation, but continuously and immediately exerts his influence on them: " 'Tis certain that when God first created matter or the various chaoses of atoms" He "designed" as well "the figures and shapes of every atom, and likewise their place." Hence, to avoid a situation where "the least wrong step in a mote may, in eternity, subvert the order of the universe," Edwards praised "the great wisdom of God" in disposing "every atom at first, as that they should go for the best throughout all eternity."[76] What arises, then, from his concept of atoms as a metaphysical-theological principle, is a universe structured according to a teleological and theological order in which God becomes the sole foundation of all natural phenomena: through the agency of the atom, his absolute sovereignty is established; and divine omnipotence, omnipresence, and omniscience are affirmed by the smallest particle in the universe, thus securing divine immanence and redemptive activity in

[69] Edwards, *Of Atoms*, pp. 214–16.

[70] Ibid., p. 214.

[71] Isaac Newton, *Opticks, or A Treatise of the Reflections, Refractions, Inflections & Colours of Light* (1704), ed. Bernard Cohen (New York: Dover, 1952), p. 400.

[72] Edwards, *Things to be Considered*, p. 231.

[73] Ibid., p. 241.

[74] Edwards, *Of Atoms*, p. 208.

[75] Ibid., p. 214.

[76] Edwards, *Things to be Considered*, pp. 265, 231.

creation. The world of nature could not be regarded as founded upon mechanistic causes and effects but was totally dependent on God's power and will.

The attempt to establish God's sovereignty through the agency of atoms was not Edwards's alone. Such a doctrine was first formulated by the Italian philosopher Giordano Bruno, according to whom "God becomes the source of all change in nature, as well as the source of its existence" via the agency of the atom.[77] Both Bruno and Edwards used the atomic doctrine to enhance nature's dependence on God's will and power. Yet there are many differences between their conceptions. In Bruno's thought the number of atoms is infinite because "matter is infinite" and the world as a whole is infinite, whereas Edwards believed that the number of atoms is finite because they are part of a finite and closed universe. (In order to secure God's absolute sovereignty in creation, Edwards rejected the notion of an infinite universe, saying that only in "the ecstasy of the imagination" could one "pronounce the world infinite.")[78] Bruno argued that the "source of atom's motion is not to be sought in another atom," but rather the "atom is a center of life, a point in which the soul of the universe is inserted. Co-eternal with God, matter is not a pre-existent chaos" nor "was it created in time," hence "it is located outside the temporal." And although matter can not be "identified with God," it is nevertheless " 'close to God'."[79] Edwards, of course, would not accept the co-eternality of matter with God or that matter exists outside the temporal dimension of time. For him atoms are created and not eternal, hence their essence and being is entirely dependent on God. Despite these differences, however, there are many similarities between Bruno and Edwards. Both argued that through the agency of atoms God is the source of all natural phenomena, and they both believed that the cause of the atom's motion stemmed from God and not from natural, mechanistic causes. Thus in Edwards the cause of "motion" is "from the immediate exercise of divine power."[80]

Edwards's views on atomism have many affinities as well with the ideas of the French philosopher and mathematician Pierre Gassendi, who attempted to Christianize the classical atomist doctrine of Epicurus and

[77] Robert H. Kargon, "Atomism in the Seventeenth Century," in *Dictionary of the History of Ideas*, 4 vols. (New York: Scribner, 1973), I, p. 133.

[78] Edwards, *Of the Prejudices of Imagination*, 1722, in *SPW*, p. 197.

[79] Michel, *The Cosmology of Giordano Bruno*, pp. 147–49. On Bruno's life and thought, see Dorothea W. Singer, *Giordano Bruno: His Life and Thought* (New York: Greenwood, 1968.) This book contains a translation of Bruno's work *On the Infinite Universe and World* (1584). See also Bruno, *Cause, Principle, and Unity: Five Dialogues by Giordano Bruno*. On Bruno's materialism, see Frederick A. Lange, *The History of Materialism: And Criticism of its Present Importance* (London: Paul Kegan, 1925), pp. 232–36.

[80] Edwards, *Of Atoms*, pp. 214–16.

Lucretius by arguing that God directs the atoms.[81] The resemblance between Gassendi's and Edwards's views regarding God's direct control of
the atom is striking; both hold that atoms are created rather than eternal
as in Epicurus or in Bruno; both argued that atoms are not infinite in
number, as Bruno thought, but rather part of a finite universe; and, finally,
both believed that atoms are an integral part of the created universe constructed by God to fulfill his redemptive purposes. Moreover, against the
mechanical philosophers' concept of motion inherent in matter, Gassendi,
and later Edwards, asserted that the motion of atoms was instilled in them
by God at creation. The "individual atoms," said Gassendi, "received
from God as he created them their corpulence, or dimensions, however
small, and their shapes in ineffable variety, and likewise they received the
capacity (*vis*) requisite to moving, to imparting motion to others, to roll-
ing about . . . to leap away, to knock against other atoms," and so on.[82]
In Edwards, not only "the exercising of the infinite power of God is necessary to keep the parts of atoms together," but "motion also, which is the
communication of body, solidity, or this resistance from one part of space
to another successively . . . is from the immediate exercise of divine
power."[83] However, Edwards diverged from Gassendi's views when he
went on to claim that it is in fact Christ who directs all the atoms in the
universe—"Every atom in the universe is managed by Christ so as to be
most to the advantage of the Christian"[84]—thus completely Christianizing
the atomic doctrine of mechanical philosophy.

Edwards's reaction against the metaphysical and theological ramifications of mechanical philosophy should be seen in the overall context of the
dialectic of God's utter transcendence and divine immanence. Edwards
utilized the atomic doctrine to advance his fundamental theological convictions, and by Christianizing atomism he sought to present it as evidence
of the created order's total dependence on God, leading to the reenchant-

---

[81] Edwards read Gassendi's *Institutio Astronomica* (London, 1653), and Gassendi's attack on Descartes in the *Disquisitio metaphysica anti-Cartesianas* [*Metaphysical Colloquy,
or Doubts and Rebuttals concerning the Metaphysics of René Descartes*] (1644) during his
senior year at Yale. See Anderson, introduction, pp. 12–13, 21–22. It is not clear, however,
whether Edwards indeed read Gassendi's *Syntagma Philosophicum* [*A Philosophical Compendium*] of 1658, where Gassendi elaborated his modernized atomic theory. On Gassendi's
life and thought, see Lynn Sumida Joy, *Gassendi the Atomist: Advocate of History in an Age
of Science* (Cambridge: Cambridge University Press, 1987); Barry Brundell, *Pierre Gassendi:
From Arisotelianism to a New Natural Philosophy* (Dordrecht: D. Reidel, 1987); and Lisa T.
Sarasohn, *Gassendi's Ethics: Freedom in a Mechanistic Universe* (Ithaca: Cornell University
Press, 1996).

[82] Pierre Gassendi, *The Syntagma: Physics* (1658), in *The Selected Works of Pierre Gassendi*, ed. and trans. Craig B. Brush (New York: Johnson Reprint Corporation, 1972), p.
400.

[83] Edwards, *Of Atoms*, pp. 214–16.

[84] Edwards, *Miscellany ff* (1722), in *MIS*, p. 184.

ment of the world of nature. The mechanistic atomic doctrine thus underwent a radical transformation to suit Edwards's religious persuasions. Whereas the "ancient atomists had made motion an inherent property of matter; hence, a Godless universe could exist and subsist,"[85] Edwards denied any inherent qualities except solidity to matter, and through the agency of the atom he claimed divine immanence in creation.

The Mechanization of Nature and the World

Opposition to the metaphysical and theological premises that often accompanied the atomic doctrine constituted only part of Edwards's general antagonism to mechanical philosophy, especially with regard to the mechanistic image of the world as a huge machine, the concept of "laws of nature," and God's relationship with his creation. The mechanization of the natural world was a feature of late-seventeenth-century science. Its "basic postulate was that nature operates according to mechanical principles, the regularity of which can be expressed in the form of natural laws."[86] Mechanical philosophers conceived of the world as a machine, "a world machine," running like a clockwork according to the mechanical laws of nature: the world of nature, wrote Boyle, is a "compounded *machine*," in which "*the laws of motion* [are] freely established and still maintained by God among its parts," and from this "results the settled order or course of things corporeal."[87] Since "the world" is but "a great piece of clockwork, the naturalist, as such, is but a mechanician."[88] In this scientific reasoning, indeed, the "whole universe (the soul of man excepted)" is "but a great Automaton, or self-moving engine, wherein all things are performed by the bare motion (or rest), the size, the shape, and the situation, or texture the parts of the universal matter it consists of."[89]

[85] Robert Kargon, introduction, in *Physiologia Epicuro-Gassendo-Charltoniana: Or A Fabric of Science Natural, upon the Hypothesis of Atoms . . . by Walter Charleton*, 1654, ed. Robert H. Kargon (New York: Johnson Reprint Corporation, 1966), p. xiii.

[86] Brooke, *Science and Religion*, pp. 117, 119. For general studies dealing with mechanical philosophy of nature, see also Richard S. Westfall, *The Construction of Modern Science: Mechanisms and Mechanics* (Cambridge: Cambridge University Press, 1977 [1971]); idem, *Force in Newton Physics: The Science of Dynamics in the Seventeenth Century* (London: Macdonald, 1971); and Margaret C. Jacob, *The Cultural Meaning of the Scientific Revolution* (New York: Alfred A. Knopf, 1988).

[87] Boyle, *A Free Enquiry into the Vulgarly Received Notion of Nature* (1686), p. 191.

[88] Boyle, *The Excellency of Theology Compared with Natural Philosophy* (1665), as quoted in Otto Mayr, *Authority, Liberty & Automatic Machinery in Early Modern Europe* (Baltimore: Johns Hopkins University Press, 1986), p. 56.

[89] Boyle, *The Excellency of Theology Compared with Natural Philosophy* (1665), as quoted in Otto Mayr, *Authority, Liberty & Automatic Machinery in early Modern Europe*, p. 56.

Changes in the natural world "did not result from the operation of internal principles and powers, as in the Aristotelian view; instead, motion
was explained by the laws of impact and the new principle of inertia."[90]

The view that nature is operated by secondary causes or natural laws,
setting an intermediate realm between God and the created order, was
unacceptable to Edwards because it radically reduced divine immanence
and redemptive activity and placed severe limitations on God's absolute
sovereignty in creation. He argued therefore that there is "no such thing
as mechanism,"[91] because the phenomena of the world cannot be explained by the mechanics of matter and motion alone, but should be understood ultimately in light of higher ends. The mechanistic image of the
world should be rejected because "if the highest end of every part of a
clock is only mutually to assist the other parts in their motions, that clock
is good for nothing at all." The analogy from this to the world is not hard
to see; however "useful all the parts of the world are to each other, if that
be their highest end, the world in general is altogether useless." Seen in
this wider teleological and theological context, the mechanistic concept
of the world as a vast machine has no warrant whatsoever: "it is nonsense
to say of a machine whose highest end is to have one part move another,"
argued Edwards, "for the whole is useless, and so every part, however
they correspond."[92] Instead "the corporeal world is to no advantage but
to the spiritual."[93] Religion, therefore, should be the main interpreter of
world phenomena: "The Book of Scripture is the interpreter of the book
of nature," by illuminating "those spiritual mysteries" that are "signified
or typified in the constitution of the natural world."[94] Believing that the
main function of the world of matter and motion, being ontologically
inferior and subordinated to a higher divine reality, is to reflect the images
and shadows of spiritual reality beyond and above it, Edwards claimed
that the "whole outward creation, which is but the shadows of beings, is
so made to represent spiritual things,"[95] or, conversely, that "the things
of the world are ordered [and] designed to shadow forth spiritual
things."[96] Here lay the main role Edwards assigned to religion in ex-

[90] Gary B. Deason, "Reformation Theology and the Mechanistic Conception of Nature,"
in *God and Nature: Historical Essays on the Encounter between Christianity and Science*,
ed. David C. Lindberg and Ronald L. Numbers (Berkeley: University of California Press,
1986), p. 168. See also Edwin A. Burtt, *The Metaphysical Foundations of Modern Physical
Science: A Historical and Critical Essay* (London: Routledge, 1967 [1924]), p. 200; Kargon,
Atomism in England from Hariot to Newton, pp. 57, 60–61.
    [91] Edwards, *Of Atoms*, p. 216.
    [92] Edwards, *Miscellany tt* (1723), in *MIS*, p. 190.
    [93] Edwards, *The Mind*, pp. 353–55.
    [94] Edwards, *Images of Divine Things*, 156 (1743), in *TW*, p. 106.
    [95] Edwards, *Miscellany no. 362* (c. 1728), in *MIS*, p. 434.
    [96] Edwards, *Images of Divine Things*, 7 (1728), p. 53.

plaining the world of nature: where the "glories of astronomy and natural philosophy consist in the harmony of the parts of the corporeal shadow of a world; the glories of religion consist in the sweet harmony of the greater and more real worlds with themselves, with one another and with the infinite fountain and original of them."[97]

The Laws of Nature

Rejecting the mechanization of the world was part of Edwards's reaction against the mechanical conception of natural laws. By rejecting the classical and medieval notion of nature as an organic being, or an organism of active bodies, mechanical philosophy denied the possibility of divine immanence in nature. The divine presence was confined to the construction of a system of external, abstract laws that could be formulated in mathematical terms, such as the laws of motion or the laws of gravity, which govern the world's phenomena. God "established *rules of motion*, and that order amongst things corporal, which we are wont to call the *laws of nature*."[98] The mechanization of the natural world led therefore to the mechanization of God's providential activity in the world. Thus, according to Boyle, once set going by God, the course of nature and the phenomena of the world are the product of mere mechanical laws and no longer manifest the divine immanence: "The universe being once framed by God, and the laws of motion being settled and all upheld by his incessant concourse and general providence, the phenomena of the world thus constituted are physically produced by the mechanical affections of the part of matter, and what they operate upon one another according to mechanical laws."[99] God's providential scheme, then, was confined mainly to the establishment and maintaining of the general, external laws of nature, which regulate the world phenomena. Thus Newton's God is a cosmic legislator, "a Universal Ruler,"[100] who, as he wrote to Richard Bentley in 1693, is "an agent acting constantly according to certain laws."[101] In other words, "God himself was confined to working through

[97] Edwards, *Miscellany* no. 42 (1723), in *MIS*, p. 224.

[98] Boyle, *About the Excellency and Grounds of the Mechanical Hypothesis*, p. 139.

[99] Ibid.

[100] Newton, "General Scholium," in *Sir Isaac Newton's Mathematical Principles of Natural Philosophy and His System of the World*, ed. Florian Cajori, II, p. 544. Newton wrote the "General Scholium" for the second edition of the *Principia* (*The Mathematical Principles of Natural Philosophy*, 1687) of 1713.

[101] Newton, "Four Letters to Richard Bentley," Letter III, February 25, 1693, in *Newton's Philosophy of Nature*, ed. H. S. Thayer, p. 54. See also Richard S. Westfall, "The Rise of Science and the Decline of Orthodox Christianity: A Study of Kepler, Descartes, and Newton," in *God and Nature*, ed. David C. Lindberg and Ronald L. Numbers, p. 233.

natural causes."[102] Exactly on this point Leibniz "chides Newton and his followers for reducing God to the status of an inferior maker/repairman" of the universe.[103]

Edwards could not accept this radical reduction of divine power. Against the mechanical philosophers' assertion that "divine operation" is "limited by what we call LAWS OF NATURE," Edwards declared that it is unwarranted to use such a concept to describe God's relation with the order of creation. For what is implied in such a mechanistic view is that God "himself in common with his creatures" is "subject in his acting to the same laws with inferiour beings" and thus ultimately deprived of his place as "the head of the universe" and as "the foundation & first spring of all."[104] Instead, believing the "material world, and all things pertaining to it, is by the Creator wholly subordinated to the spiritual and moral world," Edwards thought nature's role lay ultimately in "showing forth and resembling spiritual things." Further, divine activity in the world is not limited by natural laws, for "God in some instances seems to have gone quite beside the ordinary laws of nature." For example, "God in some things in providence, has set aside the ordinary course of things in the material world to subserve to the purposes of the moral and spiritual, as in miracles." And in order "to show that all things in heaven and earth, the whole universe, is wholly subservient" to divine power and will, "God has once or twice interrupted" the course of nature "as when the sun stood still in Joshua's time."[105] This was of course also the view of Boyle, and of Newton and his closest followers, such as Samuel Clarke and William Whiston. Indeed, in the *Opticks* Newton claimed that his conception of nature affirmed the voluntarist doctrine of divine omnipotence—everything in the world is "subordinate to him, and subservient to his will." Given that God's will was "the only causally efficacious agency in nature," God "may vary the Laws of Nature, and make worlds of several sorts in several parts of the universe."[106] Yet, it should be noted that "Newton and Whiston prefer[red] *not* to demonstrate the specially provident aspect of God's dominion over nature by recourse to miracles, if at all"; for without "God first creating and then sustaining the generally

[102] Keith Thomas, *Religion and the Decline of Magic* (New York: Charles Scribner's Sons, 1971), p. 639.

[103] James E. Force, "Newton's God of Dominion: The Unity of Newton's Theological, Scientific, and Political Thought," in *Essays on the Context, Nature, and Influence of Isaac Newton's Theology*, ed. James E. Force and Richard H. Popkin (Dordrecht: Kluwer, 1990), p. 86.

[104] Edwards, *Miscellany* no. 1263.

[105] Edwards, *Images of Divine Things*, 43 (c. 1735), p. 61.

[106] Heimann, "Voluntarism and Immanence," p. 273; Oakley, "Christian Theology and the Newtonian Science," p. 436; Gascoigne, "From Bentley to the Victorians," pp. 226–27.

regular operations of nature, there could be no ordinary concourse of natural law to describe with mathematical principles."[107]

Edwards therefore opposed the mechanistic interpretation of natural laws because these laws—setting up a mediating sphere between God and his creation and thus signifying that God governs the world only through secondary causes—restricted God's power and limited the divine immanence. Rather than detaching God from the world, Edwards attempted to heal the growing breach between the order of grace and the order of nature by restating, as in classical and medieval theology, the natural world as a special mode of reality ontologically subordinated and inferior to a higher divine reality. God "makes the inferior [world] in imitation of the superior, the material of the spiritual, on purpose to have a resemblance and shadow of them."[108] God's will was "the only causally efficacious agency in nature."

Edwards's view that God's will is the only efficacious agency in nature had a close affinity with the notions of the French philosopher and theologian Nicolas Malebranche, especially in regard to the theory of occasionalism that came to be most associated with this Catholic writer—the doctrine that finite created beings have no causal efficacy and that God alone is a true causal agent. According to Malebranche's occasionalist view of causation, natural causes, such as collisions of material bodies or human volition, are not real but only occasional causes: "everything depends upon God, because all causes can act only through the efficacy of the divine power."[109] Natural causes provide only the occasion for the operation of the one and only real cause, which is God, who is "being in general" or a "universal Being."[110] All natural phenomena are directly and immediately brought about by God, and "the will of God orders the nature of each thing."[111] God, therefore, is the cause of a corporal thing's existence. In the Malebranchian universe, individual objects and events are stripped of their causal powers. In reality what we call the cause is merely the *occasion*—hence the term "occasionalism"—for God to exercise his efficacious will. Since secondary causes have no efficacy of their own, they can only serve the all-divine purpose of God's determining will and activity: "it is by obeying His own laws that God produces everything which the secondary causes seem to produce."[112] God's "action in ordinary Providence is only the simultaneous cooperation without which secondary causes can do

---

[107] Force, "Newton's God of Dominion," pp. 87–88. For Boyle's views on miracles, see McGuire, "Boyle's Conception of Nature," p. 526.

[108] Edwards, *Images of Divine Things*, 8 (1728), p. 53.

[109] Malebranche, *Dialogues on Metaphysics and on Religion*, p. 279.

[110] Malebranche, *The Search after the Truth*, pp. 241, 618.

[111] Ibid., p. xxxiv

[112] Malebranche, *Dialogues on Metaphysics and on Religion*, p. 336.

nothing."[113] Whatever of reality there is in finite activity is a manifestation
of the divine activity. Hence "we see that it is the same Wisdom that ordered everything" in the world, "the same Power that has produced everything, the same Providence that conserves everything."[114]

Malebranche's theory of occasionalism offers a defense against the serious threats that mechanical philosophy posed to traditional Christian
thought and belief in regard to understanding the essential nature of reality. Instead of the mechanical conception of "a blind nature," characterized by impersonal forces, and in contrast to "natural philosophers" who
strove "to find out the mechanism and the relations" of natural phenomenon, Malebranche invoked the notion of the inherent teleological and
theological structure of order in the world, attempting to explain the "infinite multiplicity" of God's "marvelous works" of providence in creating,
maintaining, and preserving the whole of creation.[115] His goal was to close
the growing breach caused by "natural philosophers" between the "order
of nature and of grace,"[116] arguing that the laws of nature are the manifestation of God's general, ordinary providence: God wants that "His work
should be preserved by the natural laws which He has resolved to follow."[117] The world of nature therefore is not a blind machine, running by
the impersonal forces of its components, but a special mode of reality in
which God's redemptive activity is manifested. "In a universe sustained
in all of its parts by the will of God, and in which operations are connected
not by mechanical causation but by the constant exercise of God's conser-
vatory will," Malebranche believed, "even the so-called laws of nature
become immediate effects of special grace."[118] God "laid down general
laws [of nature] for the regulation of the ordinary course of His providence," while "Jesus Christ imitates the procedure of His Father as much
as possible by making nature subservient to Grace."[119] The theory thus
stipulated that God acts in the order of creation in accordance with his
general volitions, namely, general laws.

"Occasionalism was the vehicle most available to Edwards for shattering belief in the autonomy of nature, a mechanistic universe, and the

[113] Malebranche, *The Search after the Truth*, p. 743. See also "Elucidation Fifteen: Concerning the efficacy attributed to secondary causes," in *The Search after the Truth*, pp. 657–
86.
[114] Malebranche, *The Search after the Truth*, p. 740.
[115] Malebranche, *Dialogues on Metaphysics and on Religion*, p. 259.
[116] Ibid., pp. 259, 325.
[117] Ibid., p. 267.
[118] Fiering, *Jonathan Edwards's Moral Thought and Its British Context*, pp. 94–95.
[119] Malebranche, *Dialogues on Metaphysics and on Religion*, p. 342.

independence of second causes."[120] In such a system of reasoning, "the harmony and regularity of natural physical laws" are "essentially an expression of God's love of order."[121] Malebranche and Edwards shared this view of causation. "Malebranche's goal, like Edwards's later, was not to reduce the texture of the universe to a clocklike mechanism with an indifferent or dormant God presiding. On the contrary, Malebranche wanted to break down the artificiality of the distinction between nature and grace in order to enlarge the domain of the latter."[122] One of the sources for Edwards's theocentric metaphysics, his notion of God's absolute sovereignty in the order of creation, may thus be found in the occasionalist doctrine of Malebranche, which made "all knowledge of the physical world the immediate product of divine will and treated natural phenomena as representations of divine spirit and order."[123] Edwards's immaterialism, as well as his belief that God creates the world for his own glory, his view of the Deity as Being in general, and the definition of God's activity in creation in terms of communication, were inspired in part by Malebranche's thought.

In sum, Edwards refused to allow secondary causes the ultimate role in the regulation and operation of the world's phenomena. To accord to nature intrinsic qualities and powers of its own, and to admit that the phenomena of the world are regulated by secondary causes or natural laws, would signify that God is "making use" of "means that operate by their own power and natural forces," which might lead to the conclusion that the Deity is using "mediate causes" and "second causes" in ordering the world.[124] To admit that the phenomena of the world are governed only by laws of nature would mean that God is "limiting himself by such invariable laws fix[e]d from the beginning of the creation," thus seriously undermining his power. Edwards spoke therefore "in opposition" to the mechanistic concept that God's activity is "confined to & limited by those fix'd establishments & laws commonly called the laws of nature."[125] And he stressed time and again, "God's providence over the world consists" only "partly in his governing the natural world according to the course

[120] Fiering, "The Rationalist Foundations of Edwards's Metaphysics," p. 81. See also Fiering, *Jonathan Edwards's Moral Thought and Its British Context.* On the relationship between Edwards's and Malebranche's thought, see also Chai, *Jonathan Edwards and the Limits of Enlightenment Philosophy.*

[121] Fiering, "The Rationalist Foundations of Edwards's Metaphysics," p. 80.

[122] Fiering, *Jonathan Edwards's Moral Thought and Its British Context,* p. 94.

[123] Fiering, "The Rationalist Foundations of Edwards's Metaphysics," p. 92.

[124] Edwards, *A Divine and Supernatural Light,* 1734, in *SJE,* p. 130.

[125] Edwards, *Miscellany* no. 1263.

and laws of nature."[126] He denounced the mechanistic view that the divine activity within the created order is restricted to God's imposition of the laws of nature from infinite space above, and he was unwilling to accept that God should be confined to the status of a cosmic lawgiver who regulates world phenomena from some undefined place. Such a view of the Deity as a mechanic became more and more widespread during the eighteenth century. Increasingly Newton's achievements were associated with "revealing the watchmaker God," the image of "a Creator-Mechanic," or with the concept of "a God of order rather than with an interventionist Deity."[127] Benjamin Franklin, for example, argued that in America "God Almighty is himself a mechanic" and "he is respected and admired more for the variety, ingenuity, and the utility of his handiworks."[128]

God and the World

In mechanical philosophy the only conceivable way for God to express himself in nature was through external laws, such as the laws of motion, imposed from above on the created order. Defining God's relation with the world in mechanical terms, the new scientific culture of space and time led increasingly to the detachment of God from the processes of nature. "Natural philosophy was gradually separating itself from theological ends."[129] Indeed, God still firmly held dominion over creation, but his redemptive activity was not considered as inextricably immanent. Rather, it was defined as external to nature and expressed more and more in the laws of mechanics: no longer immanent in creation, the divine activity was assigned the role of ordering world phenomena according to mechanical laws, or general abstract rules that could be expressed in terms of the mechanics of matter and motion.

With the mechanization of the natural world, the notion of God's relationship to the creation was radically changed: "The sovereign Redeemer of Luther and Calvin became," in scientific thought, "the sovereign Ruler of the world machine."[130] The God of René Descartes "is not symbolized

---

[126] Edwards, *Notes on Scripture*, 389 (1939), in *NOS*, p. 373.

[127] Gascoigne, "From Bentley to the Victorians," p. 230.

[128] Benjamin Franklin, "Information to Those who Would Remove to America" (1782), as quoted in Liah Greenfeld, *Nationalism: Five Roads to Modernity* (Cambridge, Mass.: Harvard University Press, 1992), p. 408.

[129] Dorinda Outram, *The Enlightenment* (Cambridge: Cambridge University Press, 1999), p. 55.

[130] Deason, "Reformation Theology and the Mechanistic Conception of Nature," p. 187.

by the things He created; He does not express Himself in them."[131] The same can be said about Newton: "Newton's God was first and foremost the *kosmokrator*, ruler over everything,"[132] and not, as in classical and medieval thought, a God whose symbolic presence was manifested in the nature and harmony of creation. For him "only a God of true and supreme dominion is a supreme and true God" and this "at the expense of God's love and, apparently, God's intellect."[133]

It has been argued that the source for Newton's God of Dominion, as articulated in the General Scholium, may be found in his Arianism.[134] This precluded him from assigning a significant role to Christ in the creation; "even Jesus Christ, falls under the dominion of God."[135] Thus, "the Son receiving all things from the Father, being subject to his executing his will, sitting in his throne and calling him his God. . . . For the word God relates not to the metaphysical nature of God but to dominion."[136] Newton's disciples Clarke and Whiston adopted a similar view regarding the nature of God's dominion, along with its necessary consequence that Christ is not divine in his metaphysical nature. Obviously, this conception of the God of Dominion is opposed to the doctrine of the Trinity.

Edwards's theology, on the contrary, is Trinitarian, according Christ a crucial role in ordering and managing the created order. To safeguard the divine nature of Christ and his role in creation from Arian tendencies, Edwards argued "that God three in one, all that he is, and all that he has" does "possess all things" in creation. Christ, therefore, does "possess all things." Indeed, the "universe is [his]" or God's, "only he has not the trouble of managing of it; but Christ, to whom it is no trouble, manages it for him."[137] Things in the world therefore "are left to his ordering and government" so that "the Father reigns by the Son."[138] Christ manages

[131] Koyré, *From the Closed World to the Infinite Universe*, p. 100. For Descartes's conception of God, see Gary Hatfield, "Reason, Nature and God in Descartes," *Science in Context* 3 (1989): 175–201.

[132] Funkenstein, *Theology and the Scientific Imagination*, p. 90.

[133] Force, "Newton's God of Dominion," pp. 79, 83.

[134] Richard S. Westfall, "Newton's Theological Manuscript," in *Contemporary Newtonian Research*, ed. Zev Bechler (Dordrecht: D. Reidel, 1987), p. 130; James E. Force, "Newton's God of Dominion," pp. 75–102. For the transformation in Newton's thought concerning God's relation to his creation, see J. E. McGuire, "The Fate of the Date: The Theology of Newton's *Principia* Revisited," in *Rethinking the Scientific Revolution*, ed. Margaret J. Osler, pp. 271–96.

[135] Force, "Newton's God of Dominion," p. 80.

[136] Newton, Yahuda MS 15.1, Hebrew University, Jerusalem, as cited in Force, "Newton's God of Dominion," p. 79.

[137] Edwards, *Miscellany ff* (c. 1723), p. 184.

[138] Edwards, *Miscellany* no. 609 (c. 1733).

every "atom in the universe" to the "advantage of the Christian."[139] Not only that "the Son of God created the world"[140] and "all things" in the world "will be managed so as shall be most agreeable to his will,"[141] but the whole "works of creation and the laws of nature, and that course of nature that God established in creation, is subordinated" to Christ's "work of redemption."[142] Evidently, for Edwards the central point in his philosophical theology is God's great act of redemption in Jesus Christ.[143] In sum, his "understanding of nature was finally determined by a Christocentric construction of the world."[144]

Natural philosophy presents God's *distance* from his creation. Hence "the mechanists' God" was "a God of general providence and only rarely, in the case of miracles, a God of special providence."[145] In 1781 John Wesley described the triumph of mechanical philosophy when he claimed that the "doctrine of particular providence" is "absolutely out of fashion in England."[146] Likewise, as wrote William James, the "God whom science recognizes must be a God of universal laws exclusively, a God who does a wholesale, not a retail business. He cannot accommodate his process to the convenience of individuals."[147] The classical and medieval God intimately present in creation was thus transformed in mechanical philosophy into a cosmic lawgiver who exercises his dominion over the created order from above. No longer intrinsically related to the essence of material bodies, divine activity was conceived as external to tangible, created beings. Not open to divine activity, or imbued with the redemptive presence and activity, the world of nature was separated from the affairs of salvation. God himself, removed from the inner development of natural phenomena, could only exercise his dominion over nature by external laws expressed in terms of the mechanics of matter and motion. The mechanical philosophers radically transformed the traditional Christian dialectic of God's utter transcendence and divine immanence; his redemptive activity was restricted mainly to maintaining and preserving world phenomena. As Newton wrote in the *Opticks* (1704): "the Wisdom and Skill of a powerful ever-living Agent" is revealed in his ability "to form and reform the Parts of the Universe."[148]

---

[139] Edwards, *Miscellany ff* (c. 1723), p. 184.

[140] Edwards, *Miscellany* no. 108, p. 279.

[141] Edwards, *Miscellany ff* (c. 1723), pp. 183–84.

[142] Edwards, *Miscellany* no. 702 (c. 1737), in *MISA*, pp. 290–91.

[143] Edwards's focus on redemption in Jesus Christ is analyzed most recently in Taves, *Fits, Trances & Visions: Experiencing Religion and Explaining Experience from Wesley to James.*

[144] Wilson, introduction, pp. 47–48.

[145] Deason, "Reformation Theology and the Mechanistic Conception of Nature," p. 187.

[146] Thomas, *Religion and the Decline of Magic*, p. 640.

[147] James, *The Varieties of Religious Experience*, pp. 594–95.

[148] Newton, *Opticks*, p. 403.

Mechanical philosophy more and more emphasized God's general providence, as expressed in God's ordering and regulating the world of nature, and less and less the mystery of special providence that cannot be expressed in mechanical terms. " 'Special providence' and private revelations gave way to the notion of a Providence which itself obeyed natural laws accessible to human study."[149] For example, in his *About the Excellency and Grounds of the Mechanical Hypothesis* (1674), Boyle praised the mechanistic distinction between "the first *original of things* and the subsequent *course of nature.*" Mechanical philosophy, he continues, teaches that "God gave motion to matter" and that "in the beginning he so guided the various motions of the parts of it as to contrive them into the world he designed they should compose." God's providential scheme was confined mainly to establishing and maintaining the general, external "laws of nature," which regulate world phenomena. Once created by God, all phenomena in the corporal world "are physically produced" by mechanical causes "according to mechanical laws."[150]

The same is evident in Newton. In "the first Creation," God created the material, tangible bodies and "set them in order" according to the laws of nature. Thus, "being once form'd," the world "may continue by these Laws for many Ages."[151] And if the world machine were to incur some damage, God would be able "to reform the Parts" of it.[152] In the mechanical interpretation, therefore, God's providential activity is relegated to winding up his watch from time to time, and his redemptive activity consists mainly in the duty of providentially reforming the world machine when necessary. Within such a mechanistic cosmic economy, God is "allotted the duty of providentially reforming the system of the world when the mechanism has so far run out of gear as to demand such a reformation."[153] It is not surprising that Newton believed in an infinite universe, assuming "that the incomparable order, beauty, and the large harmony that characterizes the celestial in the large, is to be eternally preserved."[154] Edwards would not admit the world is "infinite"[155] because this would restrict divine creative and redemptive activity in creation.

The mechanistic conception of God as a cosmic legislator indeed posed a serious question regarding God's relationship to the world: "What role

[149] Thomas, *Religion and the Decline of Magic*, p. 639.
[150] Boyle, *About the Excellency and Grounds of the Mechanical Hypothesis* (1674), in *Selected Philosophical Papers of Robert Boyle*, p. 139.
[151] Newton, *Opticks*, p. 402.
[152] Ibid., p. 403.
[153] Burtt, *The Metaphysical Foundations of Modern Physical Science*, pp. 292–93.
[154] Ibid.
[155] Edwards, *Of the Prejudices of Imagination*, 1722, p. 197.

could be left for God to play in a universe which runs like a clock-work?"[156] For Edwards the danger in the Newtonian scientific system was that it placed so much emphasis on the regular working of natural laws, leading to the undermining of God's redemptive role in creation. Such a prospect, which might lead to materialism and the endorsement of fate in the regulation of the world, profoundly alarmed Edwards. It was alto-gether unacceptable. Since God exercises an "absolute and universal do-minion" over his creation, "it is fit" that his supremacy "should appear" in "those things by which he makes himself known, or by his *word* and *works*; i.e. in what he says, and in what he does." It is God's intention "that his works should exhibit an image of himself their author," and "what manner of being he is, and afford a proper representation of his divine excellencies."[157] Pervaded by divine meaning and significance, na-ture is not divorced from God's providential plan, but has a singular role to play in reflecting images and shadows of the ontologically superior divine reality beyond it:

> The Book of Scripture is the interpreter of the book of nature two ways: viz. by declaring to us those spiritual mysteries that are indeed signified or typified in the constitution of the natural world; and secondly, in actually making appli-cation of the signs and types in the book of nature as representations of those spiritual mysteries in many instances.[158]

Edwards's desire to establish God's absolute sovereignty led directly to deification of the order of creation. However, his God is not the *Deus absconditus* of Martin Luther, who hides himself and is unknown in cre-ation, but rather *Deus revelatus*, the God who reveals himself constantly in the world:

> 'Tis very fit and becoming of God, who is infinitely wise, so to order things that there should be a voice of his in his work instructing those that behold them, and pointing forth and showing divine mysteries and things more immediately appertaining to himself, and his spiritual kingdom.[159]

Edwards's deification of nature means that God constantly reveals himself in creation: "the works of nature are intended and contrived of God to signify and indigitate spiritual things."[160] Hence the natural world consti-tuted a special dimension of reality, revealing continuously the "voice or

---

[156] Brooke, *Science and Religion*, p. 118.
[157] Edwards, *Concerning the End for which God Created the World*, in *EW*, pp. 424, 422.
[158] Edwards, *Images of Divine Things*, 156 (1743), p. 106.
[159] Ibid., 57 (1737), p. 67.
[160] Ibid., 55 (1737), p. 66.

language" of God: "The works of God are but a kind of voice or language of God, to instruct intelligent beings in things pertaining to himself."[161]

Edwards's theology of nature proclaims the immediate presence of divine power and activity in the whole fabric of the universe. As such, clearly it has more affinity with medieval theology, which was based upon a "sense of God's symbolic presence in his creation, and the sense of a universe replete with transcendent meaning and hints,"[162] than with the mechanistic conception of nature, which accorded God the role of a "cosmic legislator,"[163] or a "Universal Ruler" who governs the world of nature merely according to abstract and general natural laws.[164]

The Nature of the Created Order

Mechanical philosophy's disenchantment of the world is further shown by the replacement of the classical and medieval notion of a finite cosmos organized according to a grand theological teleology of order, a great chain of being structured according to a hierarchy of values and entities, by the non-hierarchical world of nature, deprived of any value concepts. The scientific and philosophical revolution of the seventeenth century led to a new conception of the universe, which can be described as

> bringing forth the destruction of the Cosmos, that is, the disappearance, from the philosophically and scientifically valid concept, of the conception of the world as a finite, closed, and hierarchically ordered whole (a whole in which the hierarchy of value determined the hierarchy and structure of being, rising from the dark, heavy and imperfect earth to the higher and higher perfection of the stars and heavenly spheres), and its replacement by the indefinite and even infinite universe which is bound together by the identity of its fundamental components and laws, and in which all these components are paced on the same level of being.[165]

Given that all "natural bodies are essentially of the same kind," the classical and medieval "distinction between earthly and celestial bodies" and motions "has become obsolete." In such thought, evidently, the concept of nature is radically transformed: "Nature is no longer the *inner* principle out of which the motion of the body follows; rather, nature is the mode

---

[161] Ibid., 57 (1737), p. 67.
[162] Funkenstein, *Theology and the Scientific Imagination*, p. 116.
[163] Deason, "Reformation Theology and the Mechanistic Conception of Nature," p. 186.
[164] Newton, "General Scholium," p. 544.
[165] Koyré, *From the Closed World to the Infinite Universe*, p. 4.

of the variety of the changing relative positions of bodies, the manner in which they are present in space and time."[166]

Seventeenth-century scientific thought constructed a new conception of the nature of reality, a new vision "of nature as thoroughly homogeneous and therefore nonhierarchical,"[167] in contrast to the classical and medieval one in which nature "reveals God's symbolic presence, and was seen as a system of symbols, or signatures of God."[168] In medieval theology, God "authored *two* books: the Bible and the Book of Nature." In such a system, "events in nature, like linguistic expressions, are signs. To study them is to decipher God's meaning. Here natural observations do play a part in the determination of belief, but they do so *only because they are a kind of testimony* [italics in original]."[169] Thus, if for Hugh of St. Victor "the whole sensible world is like a kind of book written by the finger of God," and "each particular creature is somewhat like a figure . . . instituted by the divine will to manifest the invisible things of God's wisdom," for Galileo "the universe" is a "grand book . . . written in the language of mathematics."[170] With the developing scientific notion of a one-dimensional, homogeneous, symmetrical, uniform, and non-hierarchical nature, the "testimony" of nature became more and more problematic, as did the notion of divine immanence and activity in the created order. Because "scientists since the seventeenth century wanted their scientific language to be as unambiguous as possible," they "emptied nature of intrinsic meanings." Therefore, "no longer were natural phenomena to symbolize and reflect each other and that which is beyond them; the symbolic-allegorical perception of nature as a network of mutual references was discarded as a source for protracted equivocation." In other words, nature according to the new scientific imagination should be "homogeneous, uniform, symmetrical."[171] Hence, the "medieval sense of God's symbolic presence in His creation, and the sense of a universe replete with transcendent meanings and hints, had to recede if not to give way totally to the postulates of univocation and homogeneity in the seventeenth century."[172] Robert Greene, a fellow of Clare College, for example, attacked Newton's work on the ground that "the Philosophy of Homogeneous Matter" is a "revival of Epicureanism," and as such "undermin[es] Christian belief."[173]

---

[166] Heidegger, "Modern Science, Metaphysics, and Mathematics," pp. 286, 288, 292.

[167] Funkenstein, *Theology and the Scientific Imagination*, p. 10.

[168] Ibid., p. 49.

[169] Nancy Murphy, *Theology in the Age of Scientific Reasoning* (Ithaca: Cornell University Press, 1990), p. 5.

[170] Harrison, *The Bible, Protestantism, and the Rise of Natural Science*, p. 1.

[171] Funkenstein, *Theology and the Scientific Imagination*, pp. 28–29.

[172] Ibid., p. 116.

[173] Gascoigne, *Cambridge in the Age of the Enlightenment*, pp. 167–69.

The reason behind this strong reaction to the mechanical universe is not hard to understand. It was "of the greatest consequence for succeeding thought that now the great Newton's authority was squarely behind that view of the cosmos which saw in man a puny, irrelevant spectator . . . of the vast mathematical system whose regular motions according to mechanical principles constituted the world of nature."[174] Deprived of any integrity of its own, as well as of inner teleological development and ends, the world of nature in mechanical philosophy was transformed into a huge machine, an engine or a clockwork, based upon cold mechanical principles and operating according to abstract laws. As such, of course, it could not play any role in the mystery of divine providence.

For Edwards this process of the disenchantment of the world was totally unwarranted. To reassert God's power and will within creation, he returned to the classical and medieval notion that God had authored two books, scripture and nature, arguing that nature reflects the transcendent meanings and symbols of divine things. If there is an inherent teleological and theological structure of order in the world, scripture is the "interpreter of the book of nature," because only God's revelation can illuminate "those spiritual mysteries that are indeed signified or typified in the constitution of the natural world."[175] Thus, not only did Edwards reject the mechanical vision of a one-dimensional world of nature, but he also denounced the consequences of a view that implies the exclusion of value concepts from the order of creation. One of the main results of the mechanical view of the universe was the "discarding by scientific thought of all considerations based upon value-concepts, such as perfection, harmony, meaning and aim, and finally the utter devalorization of being, the divorce of the world of value and the world of fact."[176] This transformation affecting the whole fabric of the universe was of course unacceptable to Edwards. In his theology of nature he returned therefore to the classical (Platonic) and medieval (Neo-Platonic) notion of the great chain of being, or, as he called it "the order of creation," and strove to show that the fabric of the universe is indeed essentially founded upon a theological teleology of values, which in turn defines the ontological status of beings in creation. Attempting to save God's presence and redemptive activity in the world, Edwards invoked the notion of a hierarchically ordered universe, declaring that the whole created order is characterized by "communication between one degree of being and the next degree of being"[177] This view had previously been developed by the Cambridge Platonists,

---

[174] Burtt, *The Metaphysical Foundations of Modern Physical Science*, p. 236.
[175] Edwards, *Images of Divine Things*, 156 (c. 1743), p. 106.
[176] Koyré, *From the Closed World to the Infinite Universe*, p. 4.
[177] Edwards, *Miscellany tt* (c. 1723), p. 190.

a group of seventeenth-century philosopher-theologians including Henry More (1614–87), Ralph Cudworth (1617–1688), and John Smith (1616–52), who "adhered to the ancient doctrine of microcosm and macrocosm which they related to the great chain of being. Thus various levels of reality emanated from God in an ordered hierarchical structure."[178]

The Poverty of the Mechanistic Interpretation

Edwards sought to rescue a creation in danger of gradual detachment from divine providence, and to reconstitute the essence of natural phenomena as radically and immediately dependent on God's power and will. Although he was not able to maintain the classical and medieval notion of the union between the orders of grace and nature,[179] he nevertheless was not willing to see their extreme separation in mechanical philosophy. He admitted that nature played an important function in divine providence, being a unique mode of reality that exhibits and illuminates the images and shadows of the divine reality beyond and above it. Envisioning the universe as imbued with God's symbolic meanings and signs, he said that "spiritual beauties are infinitely the greatest, and bodies" are "but the shadow of beings" because the role of tangible, material bodies is indeed to "shadow forth spiritual beauties."[180] By instilling divine meaning into the created order, Edwards rejected the mechanical explanation that defined reality only in terms of mechanics of matter and motion. Instead, he declared, "that which truly is the substance of all bodies is the infinite exact and precise and perfectly stable idea in God's mind."[181] He indeed accepted the mechanical premise that nature is totally passive, but claimed that without God's redemptive activity nature has no existence or being of its own.

This is the source of Edwards's idealism, his view that the universe "exists nowhere but in the divine mind," and therefore "those beings which have knowledge and consciousness are the only proper and real and substantial beings, inasmuch as the being of other things is only by

---

[178] McGuire, "Boyle's Conception of Nature," p. 542. See also Hunter, *Science and Society in Restoration England*, p. 182; and C. A. Patrides, ed., *The Cambridge Platonists* (Cambridge: Cambridge University Press, 1980).

[179] On medieval views regarding God's relation with the world, see Etienne Gilson, *The Spirit of Medieval Philosophy*, trans. A.H.C. Downes (New York: Scribner, 1936), and *The Philosophy of St. Thomas Aquinas*, trans. Edward Bullough (New York: Dorset, 1972). See also note 16 above.

[180] Edwards, *Beauty of the World* (c. 1726), in *SPW*, p. 305.

[181] Edwards, *The Mind*, p. 344.

these."[182] He naturally denounced the view that human beings can "actually perceive by their senses" a true and objective picture of the world: "I hardly know of any other prejudices that are more powerful against truth of any kind than ... those of imagination." Thus, as seen above, he claimed "the ecstasy" of imagination could lead one even "to pronounce the world infinite,"[183] something he could not agree to because it undermines God's sovereignty; if the material world is infinite, then it neither needs nor even admits God's creative and redemptive action. The same can be said about his rejection of the Copernican revolution. He argued that God "contrived the diurnal revolution of the sun around the earth in perpetual successions" in order to avoid "the fatal inconvenience that would have arisen from the sun's always standing over one side of the earth."[184] Likewise, he denied "the mechanical cause of gravity," and argued that it should be "attributed to the immediate operation of God."[185] "Divine power," he declared, "is every moment exerted to the upholding of the world."[186]

To replace the mechanical explanation, Edwards formulated his own idealism; "all existence is mental," hence "the existence of all exterior things is ideal. Therefore, it is a necessary being only as it is a necessary idea."[187] Since "the substance of all bodies is the infinitely exact and precise and perfectly stable idea in God's mind,"[188] the "world is therefore an ideal one."[189] Edwards thus deprived creation of any independent ontological status and the phenomena of the world of any intrinsic teleological qualities and powers, in order to argue for the created order's absolute contingency. The realm of nature is radically dependent upon God's will and power, because "the existence of the whole material universe is absolutely dependent on idea."[190] God's absolute sovereignty in the world was thus reaffirmed and rescued from the limitations placed on it by mechanical philosophy. Edwards could conclude that "all arts and sciences, the more they are perfected, the more they issue in divinity, and coincide with it, and appear part of it."[191]

---

[182] Edwards, *Of Being*, in *SPW*, p. 206.

[183] Edwards, *Of the Prejudices of Imagination*, p. 197.

[184] Edwards, *God's All-Sufficient for the Supply of Our Wants*(1729), in *SDM*, pp. 477–78.

[185] Edwards, *Things to be Considered*, p. 234.

[186] Ibid., p. 241.

[187] Edwards, *The Mind*, p. 341.

[188] Ibid., p. 344.

[189] Ibid., p. 351.

[190] Ibid., p. 353.

[191] Edwards, *Outline of 'A Rational Account'* (c. 1740), in *SPW*, p. 397.

Edwards and the Reenchantment of the World

In constructing his theology of nature, Edwards strove to provide a philosophical and theological alternative to mechanical philosophy that would take into account his profound religious and theological persuasions regarding God's sovereignty and the divine presence in the world. To do this he adopted a twofold strategy. First, he claimed that God created the world so that "things natural" would "livelily represent things divine and spiritual."[192] Instead of understanding natural phenomena in terms of the mechanics of matter and motion, he argued that "all body is nothing but what immediately results from the exercise of divine power."[193] Since divine agency is the source of all being and existence, God's redemptive activity is secured and his immanence affirmed within the whole fabric of the universe. Conceiving in his typology the realm of nature as a specific although inferior mode of reality, ontologically subordinated to a higher divine reality, Edwards could assert that "the works of nature are intended and contrived of God to signify and indigitate spiritual things."[194] In this cosmological vision, the created order was infused with transcendent meaning, and the existence of every being in the world was endowed with theological and teleological significance.

Second, Edwards invoked the classical (Platonic) and medieval (Neo-Platonic) notion of a hierarchical universe structured according to a coherent and well-defined theological teleology of a great chain of being, or, in his words, an "order of being." In the order of "the creation," he said, "there is an immediate communication between one degree of being and the next degree of being" according "to the *order of being* [emphasis added]."[195] Edwards accepted the Neo-Platonic system that "posited divine archetypes and ectypal representations on earth."[196] Yet, because in his idealism the natural order was deprived of any contribution to and participation in the affairs of divine providence, and since "nothing else has a proper being but spirits,"[197] therefore "in the various ranks of beings, those that are nearest to the first being should most evidently and variously partake of his influence," or "be influenced by the operation of the Spirit of God."[198] In "the order of beings" the "most

---

[192] Edwards, *Miscellany* no. 118 (c. 1724), p. 284.
[193] Edwards, *Of Atoms*, p. 215.
[194] Edwards, *The Mind*, p. 66.
[195] Edwards, *Miscellany* tt (c. 1722), p. 190.
[196] Fiering, "The Rationalist Foundations of Edwards's Metaphysics," p. 84.
[197] Edwards, *The Mind*, p. 337.
[198] Edwards, *Miscellany* no. 178 (c. 1725), p. 327.

noble of all, and that which is most akin to the nature of God," is "the soul of man."[199]

The classical and medieval concept of a hierarchical chain of existence included all beings, material as well as spiritual, from the lowest in nature to the highest in heaven, and the place and value of every being in the universe was determined by "the greater or lesser distance which separate it from the First Cause."[200] However, Edwards was in spite of himself affected by the scientific reasoning that denied the created order any participation in divine providence. His hierarchical ladder of being, therefore, consisted of spirits only, because "perceiving being only is properly being,"[201] and not of material, tangible things that cannot be involved in or contribute to divine providence. Accordingly, the principle underlying his theological teleology of order inherent in the structure of the universe was the concept of excellency, which defines relationships within the hierarchy of spirits according to their consent to the supreme being, or God. Edwards defined this notion as the "consent of being to being, or being's consent to entity," which in turn defined the relationship within the hierarchy of spirits according to their consent to the supreme being, God. "So far as a thing consents to being in general," he wrote, "so far it consents to him," hence "the more perfect created spirits are, the nearer do they come to their creator in this regard." Accordingly, seeing that "the more the consent is, and the more extensive, the greater is the excellency."[202] In "the order of beings in the natural world, the more excellent and noble any being is, the more visible and immediate hand of God is there in bringing them into being; and the most noble of all" is "the soul of man."[203] God determines the ontological status of beings according to the place he accords them in the cosmological hierarchy of the chain of beings: "The nearer in nature beings are to God, so much the more properly are they beings, and more substantial . . . spirits are much more properly beings, and more substantial, than bodies."[204]

Constructing the created order's ontological status as inferior and subordinated to the divine reality beyond it, and conceiving the universe as structured according to a grand theological teleology of a hierarchical chain of beings, or spirits, was Edwards's main strategy in combating mechanistic natural philosophy. Through it he sought to close the growing gap between the orders of grace and nature and to fight the increasing

[199] Edwards, *Miscellany* no. 541, in *MISA*, p. 89.
[200] Cassirer, *The Philosophy of the Enlightenment*, p. 39.
[201] Edwards, *The Mind*, p. 363.
[202] Ibid., pp. 336–37.
[203] Edwards, *Miscellany* no. 541, in *MISA*, p. 89.
[204] Edwards, *Things to be Considered*, p. 238.

disenchantment of the world. His return to the notion of the great chain of being signified a radical departure from current scientific thought. Constructing the hierarchical order of the universe as a chain of created spirits, based upon the concept of excellency, which defined these spirits' relation to God, enabled Edwards to claim that "God created the world for the shining forth of his excellency."[205] World phenomena were thus established as a mode of reality in which "the beauties of nature are really emanations, or shadows, of the excellence of the Son of God."[206]

Disenchantment of the World, Eighteenth-Century Imagination, and the Protestant Evangelical Awakening

Edwards's response to mechanical philosophy's disenchantment of the world existed in the context of the strong negative reaction to the new scientific interpretation of the nature of reality within religious circles, mostly Protestant, during the first half of the eighteenth century. Indeed, with the scientific, mechanistic explanation of the nature of reality, the "glorious romantic universe of Dante and Milton, that set no bounds to the imagination of man as it played over space and time, had now been swept away." And instead of "a world rich with colour and sound, redolent with fragrance, filled with gladness, love and beauty, speaking everywhere of purposive harmony and creative ideals," in mechanical philosophy the "really important world outside was a world hard, cold, colourless, silent, and dead. A world of quantity, a world of mathematically computable motions in mechanical regularity."[207] This, for example, is how Joseph Addison (1672–1719), essayist, poet, and government official, saw the contradiction between the new mechanistic image of the universe as a vast mathematical system, and popular, traditional reverence and awe toward the world of nature: "We are everywhere entertained with pleasing shows and apparitions, we discover imaginary glories in the heavens, and in the earth, and see some of this visionary beauty poured out upon the whole creation." Yet all these wonders and beauties in the world of nature and heaven's glory had vanished with "that great modern discovery, which is at present universally acknowledged by all inquiries

[205] Edwards, *Miscellany* no. 332 (c. 1728), p. 410.

[206] Edwards, *Miscellany* no. 108 (c. 1727), p. 279. It should be noted, as Norman Fiering argued, that "Edwards's frequent statement that the created order is an emanation of Christ was not simply a pious metaphor or some type of mystical vision. As the second person of the Trinity, which is God's idea of himself and hence the idea of all that is, Christ is truly all being, including created being." See Fiering, "The Rationalist Foundations of Edwards's Metaphysics," p. 83.

[207] Burtt, *The Metaphysical Foundations of Modern Physical Science*, pp. 236–37.

into natural philosophy, namely that light and colours, as apprehended by the imagination, are only ideas in the mind and not qualities that have any existence in matter." Accordingly, continued Addison, people's "souls are at present . . . lost and bewildered in a pleasing delusion" because of the disenchantment of the world caused by mechanical philosophy.[208]

The reason behind this strong negative reaction is not hard to grasp. It was "of the greatest consequence for succeeding thought that now the great Newton's authority was squarely behind that view of the cosmos which saw in man a puny, irrelevant spectator . . . of the vast mathematical system whose regular motions according to mechanical principles constituted the world of nature."[209] Likewise, as Alfred North Whitehead wrote, "whatever theory" of mechanical philosophy

> you choose, there is no light or colour as a fact in external nature. There is merely motion of material. . . . Nature is a dull affair, soundless, scentless, colourless; merely the hurrying of material, endlessly, meaninglessly. However you disguise it, this is the practical outcome of the characteristic scientific philosophy which closed the seventeenth century.[210]

Deprived of any integrity, as well as of inner teleological development and goals, the world of nature in mechanical philosophy was transformed into a huge machine, an engine or a clockwork, based upon cold mechanical principles and operating according to abstract laws. As such, of course, it could not play any part in the mystery of divine providence. The natural world, therefore, became

> an engine which consists of raw masses wandering to no purpose in undiscoverable time and space, and is in general wholly devoid of any qualities that might spell satisfaction for the major interests of human nature, save solely the central aim of the mathematical physics.[211]

Reducing the phenomena of the physical, material world into the mechanics of the motion of bodies in time and space that can be expressed in abstract mathematical terms, mechanical philosophy led to the disenchantment of the world. At the same time, it raised to a high eminence the power of human reason to unveil, and hence to understand, the wonders of the created order. Thus, although the poet Alexander Pope contributed to the host of elegies and eulogies pouring out of the English press

---

[208] Joseph Addison, *Spectator* # 413, as quoted in Marjorie Hope Nicolson, "Newton's Opticks and Eighteenth-Century Imagination," in *Dictionary of the History of Ideas*, III, pp. 397–98.

[209] Burtt, *The Metaphysical Foundations of Modern Physical Science*, p. 236.

[210] A. N. Whitehead, *Science and the Modern World* (Cambridge: Cambridge University Press, 1953 [1926]), pp. 67–69.

[211] Burtt, *The Metaphysical Foundations of Modern Physical Science*, p. 299.

during 1727–28 following Newton's death in 1727, he was nevertheless very critical of the mechanical conception of nature and of the excessive role it accorded to human beings in understanding the world of nature. In "An Essay on Man" (c. 1730), Pope deplored the prominent role human beings were assigning to themselves in the cosmos, a role which in his eyes amounted to the dethroning of God and the assumption of his place in ordering the universe:

> Go, wondrous creature! Mount where Science guides,
> Go, measure earth, weigh air, and state the tides;
> Instruct the planets in what orbs to run,
> Correct the old Time, and regulate the sun . . .
> Go teach Eternal Wisdom how to rule—
> Then drop into thyself, and be a fool!
> Superior beings, when of late they saw,
> A mortal man unfold all nature's laws
> Admired such wisdom in an earthly shape,
> And showed a Newton as we show an ape.[212]

Pope of course was not alone in his dislike of the great excesses to which mechanical philosophy had gone "in elevating science and metaphysics above religion and ethics, in believing that ultimate truth was to be found in the works of mathematicians, scientists, philosophers."[213] By the end of the eighteenth century, there is much evidence that the great admiration for Newton's scientific achievements, so apparent at the beginning of that century, had undergone a change; "The End of Epicurean or Newtonian Philosophy," wrote Blake, "is Atheism."[214]

But probably the strongest negative reaction to the new scientific culture was uttered in religious circles. The impersonal God of mechanical philosophy, the Lord of the physical world and the cosmic lawgiver, was radically different from the living God of the Bible whom Christians had worshiped for many centuries—God the Savior and Redeemer, the triune God of special as well as of general providence, Jesus the personal Savior, and the Holy Spirit, the mediating power between God and human beings. In medieval theology, "God had no purpose; he was the ultimate object of purpose" in a universe structured according to an order whose harmony reflects and symbolizes God's redemptive presence. Mechanical philosophy, of course, stressed that "the cosmic order of masses in motion is itself the final good. Man exists to know and applaud it; God exists to tend and preserve it."[215]

---

[212] Alexander Pope, "An Essay on Man," II, 19–34, in *Alexander Pope: A Critical Edition of the Major Works*, ed. Pat Rogers, pp. 281–82.

[213] Nicolson, "Newton's Opticks and Eighteenth-Century Imagination," p. 397.

[214] Ibid., p. 398.

[215] Burtt, *The Metaphysical Foundations of Modern Physical Science*, p. 294.

Accordingly, in opposing the mechanistic universe, where the role reserved to God was mainly that of preserving and maintaining by general providence the intelligible, rational order and harmony of things, many revival movements during the Protestant evangelical awakening at the turn of the eighteenth century faced a tremendous task: to redefine the relationship between God and the world, to formulate a whole new set of religious convictions and persuasions that would express God's direct and immediate involvement in the order of creation, and, consequently, to construct new modes of religious faith and experience that would exhibit the living God's redemptive and saving presence within believers' lives.[216] Being unable to convince their hearers of God's immediate influence in the physical world because of the predominant scientific culture, Protestant evangelists increasingly tended to emphasize the spiritual, inner realm of the soul by developing a "theology of the heart," or a "heart religion," based upon justification by faith, conversion, new birth, and the witness of the Holy Spirit. Since "the search for the essence of true religion, as an objective 'presence of things outside myself' appeared to have bankrupted itself," Protestant revival movements developed a new theology of the heart that emphasized "the illumination of the Holy Spirit in the individual heart."[217] In other words, in their attempts to combat mechanical philosophy evangelists elevated the heart to become the locus of God's redemptive activity, and conceived of salvation and redemption as taking place within the inner sphere of the soul through the immediate presence and influence of the Holy Spirit. The soul, and not the external world of nature, was the proper domain of divine redemptive activity within the world, and the heart was conceived as the sacred dwelling place within which the Holy Spirit directly operates, affecting and transforming the human existential condition by its divine influence. To a large extent, then, revolt against the predominant mechanical culture constituted an ideological context for the growth of Protestant evangelical movements during the first half of the eighteenth century.

[216] See W. R. Ward, *The Protestant Evangelical Awakening* (Cambridge: Cambridge University Press, 1992); Crawford, *Seasons of Grace: Colonial New England's Revival Tradition in Its British Context*; and Noll et al., eds., *Evangelicalism: Comparative Studies of Popular Protestantism in North America, The British Isles, and Beyond, 1700–1990*. A discussion of the theological origins of the Great Awakening in New England can be found in Perry Miller and Alan Heimert, introduction, in *The Great Awakening: Documents Illustrating the Crisis and Its Consequences*, ed. P. Miller and A. Heimert (Indianapolis: Bobbs-Merrill, 1967), pp. xiii–lxv. An excellent bibliography of the body of secondary literature on eighteenth-century religion and society appeared in Harry S. Stout, *The Divine Dramatist: George Whitefield and the Rise of Modern Evangelicalism* (Grand Rapids: Eerdmans, 1991), pp. 288–96.

[217] Pelikan, *The Christian Tradition: A History of the Development of Doctrine*, vol. V, *Christian Doctrine and Modern Culture (since 1700)*, 1989, pp. 119–21.

An important aspect of the spread of revival movements in Protestant Europe and the British world—in England, Wales, Scotland, and the English colonies in North America—was the reaction to the scientific culture of time and space. Yet, the early history of eighteenth-century Protestant revival movements should be analyzed not in an Anglo-American context alone, but from a wider European perspective. Stimulated by the development of evangelical Pietism during the sixteenth and seventeenth centuries, the Protestant evangelical awakening began in Europe during the second half of the seventeenth century following the Thirty Years War (1618–48), and from there spread to England.[218]

In the British world itself, the awakening was manifested in various religious movements such as the evangelical revival of Methodism and the Great Awakening in the English colonies in North America. As is evident in these movements, the most acute danger evangelists faced was "the threat of rationalism," which "was extending the frontiers of natural religion at the expense of revelation." While the scientific culture tended to minimize the speculative element in religion and elevated the role of reason, leading to an emphasis on the practical implications of religion, "evangelical religion offered a solution" in terms of reaction to a religion based upon rational arguments and a search for "interior evidence of personal acceptance of Christ."[219] In their struggle against the successful, predominant mechanistic interpretation of the essential nature of reality, evangelists strove to formulate new modes of religious faith and experience founded upon a transformation of the heart through the immediate presence and influence of the Holy Spirit. They thus tried to establish all the springs of religious life upon the saving experience of conversion. It is not surprising that "conversion was at the heart of the [Methodist] Revival"[220] as well as of the Great Awakening in America. Furthermore, the "spectacle of so many striking conversions" among the evangelists in the British world "proved that God was not the impersonal *Deus absconditus* of the deists, remote from a world governed by impersonal natural laws, but the living God of the Bible."[221] In sum, the Protestant evangelical awakening was due, in part, to the revolt against the "rationalist, homocentric, spirit" of "the Age of Reason," according to which "moral behavior is conductive to temporal happiness," as well as to the rebellion

---

[218] See Ward, *The Protestant Evangelical Awakening*. The rise of Protestant revival movements during the seventeenth and eighteenth centuries was inextricable from the growth of evangelical pietism. See F. Ernest Stoffler, *The Rise of Evangelical Pietism* (Leiden: E. J. Brill, 1965).

[219] John Walsh, " 'Methodism' and the Origins of English-Speaking Evangelicalism," in *Evangelicalism: Comparative Studies of Popular Protestantism in North America, The British Isles, and Beyond, 1700–1990*, ed. Mark A. Noll et al., pp. 23, 26.

[220] Gordon Rupp, *Religion in England, 1688–1791* (Oxford: Clarendon, 1986), p. 326.

[221] Walsh, " 'Methodism' and the Origins of English-Speaking Evangelicalism," p. 26.

against reducing divine "revelation to reason, faith to philosophy, and Christian ethics to prudential morality."[222]

The evangelists thus formulated a new type of spirituality based upon experimental religion, (i.e., experienced religion), and developed the theology of the heart which stressed the Holy Spirit's direct influence on the soul and its ability to transform the human condition. So, declared John Wesley, the Holy Spirit brings about a new birth where a human being feels "the love of God shed abroad in his heart." The essence of the new birth is a profound existential change "wrought in the whole soul by the almighty Spirit of God," whereby human beings are "created anew in Christ Jesus."[223] By emphasizing the sense of the heart as the locus of religious life and experience, the evangelists claimed new birth as rooted in the experience of conversion. True, authentic religion, therefore, was not founded on the objective presence of things outside the self, but on the subjective residence of divine things within the soul as evidence of conversion. Rejecting the impersonal God of mechanical philosophy, Protestant revival movements stressed the personal God of special providence, the God of salvation and redemption. According to Wesley, "true Christianity consists in this, that one acknowledge the Lord Jesus as personal Savior and Lord."[224]

By constructing new modes of religious experience founded upon the presence of the Holy Spirit within the believer's soul, Protestant evangelical movements rejected the rationalism of the predominant scientific culture and strove to draw a correlation between the objectivity of God and the subjectivity of the self. Although the operation of the Holy Spirit did not contradict reason, they claimed, "it did transcend reason." It was considered as " 'the deity that dwelleth in' the human heart, so that 'the feeling that naturally lies in the human heart' as it moved beyond 'reasoning' to 'affective sentiments' was the proof for the existence of God and the way of discovering the attributes of God."[225] Wesley, for example, who experienced "the change which God works in the heart through faith in Christ,"[226] was convinced that the Spirit of the Lord was upon him: "The Spirit of the Lord is upon me," he declared, "because he anointed me to preach" to the world the gospel of the new birth.[227] In their "reac-

---

[222] Crawford, *Seasons of Grace*, pp. 53–54.

[223] Ronald H. Bainton, *Christianity* (Boston: Houghton Mifflin, 1964), p. 338.

[224] Pelikan, *Christian Doctrine and Modern Culture (since 1700)* (1989), p. 122.

[225] Ibid.

[226] Cragg, *The Church and the Age of Reason, 1648–1789*, pp. 142–43. For the Protestant evangelical revival in England, see also Rupp, *Religion in England, 1688–1791*; and Roland N. Stromberg, *Religious Liberalism in Eighteenth-Century England* (Oxford: Oxford University Press, 1954).

[227] Cragg, *The Church and the Age of Reason, 1648–1789*, p. 143.

tion against rationalism" the Methodists, for example, "allowed unfettered scope to the emotions." In their effort to undermine rationalist tendencies in the prevalent theology, they "deprecated intellectual pursuit
and relied on an uncritical Biblical literalism."[228] New modes of religious
experience were shaped to combat rationalism; the "heart religion" of
Count Zinzendorf and the Moravian Brethren claimed that we "cannot
know God in himself, but only through the Son, and the Son we know
essentially by feeling."[229] Instead of the mechanical God of nature of
mechanistic philosophy, evangelists proclaimed with great enthusiasm
that God is revealed not only in the structure and harmony of the physical
world of nature, but in the inner sphere of the soul or the heart, and
demanded, as was the case with Wesley himself, "the joy of surrender
to Christ."[230] Likewise, for Jonathan Edwards religion "consists in holy
affections," or "the inner working of the Spirit" in the believer's heart;[231]
it is essentially a kind of private experience evident in "the sense of the
heart" and "religious affections" which are produced by the dwelling of
the Holy Spirit in the depths of the soul.[232] Like other evangelists of his
time, Edwards emphasized the personal, unmediated experience of the
new birth and claimed that the regenerative process of "conversion by
grace" is "immediate" and totally dependent upon God's word and Spirit.[233]

The affinities between Edwards and other prominent leaders of the
transatlantic Protestant evangelical revival are manifested also in the context of his attempt to Christianize the world following his conversion.
After their conversion, Wesley and George Whitefield immediately embarked on a crusade to bring souls to Christ. During their preaching ca-
reers both men left behind them a flock of faithful converts with pierced
and penetrated hearts. After his conversion moment on May 24, 1738,
when he experienced the change "God works in the heart through faith
in Christ,"[234] Wesley immediately turned to the world "to declare in my
own country the glad tidings of salvation" and began "a ceaseless round
of evangelical activity"[235] that took him "across England and Scotland,

---

[228] Ibid., p. 153.

[229] John McManners, "Enlightenment: Secular and Christian (1600–1800)," in *The Oxford Dictionary of Christianity*, ed. John McManners (Oxford: Oxford University Press,
1993), p. 302.

[230] John Pudney, *John Wesley and His World* (New York: Charles Scribner's Sons, 1978),
p. 57.

[231] John E. Smith, introduction, in *RA*, pp. 9, 42.

[232] Jenson, *America's Theologian*, pp. 66–69.

[233] Cherry, *The Theology of Jonathan Edwards: A Reappraisal*, p. 57.

[234] Cragg, *The Church and the Age of Reason, 1648–1789*, p. 142.

[235] Rupp, *Religion in England, 1688–1791*, p. 359.

across the Irish bogs and the Welsh mountains."[236] Likewise, immediately following his conversion experience in 1735, Whitefield, "the Morning Star of the Evangelical Revival," went out to the world to preach the gospel of "the new Birth" both in the British world at home and abroad in the English colonies in America.[237]

The same can be said about Edwards himself. Following his conversion, and believing that religion can still provide objective truths about the world of nature, he turned immediately to define the essential nature of reality according to his saving experience. The outcome was, as we have seen, a radical construction of a theology of nature. Yet, given the close and inextricable affinities between space and time, nature and history, Edwards found it necessary to construct an ideology or philosophy of sacred history as well, based on a redemptive mode of historical thought, which would illuminate God's absolute sovereignty not only in the order of nature but also in the order of time.

[236] Bainton, *Christianity*, p. 339.

[237] Rupp, *Religion in England, 1688–1791*, pp. 339–40. On Whitefield's life and thought, see Stout, *The Divine Dramatist*; and Frank Lambert, *"Pedlar in Divinity": George Whitefield and the Transatlantic Revivals, 1737–1770* (Princeton: Princeton University Press, 1994).

Time

.

Four

The Ideological Origins of Edwards's Philosophy of History

What Edwards knew, what he believed in his heart and his mind, was that man was made to stand in the presence of eternal, unending absolute glory, to participate in the celebration of cosmic deliverance from everything putrid, destructive, defiling, to rejoice in the service of the stupendous artist who flung universes of stars on his canvas, sculptured the forms of angelic powers, etched with loving care miniature worlds within worlds.

(H. Richard Niebuhr, "The Anachronism of Jonathan Edwards," 1958)

Edwards's universe was orderly and intelligible only on its surface. The operation of the mind, the relation of subject to object, the existence of personal identity were all . . . dependent on the exertion, from minute to minute, of God's inscrutable will. God himself was utterly unlike the prime mover of the deists, or the benevolent contriver of natural religion, and not much more like the loving father of sentimental piety.

(Henry F. May, *The Enlightenment in America*, 1976)

WHEN THE "little revival" of 1734–35 occurred in Northampton, it took the whole community by great surprise. Edwards was indeed convinced that the "surprising work of God" was the testimony of a "remarkable pouring out of the Spirit of God" and "a very extraordinary dispensation of Providence," yet he was much confused, to say the least, about this whole affair. As he frankly noted in June 1735: "I forbear to make reflections, or to guess what God is about to do with this remarkable manifestation of His Spirit."[1] One of the main reasons for this hesitation was that in contrast to the formulation of his theology of nature, which was only a few years in the making during the 1720s, in 1735 Edwards had not yet fully developed a systematic and coherent philosophy of history. Naturally, in the absence of any well-defined historical ideology he was unable to explain the meaning of the revival in his town in a larger context of

---

[1] "Benjamin Colman's Abridgment, November 1736," in *GA*, pp. 120–21, 118; Edwards, "Unpublished Letter of May 30, 1735," in *GA*, p. 109.

sacred, providential history. At the time he tended to consider the affair mostly in terms of the operation of saving grace in converting souls, of the "converting influences of God's Spirit" and its manifestation in the "great and marvelous work of conversion and sanctification among the people here."[2] Consequently, Edwards could only think of the revival in terms of the "surprising work of God" in effecting "the conversion" of the people in his town.

In the years 1736–39, after the "little revival," there is clear evidence of a shift in Edwards's historical consciousness; he developed a whole new set of premises about the nature of time and the meaning of history, where God's redemptive activity was related more and more to the historical process as a whole. Already in 1736, in the aftermath of the "little revival," he expressed the view that the work of redemption is the "great design" of God in the order of time,[3] or that the "Work of Redemption" is the "great end and drift of all Gods works and dispensations" in history from the beginning to "the end of the work of creation."[4] By 1739, on the basis of this new historical consciousness Edwards was convinced, as can be seen in his *A History of the Work of Redemption*, that religious revivals and awakenings were inextricable from God's overall redemptive plan in the order of time, and thus constitute the heart of the entire historical process:

> from the fall of man to this day wherein we live the Work of Redemption in its effects has mainly been carried on by remarkable pourings out of the spirit of God . . . [and] the way in which the greatest things have been done towards carrying on this work always has been by remarkable pourings out of the Spirit at special seasons of mercy.[5]

However, to understand the formation of Edwards's historical consciousness, especially in regard to the content and form of his redemptive mode of historical thought—the doctrine that the process of history depends exclusively on God's redemptive activity in time, as evident in the close association between the effusion of the Spirit and its manifestation in the form of revivals and awakenings throughout history, and not on human power and autonomy—it is necessary to take into account not only the circumstances surrounding his life in provincial New England but also certain intellectual trends in the early modern period pertaining to the meaning of time and history. As was the case with the formation

---

[2] Edwards, *A Faithful Narrative*, pp. 179, 209.

[3] Edwards, *Miscellany* no. 547 in *MISA*, p. 93.

[4] Edwards, *Miscellany* no. 702 (c. 1736), in *MISA*, p. 284.

[5] Edwards, *History of the Work of Redemption*, p. 143. The central place attached to history in Edwards's theology is discussed in Stephen M. Clark, "Jonathan Edwards: The History of Redemption," (Ph.D. diss., Drew University, 1986).

of his theology of nature, Edwards's construction of the order of time and the nature of history was not done in isolation but constituted, in part, a response to the rise of certain modes of historical thought, most specifically the scientific notion of homogeneous, empty time, deprived of God's redemptive activity, and the Enlightenment historical narratives' denial of theistic explanations concerning the historical process. More specifically, Edwards's attempt to construct the order of time cannot be understood without considering the threats to the Christian theological teleology of history caused by the emergence of new modes of historical thought in the early eighteenth century, such as the increasing validity and legitimacy attached to historical time, the significance accorded to *historia humana* rather than sacred history, and the new role accorded to human agency, autonomy, and freedom in the historical process.

The understanding of Edwards's purpose in the construction of time, and the analysis of his philosophy of history, will have to deal with his rejection of the separation between the order of grace and the order of time, redemption and history. The following, therefore, is an attempt to depict the ideological context of Edwards's vision of history in light of the threats to the Christian historical explanation in the early modern period. I deal first with Edwards's argument that God should be known in the order of nature as well as in the order of time, and hence that redemptive activity is manifested not only within the subjective, spiritual sphere of the operation of saving grace in the depths of the soul, as some contemporary Protestant evangelists tended to declare. This will be followed by a discussion of the new scientific, mechanical homogeneous, empty time, the new secular conception of history and the "legitimacy" accorded to secular, historical time. Later, an analysis will be offered of Edwards's "poetics of history," or his philosophy of salvation history, placing the formation of his redemptive mode of historical thought within the larger context of the Christian ideology of history, or sacred, ecclesiastical history. A detailed discussion of the development of Edwards's philosophy of history, as well as its form and content, will appear in the next chapter.

The Disenchantment of the World and the Reenchantment of the Soul

During the first half of the eighteenth century, there is clear evidence that in face of the development and success of mechanical philosophy and Enlightenment rationalism, some Protestant evangelists, but by no means all, voluntarily withdrew from attempting to pronounce objective truths about the essential nature of reality and instead focused much of their theological energies on analyzing the mysterious working of the Holy

Spirit within the believer's soul, or to recording the inward, spiritual, and mysterious operations of God's saving grace in the heart. "In their reaction against rationalism," Protestant evangelists "allowed unfettered scope to the emotions . . . they deprecated intellectual pursuit and relied on an uncritical Biblical literalism. As a result, the evangelical movement proved comparatively sterile as a theological force."[6] In other words, they displayed "the tendency to see God at work only within the sphere of religious experience."[7] Moreover, as the scientific imagination increasingly left the world of nature bereft of God's redemptive activity and living presence, and as "the public sphere grew more impersonal and abstract, [so] the private self gained proportionate importance as the repository of spiritual experience."[8] Thus for Whitefield "true religion" was the "union of the soul with God."[9] And John Wesley believed that "the wisdom of God has, in most later ages, permitted the external evidence of Christianity to be more or less clogged and encumbered for this very end, that men (of reflection especially) . . . be constrained to look into themselves" and "attend to the light shining in their hearts."[10] For Wesley "the heart of faith was immediate knowledge" of God "in the empirical sense of personal awareness of the operation of God in life."[11] This growing trend among some eighteenth-century evangelists of the privatization of religious faith and experience was part of a larger intellectual and cultural tendency in early modern history, which some historians like to call the "sentimental revolution." The Age of Reason, according to this view, witnessed the rise of a new culture of "sense and sensibility," a growing emphasis on the role of the senses in human experience and social life.[12]

One of the main reasons for the growing privatization of religious life and experience was that during the early eighteenth century the Christian theological and teleological explanation of the nature of reality had stead-

---

[6] Cragg, *The Church and the Age of Reason, 1648–1789*, pp. 153–54.

[7] Niebuhr, *The Kingdom of God in America*, p. 108.

[8] Stout, *The Divine Dramatist: George Whitefield and the Rise of Modern Evangelicalism*, p. xvii.

[9] Lambert, *"Pedlar in Divinity": George Whitefield and the Transatlantic Revivals*, p. 11.

[10] John Wesley, *A Plain Account of Genuine Christianity*, as cited by Jaroslav Pelikan, *The Christian Tradition*, vol. 5: *Christian Doctrine and Modern Culture (since 1700)*, p. 118.

[11] Niebuhr, *The Kingdom of God in America*, p. 106.

[12] Geoffroy Atkinson, *The Sentimental Revolution* (Seattle: University of Washington Press, 1965); John Mullan, *Sentiment and Sociability: The Language of Feeling in the Eighteenth Century* (Oxford: Oxford University Press, 1988); Paul Langford, *A Polite and Commercial People: England 1727–1782* (Oxford: Oxford University Press, 1992); and the studies by Isabel Rivers, *Reason, Grace, and Sentiment: A Study of the Language of Religion and Ethics in England 1660–1780*, vol. I: *Whichcote to Wesley* (Cambridge: Cambridge University Press, 1991), and vol. II: *Shaftesbury to Hume* (Cambridge: Cambridge University Press, 2000).

ily declined in persuasiveness because of the attraction of scientific thought in interpreting the nature of the material world and the influence of the British school of moral sense, which developed the rationalist idea of disinterested benevolence as the criterion for moral judgment. In this Age of Reason, the "authority of the church was challenged in many spheres, but nowhere so seriously as in the intellectual realm."[13] More specifically, the whole relationship between reason and revelation, between human understanding and capacity and the mystery of God's will and divine revelation, was profoundly transformed. If during the Middle Ages, "the normal use of natural reason was obscured by blind faith in the absolute truth of Christian Revelation,"[14] during the Age of Reason the supremacy and primacy of divine revelation was attacked: "The role of reason was magnified, that of revelation was depressed. The scriptures were subjected to intensive and often to unsympathetic scrutiny. Miracles were challenged. Prophecy was reassessed. Christian thought faced a threat which might have stripped it of all its uniqueness."[15]

The elevation of reason over revelation crucially informed religious life and belief. Within the church itself, as can be felt in English Protestant sermons of the period, the rationalist and homocentric spirit of the time was seen to constitute a grave danger to traditional Christian piety. By "the turn of the eighteenth century, Scottish, English and American clergymen" were "convinced that piety was expiring" and they found themselves "powerless to do anything about it." The Age of Reason thus deeply affected religious thought and the Christian message in the world: "The standard message of the English sermon of the Age of Reason was that moral behavior is conducive to temporal happiness. Much in the new preaching resulted from the attempt to defend Christianity against the deistic attack by demonstrating the reasonableness of the Christian religion. Thus sermons became rational discourses. The clergy tended, in the phrase of Horton Davies, to reduce 'revelation to reason, faith to philosophy, and Christian ethics to prudential morality.' "[16]

In face of such threats to religious faith and life, some Protestant theologians gradually retreated from proposing objective explanations about the essential nature of reality and instead tried to forge new modes of religious faith and experience. "To many defenders as well as to most critics" of Christian "traditional belief, the search for the essence of true religion as an objective 'presence of things outside myself' appeared to

[13] Cragg, *The Church and the Age of Reason*, p. 12.
[14] Gilson, *Reason and Revelation in the Middle Ages*, p. 4.
[15] Cragg, *The Church and the Age of Reason*, pp. 12–13.
[16] Crawford, *Season of Grace: Colonial New England's Revival Tradition in Its British Context*, pp. 53–54. See also Horton Davies, *Worship and Theology in England: From Watts to Wesley and Maurice, 1690–1850* (Princeton: Princeton University Press, 1961); and Cragg, *The Church and the Age of Reason*.

have bankrupted itself."[17] Since divine revelation could no longer be simply understood and interpreted within the fabric of the natural realm, or provide a foundation for defining the nature of the physical world, as the mechanical, scientific interpretation had clearly demonstrated, some Protestant theologians turned to the sphere of the soul to find evidence for the power of God's revelation and his redemptive activity in the created order. The transatlantic Protestant "revival movement" in the early eighteenth century "resulted in a new tendency toward the withdrawal of the Christian community from entangling alliance with the world."[18] This shift signified an important move "from mere outside religion" to "heart religion," which "was beyond rational argument." The new theological stance was expressed in the concept of "theology of the heart," according to which "doctrinal themes involved in the defense of the objectivity of transcendent revelation" were susceptible of treatment. Instead of looking for God in the fabric of the universe, theologians of the heart referred to the "experience of the heart, the internal feeling by which the external word authenticated itself," stressing that "true Christianity consists in this, that one acknowledge the Lord Jesus Christ as personal Savior and Lord." God's place was in the heart, and only there could he fully and vividly reveal himself and be known. Accordingly, the emphasis was on " 'the Deity that dwelleth in' the human heart," because " 'the feeling that naturally lies in the human heart' as it moved beyond 'reasoning' to 'affective sentiments' was a proof for the existence of God and a way of discovering the attributes of God."[19] The disenchantment of the world led therefore to the reenchantment of the soul, or the heart, as the main locus of religious life and experience.

Facing the serious challenges of the scientific and Enlightenment construction of nature's God and nature's laws, which gradually denied the Deity's direct redemptive involvement in the created order, religious reflection regarding the relationship between God and the world gradually retreated into the inner, private, and spiritual domain. Gazing fearfully at the conquering mechanical explanation of the natural world, which led gradually to the disenchantment of the world of nature, Protestant theologians tended more and more to emphasize pietistic tendencies. To explain God's relationship with creation, they stressed the influence of the Holy Spirit and the mysterious operation of saving grace within the believer's soul, as can be seen in the successful Protestant evangelical awakening of the early eighteenth century.[20] They thus inaugurated a major transforma-

---

[17] Pelikan, *Christian Doctrine and Modern Culture (since 1700)*, p. 121.

[18] Niebuhr, *The Kingdom of God in America*, p. 119.

[19] Pelikan, *Christian Doctrine and Modern Culture (since 1700)*, pp. 119–22.

[20] For general studies dealing with the Protestant evangelical awakening in the early eighteenth century, see Ward, *The Protestant Evangelical Awakening*; and Crawford, *Seasons of Grace*.

tion in Christian thought and its attitude toward the world—the shift from finding God in the world of nature, or in the fabric of the universe, to discovering his saving presence and redemptive activity in the soul. The "private self gained" great "importance as the repository of spiritual experience."[21] Within a mechanical universe, gradually deprived of sacred, redemptive dimensions, the realm of the senses, and the validity of emotions and feelings, including the religious notion of the sense of the heart, became more and more dominant.

The flourishing of the leaders of the Protestant evangelical awakening in the British world in general and in colonial British America in particular during the first half of the eighteenth century was based to a large extent upon their ability to redefine the mysterious working of the Spirit of God and the power of saving grace within the sphere of the soul.[22] Objective truths about natural reality were relegated to science, and thus abandoned, and the way was cleared for the refashioning of the spiritual dimension, or the reenchantment of the soul, as the main locus where God could be found and known. Since the knowledge of God was sought more and more in the abysses of the soul and less and less in the objective dimension of the fabric of the universe, the inner dynamism of the spiritual sphere displaced material occurrences in time and space. More specifically, the describing of God's relationship with the created order increasingly moved from the material world into the realm of the believer's soul. Thus, for example, Whitefield declared that "true religion [was nothing less than] union of the soul with God, and Christ formed within."[23] With the gradual relinquishment of the claim to define the world of nature, several Protestant theologians constructed the spiritual sphere as the place where God can be most properly found, experienced, and known. Being no longer able to detect God's presence in the material world, which was conceived more and more as operating by general, abstract, and impersonal laws of nature and hence devoid of the power of divine revelation, theologians refashioned the soul as the main locus of God's redemptive activity. This crucial transformation signified the "domestication of the transcendence,"[24] the relegation of the divine from the world of nature

---

[21] Stout, *The Divine Dramatist*, p. xvii.

[22] The development of the religion of the heart or the theology of the heart in Anglo-American evangelicalism is discussed in Taves, *Fits, Trances, & Visions: Experiencing Religion and Explaining Experience from Wesley to James*, especially pp. 3–76.

[23] Lambert, *"Pedlar in Divinity,"* p. 11.

[24] William C. Placher, *The Domestication of the Transcendence: How Modern Thinking about God Went Wrong* (Louisville, Ky.: Westminster/John Knox, 1996). In using Placher's phrase, I have modified the meaning. Placher argues that "before the seventeenth century, most Christian theologians were struck by the mystery, the wholly otherness of God, and the inadequacy of any human categories as applied to God." However, "in the seventeenth century philosophers and theologians increasingly thought they could talk clearly about God." Thus, "they were already explaining God's difference from created things by saying

to the spiritual realm, and it had important consequences regarding the enchantment of the soul; God's place was seen, and his presence was articulated, more and more within the confines of the individual's spiritual life and not in the fabric of the external, physical world.

Edwards of course took an active part in shaping the theology of the heart.[25] However, as we have seen, he fought in his theology of nature against the disenchantment of the world. To him God's absolute sovereignty was evident not only in the soul but also in the whole created order. Hence God should be known not only through his word but also through his works, in both space and time. Indeed, as we saw in the previous chapter, the whole purpose of Edwards's natural philosophy was not only to reject the predominant scientific culture of his time, but also to provide objective truths about the essential nature of reality, and thus to supply valid proof of human ability to know God through the phenomena of nature, through his works. For he was firmly convinced that the knowledge of God is possible "in those things by which he makes himself known, or by his *word* and *works*; i.e. in what he says, and in what he does."[26] The same contention stood at the base of Edwards's construction of time. As in the construction of space, in the *theologia gloriae*, where he strove to demonstrate God's absolute sovereignty over the created order, so his goal in the order of time was to show God as Lord and author of history. In this enterprise, Edwards fought against the de-Christianization of the world and the de-divination of the historical process, against the transformation of history into *historia humana*, a length of time not contingent on divine redemptive activity.

Constructing the Order of Time

The thrust of Edwards's philosophical theology may be summarized thus: he never gave up his striving to provide objective truths about the essential nature of reality, to unveil the external evidence of Christianity in both space and time. His theology of nature, therefore, was based upon a *theologia gloriae* that emphasized the glory of God in creation and accorded him preeminence and sovereignty in the created order. His philosophy of

---

that God was *transcendent* (distant, unaffected) in *contrast* to *immanent* (close, engaged). Rather than explaining how all categories break down when applied to God, they set the stage for talking about transcendence as one of the definable properties God possesses—a quality we could understand. . . . In that sense, transcendence got domesticated, and theology suffered as a result" (pp. 6–7). I use the concept of domestication to mean the move from finding God in the world of nature to finding his presence within the soul.

[25] A comparison between Edwards and Wesley regarding the issue of explaining religious experience can be found in Taves, *Fits, Trances, & Visions*, pp. 47–58.

[26] Edwards, *Concerning the End for which God Created the World*, in *EW*, p. 422.

history in turn was based upon the notion of God's work of redemption, a mode of historical thought according to which God continuously unveils his redemptive power and activity in time and history through the close connection between the effusion of the Spirit and the emergence of revivals and awakenings. Edwards's theological and philosophical enterprise, therefore, was not confined to the exploration of the subjective sphere of the soul. Rather, he strove with all his intellectual ability to represent the existential conditions of human life and experience in space and time as based on God's absolute sovereignty and redemptive presence in creation. The main reason for this venture was no doubt his transforming conversion experience. Following that moment, Edwards sought to convert the whole world to the persuasions he had acquired. He was not only a theologian of the heart, but an original early modern philosopher who had much to say about the essential nature of reality.

During the 1720s, truly convinced that he had discovered some important and undeniable truths about the fabric of the created order, Edwards worked on his theology of nature and philosophy of history in order to show that the order of grace is inextricable from the order of nature, as is God's redemptive activity from the order of time. He believed that the "being of God" is the "first and universal principle of things, from whence results the being, the nature, the powers and motions, and sweet order of the world."[27] To emphasize God's absolute sovereignty in creation, he tended more and more to identify the operation of divine providence with that of a machine, or a wheel—language clearly borrowed from current mechanical philosophy—arguing "the providence of God is like a wheel," or "a machine composed of wheels."[28] Thus he associated God's providence with the vision of the wheels in the Old Testament book of Ezekiel, claiming that divine "providence is most aptly represented by the revolution or course of these wheels. Things in their series and course in providence, they do as it were go round like a wheel in its motion on the earth." This mechanization of God's providential work applies to both the natural and moral world because "the annual changes that appear in the natural world are as it were by the revolution of a wheel," and so "it is in the course of things in God's providence over the intelligent and moral world." Consequently, basing himself on this typology that comprehended not only scripture but also nature and history Edwards further claimed that what "comes to pass in the natural world is . . . typical of what comes to pass in the moral and intelligent world."[29]

In space and time alike God's providence directly and immediately controls the phenomena of the world so that all of creation depends on God's

---

[27] Edwards, *Miscellany* no. 383 (1729), in *MIS*, pp. 451–52.

[28] Edwards, *Images of Divine Things*, 89 (1739), p. 86.

[29] Edwards, *Notes on Scripture*, 389 (1739), pp. 373–74.

redemptive activity. To demonstrate this, Edwards first undertook a reconstruction of the dimension of space in his theology of nature. Unwilling to limit God's sovereignty to setting up abstract, general laws of nature, and opposing any attempt to restrict his redemptive activity to the sphere of the personal soul, Edwards embarked on a mission of converting every dimension of reality. The outcome, as we saw in his theology of nature, was the declaration of God's absolute majesty over the whole of creation. Constructing a theological alternative to the early Enlightenment exposition of the world of nature, Edwards enhanced God's power through co-opting the agency of the smallest particles of the atoms, and developed an idealistic phenomenology whereby spirits are properly beings and more substantial than bodies. On the basis of this reenchantment of the world, he was able to reclaim God's direct redemptive activity in the whole fabric of the universe.

The same overarching goal directed all Edwards's work in constructing the order of time and the meaning of history. If the thrust of his theology of nature was to refute contemporary scientific culture, the same ambition applied to the dimension of time; his philosophy of history, as one scholar remarked, "makes him stand out against his eighteenth-century Enlightenment background more sharply than his other writings."[30] While many contemporary Protestant theologians were gradually retreating from attempting to provide an explanation of the essential nature of reality, Edwards claimed that the Christian faith and belief could and should provide the main source for understanding the world in which human beings are placed. To restrict religious faith and life to experienced religion, or to the sense of the heart, and to limit God's redemptive activity to the mysterious operation of saving grace, would mean to abandon all pretensions on the part of Christianity to supply valid truths about the nature of the real world. The growing emphasis in Protestant evangelical circles on the subjectivity of the spiritual sphere in religious life and experience, Edwards believed, should not prevent one from seeing that Christianity ought also to define the objectivity of the natural order by explicating the material world and the course of history. Failure to do so would mean allowing materialists and mechanical philosophers to develop their own notions of a purposeless universe, in the first case, or a world that admitted only general providence, in the second.

Against attempts by "natural scientists and historians" during the eighteenth century "to leave nature and history in their own sphere and to establish them on their own soil,"[31] Edwards aimed to fight this separation by restoring God's sovereignty in space and time, nature and history.

---

[30] Ahlstrom, "Theology in America: A Theological Survey," I, p. 251.
[31] Cassirer, *The Philosophy of the Enlightenment*, p. 199.

In constructing the dimension of time he was resisting the threatened disunion of God from his creation. The world is God's; and in his philosophical and theological endeavor Edwards sought to return to God his glory within the order of time. To establish God as the sole and absolute Lord of time meant, among other things, that he controlled and directed the course and process of history. As Edwards said:

> There is doubtless some design that God is pursuing, and scheme that he is Carrying on, in the various changes and revolutions that from age to age happen in the world; there is some certain great design, to which providence subordinates all the successive changes that come to pass in the state of affairs of mankind.[32]

Edwards's interpretation of the dimension of time, therefore, was based upon a redemptive mode of historical thought, the "work of redemption," as he called it. The basis for this formulation was his refusal to recognize the scientific notion of homogeneous, empty time, without any redemptive significance, and his denial of the Enlightenment vision of *historia humana*, which admitted no supernatural power or super-historical sphere above the historical process.[33] For him history is totally subordinated to God's higher redemptive plan for human salvation, which will be made manifest at the end of the world.

Such an historical interpretation stood in clear contrast to the Enlightenment narratives of history, which were "both a historiography of state and a historiography of society";[34] its proponents were skeptical of the "chronology of Christian universal history."[35] In contrast to the Christian historical interpretation, Enlightenment historians wrote "history in the grand manner," as "a majestic authoritative narrative of political and military deeds,"[36] endeavoring "to modify or transform their readers' sense of national self-awareness through the writing of narrative history."[37] Edwards owned and read many of these works, where he discovered that the

---

[32] Edwards, *Miscellany* no. 547 (c. 1731), p. 93.

[33] Analyses of the Enlightenment new science of morals and history can be found in Cassirer, *The Philosophy of the Enlightenment*; Peter Gay, *The Enlightenment: An Interpretation: The Rise of Modern Paganism* (New York: Norton, 1995); idem, *The Enlightenment: The Science of Freedom*; Isaac Kramnick, ed., *The Portable Enlightenment Reader*; and more recently, Pocock, *Barbarism and Religion: The Enlightenments of Edward Gibbon, 1737–1764*; idem, *Barbarism and Religion: Narratives of Civil Government*; Roy Porter, *Enlightenment: Britain and the Creation of the Modern World* (London: Allen Lane, 2000); Jonathan Israel, *Radical Enlightenment: Philosophy and the Making of Modernity, 1650–1750* (Oxford: Oxford University Press, 2001).

[34] Pocock, *Barbarism and Religion: Narratives of Civil Government*, pp. 2–8.

[35] O'Brien, *Narratives of Enlightenment*, p. 10.

[36] Hicks, *Neoclassical History and English Culture*, p. 1.

[37] O'Brien, *Narratives of Enlightenment*, p. 1.

divine agency was no longer considered intrinsic to history. For example, Bishop Gilbert Burnet's *History of his Own Time* (1724–34), which enjoyed enormous commercial success in England, "recorded the triumph, in 1688–9, and precarious survival, during the reign of Anne, of Whig and Protestant ideals." Likewise, Edwards owned John Oldmixions's radical Whig *Critical History of England* (1724), which was "centrally preoccupied with the country's constitution, right and liberties." The same can be said about the most popular historical work that appeared in England during that time, Paul de Rapin-Thoyras's *Histoire d'Angleterre* (1721–31), which "provided the Whig with a secular and scholarly account of the origins of the nation's mixed and liberal constitution." Because of the enormous popularity of this work during the first half of the eighteenth century, Rapin's history played an important part "in the political education of the nation," thus helping forge England's "national self-awareness in this period."[38]

Edwards's philosophy of history was radically different as well from the Enlightenment narratives' emphasis on the role of great men in history instead of God and his Son. For example, Bolingbroke spoke about the "Patriotic King," the humanistic prince, "whose virtuous moral example will return the body politic to its lost liberty and true principles."[39] In contrast, Edwards stressed the narrative of God's redemptive activity in history: "Shall we prize a history that gives us a clear account of some great earthly prince or mighty warrior," he asked rhetorically, "and shall we not prize the history that God has given us of the glorious kingdom of his son, Jesus Christ, the prince and savior of the world."[40] These words were directed against Enlightenment historians, such as Pierre Bayle, Samuel Pufendorf, Henry St. John, Lord Bolingbroke, David Hume, and others, who spoke of "man's autonomous potentialities over against heteronomous powers which were no longer convincing,"[41] among them the "authority of the Christian church and of its dogma and ultimately the objective authority of Scripture and of transcendent [divine] revelation itself."[42]

Understanding of the nature of time and the course of history during the early eighteenth century was profoundly influenced by this Enlightenment revolt. The sense of both underwent a radical change with the separation

---

[38] Ibid., pp. 14–18; Hicks, *Neoclassical History and English Culture*, pp. 126–30, 146–50.

[39] Isaac Kramnick, introduction, in *Lord Bolingbroke: Historical Works*, ed. Isaac Kramnick, p. li. See also Lord Bolingbroke, *The Idea of the Patriotic King* (1749), in *The Works of Lord Bolingbroke*, 4 vols. (Philadelphia, 1841), II, pp. 393–97.

[40] Edwards, *History of the Work of Redemption*, p. 291.

[41] Tillich, *A History of Christian Thought*, p. 323.

[42] Pelikan, *Christian Doctrine and Modern Culture (since 1700)*, p. 60.

of redemption and history. Inheriting the scientific notion of a one-dimensional, homogeneous, symmetrical, uniform, and non-hierarchical nature, Enlightenment historical narratives envisioned time as uniform and linear. Accordingly, history was increasingly seen as devoid of the involvement of a supernatural power. Enlightenment historians refused "to recognize an absolutely supernatural or an absolutely super-historical sphere." Seen against this denial of any theistic explanation dealing with the form and content of the historical process, it is not surprising that the study of history became a central issue during the Enlightenment: "History bears the torch for the Enlightenment," because it was liberated "from the bonds of scripture dogmatically interpreted and the orthodoxy of the preceding centuries."[43] Thus construed, human history became blind and indifferent to God's providence and his message of salvation and redemption. Enlightenment writers only continued in greater earnest the attempts made by humanists during the Renaissance to liberate history from the restrictions imposed upon it by Christianity. "In the Renaissance, Humanists had joyfully embraced antique models in their horror at the tedium and superstitiousness of medieval chronicles, and had begun to liberate history writing from its subservience to theology, dependence on miracles, mythopoeic schemes of periodization, and apocalyptic expectations."[44]

These new conceptions of history impelled Edwards to his own construction of time, where he attempted to show the absolute power of God's redemptive activity in controlling world events and to establish divine revelation as inextricable from history. The belief that "the ultimate mode of expressing the meaning of Christian faith was through *Heilsgeschichte* (salvation history; sacred history)" illuminates more than anything else the specific shape of Edwards's thinking. Indeed, in this wider context of sacred, providential history, Edwards's philosophy of history "makes him stand out against his eighteenth-century Enlightenment background more sharply than his other writings. Herein may lie his most impressive originality."[45]

Homogeneous Time, Empty Time, and "Redeeming the Time"

To understand the content and form of Edwards's philosophy of history, it is necessary to take into account, among other things, some major changes in the concepts of time and history in the early eighteenth century.

[43] Cassirer, *The Philosophy of the Enlightenment*, p. 199.
[44] Gay, *The Enlightenment: The Science of Freedom*, p. 372.
[45] Ahlstrom, "Theology in America," pp. 249–51.

Edwards developed his redemptive mode of thought in part as a direct response to these changes. The scientific culture and the early Enlightenment profoundly influenced the sense of time, especially in regard to the meaning and purpose of the historical process. The legitimacy of historical time was confidently asserted, and the secularity of time was established together with belief in the realization of human freedom and happiness within history. The meaning of history was no longer sought solely in a supernatural order beyond and above the historical process. This transformation radically influenced the Christian theological teleology of history and gave rise to a whole new mode of historical consciousness. That change is evident in the notion of scientific, homogeneous, empty time, the decline of the Christian interpretation of history, the gradual eclipse of biblical narrative, and attempts to separate divine revelation from history. The result was, according to Rudolf Bultmann, "the secularization of theological teleology of history" announced by the Enlightenment of the eighteenth century.[46] Once considered as the source and foundation of all historical understanding, during the eighteenth century the Christian interpretation of history lost much of its power.

The new scientific ideas gave rise to the notion of a one-dimensional, homogeneous, symmetrical, uniform, and non-hierarchical world of nature, detached from divine providence. God set the world in motion at the moment of creation, and after establishing the abstract general laws of nature that since then have ruled the created order, he has let the world run by itself like a machine. Against this interpretation of the nature of reality, as we have seen, Edwards strove to reconstitute God's absolute sovereignty and redemptive activity in the physical world by arguing that he controls the smallest particles of atoms, and hence all natural phenomena. The same purpose directed Edwards in his exploration of time and history. The new scientific thought not only stripped nature of teleological and theological meaning, but it led to the notion of homogeneous, empty time—time deprived of any redemptive significance. This notion eventually led to the Enlightenment historians' refusal to recognize any supernatural power beyond history and to the denial of any connection between history and *mysterium salutis* (the mystery of salvation) or between time and *mysterium gubernationis Dei* (the mystery of God's providence). In the new conception of secular time, denying the theistic interpretation of the historical process, the course of history is no longer directed by divine providence nor is it pervaded by redemptive activity. To a large extent, then, the mechanical notion of empty, uniform, secular time greatly influ-

---

[46] Rudolf Bultmann, *History and Eschatology* (Edinburgh: The University Press, 1957), p. 65.

enced the process of separating grace and time, and thus led to the detachment of redemption from the historical process.[47]

In his "Theses on the Philosophy of History" (1940), Walter Benjamin invoked the term "homogeneous, empty time" to distinguish between the scientific, mechanical time reckoned by clocks and the historical time measured by calendars: "the calendars do not measure time as the clocks; they are monuments of historical consciousness." Hence the meaning of history is always inextricable from historical consciousness: "History is the subject of a structure whose site is not homogeneous, empty time, but time filled by the presence of the now. Thus, to Robespierre ancient Rome was a past charged with the time of the now which he blasted out of the continuum of history."[48] Scientific, empty time, then, is radically different from historical time. "The soothsayers who found out from time what it had in store certainly did not experience time as either homogeneous or empty."[49] Scientific time is an undifferentiated linear continuum, whereas historical time is a time charged with meaning. The first is empty because it knows nothing of human existence and experience. Historical time, on the other hand, which constitutes the source for historical consciousness, is filled with meaning reflecting the conditions of human existence. Furthermore, scientific time is empty because it allows for no possibility of a new and surprising event. Historical time admits the possibility of transformation that could lead to the realization of various utopian and redemptive goals and aims.

These notions about the nature of historical time are useful in considering the formation of Edwards's sense of time and vision of history. Scientific time—the modern concept of "arrow of time," whether cosmological, biological, or evolutionary—is indifferent to human existence and experience. It cannot account for the passage of history, nor does it explain its direction or its meaning. Edwards's experience of time was radically different; he boldly rejected the concept of homogeneous, empty time and argued instead that time is filled with the presence of divine, redemptive activity. Thus, already in 1723 he began to define historical time as a special expanse within which God's work of redemption takes

---

[47] For recent studies dealing with the transformation of the Christian theology of history during the Enlightenment, see Robert E. Frykenberg, *History and Belief: The Foundation of Historical Understanding* (Grand Rapids: Eerdmans, 1996); Kelley, ed., *Versions of History from Antiquity to the Enlightenment*; Frederick C. Beiser, *The Sovereignty of Reason: The Defense of Rationality in the Early English Enlightenment* (Princeton: Princeton University Press, 1996); and Marcel Gauchet, *The Disenchantment of the World: A Political History of Religion* (Princeton: Princeton University Press, 1997).

[48] Benjamin, "Theses on the Philosophy of History," p. 261.

[49] Ibid., pp. 262–64.

place.[50] Later he declared that because "salvation is the sum of all those works of God" in the creation of the world,[51] the "works of creation & the laws of nature and that course of nature that God established," in sum the entire created order, "is subordinate to the work of redemption."[52] Refusing the detachment of creation from the Creator, for Edwards the testimonies of the Old and New Testaments are evidence of the sovereignty of God and the realization of his redemptive power in time, establishing him as the true Lord of history. Since the Bible is a divine commentary on divine acts in history, the prophetic revelations closely foretell the entire progress of history. That belief was inherent in medieval thought, but with the secularization of theological teleology of history during the Enlightenment, salvation history found itself in decline.

From the beginning of his construction of the order of time, Edwards believed that redemption is inextricable from history and vice versa, although it would take him many years to develop this connection into a coherent philosophy and theology of salvation history. Since the purpose of history is God's redemptive activity, Edwards faced the acute problem of how to demonstrate God's sovereignty and redemptive activity to an age in which scientific discoveries were bringing about the disenchantment of the world. More specifically, the most pressing issue was the reconstitution of the *series temporum* (the stage of time) as inseparable from God's redemptive plan. For, as Jürgen Moltmann wrote,

> if the rule of God is the scarlet thread running through the writings of the Old and New Testament, then the *mysterium salutis*—the mystery of salvation—is one and the same as the *mysterium gubernationis Dei*—the mystery of God's providence; for salvation is effected in a redemptive history in accordance with God's salvific plan.[53]

Edwards's efforts, then, were directed toward bringing together the mystery of salvation and history, the order of grace and the order of time, and thus to make history equivalent to God's plan for salvation and redemption.

In the traditional Christian interpretation of history, the whole space of time is pervaded with sacred, divine meaning; it is not uniform and empty, but endowed with sacred significance and prophetic revelation. This is especially true in regard to the future as a special dimension of time in which the all time drama of human salvation and redemption will be realized. "Until well into the sixteenth century, the history of Christianity is a history of expectations, or more exactly, the constant anticipation

---

[50] Edwards, *Miscellany* no. 38 (c. 1723), p. 221.
[51] Edwards, *History of the Work of Redemption*, p. 115.
[52] Edwards, *Miscellany* no. 702 (c. 1736), in *MISA*, p. 290.
[53] Moltmann, *The Coming of God*, p. 7.

of the End of the World on the one hand and the continual deferring of the End on the other." But this sense of time underwent a major change in early modern history. Between "1500 to 1800," the period "in which modernity is formed," according to Reinhart Koselleck, "historical time gained" more and more a "new quality" signified by the "temporalization of history," an important quality that "characterizes modernity."[54] One mark of modernity, among others, is the increasing difference between the "space of experience" and the "horizon of expectations."[55] Visions focused on what lay beyond and above history gradually declined, and a new consciousness of time arose regarding the historical process itself. At this period, instead of Christian vertical expectations placing the end of time *beyond* the confines of history, "there [was] an inversion in the horizon of expectations" for the fulfillment of human destiny within history.[56] Where the Christian ideology of history emphasized redemption *from*, and hence *beyond*, history, modern temporalization of history signified redemption *of* or *in* history, stressing human ability to bring about the perfecting of human nature, as well as of social and political institutions, within history itself. The structure of temporality was thus greatly modified and gained crucial importance in the process of history and the historical consciousness and imagination.

The transformation can be easily discerned in a comparison between Luther's and Robespierre's sense of time and vision of history. Profoundly convinced that the Protestant Reformation was situated at the end of time and history, Luther, in accordance with his eschatological expectations and apocalyptic visions, thought that when the world "was speeding" toward its end God "would shorten the final days." For him "the compression of time is a visible sign that, according to God's will, the Final Judgment is imminent, that the world is about to end." Two hundred and fifty years later, the historical imagination had changed drastically. Robespierre, leader of the French Revolution, believed that the "progress of human Reason has laid the basis for this great Revolution, and the particular duty of hastening it has fallen" upon human beings' actions and deeds. Thus, "the acceleration of time is a task of man leading to an epoch of freedom and happiness, the golden future" within this world and in history. The Christian conception of time, which assigned to God the ultimate role in history, gave way to the temporalization of history,

[54] Koselleck, "Modernity and the Planes of Historicity," in *Futures Past: On the Semantics of Historical Time*, pp. 5–7. For the debate concerning modernity, see Blumenberg, *The Legitimacy of the Modern Age*; and Jürgen Habermas, *The Philosophical Discourse of Modernity* (Cambridge, Mass.: MIT Press, 1993 [1985]).

[55] Koselleck, " 'Space of Experience' and 'Horizon of Expectations': Two Historical Categories," pp. 267–88.

[56] Koselleck, "Modernity and the Planes of Historicity," p. 7.

the belief that historical space constitutes a dimension of time in which human beings can achieve freedom and happiness. The Christian quest for redemption *from* history in order to reach the promise of eternal life that lay beyond it,[57] was gradually displaced in modern historical consciousness by the belief in redemption *of* or *in* history. In other words, the crucial change in historical imagination was the "setting free of a *historia humana* and the turning away from sacred history."[58] Facilitating this change was the gradual moving away from the theological explanation of history; "the seventeenth and eighteenth centuries" marked "the transformation of Christian Scripture, the legibility of religious cosmos, into pure 'representations' or 'superstitions' marginalized by an ethical and technical system of practices capable of building a human history."[59] History was increasingly liberated from the portrayal of "human history as the realization of a divine plan" and instead became a dimension of time for achieving human freedom and happiness.[60]

The eclipse of biblical narrative and its gradual detachment from historical occurrences also facilitated the transformation from sacred to human history in historical imagination. Hans Frei writes: "Western Christian reading of the Bible in the days before the rise of historical criticism in the eighteenth century was usually strongly realistic, i.e. at once literal and historical, and not only doctrinal or edifying. The words and sentences meant what they said, and because they did so they accurately described real events and real truths that were rightly put only in these terms and no others." Until the eighteenth century it was assumed, first, that if "a biblical story was to be read literally, it followed automatically that it referred to and described actual historical occurrences." Second, it was the accepted belief that "the several biblical stories narrating sequential segments in time must fit together into one narrative," and the "interpretive means for joining them" together into that one narrative "was to make earlier biblical stories figures or types of later stories and of their events and patterns of meaning." Third, not only did biblical "interpretation bec[o]me an imperative need," but over time it constantly incorporated "extra-biblical thought, experience, and reality into one real world detailed and made accessible by the biblical story." During the eighteenth

---

[57] See, for example, H. Richard Niebuhr: "To the Protestant . . . life seems a pilgrim's progress which, whether made solitarily or in company, proceeds through unpredictable contingencies and crises toward the destination beyond life and death where all the trumpets blow." Niebuhr, "The Protestant Movement and Democracy in the United States," I, p. 23.

[58] Koselleck, "Modernity and the Planes of Historicity," pp. 7, 9.

[59] Michel de Certeau, *The Writing of History* (New York: Columbia University Press, 1988 [1975]), p. xxvi.

[60] Gay, *The Enlightenment: The Science of Freedom*, p. 373.

century, this "overarching story," or this "mode of interpretation and the outlook it represented broke down with increasing rapidity." The process marked "the breakup of the cohesion between the literal meaning of the biblical narratives and their reference to actual events" in history; and it signified above all the "detachment of the 'real' historical world from its biblical description." From then on the "real events of history constitute an autonomous temporal framework of their own under God's providential design." The gradual liberation from the "overarching story" of biblical historical narrative, or the Christian philosophy of history, and the emergence of an "autonomous temporal framework," signified the growing legitimacy accorded to the historical process and to historical time.[61] No longer described as the realization of the divine plan, human history accorded its own legitimacy and validity was seen as that space of time in which human beings could exercise their autonomy.

What is important to our discussion is the gradual disunion between grace and time, redemption and history, hence the disenchantment of the historical time. History became increasingly blind to divine providence and indifferent to God's redemptive activity, and open to human existence and experience. Human life was freed from dependence on the transcendental aims and goals that lay beyond and above history; instead, history became a dimension of time in which human beings could realize freedom and autonomy.

It is in this wider context of the secular mode of historical thought that Edwards's goal in his construction of time may be placed. In response to Enlightenment historians' emphasis on the autonomy of human beings, along with their ability to realize their goals within history, Edwards endeavored to prove God's absolute power and will in controlling the course and passage of history. In the early 1720s, he developed the concept of God's work of redemption, a concept defining the close and essential relationship between redemption and history, arguing that history is inextricable from God's work of redemption and vice versa. Edwards sought to refute both the scientific concept of homogeneous, empty time and the Enlightenment notion of secular historical time. His philosophy of history signified that the whole of history is based upon God's redemptive activity; thus redemption is inseparable from the creation of the world and hence from the process and aim of history. For "the wisdom of God in creating the world," declared Edwards, is evident in that he "has created it for such an excellent use, to accomplish in it so glorious a work" as "this Work of Redemption."[62]

[61] Hans W. Frei, *The Eclipse of Biblical Narrative: A Study in Eighteenth and Nineteenth Century Hermeneutics* (New Haven: Yale University Press, 1974), pp. 1–5.
[62] Edwards, *History of the Work of Redemption*, p. 524.

Thus, whereas for the Enlightenment mind salvation has nothing to do with time and history, for Edwards the contrary was the case—there is no possible explanation of history without God's work of redemption. Salvation is inseparable from the fate of the universe in general, and that of human history in particular. There is no history without redemption and there is no redemption without history, because the mark of God's redemptive activity is not only the salvation of particular individuals, the elect, but also of "redeeming the time" as a whole.[63] God accomplishes his redemptive plan in history although its results lie beyond history. For the "greatest fruits" of the "Work of Redemption" are only manifested "after that," namely, after the end of history.[64] Thus, since history, or the mystery of salvation and redemption, has a transcendental goal and aim beyond itself, it is only with the final consummation of history that God's work of redemption will be fulfilled. Redemption *from* history was the mark of Edwards's singular mode of historical thought. For him there "is never redemption *in* history . . . but there is a history *of* redemption."[65]

History, Ideology, and Redemption

Responding to the changing climate of ideas in Europe, Edwards shaped his historical philosophy within the process in which the Christian ideology of history suffered steady decline in face of the new historical consciousness of the Enlightenment. In this sense, indeed, Edwards's enterprise in the sphere of time resembled much of his venture in constructing the dimension of space, his theology of nature. In both cases the threat to the traditional Christian mode of thinking led him to react with all his intellectual power. Yet the matter of constructing time and history proved much more difficult because from the beginning he found it necessary to establish a connection between the operation of saving grace in the personal experience of conversion, as the manifestation of God's redemptive activity in the soul, and the external, providential scheme of time, and to show that personal salvation was inextricable from sacred, providential history. Having found the evidence of saving grace during his moment of conversion, Edwards attempted to construe the whole space of time according to this saving experience. The outcome was the formation of a philosophy of history based upon divine agency in history.

Edwards's invention of an ideology of history signifies an important stage in the development of his thought: the move to define the power of

---

[63] Edwards, *The Preciousness of Time*, 1734, in *SDL*, p. 246.

[64] Ibid., p. 119.

[65] Miller, *Jonathan Edwards*, p. 314.

divine agency in shaping the historical process. His construction of the dimension of time is inseparable from the formation of his own religious self during his conversion, and the formation of his theology of nature, the constructing of the dimension of space, during the early 1720s. Edwards himself defined his quest as follows: the "very thing I now want, to give me a clearer and more immediate view of the perfections and glory of God, is as clear a knowledge of the manner of God's exerting himself, with respect to spirits and mind, as I have, of his operations concerning matter and bodies."[66] Yet, establishing a close and meaningful relationship between the dimensions of the spiritual and the spatial was not easy. Conversion illuminates the dynamism involved in the operation of saving grace in the soul, while the spatial dimension defines the ontological status of beings in space and not their teleological place in God's plan of redemption. To overcome this difficulty, Edwards formulated the concept of excellency. Arguing that only spiritual beings are real beings, he placed humans at the top of the great chain of being. The concept of excellency, however, defined only the structure of reality, or the order of being, and the ontological status of created, spiritual beings in the grand chain of being according to their relationship with God, but not yet their role in God's work of redemption. In contrast to mechanical philosophy's concept of a one-dimensional image of reality, Edwards's excellency established a hierarchical cosmological order in which created beings are attached or related to the supreme being.

What was obviously lacking was the dynamism entailed in the order of grace, the power of divine agency and redemptive activity in time and its relationship to history. In other words, Edwards's theology of nature referred to the essential nature of reality, but not to the nature of time or the meaning and goal of history. Nor did it account for the role of God as the Lord of history, or for the theological teleology of order inherent in history. Accordingly, in constructing the dimension of time, Edwards's main goal was to establish an association between redemptive activity in the soul and its manifestations in time. His aim was to transport the dynamism revealed in saving grace from the inner sphere of the soul into the whole realm of history, and thus to show the presence of God's redemptive activity within the whole of history.

Edwards embarked on the task of exploring the nature of time and the meaning of history shortly after his conversion moment. As he recalled in his *Personal Narrative*, following his conversion his "heart has been much on the advancement of Christ's Kingdom in the world. The histories of the past advancement of Christ's kingdom have been sweet to me." The conversion evidently led to the formation of a new historical conscious-

---

[66] Edwards, *Diary*, February 1725, p. 787.

ness, which entailed a search for books dealing with the emergence of Christ's kingdom: "When I have read histories of past ages, the pleasantest thing in all my reading has been, to read of the kingdom of Christ being promoted." His mind was "much entertained and delighted, with the Scripture promises and prophecies, of the future glorious advancement of Christ's kingdom on earth."[67] As is made evident in these passages, Edwards had cultivated a fascination not only with the millennial prophecies, but with history as such. Further evidence for his turn to history can be found in his *Notes on the Apocalypse*, of which the first entries were written "in late spring or early summer of 1723,"[68] as well as in the *Miscellanies* written in the early 1720s, where he began to struggle with the issue of God's "Work of Redemption."[69] It is not surprising that he adopted this concept since his thoughts were directed by a desire to prove God's redemptive activity in time. Here indeed one can find the genesis of Edwards's ideology of history. Faithful to his theistic metaphysics, he endeavored to understand the aim of God's redemptive activity in time. From his conversion experience he had learned that there is no salvation without conversion. Hence the connection he made between the effusion of the Spirit and revival, which constituted the core of his philosophy of salvation history.

Conversion, it should be recalled, is essentially association with sacred time: "Conversion and the rebirth of a new life change time and the experience of time, for they make-present the ultimate in the penultimate, and the future time in the midst of time."[70] Thus, whereas Edwards's construction of the nature of reality was confined to the spatial dimension of the material world, and had almost nothing to do with the fate of human beings in time and history—except for describing their highest place in the ontological hierarchy of created beings—his construction of the order of time illuminates the essential convergence between conversion and redemption. History, defined as God's work of redemption, deals with the inner movements or operations of conversion and salvation. Edwards's construction of time was thus a formidable task, aiming at nothing less than the establishment of a coherent relationship between the self and history.

An important dimension of Edwards's ideology of history was his striving to establish a close relationship between God's redemptive activity and the process of history. This was most clearly manifested when the theme of the wisdom of God in the work of redemption became more and

---

[67] Edwards, *Personal Narrative*, p. 800.
[68] Stein, introduction, in *AW*, p. 77.
[69] Edwards, *Miscellany* no. 38 (c. 1723), p. 221.
[70] Moltmann, *The Coming of God*, p. 22.

more significant in his writings.[71] His discourse attempts to describe the relationship between grace and time, God's redemptive activity within the boundaries of history and the role of creation in God's providence:

> There is doubtless some design that God is pursuing, and scheme that he is Carrying on, in the various changes and revolutions that from age to age happen in the world. . . . All revolutions from the beginning of the world to the end, are doubtless but various parts of one scheme, all conspiring for the bringing to pass the great event which is ultimately in view.[72]

Redemption and history are essentially intermingled because the ultimate mark of history is God's redemptive activity. Not only private conversion and salvation, but the whole internal dynamism behind all historical phenomena is evidence of God's redemptive plan from the beginning to the end of history.

Given that he lived in a Puritan religious culture that accorded high prominence to revivals and awakenings as a manifestation of God's saving grace,[73] it is not surprising that Edwards established an essential connection in his theology of history between religious revivals and salvation history. The "little revival" of 1734–35 at Northampton assisted him in reshaping his view of the relationship between grace and time, redemption and history.[74] In this saving event he found an important clue to the mystery of salvation history, or how God's redemptive activity and the general historical scheme of his work of redemption are manifested within the confines of history. The revival demonstrated to him that the operations of saving grace were inextricable from God's great design in time, and that they are not confined only to the private sphere of individual conversions. Redemption, in other words, concerns not only the realization of divine grace within the soul; it is inseparable from salvation history. Hence Edwards's claim that God's work of redemption in history should "be looked upon as the great end and drift of all Gods works & dispensations from the beginning & even the end of the work of creation it self."[75] Describing the work of redemption as the ultimate cause and reason for

---

[71] For the genesis and development of Edwards's concept of God's work of redemption, see Wilson, introduction, in *HWR*, pp. 13–16; and Ava Chamberlain, introduction, in *MISA*, pp. 29–34.

[72] Edwards, *Miscellany* no. 547 (c. 1731), pp. 93–94.

[73] An analysis of the rich religious culture of revivals and awakenings in New England can be found in Crawford, *Season of Grace*; Goen, introduction, in *GA*; Harry S. Stout, *The New England Soul: Preaching and Religious Culture in Colonial New England* (New York: Oxford University Press, 1986); and Heimert, *Religion and the American Mind*.

[74] According to Stein, in "no period was Edwards's public discretion on apocalyptic issues more evident than at the time of the surprising conversion in Northampton" during that revival. See Stein, introduction, in *AW*, p. 19.

[75] Edwards, *Miscellany* no. 702 (c. 1736), p. 284.

the creation of the world, Edwards found a clear and plausible historical agent—revival or awakening—by which to depict God's relationship with the historical process. The phenomenon of revival is evidence for the effusion of Holy Spirit and its immediate involvement in history, and for the power of God's hand in directing and controlling the affairs of human beings. God therefore is not only known through his structuring of the natural realm by abstract laws of nature, as some mechanical philosophers claimed, and the scope of his redemptive activity is not confined to the operation of saving grace in conversion, as some Protestant evangelical theologians held, but it constitutes the very foundation of creation and the historical process is grounded on it. Thus Edwards declared in 1739: "It may here be observed that from the fall of man to this day wherein we live the Work of Redemption in its effect has mainly been carried on by remarkable pourings out of the Spirit of God" at "special seasons of mercy," or revivals and awakenings.[76]

Revival thus represented the historical agent upon which Edwards could establish his ideology of history. God's redemptive activity in time is manifested through the effusion of the Spirit at religious awakenings throughout sacred, ecclesiastical history, such as the decisive revivals that took place during the "apostolical [sic] age," or in the time of "the [Protestant] Reformation" and the Great Awakening in New England, to name only a few.[77] Through the phenomenon of revival, therefore, Edwards could assert divine agency in time; it constituted the clue to and the main locus of God's work of redemption and hence of salvation history as a whole. Redemption and history are inextricable since, from the creation of the world to its end, God's redemptive power defines and directs the historical process. The search for God's power and will in creation led Edwards in the realm of space to show God's sovereignty through the agency of the atoms, and in the dimension of time to invoke God's work of redemption, according to which the historical process is determined by God's redemptive activity. In the world of nature this divine activity is asserted through the agency of the atoms, or through God's ordering and placing the atoms in their exact position, which is the essential condition of the perseverance of bodies; in the dimension of time it is affirmed through a series of historical turning points marked by an effusion of the Spirit of God as manifested in revivals and awakenings. In both dimensions Edwards strove to find an agent—the atom in the physical realm and revival in history—through which to affirm God's absolute sovereignty.

It is clear that in his reconstruction of time Edwards was not responding only to some provincial affairs in colonial New England, but to intellec-

---

[76] Edwards, *History of the Work of Redemption*, p. 143.
[77] Edwards, *Distinguishing Marks*, pp. 226, 245, 260.

tual developments in early-eighteenth-century Europe concerning the nature of time and the significance of history. Yet, he developed his redemptive mode of historical thought in order to reshape the notion of time in
a way most fitted to his own religious experience, namely, conversion and
revival. Since he lived in a Puritan culture that constantly sought for signs
of revivals and awakenings as a manifestation of God's saving grace, one
of the main themes of Edwards's philosophy of history became the association between religious revivals and salvation history. By placing the effusion of the Spirit and its historical manifestations in the form of revivals
at the center of the narrative of God's work of redemption, he transformed his own religious experience into a framework for sacred, salvation history, and thus could go on to describe the meaning of history
according to the rise and decline of revivals and awakenings throughout
the existence of the Christian church. He thus found a solution to the
breach in early-eighteenth-century historical thought between history and
redemption, and an answer to the dialectic of God's utter transcendence
and divine immanence in time and history. For him saving grace, as expressed in revivals, was the locus of history because only it could give
meaning to the passage of time and show the way to the eternal promise
that lay beyond history at the end of the world.

One of the great advantages of this historical explanation, of course, is
the link established between the self and history. In other words, in contrast to theories based upon the alienation between human actions and
impersonal historical forces, such as economics, or social and political
powers, for Edwards history is based upon a close and essential association between personal experience and historical events; God's redemptive
activity in religious revival affects the whole condition of human beings.
Hence the personal sphere is informed by God's saving and redemptive
grace. Individual existence again acquires a central role in history. Edwards thus overcomes the sense of alienation from history, and brings
about a reconciliation between God and humanity. Throughout his sermons on the *History of the Work of Redemption* (1739), Edwards thus
passionately pleaded with his audiences to assume their historical responsibility by taking an active part in understanding and advancing the sacred
cause of revival and redemption.

Edwards's Poetics of History

Study of Edwards's philosophy of history brings to mind H. Richard Niebuhr's famous remark in *The Kingdom of God in America* (1937), reserv-
ing for Jonathan Edwards together with St. Augustine a prominent place
among church historians because of their ability to reconstruct the history

of the Christian church in the midst of historical transformations within
the civilizations of their own time—Augustine during the fall of Rome
and Edwards in the eighteenth century.[78] Seen in this context, Edwards
was indeed an ecclesiastical historian of importance,[79] one who took on
himself the task of responding to the grave threats which he thought confronted Christianity during the early eighteenth century with the appearance during the Enlightenment of new scientific ideas, new modes of historical thought and moral philosophy, and the growth of deism[80] and
Arminianism.[81] It is necessary, therefore, to examine Edwards's philosophy of history within the wider context of the Christian ideology of history, and to show how his interpretation of salvation history constituted
a response to the changing circumstances in which the Christian church
then found itself. Placing Edwards's mode of historical thought in such a
wider context will contribute to the appreciation of him as a major church
historian who belongs to the rich tradition of ecclesiastical history extending from Eusebius and Augustine to the eighteenth century, and less
as an American theologian, whatever the term "America" may have signified in early-eighteenth-century colonial British North America.

   In recent years Hayden White's studies in the history of narrative have
considerably transformed our consciousness of the nature and structure
of historical discourse.[82] For, as he reminds us, "the historian has to inter-

   [78] See Niebuhr, *The Kingdom of God in America*, p. xiv: "My greatest hope is that such
a work [*The Kingdom of God in America*] as this may serve 'even as a stepping stone' to
the work of some American Augustine who will write a *City of God* that will trace the story
of the eternal city in its relation to modern civilization instead of to ancient Rome, or of
Jonathan Edwards *Redivivus* who will bring down to our time the *History of the Work of
Redemption*."
   [79] Today the common usage of the term "ecclesiastical history," or "church history,"
refers to the history of churches as institutions. The reader will immediately recognize, however, that in my use of the term "ecclesiastical history" throughout this study I am referring
to a coherent, well-defined Christian philosophy of salvation history (*Heilsgeschichte*).
Throughout the history of Christianity, this usage of ecclesiastical history to signify a mode
of historical thought, or a unique Christian ideology of salvation history, was common
among church historians. Therefore, in using the term "ecclesiastical history," or "church
history," to denote a Christian philosophy and ideology of history, I follow, for example,
such writers as Eusebius Pamphili, "the father of church history" (*Ecclesiastical History*,
323), John Foxe (*Acts and Monuments*, 1570), and Cotton Mather (*Magnalia Christi Americana*, 1702).
   [80] Edwards's response to deism can be found in McDermott, *Jonathan Edwards Confronts the Gods*.
   [81] The threat of Arminianism in early-eighteenth-century New England is discussed in C.
C. Goen's introduction, in *GA*, pp. 4–19.
   [82] Hayden White, "The Historical Text as Literary Artifact," in *The Writing of History:
The Literary Form and Historical Understanding*, ed., Robert H. Canary and Henry Kozicki
(Madison: University of Wisconsin Press, 1978), pp. 41–62; "The Structure of Historical
Narrative," *Clio* 1 (1972): 5–20; *Metahistory: The Historical Imagination in Nineteenth-*

pret his materials in order to construct the moving pattern of images in which the form of the historical process is to be mirrored" or understood.[83] The fact that Christians for many centuries (and even now) have profoundly believed in sacred, providential history based upon a universe of biblical imaginings and prophetic revelations should not prevent us from seeing that this Christian interpretation of salvation history is the ultimate example of the "Poetics of History," to use White's phrase; namely, "an imaginative construction of history in terms of 'plot-structure or mythos.' "[84] For historical narratives, or "the forms of historical representation"[85]—the story of the course and progress of time—"are not only models of past events and processes, but also metaphorical statements," which "endow" historical events "with culturally sanctioned meanings."[86] Historical narratives, therefore, should be understood as "symbolic structures" mediating "between the events reported" in them "and the generic plot-structures conventionally used in our culture to imbue unfamiliar events and situations with meanings."[87] This analysis of the nature of historical narrative would eventually lead to abolishing the distinction between historical narrative and fictional narrative, and would oblige us to consider the Christian interpretation of sacred, redemptive history together with its prophetic narrative as an example of the poetics of history, or as a great Christian theological poem.[88]

Edwards's redemptive mode of historical thought is indeed a model of Christian poetics of history. Writing against the mechanistic conception of a clockwork universe ruled by natural laws and against Enlightenment historical narratives that were coming to view God as external to history and human experience, and in fierce opposition to deism, which denounced revealed religion, and Arminianism, which opposed total depravity and salvation by grace alone, Edwards constructed a unique re-

---

Century Europe (Baltimore: Johns Hopkins University Press, 1973). (The term "The Poetics of History" appears in the title of White's introduction to *Metahistory*.) See also White's study, *The Content of the Form: Narrative Discourse and Historical Representation* (Baltimore: Johns Hopkins University Press, 1987). On the relationship between history and literature, see also Gossman, "History and Literature: Reproduction or Signification," in *The Writing of History*, ed. R. H. Canary et al., pp. 3–40. For narrative form in the cognitive process, see Louis O. Mink, "Narrative Form as a Cognitive Instrument," in *The Writing of History*, ed. R. H. Canary et al., pp. 129–50.

[83] White, "The Historical Text as Literary Artifact," p. 51.

[84] Ibid., p. 47.

[85] Ibid., p. 41.

[86] Ibid., p. 51.

[87] Ibid., p. 52.

[88] See, for example, Avihu Zakai, "The Poetics of History and the Destiny of Israel: The Role of the Jews in English Apocalyptic Thought during the Sixteenth and Seventeenth Centuries," *Journal of Jewish Thought and Philosophy* 5 (1996): 313–50.

demptive mode of historical thought—interpreting the whole of salvation history, and hence the history of the Christian church, primarily in light of God's redemptive activity in the form of "glorious revivals of religion"[89]—that emphasized his sovereignty over the world and his direct involvement in history: "And time after time," declared Edwards, "when religion seemed to be almost gone and it was come to the last extremity, then God granted a revival" and "poured out his spirit with . . . awakening providences."[90] This mode of thought dwells on the workings of God in terms of the effusion of his Spirit and its historical manifestations through religious revivals and dispensations throughout the history of the church. "It may here be observed that from the fall of man to this day wherein we live the Work of Redemption in its effects has mainly been carried on by remarkable pourings out of the spirit of God." And "the way in which the greatest things have been done towards carrying on this work always has been by remarkable pourings out of the Spirit at special seasons of mercy."[91] Thus, in accordance with the Enlightenment historians' belief that history exhibits unmistakable progress in terms of human life, Edwards's philosophy of history dwelt on progress as based ultimately upon God's "grand design"[92] for human salvation and redemption. For he believed that things "in their series and course in providence" clearly manifested "a progress towards a certain final issue of things, and every revolution brings nearer to that issue,"[93] or the accomplishment of God's work of redemption.

Religious revivals, then, constituted the main mark of the history of redemption, inaugurating a special dimension of sacred time, or "special seasons of mercy"[94] and grace, in which God's divine providence directly transformed human experience upon the earth and hence the course and progress of salvation history as a whole. Throughout the history of the church, revivals and awakenings signified that "God was pleased to grant a more large effusion of his Spirit for the bringing in an harvest of souls to Christ."[95] In contradistinction to traditional Christian interpretations of salvation history, which were based upon political, social, and religious changes and transformations regarding the fate of the church as a worldly institution, such as the rise and fall of empires, nations, and states, and the struggle against Antichrist, Edwards's philosophy of history and his interpretation of church history deal with religious revivals and dispensa-

---

[89] Edwards, *History of the Work of Redemption*, p. 457.

[90] Ibid., pp. 195, 190.

[91] Ibid., p. 143.

[92] Ibid., p. 121.

[93] Edwards, *Notes on Scripture*, 389 (1739), p. 375.

[94] Edwards, *History of the Work of Redemption*, p. 143.

[95] Ibid.

tions as the ultimate manifestations of God's redemptive activity in time; the locus of salvation history is situated in religious revivals within the history of the Christian church and their manifestation within the individual soul. Hence redemptive history does not deal with social and political institutions, but with religious revival and awakening aiming at the restoration of corrupted human nature. There is an essential relationship between the self and the history of God's work of redemption. "Man's soul was ruined by the fall, the image of God was ruined, man's nature corrupted and destroyed, and man became dead in sin. The design [of the work of redemption] was to restore the soul of man in conversion and to restore life to it, and the image of God in conversion and to carry on the restoration in sanctification, and to perfect it in glory."[96] Viewing providential history in light of religious revivals and awakenings taking place within the church, from the fall to the end of the world, Edwards's redemptive history sought to rescue the Christian conception of salvation history from the menace of the mechanistic, scientific worldview and the Enlightenment conception of *historia humana*, and thus to restore sacred meaning and significance to human life and experience upon earth.

The uniqueness of Edwards's philosophy of history becomes clear when we compare his redemptive mode of historical thought with the formulations of church historians who wrote in different historical and ideological contexts.[97] There are indeed many similarities between Edwards's and St. Augustine's assumptions regarding the meaning and goal of history; both held that the culmination of the redemptive process would be realized only *beyond* time and history. Both believed in redemption *from* history and not *in* history. After the sack of Rome in 410, Augustine preached to his fellow Christians in Carthage: "Citizens of Jerusalem, O God's own people, O Body of Christ, O high-born race of foreigners on earth—you do not belong here, you belong somewhere else."[98] And Edwards, preaching to his congregation in Northampton during the 1730s, echoed almost word-for-word Augustine's sermon of more than 1,300 years earlier when he said:

[96] Ibid., p. 124.

[97] Among the studies concerned with the Christian view of history, see Langdon Gilkey, *Reaping the Whirlwind: A Christian Interpretation of History* (New York: Seabury, 1976); Gerhart B. Ladner, *The Idea of Reform: Its Impact on Christian Thought and Action in the Age of the Fathers* (Cambridge, Mass.: Harvard University Press, 1959); Bultmann, *History and Eschatology*; Moltmann, *The Coming of God*; C. A Patrides, *The Phoenix and the Ladder: The Rise and Decline of the Christian View of History* (Berkeley: University of California Press, 1964); idem, *The Grand Design of God: The Literary Form of the Christian View of History* (London: Routledge and Kegan Paul, 1972); and Richard Sorabji, *Time, Creation and the Continuum: Theories in Antiquity and the Early Middle Ages* (Ithaca: Cornell University Press, 1983).

[98] Brown, *Augustine of Hippo*, pp. 313–14.

This world is not our abiding place. Our continuance here is but very short. Man's days on earth, are as a shadow. . . . It was never designed by God that this world should be our home. . . . The future world was designed to be our settled and everlasting abode. There it was intended that we should be fixed; and there alone is a lasting habitation, and a lasting inheritance.[99]

But there are essential differences between Edwards's and Augustine's philosophies of history, due to the different historical and ideological contexts in which they constructed their sense of time and vision of history. These concern the issues of the "deeschatological process,"[100] the millennium, and the possibility of human progress within history. Edwards, who rejected Augustine's dissociation of history and prophecy, redemption and history, denied the gradual displacement of sacred prophetic revelations, such as Christ's second coming, from this world to "the world to come," making eschatology and apocalypse stand outside the boundaries of history—which Augustine advocated.[101] Consequently, while Au-

---

[99] Edwards, *The Christian Pilgrim*, in *Jonathan Edwards: Representative Selections*, ed. Clarence H. Faust and Thomas H. Johnson, p. 130.

[100] The process of deeschatologization in early Christianity is related to the major changes introduced by the fathers of the church from Eusebius to Augustine into the Christian philosophy of history, especially concerning the apocalyptic and eschatological dimensions of history and the nature and meaning of the millennium. See Alfred Braunthal, *Salvation and the Perfect Society* (Amherst: University of Massachusetts Press, 1979); and Zakai and Mali, "Time, History and Eschatology," pp. 393–417. For studies dealing with the reemergence of eschatological visions and apocalyptic and millennial expectations, as well as with apocalyptic thought and apocalyptic imagery, from early Christianity to the Protestant Reformation, see Bernard McGinn, *Vision of the End: Apocalyptic Traditions in the Middle Ages* (New York: Columbia University Press, 1979), and "John's Apocalypse and the Apocalyptic Mentality," in *The Apocalypse in the Middle Ages*, ed. Richard K. Emmerson and Bernard McGinn (Ithaca: Cornell University Press, 1992), pp. 3–19; Marjorie Reeves, *The Influence of Prophecy in the Later Middle Ages: A Study in Joachimism* (Oxford: Oxford University Press, 1969), and *Joachim of Fiore and the Prophetic Future* (London: SPCK, 1976); Norman Cohn, *The Pursuit of the Millennium: Revolutionary Millenarians and Mystical Anarchists in the Middle Ages* (New York: Oxford University Press, 1961); Robert Lerner, *The Power of Prophecy: The Cedar of Lebanon Vision from the Mongol Onslaught to the Dawn of the Enlightenment* (Berkeley: University of California Press, 1983); Robert Lerner, "Medieval Prophecy and Religious Dissent," *Past and Present* 72 (August 1976): 3–24, and "The Black Death and Western European Eschatological Mentalities," *American Historical Review* 86 (June 1981): 533–52; Richard K. Emmerson, *Antichrist in the Middle Ages: A Study of Medieval Apocalypticism, Art and Literature* (Seattle: University of Washington Press, 1981), and "The Apocalypse in Medieval Culture," in *The Apocalypse in the Middle Ages*, ed. Richard K. Emmerson and Bernard McGinn, pp. 293–332; Barbara Nolan, *The Gothic Visionary Perspective* (Princeton: Princeton University Press, 1977); Austin Farrer, *A Rebirth of Images: The Making of St. John's Apocalypse* (New York: SUNY Press, 1986 [1949]); Frank Kermode, *The Sense of Ending: Studies in the Theory of Fiction* (Oxford: Oxford University Press, 1967).

[101] Zakai and Mali, "Time, History and Eschatology," pp. 393–417.

gustine's millennium already takes place in history within the boundaries of the established church and is devoid of eschatological significance and apocalyptic meaning, for Edwards this glorious period is yet to come in the future.[102] In contrast to Augustine, who denied any room for human improvement within history, Edwards's redemptive process featured human progress as intrinsic to redemptive history—through the mechanism of religious revivals, greater understanding of sacred, prophetic revelation, further advancement of learning, growth of knowledge, and so forth.[103]

Peter Brown points out that there are "no verbs of historical movement in the *City of God*, no sense of progress to be achieved in history," and it appears from Augustine's writings that "the most obvious feature of man's life in this *saeculum* is that it is doomed to remain incomplete."[104] According to Robert Markus, to Augustine's mind profane, secular history was devoid of any significance: "Since the coming of Christ, until the end of the world, all history is homogeneous . . . it cannot be mapped out in terms of a pattern drawn from sacred history . . . [and] it can no longer contain decisive turning-points endowed with significance in sacred history."[105] Edwards's redemptive mode of historical thought, however, endowed history with sacred meaning by defining revival as the locus of history and awakening as the main agent in the historical process. Furthermore, understanding progress within history in terms of conversion and awakening, he defined history as a span of time in which the drama of salvation and redemption is played out before the end of the world.

Edwards's philosophy of history shows that he was a true heir of sixteenth- and seventeenth-century Protestant and Puritan historiography, which was founded upon an apocalyptic interpretation of history, although he radically transformed some of its basic assumptions.[106] Ed-

---

[102] For Edwards's views of the millennium and the progress entailed in this period from the point of view of the advancement of human learning and enlightenment, see, among others, *Miscellany* no. 26 (c. 1723), in *MIS*, pp., 212–13; *Miscellany* no. 262 (c. 1726), p. 369; *Miscellany* 351 (1728), pp. no. 426–27; and *Miscellany* no. 613, in *MISA*, pp.145–46. See as well Edwards's discussion of the millennium in *History of the Work of Redemption*, especially pp. 471–86, and in *Notes on the Apocalypse* and *An Humble Attempt*, both in *AW*.

[103] See especially *Miscellany* no. 26 (1723). However, it should be noted that Edwards's religious concept of progress is clearly different from that of the Enlightenment, which rejected an absolutely supernatural or an absolutely super-historical sphere above and beyond history.

[104] Brown, "Saint Augustine," p. 11.

[105] Markus, *Saeculum: History and Society in the Theology of St. Augustine*, pp. 20–21.

[106] For general studies dealing with the development of Protestant historiography during the sixteenth century, see A. G. Dickens, *The Reformation in Historical Thought* (Cambridge, Mass.: Harvard University Press, 1985); Donald R. Kelley, *Foundations of Modern*

wards inherited the quest to establish the closest possible link between prophecy and history, as can be seen in his various apocalyptic writings,[107] thus constructing the dimension of history as intrinsic to prophecy and vice versa. Yet, in contrast to the Protestant assumption that the historical process is based ultimately on social, political, and ecclesiastical changes, such as the struggle against the Church of Rome, Edwards held that the principal source governing the historical process is God's redemptive plan, the pouring out of the Spirit of God, as made evident in revival and awakening—that is, a spiritual experience of saving grace and its embodiment in decisive historical moments in the history of the Christian church rather than external historical transformations. On the other hand, in contrast to New England Puritan historians who construed the Puritan migration to America during the seventeenth century as a great eschatological and apocalyptic event, establishing an essential gulf between the Old and New Worlds, Edwards abandoned the vision of the glorious New World in providential history.[108] The redemptive process concerned all Protestants, regardless of their location. For example, Edwards understood the Great Awakening in New England as inseparable from the wider transatlantic Protestant awakening of the early eighteenth century, or other revivals taking place at the time in the Protestant world in Europe, such as the "remarkable reviving of religion" in "Saxony"[109] and "the narrative" of God's "glorious work" in the revival in Kilsyth, Scotland, 1740.[110] In other words, Edwards rejected the eschatology and

---

Historical Scholarship: Language, Law and History in the French Renaissance (New York: Columbia University Press, 1970); Rubin B. Barnes, *Prophecy and Gnosis: Apocalypticism in the Wake of the Lutheran Reformation* (Stanford: Stanford University Press, 1988); Zakai, *Exile and Kingdom*; idem, "Reformation, History and Eschatology in English Protestantism," *History and Theory* 26 (October 1987): 300–318; and idem, "The Poetics of History and the Destiny of Israel," pp. 313–50.

[107] These works, which include *Notes of the Apocalypse*, *An Humble Attempt*, and more, appeared in Edwards, *AW*.

[108] For studies dealing with the apocalypse and eschatology of the Puritan migration to America, see Theodore D. Bozeman, *To Live Ancient Lives: The Primitivist Dimension in Puritanism* (Chapel Hill, 1988); Philip Gura, *A Glimpse of Zion's Glory: Puritan Radicalism in New England, 1620–1660* (Middletown: Wesleyan University Press, 1984); Avihu Zakai, *Exile and Kingdom*, and *Theocracy in Massachusetts: Reformation and Separation in Early Puritan New England* (New York: Mellen University Press, 1994). For recent studies dealing with Puritan historiography in New England, see Stephen Carl Arch, *Authorizing the Past: Rhetoric of History in Seventeenth Century New England* (DeKalb: Northern Illinois University Press, 1994); and Michael P. Winship, *Seers of God: Puritan Providentialism in the Restoration and the Early Enlightenment* (Baltimore: Johns Hopkins University Press, 1996).

[109] Edwards, *Much in Deeds of Charity*, p. 210; *Some Thoughts Concerning the Revival*, in *GA*, p. 528.

[110] Edwards, "To the Rev. James Rose," May 12, 1743, in *LPW*, p. 108.

apocalypse of the Puritan migration to, and experience in, New England, and the Puritan tendency to glorify New England as the vanguard of redemptive history;[111] instead, he argued that the history of the Christian church in general was radically transformed through a series of decisive religious revivals taking place from the fall to the end of the world. As we will see later, out of this conception Edwards reconstructed the whole history of the Christian church upon earth in his *History of the Work of Redemption* (1739).

Ecclesiastical History as a Mode of Christian Historical Thought

To understand more fully the formation of Edwards's singular redemptive mode of historical thought, and hence his attack on Enlightenment narratives of history, based on the concept of secular, historical time, which posed a threat to the traditional theological teleology of history, it is necessary to examine the tradition of Christian historical writings to which he belongs and his particular contribution to it. As with his construction of space and the nature of reality, where his philosophical and theological interests reached well beyond the narrow intellectual life of colonial British North America, in formulating his ideology of history Edwards addressed himself to the broader issues of the contemporary philosophy of history rather than to the limited, provincial historiography of New England. He was not Cotton Mather, who wrote the *Magnalia Christi Americana*, "the ecclesiastical history of New England," in the attempt to delineate the origins of the Puritan migration to New England by finding its cause in the flight of the true church, or the "church of the wilderness," into the American wilderness.[112] Edwards had no need for such justification; more than one hundred years later he accepted the existence of Puritan New England at face value. He thus strove to compose a universal ecclesiastical history, or a general history of the Christian church, where New England would play only a small role. Hence, we must examine the broader ideological and theological notion of ecclesiastical history as a unique mode of Christian historical thought, for the full meaning of Edwards's construction will emerge only within this wider context of Christian historical writing.

---

[111] Edwards's radical departure from the eschatology and apocalypse of Puritan New England is discussed in McDermott's study, *One Holy and Happy Society: The Public Theology of Jonathan Edwards*, especially chapters I and II.

[112] Cotton Mather, *Magnalia Christi Americana, or, the Ecclesiastical History of New England* (London, 1702). For the Puritans' identification of their migration to New England with the prophetic symbol of the church of the wilderness, see Zakai, *Exile and Kingdom*, pp. 143–206.

To appreciate Edwards's ideology of history, one must consider the formation of a specifically Christian mode of historical thought, the philosophy of salvation history—*Heilsgeschichte*, the revelation of God's plan of salvation and redemption through the annals of sacred ecclesiastical history. With the conversion of Constantine, making Christianity the official faith of the Roman Empire during the fourth century, Christians developed the idea of church history as a mode of thought according to which the whole of history is explained exclusively in light of the progress of the Christian church. The establishment of ecclesiastical history as a new mode of historical thought coincided with the transformation of Christianity from a persecuted sect into the official church and faith of the Roman Empire. As Christianity became predominant in the Western world, ecclesiastical history constituted the most important and dominant mode of historical interpretation in Christian Europe until the Enlightenment of the eighteenth century.

"The story of the development of man's consciousness of history," wrote Herbert Butterfield, "involves a large-scale aspect of the whole evolution of his experience. It is a major part of his attempt to adjust himself to the world in which his life is set."[113] This comment may offer a useful point of departure for an examination of the development of the Christian philosophy of history. In such a system of thought the church is the main agent in history, and history is perceived as evolving during time mainly in light of the progress of the church, or God's chosen people, in the world. Ecclesiastical history is sacred history, for it concerns the divine dispensation of God and his revelatory redemptive acts, or more precisely, the whole of Christ's divine economy of salvation and redemption on earth.[114]

Ecclesiastical history constituted the dominant mode of historical thought from the rise of Christianity to predominance in the Western world during the fourth century until "the secularization of theological teleology of history" announced by the Enlightenment of the eighteenth.[115] "Any history written on Christian principles," wrote R. G. Col-

---

[113] Herbert Butterfield, *The Origins of History* (London: Methuen, 1981), p. 14.

[114] On the development of the Christian philosophy of history, or ecclesiastical history, see H. Butterfield, *The Origins of History*, and *Christianity and History* (London: Bell, 1960); J. Daniélou, *History of Early Christian Doctrine before the Council of Nicaea*, 3 vols. (London: Longmans, 1964); Markus, *Saeculum: History and Society in the Theology of St. Augustine*, and *From Augustine to Gregory the Great* (London: Variorum Reprints, 1983); R. G. Collingwood, *The Idea of History* (Oxford: Oxford University Press, 1961); Gilkey, *Reaping the Whirlwind*; and Karlfried Froehlich, "Church History and the Bible," in *Biblical Hermeneutics in Historical Perspective*, ed. Mark S. Burrows and Paul Rorem (Grand Rapids: Eerdmans, 1991), pp. 1–18.

[115] Bultmann, *History and Eschatology*, p. 65.

lingwood, "will be of necessity universal, providential, apocalyptic, and periodized."[116] Ecclesiastical history, by its very nature as the history of the progress of the Christian church upon the earth, is obviously the supreme example of this mode of historical thought. It is universal history, inasmuch as the church claims universal validity for its teaching of the gospel of salvation and redemption, appealing to the whole world and not to one particular nation, dealing with the origins of human beings and the universal promise of God, with creation and the end of history. Since ecclesiastical history considers the church to be the central agency in the providential drama of human salvation and redemption, it has no particularistic center such as race, nation, or people. Ecclesiastical history is providential history because it espouses the belief that the whole universe is a theocratic one ruled directly and immediately by God; hence, history is God's domain, a space of time regulated and controlled by God's divine providence, a play preordained and directed by his hand. It is periodized, because it is divisible into past, present, and future according to sacred prophetic revelations. These epochs in God's all-embracing providence include the period before Christ, that after his first coming, and that which is to unfold after the anticipated second coming. Finally, ecclesiastical history is apocalyptic, dealing with sacred revelations based on visions in the New Testament, especially in the book of Revelation, and founded upon the belief in providence and the anticipation of the fulfillment of divine prophecies and revelations. Because it progresses in a continuum from historical revelation to the future unveiling glory, from the promise made in Christ's first coming to its realization in the second coming, each age comes to perceive this apocalyptic and eschatological dimension of history differently.

Founded upon a coherent Christian conception of history, or more precisely, upon a historical economy of salvation, ecclesiastical history is a system of thought in which history is defined exclusively as the story of salvation and redemption, comprising a special dimension of sacred space and time in which progress is made from promise to fulfillment, from prophecy to realization. Unlike secular history, which deals with people, societies, and institutions during time, sacred history deals with the unfolding of God's plan of salvation. Indeed, all history, secular and sacred, displays the workings of God's providence. Yet it is only sacred, ecclesiastical history that ascribes meaning and significance to historical events in the divine scheme of salvation. The basis of sacred, redemptive history is therefore the biblical narrative of God's work among his chosen people, the promise made in the Old Testament and the fulfillment in the New, as

---

[116] Collingwood, *The Idea of History*, p. 49.

well as the prophetic revelations concerning Christ's second coming and the transformation of the world into the kingdom of God.

At the center of ecclesiastical or salvation history stands Christ, the focus of church history. It is through faith in Christ and by belonging to the church—his symbolic body on earth—that the believer can secure participation in salvation. Moreover, since Christ's first coming is perceived as a historical revelation, all of history prior to his arrival becomes infused with meaning, and all subsequent history is seen to bear his mark until the anticipated second coming—an event signifying the end of time and history. With the first coming, Christ entered time and history as the Son of God; his second coming is inseparable from occurrences within time or developments in the history of the church.

The church, as the spiritual body of Christ, necessarily assumes a central place in the history of salvation, since until the second coming history is determined by the revelation of Christ as embodied in the church and its faith. Further, since the process of history has a real significance and meaning in ecclesiastical history, history becomes a divine epic, stretching back in time to creation and pointing forward to that magnificent event of the transformation of the world into the kingdom of God and his Son Christ. For throughout the vicissitudes of time and history since the fall, God's providence has selected, elected, and predestined certain people to restore humanity and reconcile it with its Creator. In this divine epic of salvation and redemption the expulsion from Eden (as, for example, St. Augustine argued) marked the beginning of sacred, providential history, whose essential feature is the apocalyptic struggle between the "city of God," or the church, and the "city of Satan."

Within the context of ecclesiastical history the church thus becomes the necessary, perhaps even the main, instrument of salvation without which there is no grace and without which Christ's second coming is unimaginable; and which is, consequently, essential to the transformation of the world into the kingdom of God. In this divine economy of salvation— that is, the historical process of human salvation and redemption in which humanity sins against God and God is willing to redeem it—the history of the church (hence the term "ecclesiastical history," or "church history") has a most prominent place. By denying any possibility of salvation outside itself (*extra ecclesiam nulla salus*), the church thus transformed itself into the primary means through which humankind, alienated from God, could become reconciled with him. Ecclesiastical history is based on the notion of human sin and divine saving grace; for without sin and redemption, history, as the space of time from the fall to Christ's second coming, has no meaning.

Ecclesiastical history, then, is essentially the story of attempts to reconcile the fallen world with God—with the church as the central agency in the drama of human salvation. It is a history that deals with the vicissitudes of the church during time—its struggles, persecutions, and triumphs. And indeed in Christian historiography this focus became the very theme of history itself. To be more precise, within ecclesiastical history, earthly events are significant only insofar as they relate to the sacred history of the church. However, in this Christian scheme of time and history, past and present events obtain their full meaning not only in relation to the history of the church, but mainly and more fundamentally in relation to the eschatological future and the decisive apocalyptic event of salvation and redemption that is to transpire at the end of time and history. The apocalyptic and eschatological revelation of God at the close of history, the culminating event in which his glory is proclaimed along with the salvation of the elect, is the stated goal of ecclesiastical history. Thus, it is only in relation to this eschatological scenario that historical events acquire their significance.

The relation between sacred, prophetic revelation and the goal of history is the main concern of ecclesiastical history. From the beginning of time the grand design of God's miraculous providence has been unfolding, a divine scheme directing, conditioning, and controlling every event in history. History, therefore, is linear and teleological. The task of ecclesiastical history is to record and illuminate the sacred, providential, and redemptive course of events in the history of salvation. The past is perceived as replete with symbols and prophecies pointing to the glorious future, Christ's second coming, the millennium, the kingdom of God, the heavenly city of God—the New Jerusalem. These eschatological and apocalyptic visions and symbols appear in Revelation, and it was through this work of Christian "eschatological fiction"[117] that Christians learned how to interpret the meaning of their time in the general context of salvation history.

Edwards's redemptive mode of historical thought should be considered within this wider context of Christian historical philosophy, for his construction of the redemptive process in time and history took shape within the larger tradition of Christian interpretation of salvation history. Yet, as with other ecclesiastical historians throughout the centuries, Edwards wrote within a specific context which informed the content and form of his philosophy of history and contributed to the formation of his redemptive mode of historical thought.

[117] Kermode, *The Sense of Ending: Studies in the Theory of Fiction*, p. 35.

The Protestant and Puritan Ideology of History

Before the Protestant Reformation of the sixteenth century, Christian philosophy of history was largely grounded upon the legacy of the fathers of the church, most notably St. Augustine, whereby eschatology and apocalypse were removed from the process of history, and the entire culmination of the redemptive process was placed beyond time. The fulfillment of sacred prophecies and revelations—such as Christ's second coming, his millennial role with his saints upon earth, and the transformation of the world into the kingdom of God, at first considered an intrinsic dimension of history itself, as reflected in the chiliastic expectations of early Christianity[118]—was sought outside the boundaries of history. During the patristic period, this deeschatologization process gradually displaced Christ's second coming from the stage of this world to the world to come and irrevocably separated prophecy from history. No longer considered an intrinsic part of the historical process, eschatological revelation receded into some undefined realm outside the boundaries of history. Thus, the eschatological day of judgment inaugurating Christ's second coming and the millennium itself, was removed from the dimension of history and was no longer considered a historical event.[119]

From Augustine to the late Middle Ages, the Christian doctrine of salvation history tended to play down the historical significance of the apocalyptic scheme of history, or the apocalyptic mode of historical thought, especially as regards Christ's second coming and his millennial role with his saints upon earth. Following Augustine, church authorities held that although the advent of Christ indeed marked a new dispensation in the history of salvation and redemption, yet the promise of eschatological salvation had nothing to do with the course and progress of history. Again following Augustine, the Church of Rome assumed the sole means and modes of salvation; no essential transformations would occur in history until the last judgment. This attitude changed profoundly with the Protestant Reformation of the sixteenth century.

In the ecclesiastical and theological controversies surrounding the Reformation and Counter-Reformation during the sixteenth century, Protestants turned increasingly to history, to the study of past events and the interpretation of their significance, to find meaning for the Reformation within sacred, providential history. The pursuit of religious reformation led to the creation of a particular mode of historical thought: Protestant historiography based on an apocalyptic interpretation of history, or on an apocalyptic mode of historical thought. Based on a close correlation between history and prophecy, Protestant historiography was primarily characterized by an apocalyptic view of history, which in turn gave rise to a new form of historical consciousness. Not only did the study of history become a crucial dimension of the religious wars that the Protestants waged against the Church of Rome, but the whole attitude toward profane, secular history radically changed from what had been traditionally accepted in Christianity. Protestant historiography was based upon a historical interpretation of prophecies and it stressed the apocalyptic scheme of events, that is, that the Apocalypse was to be regarded as the sole guide to history. In this context the Protestant Reformation was situated at the end of time and history, as an eschatological event preceding that moment when the whole mystery of providential history would be resolved.[120]

The Protestant Reformation initiated a most revolutionary transformation in the Christian philosophy of history. Not content with the restitution of the power of God in religious faith and experience, the Protestant reformers strove also to restore God's glory and his absolute sovereignty in a theocentric universe and to return to him his direct role within time and history. By viewing history as the proper domain of the "theatre of God's judgment,"[121] as the dimension of time which is the subject of divine revelation, the Reformation gave rise to a new historical consciousness based upon a close reading of scripture and its correlation to historical events. Directed by the literal rather than the allegorical interpretation of divine prophecy, the Protestants turned to history in order to explain the historical process in light of God's word, endeavoring to prove that it was the force of God's hand which directed the course of historical events and the progress of history. Protestant historiography may be characterized as an apocalyptic mode of historical thought that viewed history as a dimension of time subject to prophecy. In it eschatology and apocalypse— and hence the millennium—were once again firmly situated within the boundaries of time and history. Within this prophetic and redemptive in-

---

[120] For general studies of Protestant historiography, see Dickens, *The Reformation in Historical Thought*; James W. Thompson, *History of Historical Writings*, 2 vols. (New York: Macmillan, 1942); Denys Hay, *Annalists and Historians: Western Historiography from the Eighth to the Eighteenth Centuries* (London: Methuen, 1977); Harry E. Barnes, *A History of Historical Writings* (New York: Dover, 1962); Ernst Breisach, *Historiography: Ancient, Medieval & Modern* (Chicago: University of Chicago Press, 1983); Kelley, *Foundations of Modern Historical Scholarship: Language, Law, and History in the French Renaissance*.

[121] According to Philip Melanchthon, "the world is God's theatre in which he displays examples of all our duties." Quoted from A. G. Dickens, *The German Nation and Martin Luther* (London: Edward Arnold, 1974), p. 205. See also Thomas Beard, *The Theatre of God's Judgments* (London, 1621). Beard was Oliver Cromwell's schoolmaster.

terpretation of history, the Reformation itself stood at the end of time, as a great revelatory and eschatological event preceding that moment when the whole mystery of salvation history would be revealed. "Much more than Catholics or Calvinists," according to a recent study, "Lutherans kept alive" eschatological visions and millennial expectations "that had characterized the late Middle Ages." Luther especially "believed in the imminence of the end of the world and the Last Judgment; [and] this belief was widely shared among his colleagues and followers." Moreover, "For Luther, Christ stood poised to return, to deliver his own, and to deal the final blow to a corrupt world. The faithful could rejoice in the recovery of God's Word and the nearness of their salvation."[122] Protestants' attitudes toward history were shaped by an apocalyptic and eschatological imagination: they discovered Antichrist in the bosom of the Church of Rome; they were fearful of the Turks and other enemies of the gospel who were threatening to destroy Christendom; they identified the Turkish invasion of Europe with the advent of Gog and Magog. They saw themselves living in the final stage of providential history, a sacred eschatological time when the whole drama of salvation and redemption would be finally resolved. Thus, while Satan and his minions were ravaging the earth, Protestants believed that Christ's second coming was imminent, and that his saints would be delivered.

With Protestant historiography, then, eschatology and apocalypse—and hence the millennium—were again brought within the boundaries of time and history. This approach brought about a radical change in the Christian attitude toward history, as exemplified by Augustine. Divine providence, Augustine believed, is concerned with salvation, not with history as such, and therefore the intrinsic dualism characterizing the historical process, the struggle between the heavenly and profane cities, would be resolved only beyond time and history. Firmly intertwined with one another in history, these two cities signified by their contest the essence of history and the immanent feature of the historical process.[123] History is the arena in which the struggle between the two cities takes place, and only on the eschatological day of judgment will it be resolved. An integral part of this dualistic view of history is Augustine's conception of *saeculum*, or secular history, and of man's existence in the world.

The most obvious feature of man's life in this *saeculum* is that it is doomed to remain incomplete. No human potentiality can ever reach its fulfillment in it; no human tension can ever be resolved. The fulfillment of human personality lies beyond it; it is infinitely postponed to the end of time, to the Last Day and the glorious resurrection.[124]

---

[122] Barnes, *Prophecy and Gnosis*, pp. 261, 3.
[123] Harrison, *Augustine: Christian Truth and Fractured Humanity*, pp. 195–222.
[124] Brown, "Saint Augustine," p. 11.

History, devoid of human progress, was regarded by Augustine as without meaning, and his attitude toward history, and hence the world, was
based upon alienation from it, and not upon reconciliation. It is within
this context that the revolutionary character of Protestant historiography
is most striking. With its apocalyptic orientation to history and strict correlation between history and prophecy, Protestant historiography infused
the *saeculum* with divine significance, thereby transforming the role
which the world and secular history assumed in sacred, providential history. This mode of thought first of all bears witness to the increasing belief
in human ability to comprehend history. Second, by incorporating the
saeculum into the framework of sacred history, Protestant historiography
abolished the Augustinian dualistic view of history. Eschatology and
apocalypse, excluded from time and history by pre-Reformation church
thought, were thus reestablished within the boundaries of history and
made intrinsic to the historical process; divine providence was conceived
as working out through and within history. Finally, human existence in
the world, and especially the saints' role in history, was changed from
that of alienation from the world to active participation within it. With
history situated in the dimension of divine prophecy, God's people, as
Christ's army, took their stand beside him, to play their singular role in
the unfolding drama of human salvation.

This approach is especially conspicuous in England, where the development of Protestant historiography during the sixteenth and seventeenth
centuries led to the creation of a singular interpretation of English national history in which the Church of England, thanks to its apostolic
origins, was to play a central role in the final stage of providential history,
which began with the Reformation. Expectations ran high among Protestants that the Reformation in England would reveal the full significance
of the nation's singular mission in providential history. Further, by adapt-
ing the premises of the Protestant apocalyptic interpretation of history,
English reformers claimed that pure apostolic Christianity had been trans-
ferred intact to England well before the intrusion of the Church of Rome
during the seventh century. Thus, it was the Church of England that was
founded upon apostolic origins, and Rome was the usurper. From this
point of view, English history appeared as an unending apocalyptic struggle of the pure English Church and monarchy against Rome's appropria-
tion of regal and ecclesiastical powers.

From the beginning of the English Reformation, the search for religious
reform "stimulated a patriotic interest in the past as well as a desire to
justify the break with Rome."[125] From the outset of the English Reformation, "the new learning of humanists was put to the test of political and

---

[125] J. R. Hale, *The Evolution of British Historiography* (London and Melbourne: Macmillan, 1967), p. 11.

theological debate." "Increasingly, after the 1530s," or when the official break with the Church of Rome took place, "scholars and statesmen turned to history to justify the ways of church and state to Englishmen."[126] Due to the special conditions of the Reformation in England as a national movement aiming to free both state and church from papal usurpation, ecclesiastical controversies in England "became more consciously historical," as the Protestants "made purposeful use of history for specific polemical ends."[127] What eventually emerged in Tudor and Stuart England was "a unified Protestant literary tradition,"[128] and in particular a distinct mode of historical thought—the English Protestant "apocalyptic tradition,"[129] based upon an apocalyptic view of English history and coming to define the Reformation in England in eschatological and apocalyptic terms. This tradition exercised enormous influence on the English Reformation, especially from Elizabeth's accession to the throne up to and during the Puritan Revolution of the seventeenth century. Perhaps the ablest and certainly the most influential apocalyptic writer in Protestant England was John Foxe, the author of *Acts and Monuments*, usually called the *Book of Martyrs* (1563).[130] In the hands of this martyrologist the English people were transformed into God's elect nation, whose history from beginning to end revealed the course of sacred, providential history leading to prophetic realization.

By the end of the Elizabethan period, the English were convinced by the arguments of the Protestant apocalyptic tradition that they were a chosen people dwelling in a holy land consecrated by God's divine providence. Their profound persuasion of the singularity of the reformed Church of England led directly to the glorious vision of the English nation as God's elect nation, a chosen people dwelling in a sacred land. Sacred

---

[126] F. Smith Fussner, *The Historical Revolution: English Historical Writing and Thought* (London: Routledge and Kegan Paul, 1962), p. 17.

[127] Arthur B. Ferguson, *Clio Unbound: Perceptions of Social and Cultural Past in Renaissance England* (Durham: N.C.: Duke University Press, 1979), p. 171.

[128] John F. King, *English Reformation Literature: The Tudor Origins of Protestant Tradition* (Princeton: Princeton University Press, 1982), p. 407.

[129] On the development of the Protestant apocalyptic tradition in England, see Katharine R. Firth, *The Apocalyptic Tradition in Reformation Britain, 1530–1645* (Oxford: Oxford University Press, 1979); Richard Bauckham, *Tudor Apocalypse: Sixteenth Century Apocalypticism, Millenarianism and the English Reformation, from John Bale to John Foxe and Thomas Brightman* (Oxford: Oxford University Press, 1978); C. A. Patrides and Joseph Wittreich, eds., *The Apocalypse in English Renaissance Thought and Literature* (Ithaca: Cornell University Press, 1984); Ernst Cassirer, *The Platonic Renaissance in England* (Austin: University of Texas Press, 1953); Paul Christianson, *Reformers and Babylon: English Apocalyptic Vision from the Reformation to the Eve of the Civil War* (Toronto: University of Toronto Press, 1978).

[130] John Foxe, *Acts and Monuments* (1563), ed. G. Townsend and G. R. Cattley, 8 vols. (London, 1837–41).

time and sacred space, the two essential dimensions within which prophetic revelation would be realized, comprised the very essence of the
apocalyptic interpretation of history. As William Haller writes:

> The idea of a predestined salvation reserved for the elect, of the Church as a
> communion of elect souls beset in all ages by enemies without and within, of
> the progression of the elect from age to age towards an apocalyptical vindica-
> tion—these conceptions assumed in many minds a meaning and application
> which went beyond their merely religious context . . . For the Church as they
> conceived it appeared now as one with the nation . . . [and] the nation itself
> assumed something of the nature of a mystical communion of chosen spirits, a
> peculiar people set apart from the rest of mankind.[131]

However, with Puritan hope in the reforming zeal of the monarchy
fading rapidly during the reigns of James I and Charles I, and with the
Church of England becoming increasingly rotten in Puritan eyes, a crisis
of terrifying proportions developed as many feared that England would
soon be called to account. With corruption flourishing in the church, these
Puritans believed, England could expect nothing but the wrath of God.
Following Thomas Brightman's apocalyptic scenario, which reversed the
role of England in providential history from that of Foxe's elect nation to
doomed Laodicea, the most sinful church in the book of Revelation, Puritans could not but await the Lord's final judgment. This divine wrath was
a very real possibility to generations of Puritans accustomed to viewing
their time and place as the historical application of prophetic revelation.
To a large extent, the course of the Puritan movement up to and during the
Puritan Revolution was determined by Brightman's correlation between
England and Laodicea.[132]

The Puritan migration to New England was based on a denial of England's title as the elect nation, and hence of its prominent role in sacred,
providential history. With the Church of England failing to execute a true
reformation according to Puritan premises, some radical early-seven-
teenth-century Puritans looked to New England as a place where they
would be able to realize their eschatological expectations and millennial
visions. To them New England became the Holy Land consecrated by
God's providence and destined to play a singular role in the history of
salvation. Moreover, by denying England any important part in salvation
history except that of apostasy, the Puritan emigrants emphasized time
and again the essential apocalyptic gulf separating England and New England, or the Old World and the New, in the history of salvation. Their

---

[131] William Haller, *The Elect Nation: The Meaning and Relevance of Foxe's Book of Martyrs* (New York: Harper & Row, 1963), pp. 244–45.

[132] Zakai, *Theocracy in Massachusetts*, pp. 59–116.

migration to America was based, to a large extent, on a deep eschatological consciousness of the true church, or the "church of the wilderness," fleeing into the wilderness in America in face of the imminent fate soon to befall sinful England and the Old World in general.[133]

The Protestant and Puritan traditions of historical interpretation exercised a great influence on the formation of Edwards's philosophy of history. He adopted the close relationship between history and apocalypse advocated by Protestant historiography, which enabled him to view the whole space of history as one long and continuous realization of sacred, prophetic revelations. However, unlike Protestant and Puritan historians, Edwards did not describe the historical process in political, social, and ecclesiastical terms. Protestant historiography was based on the struggle between Rome and the true Reformed church, and consequently it emphasized the apocalyptic struggle between the forces of Reformation and Counter-Reformation. Puritan historiography too was based on the struggle between the corrupt Church of England and the true church. In both cases social, political, and ecclesiastical considerations molded the presentation of history. Edwards, however, was not interested in these considerations; rather, his historical explanation was based on the relationship between the order of grace and the order of time, redemption and history. The main source of the historical process lay in the effusion of the Spirit of God and its manifestations in the form of revivals throughout history. The locus of sacred, ecclesiastical history is not based on an apocalyptic struggle between various historical forces, but is grounded in the saving operation of the Holy Spirit leading to spiritual changes, as evidenced in successive awakenings throughout the history of the Christian church. God's redemptive activity, in other words, is not concerned primarily with political, social, and institutional changes, but is ultimately reflected in the workings of the Holy Spirit's saving grace in awakening and revival.

Edwards as an Ecclesiastical Historian

A reading of writers of ecclesiastical history, those who like Edwards interpreted the course of history according to the progress of the Christian church, shows that all of them wrote their church histories in response to dramatic changes in the world around them and as part of their attempt to adjust the church to new historical circumstances. Crucial events therefore compelled them to redefine the relationship between the order of grace and the order of time, the world and the Christian church,

[133] Zakai, *Exile and Kingdom*, pp. 156–206.

and to justify the role of the church within the changing world, not least within history.

Eusebius Pamphili (c. 260–c. 340), bishop of Caesarea and the father of church history, wrote his *Ecclesiastical History* (323) in the early fourth century following the conversion of Constantine the Great to Christianity and the subsequent transformation of the Christian church from a persecuted sect into the official faith of the Roman Empire.[134] Reflecting these major historical events, Eusebius inaugurated "the new form of ecclesiastical history with its peculiar techniques for following up the growth of the [Christian] church or churches" in the world;[135] his book served as "a model for ecclesiastical history writing. Its form and its choice of themes both set the pattern for all the Church historians at least until the end of the sixth century."[136]

Eusebius considered Constantine's conversion as an act of the highest historical proportion and of providential magnitude, "a divine act, establishing Christianity in the citadel of government decision as a means to its further extension" and "an essential step in the diffusion of the gospel throughout the empire."[137] "For Constantine," Eusebius wrote, "God was Friend, Protector, and Guardian," and it was for this reason that Constantine and his sons "cleansed the world of hatred for God."[138] Out of the persecution and suffering that had characterized the history of Christianity from the time of Christ until the time of Constantine, the Christian church had now risen up and Christianity had finally been acknowledged as the faith of the empire. Eusebius closely identified this major historical development of the advance of the church in the world with God's redemptive scheme of history. The conversion of Constantine was for him a supreme illustration of God's providence, and in composing his work he seized on this notion of providential and redemptive intervention in order to endow the triumph of Christianity with a new significance in terms of world history. In this divine Christian epic, the *Ecclesiastical History*, the advent of the first Christian emperor stirred Eusebius's messianic hope in "a day bright and radiant, with never a cloud casting a shadow upon it, [shining] down with rays of heavenly light upon the churches of Christ throughout the whole world."[139] He believed that sa-

---

[134] Eusebius Pamphili, *Ecclesiastical History*, trans. R. J. Deferrari, 2 vols. (Washington: Catholic University of America Press, 1981).

[135] Arnaldo Momigliano, "Historiography of Religion: Western Views," in *On Pagans, Jews, and Christians* (Middletown, Conn.: Wesleyan University Press, 1987), p. 19.

[136] Robert Markus, "The Last Times," in *The End of Ancient Christianity* (Cambridge: Cambridge University Press, 1990), pp. 91–92.

[137] Henry Chadwick, *The Early Church* (Harmondsworth: Penguin, 1982), p. 71.

[138] Eusebius, *Ecclesiastical History*, II, pp. 282, 288.

[139] Ibid., II, p. 241.

cred, providential history had reached its zenith with the conversion of Constantine, and that Christianity would soon spread throughout the whole world. Indeed, he saw the conversion of Constantine as the culmination of providential history and associated the Roman Empire with the realization of God's redemptive plan in history. In other words, he "understood the events of his time as controlled by God's providence and grace," and "expressed his understanding of the events through language perhaps more imperial than Christian."[140]

In the eyes of Eusebius, as well of most Christians at the time, the conversion of Constantine and the establishment of Christianity as the official faith of the empire was an act of divine providence, inaugurating a new period in sacred history; empire and church "were providentially allied in order to convert the empire to Christianity and to bring the Church under Imperial protection."[141] With this major historical transformation, sacred, ecclesiastical history entered a new and crucial stage; people were living "in 'Christian times'—*tempora christiana*—a term which served for Christians to refer to the era following Christ's incarnation and especially to the time of Christianity's triumph."[142] These were indeed Christian times, inaugurating a new dispensation in world history. In face of such a great event, Eusebius developed his "imperial theology," depicting the emperor in messianic terms; Constantine was "divinely ordained to deliver the Empire from the forces of paganism and to ensure its salvation in the Christian Church."[143] The course of history thus bears witness to the unfolding realization of God's redemptive plan in time; hence Eusebius's optimistic belief that the triumph of Christianity would be realized *in* history. In sum, responding to this major historical change, Eusebius constructed an interpretation of salvation history maintaining that its movement is evidence of the gradual yet inevitable triumph of the church throughout the world—hence that the triumph of Christianity would be realized within historical time.

In *The City of God*,[144] composed between 413 and 426, St. Augustine further elucidated the Christian philosophy of time, and particularly the church's role in providential history, so persuasively that his views came to be identified with the essence of Christianity until the Protestant Reformation. *The City of God* was written in a totally different historical context than Eusebius's *Ecclesiastical History*; hence the radical departure of the Doctor of the Church from the father of ecclesiastical history in terms

[140] Robert M. Grant, *Eusebius as Church Historian* (Oxford: Oxford University Press, 1980), p. 146.
[141] Harrison, *Augustine*, p. 203.
[142] Ibid., p. 203; Markus, "The Last Times," pp. 89–90.
[143] Harrison, *Augustine*, p. 202.
[144] Augustine, *City of God*, trans. J. O'Meara (Harmondsworth: Penguin, 1984).

of constructing salvation history as well as in the meaning both conferred on history. While Eusebius composed his work at the time of Constantine's conversion and the rise of the church to world prominence, Augustine wrote under the shadow of the sack of Rome. More specifically, Augustine's main goal in his book was to defend Christ and Christianity against the charges that they were responsible for the great disaster of the year 410, when Alaric and the Goths sacked Rome, a city that had been free from the fear of attack for over 800 years.[145] Living in this new historical context, Augustine, unlike Eusebius, was unable to confirm the optimistic belief that the triumph of Christianity would be realized *in* history, or that history bore witness to the gradual yet inevitable triumph of the church. He notes that in their attempt to explain the disaster there were many in Rome who pointed an accusing finger at the "Christian era" under whose influence their city had been living, and held "Christ responsible for the disasters which their city endured."[146] After generations of success in the Roman Empire, Christians were once again being confronted by hostility and opposition in the world. Once again they had to contend with the notion that this world was not theirs, for theirs was another kingdom. In such a context the whole relationship between sacred, ecclesiastical history and the history of the world underwent a radical transformation.

Impelled by urgent historical circumstances, Augustine was unable to accept Eusebius's optimistic imperial theology but attempted a whole new evaluation of the relationship between church and empire, sacred and profane history. He believed that not reconciliation with the world but alienation from it, not conquest but permanent pilgrimage upon earth, was essentially the business of the Christian in the world. The essential state of a Christian is to be a "pilgrim and stranger in the world . . . predestined by grace and chosen by grace, by grace pilgrim, and by grace citizen above."[147] This is the aspect of Christian life upon which Augustine constructed his *City of God*. Here the world is no longer the realm in which the church rises to dominance and glory within history, as Eusebius had shown, but is the arena for the crucial contest between the church (the City of God) and the world (the earthly, profane city). The heavenly and the earthly cities are the locus of the unfolding of time, and the struggle between the two constitutes the essence of history, which is to culminate in their disentanglement at the last judgment. "My task," wrote Au-

---

[145] See Markus, *Saeculum*, pp. 22–44, and "The Last Times," pp. 87–96; Harrison, *Augustine*, pp. 194–206; Brown, *Augustine of Hippo*, pp. 313–29. See also Scott, *Augustine: His Thought in Context*; and Bonner, *St. Augustine of Hippo: Life and Controversies*.

[146] Augustine, *City of God*, p. 6.

[147] Ibid., p. 596.

gustine, "is to discuss . . . the rise, the development and the destined ends of the two cities, the earthly and the heavenly, the cities which we find, as I have said, interwoven, as it were, in this present transitory world, and mingled with one another."[148] Only at the end of time and history would this dualism disappear and both cities finally be separated from one another. In the final scenario, the "two cities, the earthly and the Heavenly, which are mingled together from the beginning to the end of history," will be "separated by the final judgment . . . [when] each receives her own end, of which there is no end."[149]

Augustine's *City of God* thus broke radically with Eusebius's imperial theology. The empire has no place in his dualism of the two cities. "In Augustine's hand the Roman Empire has lost its religious significance. Rome was removed from the *Heilsgeschichte*, the Empire is no longer seen as God's chosen instrument for the salvation of men. It is no longer indispensable for the unfolding of his providential plan in history."[150] For Augustine history is not the story of God's unfolding providence. "In the place of ordered progress, achievement, or culmination he saw only an absolute antithesis between the city of God and the city of the world, the righteous and the unrighteous, the predestined elect and the reprobate." Instead of the imperial theology he "abandoned the idea of pattern, progress, and meaning in secular history"; and given that the state of Christians in the world is one of suffering the vicissitudes of history, "they will ultimately leave it behind in the eschatological city which they will attain after this life." Augustine's historical thought reveals "diminishing optimism and lack of conviction in expounding any sort of plan or pattern in human history."[151] History is not the realization of God's redemptive activity. Divine providence, Augustine believed, in contrast to Eusebius, is concerned with salvation, not with history as such, and therefore the intrinsic dualism characterizing the historical process, the struggle between the heavenly and the profane cities, would be resolved only *beyond* time and history. History indeed is the stage upon which the struggle takes place, but by its nature it is devoid of any notion of progress and culmination, since only on the eschatological day of judgment will that struggle be resolved. Divine providence has nothing to do with the course of history; hence, says Augustine, Christians cannot look to history for evidence of God's redemptive activity in time.

The Protestant Reformation of the sixteenth century initiated another decisive revolutionary transformation in Christian historical thought. In

---

[148] Ibid., p. 430.
[149] Ibid., p. 842.
[150] Markus, *Saeculum*, pp. 54–55.
[151] Harrison, *Augustine*, pp. 204–6.

the attempt to justify the break between the Protestant and Catholic churches, and to establish a historical role for the Reformation in the history of the church, Protestant historiography broke with Augustine's interpretation of salvation history. Instead of Augustine's disassociation of salvation and history, Protestant historians developed a new mode of historical consciousness based upon the utmost association between prophecy and history, providence and historical occurrences, and grounded in an apocalyptic interpretation of history. This attitude can be clearly seen in Philip Melanchthon's revision of *Carion's Chronicle* (1532), Robert Barnes's *The Lives of the Popes of Rome* (1535), Martin Luther's "Preface to the Revelation of St. John" (1545), and Matthias Flacius Illyricus's monumental *Magdeburg Centuries* (1559–74). As these works and many others by Protestant historians show, eschatology and apocalypse—and hence the millennium—were again brought within history. Divine providence works out within history, in fact, determines the whole process, in order to advance God's redemptive plan for fallen humanity. Salvation is inseparable from and intrinsic to the historical process, and vice versa.

This approach brought about a radical change in the Christian sense of time and history. In contrast to Augustine, Protestant historiography infused the *saeculum* with divine significance, transforming the role assigned to the world and secular history in sacred history. The Protestant apocalyptic mode of historical thought testified to the emerging belief in human beings' ability to comprehend, shape, and influence history. Instead of alienation from the historical world, Protestant historians emphasized reconciliation with it. Further, unlike Augustine, who believed that history is homogeneous and cannot be described in terms of a pattern drawn from sacred history, or that it can exhibit decisive turning points imbued with redemptive significance in sacred history, Protestant historiography claimed that history is the realization of sacred, prophetic revelations, as attested by the Reformation itself. Hence progress could be made *in* history conceived as designated for the fulfillment of divine prophecies; history is infused with sacred meaning and situated within the apocalyptic dimension of time. Second, Protestant historiography denied Augustine's dualistic view of history. Eschatology and apocalypse, excluded from time and history by pre-Reformation church thought, were firmly reestablished and made intrinsic to the historical process. Third, human beings' existence in the world and their role in history was changed from that of alienation to active participation. They are to advance religious reformation in order to establish the kingdom of God and his Son in the world. With history situated along the dimension of prophecy, the saints, as Christ's army, take an active stand beside him, playing a role in the drama of salvation *within* history.

Another transformation in the Christian interpretation of salvation history took place during the English Reformation. In Tudor and Stuart England the English Protestant "apocalyptic tradition"[152] increasingly came to regard the Reformation in England in eschatological and apocalyptic terms, as can be seen in John Bale's *Image of Both Churches* (1541–47)[153] and Foxe's *Acts and Monuments* (1563). Foxe, for example, compared Elizabeth's coming to the throne in 1558 to Constantine's conversion and the establishment of Christianity as the official faith of the empire, thus assigning her an important role in sacred, ecclesiastical history: under a godly prince, like Constantine in the past, the triumph of Protestantism was assured in England and thus the advance of the true reformation was secured in this realm. Like Constantine in the past, Foxe believed, a godly prince in England had received a command from heaven to advance God's redemptive plan by establishing the Protestant religion in that country. Toward the end of the sixteenth century, when the Puritan attempt to reform the Church of England was evidently not succeeding, people began to think that the prince had failed in the long-awaited reformation of the Church of England. It was at that time that Thomas Brightman wrote *A Revelation of the Revelation* (1616), directing zealous Puritans to realize their eschatological visions and millennial expectations outside the Church and state of England.[154] Finally, with the emigration to New England during the seventeenth century, Puritan historians in America constructed an eschatology and apocalypse of the Puritan migration, claiming that a great and unbridgeable eschatological gulf separated the Old and doomed World from the promise of the New in the drama of salvation history, as can be seen in Thomas Hooker's sermon *The Danger of Desertion* (1631), John Cotton's *An Exposition upon the Thirteenth Chapter of the Revelation* (c. 1640), Increase Mather's *The Mystery of Israel's Salvation* (1669), and Cotton Mather's *Magnalia Christi Americana* (1702).[155]

Edwards, however, developed his own philosophy of salvation history; it was concerned primarily with events related to the effusion of the Spirit and its manifestation in the form of revivals and awakenings. To him the

---

[152] Firth, *The Apocalyptic Tradition in Reformation Britain, 1530–1645*; Michael Fixler, *Milton and the Kingdoms of God* (London: Faber and Faber, 1964); and Zakai, "Reformation, History and Eschatology in English Protestantism," pp. 300–318.

[153] John Bale, *Image of Both Churches* (1550), in *Selected Works of John Bale*, ed. H. Christmas (Cambridge, 1849).

[154] Thomas Brightman, *Apocalypsis Apocalypseos, or a Revelation of the Revelation* (Leyden, 1616).

[155] Thomas Hooker, "The Danger of Desertion" (1631), in *Thomas Hooker: Writings in England and Holland, 1626–1633*, ed. George H. Williams et al. (Cambridge, Mass.: Harvard University Press, 1975); John Cotton, *An Exposition upon the Thirteenth Chapter of the Revelation* (London, 1655); Increase Mather, *The Mystery of Israel's Salvation* (London, 1669); Cotton Mather, *Magnalia Christi Americana* (London, 1702).

true mark of sacred, ecclesiastical history was not the social and political event but the religious revival, whereby the Spirit of God transformed the human condition. Edwards's theology of history was thus based not on alienation from the world but on reconciliation with it through revivals and awakenings, leading to its transformation into the kingdom of God. He was undeniably a true heir of the Protestant historiography based on an apocalyptic mode of thought, affirming that history has a meaning and that the Deity constantly reveals his redemptive plan within history. Yet, he did not conceive salvation history as based mainly on the struggle between the true Protestant church and the Church of Rome. His historical interpretation was not founded upon the dualism of Bale's *Image of the Two Churches*, or Foxe's *Acts and Monuments*, which records the suffering of the Christian martyrs through the centuries under the Catholic Church. Edwards's interpretation of sacred history left little room for the suffering of the martyrs; his goal was not to describe the fate of human beings but the acts of divine providence in history, the effusions of the Spirit in the form of revivals and awakenings. Neither did he adopt the New England visions and expectations surrounding the flight of the true church into the American wilderness. For Edwards, earthly occurrences are not the mark of sacred, providential history. The history of God's work of redemption concerns primarily the saving acts of God in time and does not depend on worldly affairs.

In each age ecclesiastical historians interpreted the significance of their own time in salvation history in light of the historical circumstances in which they found themselves. Jonathan Edwards's philosophy of history was no exception. Maintaining that all movements in time are based solely on God's redemptive plan for human beings ("the Work of Redemption is the greatest of all God's works", and this is "the end of all his other works"),[156] he denounced the mechanistic image of a clockwork universe and proclaimed " 'Tis an evidence that all Gods works all the things that God has made in heaven & earth have relation as God has made & constituted 'em to the great work of redemption."[157] Further, he rejected the Enlightenment notion of *historia humana* and its claims regarding human beings' power to interpret the world around them and to understand history according to their reason, invoking God's purpose "to show his own glory, and exalt his own sovereignty, power and all-sufficiency" in the world and his aim to "pour contempt on all that human strength, wisdom, prudence and sufficiency."[158]

---

[156] Edwards, *History of the Work of Redemption*, p. 512.
[157] Edwards, *Miscellany* no. 1063.
[158] Edwards, *Some Thoughts*, p. 294.

*Five*_____

God's Great Design in History:
The Formation of Edwards's Redemptive Mode
of Historical Thought

There is doubtless some design that God is pursuing, and scheme
that he is Carrying on, in the various changes and revolutions that
from age to age happen in the world; there is some certain great design, to which providence subordinates all the successive changes
that come to pass in the state of affairs of mankind. All revolutions
from the beginning of the world to the end, are doubtless but various parts of one scheme, all conspiring for the bringing to pass the
great event which is ultimately in view. And the scheme will not be
finished, nor the design fully accomplished, the great event fully
brought to pass, till the end of the world and the last revolution is
brought about. The world, it is most evident, is not an everlasting
thing; it will have an end: and God's end in making and governing
the world will not be fully obtained, nor his scheme be finished, till
the end of the world comes.
  (Edwards, *Miscellany* no. 547, 1731)

And that work of Gods providence to which all other works of
providence both in the material & immaterial part of the creation,
are subservient, is the work of redemption. All other works of providence may be looked upon as *appendages* to this great work, or
things which God does to subserve that grand design. The work of
redemption may be looked upon as the great end and drift of all
Gods works & dispensations from the beginning & even the end of
the work of creation it self.
  (Edwards, *Miscellany* no. 702, c. 1736)

SOME TIME AGO Quentin Skinner warned intellectual historians against
some common "mythologies" that have long pervaded and seriously un-
dermined the field of the history of ideas. Prominent among these is the
"mythology of coherence"—the search for a precise and coherent system
of thought in the writings of certain classical authors, and the strong inclination to portray their works as a well-defined intellectual enterprise from

beginning to end. This approach, however, is indifferent to the ideological modifications in the universe of thought of such a writer and does not acknowledge the changing historical context within which it was formulated. Skinner therefore counseled historians of ideas against falling into the trap of "the mythology of coherence," or the attempt to give "the thought of various classic writers a coherence and an air generally of a chosen system, which they may never have attained or even meant to attain." Such an approach "very readily ceases to be an historical account of any thoughts which were actually thought." And the "history thus written becomes a history not of ideas at all, but of abstractions: a history of thought which no one ever actually succeeded in thinking, at a level of coherence which no one ever actually attained."[1]

This warning is applicable with respect to the development of Edwards's universe of thought, most particularly in relation to his interpretation of the order of time. For Edwards struggled much and hard to develop his philosophy of history over a period of almost twenty years, constantly modifying the content and form of his redemptive mode of historical thought in accordance with the changing historical and ideological context in which he found himself. In fact, until his final year he wrestled with the concept of God's work of redemption to get a better understanding of the "affairs of redemption,"[2] or the relation between the order of grace and the order of history.

For many years Edwards endeavored to understand "the disposition of things in redemption"[3] and the designs of providence in history. Following the "little revival" in Northampton (1734–35), and struggling "unremittingly to retrieve the halcyon days when Northampton was 'a city set on a hill,' "[4] in 1739 he launched a long series of sermons, entitled *History of the Work of Redemption*, which constituted the fullest and most systematic exposition of his philosophy of salvation history and his most comprehensive account of sacred, ecclesiastical history. Compared with his construction of space, or his theology of nature, which was only a few years in the making during the 1720s, Edwards's attempt to decipher God's "grand design"[5] within the order of time, and to understand his ultimate aim in the affairs of redemption and in the disposition of things in redemption, was a much more complex theological and philosophical task. Evidently, the main problem was the understanding of the content and form of God's work of redemption in the process of history and the

---

[1] Quentin Skinner, "Meaning and Understanding in the History of Ideas," *History and Theory* 7 (1969): 3–53.

[2] Edwards, "To the Trustees of the College of New Jersey," October 19, 1757, p. 728.

[3] Edwards, *God Glorified in the Work of Redemption*, July 8, 1731, in *SJW*, p. 78.

[4] Goen, introduction, in *GA*, pp. 47–48.

[5] Edwards, *Miscellany* no. 702 (c. 1736), in *MISA*, p. 284.

finding of an historical phenomenon, or an agent, on the basis of which the divine agency could be firmly established and fully asserted. For Edwards's goal was to reveal and explain God's role and power as the sole author and true Lord of history, or, in his words, "God's end in making and governing the world."[6]

In his theology of nature, and in accordance with the mechanical philosophy of his time, as we have seen, Edwards almost immediately found that agent in the phenomenon of the atoms. Yet as concerns the dimension of time, he spent many years in search of the necessary historical phenomenon enabling him to prove the "wheels of providence"[7] within the course and progress of history. He constantly changed his mind regarding the most appropriate agent by which to demonstrate God's sovereign power and will in time, the "design that God is pursuing, and [the] scheme that he is Carrying on, in the various changes and revolutions that from age to age happen in the world."[8] Eventually, during the late 1730s he found that historical agent in revival, claiming that the close connection between the effusion of the Spirit and its historical manifestation in the form of remarkable awakenings throughout history constituted the locus of God's work of redemption, or salvation history.

As early as 1723, following his conversion experience, Edwards adopted the term "God's work of redemption" to describe the relationship between the order of grace and the order of time.[9] From then on he used it persistently in explaining God's redemptive activity and his divine scheme in history. Yet this term, as he soon found, was too general for describing in actual, historical terms the content and form of God's absolute sovereignty in the order of time and too abstract to proclaim the glory of God as the Lord of history. At the same time Edwards began his *Notes on the Apocalypse*, in which he wrote the first entries "in late spring or early summer of 1723,"[10] where he attempted to correlate sacred prophecies and historical events. Apocalyptic thought, as he learned from the rich tradition of Protestant and Puritan apocalyptic interpretation of history, strove to establish a close association between prophetic revelations and the course and progress of history. Yet, Edwards's quest was more ambitious: to find a plausible historical agent which he could claim to show the vivid presence and immediate influence of divine agency in history. For almost two decades he struggled to lay down the ideological and theological premises regarding the form and content of the work of redemp-

---

[6] Edwards, *Miscellany* no. 547 (c. 1731), in *MISA*, p. 93.

[7] Edwards, *History of the Work of Redemption*, p. 128; *Notes on Scripture*, in *NOS*, p. 373.

[8] Edwards, *Miscellany* no. 547, p. 93.

[9] Edwards, *Miscellany* no. 38 (1723), in *MIS*, p. 220.

[10] Stein, introduction, in *AW*, p. 77.

tion. Edwards knew from his own conversion experience that this work involved, among others, the operation of saving grace in the soul. Hence, one of the main problems he faced in developing his philosophy of history was how to establish a close association between the personal experience of saving grace in the soul and the operations of redemptive activity in history as a whole, for his own tremendous conversion experience had convinced him that God's work of redemption is inseparable from the working of saving grace in conversion.

Given his theistic metaphysics and his emphasis upon God's absolute sovereignty, Edwards had to incorporate the work of redemption into the whole sacred web of the universe. Striving to establish the connection between redemption and history, he looked more and more at the theological and teleological structure inherent in the fabric of the world, expanding his concept of God's redemptive plan to the theological teleology of sacred order inherent in creation in space and time. To better understand God's work of redemption, Edwards found it necessary to expound the "great design, to which providence subordinates all the successive changes that come to pass in the state of affairs of mankind."[11] For he believed the work of redemption encompassed the whole reason and goal of creation, and thus was necessarily inextricable from the sacred structure of order inherent in the world. God's redemptive activity concerns not only personal conversion and individual salvation but the whole fabric of the universe. As he claimed, "the Work of Redemption is, as it were, the sum of God's works of providence."[12]

For almost two decades Edwards worked to redefine the meaning of God's work of redemption, an effort that resulted in the laying down of the main ideological and theological premises of his philosophy of salvation history. He sought God's absolute sovereignty in the order of time. Accordingly, he tried to formulate the concepts upon which he could found his notion of the proper relationship between grace and time, and thus more concretely illuminate the link between redemption and history. This was an enterprise of great difficulty. In forming his theology of nature, Edwards could work at his private desk, battling only in his mind against the menacing ideas of science and the Enlightenment. In the construction of his ideology of history, however, he had to be attentive to the social and ecclesiastical context in which he lived. Above all, he was obliged to take into account certain historical events and transformations that affected his own life as well as that of his congregation.

Shortly after the "little revival" of 1734–35, Edwards came to the conclusion that the work of redemption constituted "the great end and drift

[11] Edwards, *Miscellany* no. 547, p. 93.
[12] Edwards, *History of the Work of Redemption*, p. 513.

of all Gods works & dispensations from the beginning & even the end of the work of creation it self."[13] Here the main source can be found for his exploration of the work of redemption as the ultimate concern of God's activity from the creation of the world to its end, as is made evident in his sermons on the *History of the Work of Redemption* of 1739. He now turned his attention to the purpose for which God had created the world, attempting to explain God's work of redemption as part of the whole fabric of creation. Faithful to his sense of God's absolute sovereignty over the created order, Edwards claimed that the work of redemption constituted the essential dynamism behind the theological teleology of sacred order inherent in the structure of the universe. The affairs of redemption, he came to think, dealt ultimately with the cause and destiny of creation itself.

This contention helped Edwards to formulate the ideological and theological premises of his redemptive mode of historical thought. The essence of this ideology of history is the radical way in which Edwards associated God's work of redemption and the wider issue of the ultimate cause and reason for which God created the world. In other words, he identified God's work of redemption with the whole span of history. As he came to believe, there is no history without redemption, no redemption without history. By making such an historization of God's work of redemption, and claiming it constituted the essence of the entire historical process, Edwards was finally able to assert God's absolute sovereignty in time and history. The radicalism embodied in such an historical interpretation should be considered, in part, in light of the Enlightenment historical narrative based on secular, historical time. At the source of Edwards's thought stood the dimension of sacred time.

Edwards's construction of the order of time stipulated that the whole process of history was founded ultimately on God's work of redemption. This enabled him to claim, in contrast to St. Augustine, for example, that history is intrinsic to redemption and vice versa, or that divine providence concerns history and not only salvation as Augustine taught. Being an inseparable part of God's redemptive activity and the stage upon which the work of redemption unfolds, history was accorded legitimacy and validity. God is not indifferent to the process of history, or blind to the life of human beings in time. On the contrary, God consistently accomplishes his great design throughout the whole span of history, although its final realization will take place only beyond history, after the end of the world: "God's end in making and governing the world will not be fully obtained, nor his scheme be finished, till the end of the world comes."[14]

---

[13] Edwards, *Miscellany* no. 702, p. 284.
[14] Edwards, *Miscellany* no. 547, p. 94.

The Quest for God's Absolute Sovereignty in the Order of Time

The establishment of God's absolute sovereignty in the order of time was one of the most difficult tasks that Edwards undertook in his entire theological and philosophical enterprise. Even during his final years he continued to struggle with the issue of the proper relationship between the order of grace and the order of time. "I have on my mind and heart, (which I long ago began, not with any view of publication,) a great work," he wrote to the trustees of the College of New Jersey in October 19, 1757, a year before his death, "which I call a *History of the Work of Redemption*." The principal aim of this work was to lay out "all parts of" God's "grand scheme" in "the affairs of redemption,"[15] that is, to provide an explanation of the nature of time and the meaning of history. For many years Edwards was deeply preoccupied with this ambitious work, which "long engaged and swallowed up" his mind,[16] as he admitted, even during the final decade of his life. In fact, he never relinquished his desire to present to the world in a systematic way his construction of time and history. With his untimely death in 1758, this project remained incomplete. We have therefore only the long series of sermons on the *History of the Work of Redemption* of 1739 as the fullest exposition of Edwards's philosophy of history.

One of the main reasons why Edwards found it so difficult to construct the order of time is that, in contrast to the spatial dimension, where God's absolute sovereign will and power could be proved fairly easily through the ontological argument, the cosmological argument, the argument from design, and the teleological argument[17]—in sum, through the order, structure, and direction of the universe—the establishment of God's sovereignty in time and history entailed the finding of a sacred, redemptive dynamism inherent in the framework of the universe. This fundamental dynamism, intrinsic to the aim of creation, had to be defined before a coherent ideology of providential history could be formulated. Space could be defined by some order and structure, such as the great chain of being, or Edwards's order of creation, but time denoted change, governed by a teleological principle, and a sense of a beginning and an end. Grasping the sense of time was very different from expounding the structure of the spatial dimension in which human beings are placed, for the former signified some inherent teleological aim. Edwards's most acute problem

---

[15] Edwards, "To the Trustees of the College of New Jersey," pp. 728–29.

[16] Winslow, *Jonathan Edwards*, pp. 314–15.

[17] A good summary of these arguments can be found in Brian Davies, *An Introduction to the Philosophy of Religion* (Oxford: Oxford University Press, 1993).

was how to show and prove a dynamism propelling the arrow of sacred time as it moves from creation to the eternal promise that lies beyond history. The task, then, was to explain the dialectic of God's transcendence and immanence in the order of time.

The concept of God's work of redemption, which Edwards had already defined in 1723, signified such a sacred dynamism. History is the stage upon which God realizes his grand design and there unfolds his redemptive plan. Edwards could of course rely on the Protestant and Puritan apocalyptic interpretation of history, but this solution was too general and abstract for his mind. Indeed, in 1723 he began his *Notes on the Apocalypse*, attempting to correlate sacred prophecies and historical occurrences along the lines of the Protestant and Puritan apocalyptic interpretation. Edwards's aim, however, was to construct a philosophy of history capable of revealing the main forces operating in history and directing its course. In this sense, his goal was to prove God's sovereignty *within* history and not only to demonstrate his power in determining and controlling human affairs from an undefined space above. Hence Edwards attempted to show the Deity's manifestations in regulating the entire historical process. In other words, Edwards wanted to find a feasible and concrete agent in history itself through which he might confidently proclaim the glory of God's sovereignty in time and show him as the Lord of history. Rather than depend on a general association between prophetic revelations and historical events, he tried to show the actual ways and means by which God realizes his redemptive activity within the historical process. In this sense Edwards was much more historically minded in his approach than earlier Protestant and Puritan historians.

On the other hand, since Edwards had already contended in his theology of nature that only spiritual, created beings are properly beings, and that matter is totally passive, it was evident to him that the redemptive process would concern intelligent beings alone. Yet, faithful to his theistic metaphysics, he was reluctant to identify God's work of redemption with conversion, which would have allowed the operation of saving grace to serve as a locus for the unfolding of God's work of redemption in history. There were of course good reasons for such an approach since conversion denotes a special relationship between grace and time. "Conversion and the rebirth to a new life change time and the experience of time," because "they make-present the ultimate in the penultimate, and the future of time in the midst of time." As the private, spiritual experience of saving grace, conversion indeed signifies God's indwelling in time, but it does not accord him his due preeminence as the Lord of history. For in conversion, saving grace mediates only between the spiritual welfare of the individual and the eschatological future of salvation, thus granting that "the future is God's mode of being in history." Yet it does not explain historical time, or the initial cause inherent in time or the teleological goal toward which it is reaching. For the "unity between the divine coming," in the form of saving grace, "and human conversion" indicates indeed sacred "fulfilled time" but not historical time.[18] There is of course a great difference between God's presence in time and his power in controlling and directing history. For Edwards the main shortcoming of such an approach was that it entailed the anthropocentric dimension of the redemptive process in the form of individual conversion, something that in his theistic metaphysics he tried to avoid. To narrow God's redemptive activity down to the saving grace in personal conversion meant to severely restrict his power as the Lord of history.

Based on his profound sense of God's absolute sovereignty in the created order, Edwards strove to get a broader understanding of the relationship between grace and time, which would manifest God's work of redemption within history as a whole. In order to do so he had to redefine the very nature of the historical process and make it totally and absolutely dependent on God's providence. Such an effort to expand God's redemptive activity into the whole span of history can be found in 1731, when Edwards claimed "there is some certain great design, to which providence subordinates all the successive changes that come to pass in the state of affairs of mankind."[19] It is clear that Edwards was not only endowing the historical process with sacred, redemptive meaning, but establishing redemption as inseparable from the process of history. The redemptive process is made inextricable from God's aim in creation. Since history is a special dimension of the sacred order of time, Edwards could argue that the ultimate concern of God's work of redemption is the whole span of history—"the fall of man, the beginning, and the end of the world—the Day of Judgment—its end."[20] Redeeming time, in terms of the realization of God's grand design in history, in this way became the essence of the work of redemption. That shift in Edwards's mind to the objective historical goal of redeeming time and to the general issue of God's grand design in history was to be the essential mark of his philosophy of history. The nature and meaning of history, in other words, were to be understood in the wider context of God's overall redemptive plan in creation whose final realization lies beyond history after the end of the world. For, the "world, it is most evident, is not an everlasting thing; it will have an end: and God's end in making and governing the world will not be fully obtained, nor his scheme be finished, till the end of the world comes."[21] Edwards's

---

[18] Moltmann, *The Coming of God*, pp. 22–24.
[19] Edwards, *Miscellany* no. 547, p. 93.
[20] Edwards, *History of the Work of Redemption*, p. 116.
[21] Edwards, *Miscellany* no. 547, p. 94.

philosophy of history was not based on *redemption in* or *of history*, as some Enlightenment historians tended to think, but on *redemption from* and hence *beyond history*. God's work of redemption takes place in history, but its ultimate realization is beyond history.

Redemption *from history* immediately brings into question the legitimacy of historical time and with it the validity of the redemptive process. For to claim that history's meaning lies beyond it entails the devaluation of what happens within history. In the dialectic of God's transcendence and immanence in history, this was one of the main problems Edwards faced in defining the meaning of the work of redemption. To establish the validity of the historical process, he had to show that divine activity in time does not compromise God's sovereignty, but that the sacred, historical work of redemption by definition constitutes an essential part of the eternal promise that lies beyond history. Thus Edwards accorded the process of history a legitimacy of its own as the span of time in which God continuously unveils his redemptive plan. If history is only the "theatre of God's judgments," as some Protestant and Puritan historians argued, God is totally arbitrary, and how can one perceive the providential scheme which lies in history? Edwards's concept of God's work of redemption, on the other hand, accords history its own validity as a special dimension of time within which God's redemptive plan unfolds. For Edwards history is the evident theater of God's work of redemption. God is neither alien nor blind to history, but involved in the temporal process through the work of redemption. The reason is, as Sang H. Lee puts it, that for Edwards "God is not only *in* history" but he "seeks to redeem and sanctify history itself by God's own self-extension through history."[22] The historical process has its own legitimacy as the theater in which God reveals his redemptive design. In constructing this redemptive mode of thought, claiming that history is intrinsic to God's work of redemption, Edwards showed that for him history was more than the theater of God's judgments, and that human beings are able to unveil the redemptive course of time, to understand the mystery of salvation history, and to take an active part in its realization.

Edwards's quest was necessarily for the reenchantment of creation and time. His concept of God's work of redemption was aimed at reenacting the sense of the sacred in time and placing history in a larger and wider sacred whole. Whereas in his theology of nature he strove to show that Christian belief and thought led to a better understanding of humanity's place in the universe, so now he wished to show that the historical process cannot be properly understood apart from God's redemptive activity in time. Since the religious mode of being demanded a radical reenchantment

---

[22] Lee, *The Philosophical Theology of Jonathan Edwards*, p. 214.

of the world, Edwards set out to apply it to space and time alike. Entailed in this position is the belief in the sacred cohesion of creation as well as of time. Hence, against the scientific culture of his time and the Enlightenment perception of history, which attacked the notion of sacred powers and emptied the cosmos of divine forces to make way for human autonomy and freedom, Edwards's aim was to reinforce the religious mode of being and to fight the dispossession of the sacred from space and time. In the order of time, more specifically, he attempted to bring the whole span of history under one supreme principle: redemption.

Edwards's concept of the work of redemption thus recharged history with sacred meaning, constituting it not only as the theater where God poured out his wrath on sinful humanity, but also as the essential stage in the unfolding of God's redemptive plan whose realization would come after the end of the world.

The Formation of the Redemptive Mode of Historical Thought: The Early *Miscellanies*

Edwards's attempts to formulate his philosophy of history went on slowly and gradually during the early 1720s, as attested in his *Miscellanies* written during that period. At the time, as he was trying to convert the whole world around him according to the deep persuasions he had acquired during his experience of conversion, the inception of his new sense of time and vision of history was inextricable from his general quest to reconstruct the essential nature of reality. Interpreting the nature of time and the meaning of history was inseparable from his main quest to explain the essential structure of reality, and to provide a plausible alternative to the predominant scientific explanation of the world of nature. While endeavoring throughout the 1720s to reconstruct the dimension of space against prevailing scientific notions, Edwards gradually began to develop his views on history. Yet, as he became increasingly more occupied with his theology of nature, as evidenced in his growing body of scientific writings, Edwards came to the conclusion that the issue of time and history is radically different from that of space. The latter involves the spatial structure and order of the universe, while the first deals with the dynamism of redemptive activity, or what Edwards defined in the late 1730s as the "wheels of providence,"[23] concerning the ultimate aim of creation. Signs of this growing theological and philosophical engagement with time as a special field of inquiry can be found in the early *Miscellanies*.

---

[23] Edwards, *History of the Work of Redemption*, p. 128; "Notes on Scripture," in *NOS*, p. 373.

The early formulations of Edwards's sense of time and vision of history appeared in the *Miscellanies* written in 1722.[24] Naturally, these early statements were closely interwoven with those relating to space, so that in expounding the essential nature of reality Edwards also began the construction of his redemptive mode of historical thought. Overall, the conversion experience was chiefly responsible for the development of Edwards's thought during the early 1720s; at this formative period, in his attempts to convert the world around him he began with much zeal and enthusiasm to write his *Resolutions*, as well as the *Diary*, the scientific and philosophic Writings, the *Miscellanies*, the *Notes on the Apocalypse*, and the *Notes on Scripture*.[25] In this context of conversion and the growth of his theological and philosophical consciousness, Edwards began to deal with the issue of Christ's role as the Lord of the universe, whose redemptive activity lies in advancing the Christian church's cause in the world. "The universe is" God's, he said in 1722, "only he has not the trouble to managing it; but Christ, to whom it is no trouble, manages it for him." Accordingly, every "atom in the universe is managed by Christ so as to be most to the advantage of the Christian, every particle of air or every ray of the sun."[26]

Defining Christ as the ruler of the universe evokes the relationship between the Son and the Father, or the "Harmony of God's Attributes in the work of redemption." (This, in 1723, is the first time that Edwards used the term "God's work of redemption.") Hence, he argued, Christ's message of salvation cannot be separated from God's work of redemption. "The redemption by Christ is particularly wonderful upon this account," wrote Edwards, "inasmuch as the justice of God is not only appeased to those who have interest in him, but stands up for them." For God is "not enemy but a friend."[27] History therefore is not only the grand theater of God's judgments, but also and more important the stage upon which the Deity reveals the power of saving grace and mercy as manifested in Christ's message of salvation. Christ's promise of salvation, therefore, not only manifests the justice of God but also the essential connection between God's work of redemption and the course of history. In 1723 Edwards recast the claim he had made in 1722 regarding Christ's

---

[24] John F. Wilson argues that the " 'Miscellanies' contains traces or foreshadowing of the Redemption Discourse throughout." See Wilson, introduction, in *HWR*, p. 13. See also Chamberlain, introduction, in *MISA*, pp. 29–34.

[25] According to Stephen J. Stein, "Edwards wrote his earliest comments on the Revelation" in 1722–23 while serving as a minister at the Presbyterian church in New York City. See Stein, introduction, in *AW*, pp. 10, 77. Edwards wrote the first entries in his *Notes on Scripture* during 1724. See Stein, introduction, in *NOS*, p. 41.

[26] Edwards, *Miscellany ff* (c. 1722–23), in *MIS*, p. 184.

[27] Edwards, *Miscellany* no. 38 (c. 1723), p. 221.

absolute role in ordering and structuring physical reality, and tended to emphasize Christ's singular function as the Lord of history. In this capacity Christ's government is not confined to the spatial dimension of physical phenomena but extends to the passage of time: "he rules all events, every change, and every part of the universe so as to conduce to the good of his church, and to bring to pass the end of his mediation, and to suit the purposes of his kingdom of grace."[28] Conceived as a cosmic ruler as well as the Lord of history, "the Son created and doth govern the world,"[29] and the order of creation is totally subordinated to his mediating office: "the motion of every atom is under his mediatorial government, that he guides so as shall be best for his church." Due to Christ's providential and redemptive role in the cosmos, the dimension of time and history becomes inseparable from his "mediatorial government of the universe" because "the great end of his mediation" is "the conquering of all his church's enemies,"[30] or the defeat of those traditional powers, such as Satan and Antichrist, who oppose him and the Christian church throughout history. Christ's message of salvation, then, included the whole of creation, because he "possesses" the whole universe and has it "managed as much as possible according to his will." This doctrine, thought Edwards, is "not a probable scheme, but absolutely certain."[31]

At this stage, abstract ideas mark the development of Edwards's historical thought. Defined mainly by general concepts pertaining to Christ's role in history, the work of redemption is devoid of any specific notion concerning the relationship between grace and time and thus does not reflect the actual historical process. During the early 1720s Edwards's chief aim was the development of his theology of nature; the reconstruction of time was only a by-product. However, the fact that he began his consideration of time and history during the period when his primary concern was to explain the essential nature of reality, shows how inescapable the effect of his conversion moment was on his construction of both space and time. But whereas in his scientific writings Edwards was attacking the prevailing scientific culture of his time, or more specifically the mechanical interpretation of the nature of reality, at the beginning of his work on time he did not single out any definite school of historical thought for refutation.[32] The growth of Edwards's historical, like his sci-

---

[28] Edwards, *Miscellany* no. 86 (c. 1723), p. 250.

[29] Edwards, *Miscellany* no. 104 (c. 1724), p. 273.

[30] Edwards, *Miscellany* no. 86 (c. 1723), p. 250.

[31] Edwards, *Miscellany ff* (c. 1722–23), p. 184.

[32] In his recent study Gerald R. M. McDermott shows that Edwards was engaged in debating deism from the early 1720s on. See McDermott, *Jonathan Edwards Confronts the Gods: Christian Theology, Enlightenment Religion and Non-Christian Faiths.* Notwithstanding the lack of direct references to deistic writers in his *Miscellanies* of that time, Ed-

entific, consciousness at this early period may be taken, then, as being based on his conversion, which led him to understand history as inseparable from Christ's message of redemption.

The redemptive office of Christ and his rule over the created order implies that "God did not create the world for nothing." On the contrary, there is a grand theological teleology inherent in creation, which leads Edwards to conclude "religion must be the end of this creation, the great end, the very end." And since, as he believed, only intelligent beings can comprehend the essential theological and teleological structure inherent in the universe, therefore "religion is the very business, the noble business of intelligent beings, and for this end God has placed us upon earth."[33] As can be seen in these early formulations, the reconstruction of sacred space led Edwards directly to the construction of sacred time, namely, to a vision of history as directly controlled by God's plan of salvation as manifested in Christ's redemptive office. Moreover, since the universe has no autonomous existence apart from its Creator, the world was created ultimately to serve some transcendental aim that lies beyond it. Thus, in accordance with his theistic metaphysics, Edwards declared "the end of creation is that the creation will glorify" God, or conversely, "God has created the whole world for his own glory, that therefore he will glorify himself transcendently."[34] Viewing creation in such wide teleological terms, Edwards constructed a sacred dimension of time with high praise for the great "enchantment" evident in "Scripture history." For it is in the sacred books that the whole redemptive dimension of history is most evident. Although "it is destitute of all rhetorical ornaments," scripture history is "vastly more pleasant, agreeable, easy and natural, than any other history whatever. It shines brighter with the amiable simplicity of truth." One of Edwards's main reasons for this approval is that scripture shows the providential scheme of history and human beings' essential involvement in it: "Scripture sets forth things just as they happened" so that "we insensibly fancy not that we are readers but spectators, yea actors in the business."[35]

In constructing the dimension of sacred space, and declaring the whole of creation's absolute dependence on God's will and power, Edwards began his exposition of the nature of time and the meaning of history. The question of Satan, for example, is inseparable from history because

---

wards's reconstruction of time could thus also be seen in the context of the deistic debates of the early eighteenth century.

[33] Edwards, *Miscellany gg* (c. 1722–23), p. 185.

[34] Edwards, *Miscellany* no. 3 (c. 1723), pp. 199–200; *Miscellany* no. 106 (c. 1723–24), p. 276. Later Edwards developed this argument more fully in *Dissertation Concerning the End to which God Created the World* (1755).

[35] Edwards, *Miscellany* no. 6 (c. 1723), pp. 202–203.

"God contrived [it] on purpose, to make way for Christ's kingdom and the spreading of his gospel through the world." Accordingly, the establishment of Christ's kingdom in the world created a strong apocalyptic trend—history became a crucial stage for the progress of God's divine revelation and acquired an eschatological dimension. If the whole course of history is conceived in eschatological terms, it is evident that divine revelation "rendered the time the fittest for Christ's appearing of any that ever had been, [and] this was the fullness of time." The rhythms of time and history are thus all subordinated to God's sovereign will and power. For example, divine providence very prudently calculated Christ's first coming during the time of the Roman Empire, when "the world became one body; which was a vast advantage to the quick propagating of the Gospel throughout the whole" world.[36] Historical occurrences signified the eschatological scheme. At this stage, Edwards was following rather closely the Protestant and Puritan apocalyptic interpretation of history, according to which God's redemptive activity is most evident in terms of the realization of prophetic revelation, as manifested in certain decisive historical events.

Clearly, in this redemptive context, not only are "all creatures and all the operations of the universe . . . only the immediate influence of God,"[37] but divine providence directs the whole time and every event in history, because "God created the world for his Son, that he might prepare a spouse or a bride for him to bestow his love upon."[38] Historical occurrences, therefore, are intelligible only in this broader scheme. History is essentially apocalyptic, illuminating the unfolding revelation of God's redemptive plan in time. So, for example, "God first revealed the laws with thunders and lightning from Mount Sinai before the full revelation of his grace by Christ, to prepare the more for the reception of that grace, and so in the destruction of Jerusalem before the preaching [of] the Gospel to the gentile world, and the dreadful destruction of Antichrist before the full revealing of his grace to the whole world."[39] In the mystery of salvation, then, historical events are closely intertwined with prophetic revelations and vice versa; history and prophecy are inextricable.

As can be seen at this early stage of Edwards's construction of time during the 1720s, his interpretation of history was based upon abstract notions and founded on a simple and naive correlation between prophetic revelations and events. Structured according to a redemptive plan, historical occurrences served, Edwards thought, as a sure sign in unveiling the

---

[36] Edwards, *Miscellany* no. 156 (c. 1725), p. 306.
[37] Edwards, *Miscellany* no. 177 (c. 1725), p. 326.
[38] Edwards, *Miscellany* no. 271 (c. 1727), p. 374.
[39] Edwards, *Miscellany* no. 337 (c. 1728–29), p. 412.

mystery of salvation history. On the other hand, prophetic revelations constituted the main source for unrestricted progress (an important concept of the early Enlightenment) in history, as can be seen, for example, in Edwards's explanation of the advancement of learning. "The increase of learning in philosophy in the Christian world is owing to revelation: the doctrines of the Word of God are the foundation of all useful and excellent knowledge." This correlation between divine revelation and learning signified that the progress of divine revelation would usher in the advancement of all sorts of knowledge: "Revelation is that light in the world from whence has beamed forth not only the knowledge of religion, but all valuable truths; 'tis the fountain of that light which has lightened the understanding of men with all sorts of knowledge" such as in regard to "the world, human nature, spirits, providence, time, eternity."[40]

In contrast to the development of his theology of nature during the 1720s, Edwards did not formulate during that decade any precise notions pertaining to time or suggest a distinct interpretation regarding the historical process. In his construction of space he established God's sovereignty over the order of creation through the agency of the atomic doctrine. Yet as concerns the dimension of time he was unable as yet to find a similar concrete agent in history through which he would be able to show God's sovereignty in time. He did not succeed in isolating an historical phenomenon to assist him in proclaiming God as the Lord of history and to throw light on his redemptive activity. Rather, he followed the premises of the Protestant and Puritan apocalyptic philosophy of history, which depended on the close association between history and prophecy. Although he had already coined the concept of God's work of redemption, Edwards continued to speak in general, abstract terms about the relationship between redemption and history. At this stage in the development of his historical thought there is no sense of actual historical change, or of concrete redemptive activity within time, and accordingly no clear definition of the nature of God's work of redemption.

During the 1730s, however, this picture was greatly transformed. A change took place in Edwards's mind regarding God and the work of redemption, and, consequently, about time and history. The correlation he had made between prophetic revelations and history appeared too simple to his mind, because it did not really encompass the complex issue of salvation history. Having been unable to identify the main historical forces operating in the theater of history, Edwards felt that he ought to redefine the relationship between grace and time in order to establish God's redemptive activity in creation. He was conscious that his early

[40] Edwards, *Miscellany* no. 350 (c. 1729), p. 424.

formulations did not take into account the specific, concrete historical means and manifestations by which divine providence directs earthly, historical events, nor the essence of the redemptive process within time and history. To overcome this problem, and striving to prove God's sovereignty in time, Edwards tried to better define the connection between redemption and conversion. Since from his own conversion experience he knew the tremendous effect of God's saving grace on the soul, he strove to establish a close connection between the personal experience of conversion, as the manifestation of God's redemptive activity, and the external, providential scheme of time, and to show that personal salvation was inextricable from sacred, providential history.

The Work of Redemption and the Work of Conversion

There is evidence that, in the early 1730s, Edwards tried to acquire a more serious understanding of God's work of redemption. At the time he struggled with the meaning of "the affairs of redemption"[41] and strove for deeper knowledge and understanding of God's redemptive activity. The theme of the "Wisdom of God in the Work of Redemption," or the "Redemption Discourse," to use John F. Wilson's phrase, emerged as a "significant" issue "in the early 1730s."[42] Searching for some historical phenomenon by which to delineate God's redemptive activity in the world, Edwards argued that "redemption is often spoken of as a work of wonderful power as well as grace," because "it is a more glorious work of power than mere creation, or raising a dead body to life."[43] This definition of course springs from Edwards's own conversion experience.

Having made a connection between redemption and conversion, in the early 1730s Edwards strove to describe the relation between God's redemptive activity and human beings' spiritual welfare. His discourse did not deal with historical events or history as a whole. Thus, for example, he argued that it is "so ordered in redemption, that thereby man's dependence should become greater on God, and man should be brought nearer to God";[44] hence, "whatever natural inclination there is in us," God "may be the center of it, and that God may be all in all."[45] The reason for this is that the "creature was God's before, as he created it, and as it was

---

[41] Edwards, *God Glorified in the Work of Redemption*, in *SJE*, p. 78.
[42] Wilson, introduction, p. 14.
[43] Edwards, *God Glorified in the Work of Redemption*, p. 72.
[44] Edwards, *Miscellany* no. 508 (c. 1731), in *MISA*, p. 54.
[45] Edwards, *Miscellany* no. 510 (c. 1731), in *MISA*, p. 54.

absolutely dependent on God for its being." This dependence, however, is much more urgent after the conversion moment since " 'tis God's as he has created it again. 'Tis God's as he hath redeemed [it] from a state infinitely worse than nothing, and brought it to a state vastly better than its former being before the fall."[46] In this context, the work of redemption in the form of private conversion and salvation was accorded a high cosmological and teleological significance in the order of time:

> That God should so lay out himself, and do things so astonishingly great to redeem man, argues the exceeding greatness of his misery; and so doth the work of redemption's being made so much of, that all the great works of God that were wrought in the world before, and all laws and divine constitutions, must be so contrived as to be only introductory to it. Everything must be so ordered as to be a shadow; it must be so much prophesied of, spoken of so often in such an exalted manner, in songs and psalms, that all the events in the world must be only so many preparations for it. Doubtless 'tis a redemption from a very great misery, as well as to a great happiness, or it would not be made so much of.[47]

Redeeming the soul, dealing with inner spiritual welfare, is an essential concern of God's work of redemption. More particularly, redemption through the mysterious operation of God's saving grace in conversion is one of the main manifestations of God's redemptive activity in time.

Perhaps the clearest manifestation of this close connection between God's work of redemption and conversion is Edwards's famous 1731 Boston sermon, *God Glorified in the Work of Redemption*. Indeed, the main argument of this sermon, in term of God's work of redemption, is the close association of redemption with the personal, saving experience of conversion, which may explain why it is almost devoid of reference to history. No historical movements are introduced in this sermon, nor is there a sense of progress in history; the sermon proposes no definite goal to be achieved in the historical realm or a vision of redeeming time as a whole. "God glorified in the work of redemption," or "the marvelous wisdom of God, in the work of redemption,"[48] denotes almost exclusively the work of conversion. Since the locus of redemption was seen mostly in terms of the private experience of saving grace in conversion, Edwards's exegesis in this sermon of God's redemptive activity did not deal with time and history. "What God aims in the disposition of things in the affairs of redemption," he declared, was that "man should not glory in himself, but

[46] Edwards, *Miscellany* no. 508 (c. 1731), p. 54.
[47] Edwards, *Miscellany* no. 509 (c. 1731), in *MISA*, p. 54.
[48] Edwards, *God Glorified in the Work of Redemption*, p. 79.

alone in God." This means, among other things, that human redemption is based upon "absolute and immediate dependence" upon God; therefore, "the work of redemption" signifies an "absolute and universal dependence of the redeemed on him."[49] Seeing that human beings' "redemption is often spoken of as a work of wonderful power as well as grace," evidently the "great power of God appears in bringing a sinner from his low state from the depth of sin and misery, to such an exalted state of holiness and happiness." The affairs of redemption here have to do first and foremost with the private and spiritual saving experience of conversion, which reveals how much human beings are "dependent on God's power through every step of our redemption," and not so much with God's redemptive activity in history:

> Yea, it is a more glorious work of power than mere creation, or raising a dead body to life, in that the effect attained is greater and more excellent. That holy and happy being, and spiritual life which is produced in the work of conversion, is a far greater and more glorious effect, than mere being and life. And the state from whence the change is made—a death in sin, a total corruption of nature, and depth of misery—is far more remote from the state attained, than mere death or non-entity.[50]

The affairs of redemption, in this sermon, have almost nothing to do with history; they relate mainly to the spiritual operation of saving grace. Thus, as far as the spiritual, private dimension of the soul is concerned, it is "certain that what God aims at in the disposition of things in redemption" is to show that "God should appear all, and man nothing."[51] No historical movements, or historical changes, are presented in the sermon, but only various descriptions of the mighty power of God's saving grace in transforming a dead body into life. The effect of this saving power in conversion is considered greater than the creation of the whole material world. Redemption is not associated with historical time, or with the grand progress of history, but mostly with inner spiritual movements and changes within the soul. Since the dimension of history is alien to the dimension of the spirit and indifferent to it, there is no movement from the private saving experience of conversion in the soul, the exclusive domain of redemption, to the stage of history. The progress of the work of redemption has no relation to history as such, but is identified with an existential change within the spiritual domain attained through the power of saving grace in conversion.

[49] Ibid., pp. 68–69.
[50] Ibid., p. 72.
[51] Ibid., p. 79.

God's Great Design in History

An examination of Edwards's writings during the 1730s shows that a gradual yet very significant transformation was taking place in his mind. As seen in the *Miscellanies* of 1731, he began to reconsider the relationship between grace and the created order, redemption and history, striving to get a clearer notion of God's overall aim in the creation of the world in order to fully understand the affairs of redemption and God's purpose "in the disposition of things in redemption."[52] Accordingly, he began to explore the dialectical relationship between God's transcendence and immanence in creation. For God had a definite end in the creation of the world and this end was essential to the order of time and the course of history:

> That God takes care of and governs the world is evident, because the same ends, designs, and motives (whatever they were) that induced God to create the world, will oblige him forever to take care of it and look after it. . . . For whatever end it was, that [God] gave the world a being, to be continued in being; it must be supposed that the continuance of the being of the world, so long as God does continue [it] in being, or so long as he made it to be continued in being, is that which as much concerns the obtaining of God's end, as the first giving of it being.[53]

As this passage attests, Edwards increasingly dwelt on the overall issue of God's aim in creation and strove to illuminate the great design and scheme in time and history. His efforts led him to a conclusion regarding the relationship between grace and created order. From that moment Edwards was more confident about the question of "God's end in making and governing the world," and hence about the broader meaning of providential history:

> There is doubtless some design that God is pursuing, and scheme that he is Carrying on, in the various changes and revolutions that from age to age happen in the world; there is some certain great design, to which providence subordinates all the successive changes that come to pass in the state of affairs of man-

---

[52] According to Ava Chamberlain, Edwards's long involvement during the 1730s with the issue of God's work of redemption should be considered in the broad context of his struggle against deism. In that period, out of his effort "to confute deistic claims," Edwards became "increasingly confident that the argument from history was more persuasive than the argument from reason." See Chamberlain, introduction, in *MISA*, pp. 30–31. For Edwards's debate with deism, see McDermott, *Jonathan Edwards Confronts the Gods: Christian Theology, Enlightenment Religion and Non-Christian Faiths*.

[53] Edwards, *Miscellany* no. 525 (c. 1731), in *MISA*, p. 68.

kind. All revolutions from the beginning of the world to the end, are doubtless but various parts of one scheme, all conspiring for the bringing to pass the great event which is ultimately in view. And the scheme will not be finished, nor the design fully accomplished, the great event fully brought to pass, till the end of the world and the last revolution is brought about. The world, it is most evident, is not an everlasting thing; it will have an end: and God's end in making and governing the world will not be fully obtained, nor his scheme be finished, till the end of the world comes. If it were, he would put an end to it sooner; for God won't continue the world, won't continue to uphold it, and dispose and govern it, and cause changes and revolutions in it, after he has nothing further that he aims at by it.[54]

Written during 1731, these words reflect the development of Edwards's historical consciousness regarding God's ultimate goal in time. Thus defined, God's relationship with the created order led directly to a rethinking of history. From the beginning of the world to its end, the divine plan unfolds, a sacred scheme for the sake of which God has created the world and "to which providence subordinates all the successive changes that come to pass in the state of affairs of mankind."[55] All occurrences in time, all the passages of history, are only a "various part" of that overarching goal, and therefore subordinated to this great design. Every historical event is tightly interwoven into this theological and teleological framework. A sacred plan directs the whole of time from the creation to the end of the world. So constituted, God's great design manifests the essence and goal of the historical process itself. History, being a special dimension of time regulated by and subordinated to the sacred transcendent aim that lies beyond it, is situated between the eternity before creation and the eternity that will ensue after the end of the world, the "eternity after time shall be no more."[56] God's sovereignty was thus firmly asserted within time. Edwards seems to have been pleased with this new conceptual framework because he incorporated it in later major works, such as the *History of the Work of Redemption* (1739) and the *Dissertation Concerning the End for which God Created the World* (1755).

Constructing God's great design and scheme in this way, Edwards could go on to say that divine providence directs all "the state of affairs of mankind . . . from the beginning of the world to the end."[57] One characteristic of this theological teleology of history is the dimension of progress

---

[54] Edwards, *Miscellany* no. 547 (c. 1731), pp. 93–94. Edwards wrote this entry after his Boston lecture *God Glorified in the Work of Redemption*, preached on July 8, 1731.

[55] Edwards, *Miscellany* no. 547, p. 93.

[56] Edwards, *History of the Work of Redemption*, p. 508.

[57] Edwards, *Miscellany* no. 547, p. 93.

inherent in time, a notion which the Enlightenment introduced into historical discourse in the early eighteenth century, and which Edwards embraced. "Things in their series and course in providence," so he believed,
or the whole course of providential history, clearly manifested "a progress
towards a certain final issue, and every revolution brings nearer to that
issue," namely, "Christ's second coming" and the last judgment.[58] For
God does not accomplish his scheme in time, nor does he realize his great
design in history in one singular act but rather constantly causes more
progress in order to achieve his overall grand plan, although its full realization will occur only after the end of the world. The belief that God
accomplishes his goal in history in one decisive saving act, Edwards was
careful to explain, may lead to the unsound and dangerous contention
that there is no change in time and thus deprive God of his role as the
absolute Lord of history. Rather, God constantly directs and transforms
the course and progress of time according to his grand design:

> God don't fully obtain his design in any one particular state that the world has
> been in at one time, but in the various successive states that the world is in, in
> different ages, connected in a scheme. 'Tis evident that he don't fully obtain his
> end, his design, in any one particular state that the world has ever been in; for
> if so, we should have no change. But God is continually causing revolutions;
> providence makes a continual progress, and continually is bringing forth things
> new in the state of the world, and very different from what ever were before;
> he removes one that he may establish another. And perfection will not be ob-
> tained till the last revolution, when God's design will be fully reached.[59]

Defined in these terms, history is a great revelatory play bearing the
mark of God's redemptive plan in creation. It is apocalyptic and eschatological, for it concerns the unveiling and accomplishing of God's grand
scheme in time. What is significant here, moreover, is that the historical
process acquires its own legitimacy and validity—God's plan is closely
connected to a definable change and progress within history. In such a
close-knit system of thought, there is not, and cannot be, any separation
between grace and time, as Augustine thought, for history has been structured since eternity to manifest the unfolding of God's plan. The order of
time, thus, is inseparable from the order of grace because divine providence determines the passage of time and the course of history. No divorce
is possible between God's aim in creation and the movement of history.
Since time is carefully structured according to the divine plan, every event
in history has its own redemptive meaning and revelatory significance in
the overall great design:

[58] Edwards, *Notes on Scripture*, 389 (1739), pp. 375, 378.
[59] Edwards, *Miscellany* no. 547, p. 94.

Nor yet are the past states of the world abolished by revolutions because they are in vain, or don't do anything towards promoting his design in creating the world; if so, providence would never have ordered them, the world never would have been in such a state. There remains therefore no other way, but that the various successive states of the world do in conjunction, or as connected in a scheme, together attain God's great design.[60]

Edwards's God is clearly not *Deus absconditus*, who hides himself and his plans in time and space, but rather *Deus revelatus*, a God who constantly reveals himself and exhibits His work of redemption in history as in nature. Moreover, God's plan in time raises the central issue of the purpose of creation. Edwards found the answer to this question in what lay beyond history. For all this great design is of no avail if "the perception of the intelligence of the world don't remain after the world comes to an end." Without some perceiving beings continuing to exist after the end of the world and history, "the world and all that is pertain to it, and its various successive states and revolutions, the whole absolutely ceases and comes to nothing." Edwards had already developed these arguments during the 1720s in his scientific writings,[61] and now he integrated them into his conception of time and history. The whole divine plan in creation has no meaning if some beings existing in history do not transcend the end of the world. For then "no benefit, nor glory, nor honor to God himself, nor to any other, remains." Without perceiving beings "at the end of the world, at the close of all things, when the great design of the whole scheme is to be fully attained, nothing at all is attained."[62] Consequently, "the intelligent beings of the world should be made acquainted with" God's "providential disposition of things," for "God's great design, is something concerning them; and the revolution by which it is to be brought to pass are revolutions among them and in their state." History is neither strange to nor alienated from God's ultimate aim in creation. Rather, it is a special dimension of time constructed for teaching and educating human beings in the mystery of God's design in the creation of the world and the eternal promise that lies beyond it. For it is "most rational to suppose, that God should reveal the design he has [been] carrying on, to his rational creatures: that as God has made them capable of it, they may actively fall in with it and promote it, and act therein as the subjects and friends of God."[63] The validity of the historical process is thus established since human beings have an important role to play in the executing of God's grand plan. The view Edwards advances here is that modes of conviction

---

[60] Ibid.

[61] See, for example, *Of Being*, pp. 203–4.

[62] Edwards, *Miscellany* no. 547, pp. 94–95.

[63] Ibid., p. 95.

should direct modes of action, or that historical consciousness is essential to any participation of human beings in shaping the course of history. Thus, as in his theology of nature, Edwards believed that God's design in time and history is most intelligible and rational and can be deciphered by human reason.

This was Edwards's first systematic interpretative framework for God's scheme in history, founded on the essential congruity between God's grand design and human beings' ability to understand it, and consequently upon their participation in its execution and accomplishment. From then on, his efforts would be directed toward discovering this great design in time and history. The concept of the essential relationship between God and creation places the dimension of history within an apocalyptic dimension of time. Not only does the divine goal invest time with sacred meaning, but history itself shows the unfolding of divine revelation. Thus,

> Christ came in the fullness of time. It would not have been so well for Christ to have come presently after the fall; for it was needful, that men should be first seen in a fallen [state] after the world was peopled, that it might be seen and thoroughly proved and remembered, what calamity and misery mankind were under before the redemption, what a doleful state the world was in while left under the dominion of Satan. It must not be before the flood; because then it would not be within memory, as it is now. It must not be soon after the flood; for then it would be before the world is well peopled, and before the apostasy from the true God to heathenism is so great universal [sic], which was needful in order to the redemption's being conspicuous.[64]

Since history is inseparable from the progressive realization of God's revelation, historical conditions are essential to the unfolding of the divine plan in time. To advance its redemptive design, divine providence has very carefully calculated the time and season for the realization of prophetic revelations according to certain historical conditions.

However important to the development of Edwards's historical thought, all these various descriptions of God's grand design were in fact too general and abstract in character and lacked a specific locus in history. So far, Edwards's understanding of God's scheme in creation was devoid of any concrete, particular historical agents. He had not yet been able to find some plausible phenomenon characterizing God's plan in time, nor a distinct agent by which to demonstrate the materialization of divine providence in history. Several years passed before he was ready to identify his sense of God's great design with the work of redemption, and to de-

---

[64] Edwards, *Miscellany* no. 569, in *MISA*, pp. 105–6.

clare the phenomenon of revival and awakening as its ultimate realization in time and history.

The 1730s witnessed, then, an expansion of Edwards's historical thought that was based on a change in his understanding of the dialectic of God's transcendence and immanence in creation. According to his theistic metaphysics, God's absolute sovereignty encompassed the whole of creation, and therefore he began to consider in earnest the concept of God's great design in creation. However, an explanation of historical events always depends on an interpretative framework, or on some ideology of history. Edwards had not yet developed a coherent philosophy of history when the "little revival" of 1734–35 engulfed Northampton and the Connecticut Valley; thus, he possessed no clear interpretation into which he could incorporate this event and explain its significance in the general context of salvation history. As he himself admitted, he did not at first know how to understand this manifestation of the pouring out of the Spirit of God. Throughout the awakening, therefore, Edwards never attempted to place it within a wider context of providential history, or within God's great design in creation. Only several years after the decline of the revival did he finally realize that providence had indeed revealed to him the very historical agent he was seeking in order to establish the proper relationship between grace and time. Only then, when he defined revival and the effusion of the Spirit as the locus of sacred, ecclesiastical history, could he at last develop a well-defined historical philosophy based upon a redemptive mode of historical thought. First, however, we shall see why the revival of the 1730s caught Edwards by surprise and why he was so reluctant to draw from it some lessons with regard to history.

Conversion, Revival, and Redemption—The "Little Revival," 1734–1735

Although for many years Puritan New England had been accustomed to the phenomena of revivals and awakenings, the "little revival" caught Edwards and his Northampton congregation unawares. When they encountered the first wave of the revival, many in New England "seemed not to know what to make of it."[65] Contributing to this bewilderment was the sheer extent of the phenomenon: "The surprising work of the Spirit of God," as Edwards said, "seems to be upon every account an extraordinary dispensation of providence. Tis extraordinary upon the ac-

---

[65] "Benjamin Colman's Abridgment, November 1736," pp. 118–27.

count of [the] universality of it in affecting all sort, high and low, rich and poor, wise and unwise, old and young, vicious and moral."[66]

Edwards of course had many reasons to be proud of the very "extraordinary circumstances of this town" in regard to "God's Spirit being so remarkably poured out" on his congregation.[67] The revival was a test of his growing maturity and ability as the ecclesiastical and spiritual leader of the church in Northampton after the death of Solomon Stoddard in 1729. In fact, Stoddard's tenure had been blessed with many revivals. "There had been five 'harvests' [revivals] during Stoddard's sixty-years pastorate" in Northampton: "in 1679, 1683, 1696, 1712, and 1718."[68] Edwards of course knew this chronology.[69] In the series of harvests in Northampton, the revival of 1734–35 would have been the sixth, but for Edwards it was the first under his own spiritual leadership, and it was dear and precious to him to see this "extraordinary dispensation of providence," which might place him directly in the line of his grandfather's most celebrated spiritual and ecclesiastical heritage. Having so far worked in the shadow of Stoddard, Edwards naturally spared no effort to make a distinction between his own harvest and those of his famous predecessor, claiming that in contrast to his grandfather's revivals, which manifested "nothing of any general awakening," under his own leadership the revival of 1734–35 was rather "extraordinary upon the account of [the] universality of it in affecting" all sorts of people.[70] The geographical extent of the revival, which included the Connecticut River Valley as a whole, added to his satisfaction. "Nothing like it had ever occurred before in New England, where previous revivals were largely sporadic and isolated instances."[71] In sum, the "results of the revival deeply gratified Edwards." The "Spirit of God appeared to be creating an entire society of saintly men, submissive to God and exquisitely sensitive to religion, a society which confirmed and supported the identity Edwards himself had assumed in his own conversion."[72]

[66] Edwards, "Unpublished Letter of May 30, 1735," p. 107.

[67] Ibid., pp. 99, 107.

[68] Goen, introduction, in GA, p. 5.

[69] Stoddard "had five harvests, as he called them," wrote Edwards in his letter to the Reverend Benjamin Colman in November 6, 1736. See "Benjamin Colman's Abridgment, November 1736," p. 114. See also Edwards, A Faithful Narrative of the Surprising Work of God, 1737, p. 146.

[70] Edwards, in "Benjamin Colman's Abridgment," p. 115; "Unpublished Letter of May 30, 1735," p. 107.

[71] Goen, introduction, in GA, p. 25.

[72] Richard L. Bushman, "Jonathan Edwards as Great Man," in Religion in American History: Interpretive Essays, ed. John M. Mulder and John F. Wilson (Englewood Cliffs, N.J.: Prentice-Hall, 1978), p. 124.

However, Edwards was very cautious with regard to understanding the revival phenomenon. Thus, for example, he wrote in June 1735: "I forbear to make reflections, or to guess what God is about to do" with this remarkable outpouring of his Spirit.[73] Since he had not yet fully established the proper link between redemption and history, he was reluctant to come to any radical conclusion regarding the meaning of the awakening in the larger context of providential history. Much of his writing and correspondence during the revival shows that he considered this event almost solely in terms of the operation of saving grace in converting the souls of his congregation and not as an essential part of God's overall grand design in time and history. The main "design of the spirit of God" in the "little revival," he was convinced, "seem[s] to issue in conversion,"[74] and the means God used "in promoting this work among us," he explained, was in "the awakening [of] sinners."[75]

The suddenness of the revival left Edwards much puzzled regarding God's intention in causing such a visitation of his Spirit in New England. Not only he, of course, but many in New England found it hard to understand this surprising event. "When this work of God first appeared, and was so extraordinarily carried on among us in the winter" of 1734–35, admitted Edwards, his congregation and "others round about us seemed not to know what to make of it." All he was sure of was that these "remarkable pourings out of the Spirit of God" were not limited to his town but "extended from one end of the country to the other." It was something more general than the traditional harvest Northampton had been accustomed to for many years. Edwards was therefore confident that this event signified something unusual in terms of the mystery of divine providence: "That it seems a very extraordinary dispensation of Providence beyond God's usual way of working, on this account of the universality of it" in effecting the "experience of the work of conversion." Following the Puritan tradition of describing revivals in terms of the operation of saving grace, conversion, and reformation, Edwards stressed the morphology of conversion as the ultimate concern of the Spirit of God, and not any historical implication that might be attached to this awakening in God's grand design in history. The significance of the revival lay therefore in transforming the people of Northampton into "a reformed people"; the most obvious outcome was that "God has evidently made us a new people." Understood in such terms, Edwards concluded, "so it has pleased God to work, and we are evidently a people blessed of him; and in this

---

[73] Edwards, "Unpublished Letter," p. 109.
[74] Edwards, in "Benjamin Colman's Abridgment," p. 123.
[75] Edwards, *Faithful Narrative*, p. 177.

corner of the world God dwells and manifests his glory." The main consequence of the revival lay in effecting religious reformation, not in changing or transforming history, and in this capacity it was a model to be
emulated by others in the Christian world because "A City set upon the
hill cannot be hid [Matt. 5:14]."[76] In his early account of 1736, Edwards
did not find any specific historical ramifications in the "little revival," nor
did he attach to it any redemptive implications for the course of sacred,
providential history. Accordingly, "Edwards ascribed no millennial significance or preparatory role to this awakening."[77]

It was left therefore to certain ministers in England to extract the redemptive and revelatory historical significance of the "little revival." In
their preface to the first edition of Edwards's *A Faithful Narrative of the
Surprising Work of God* (1737), the English ministers Isaac Watts and
John Guyse provided the earliest attempts to understand the New England revival in the broader context of ecclesiastical history. Never did
we "hear or read," they wrote, "since the first ages of Christianity, any
event of this kind so surprising as the present" awakening in New England. Overcome by the display and extent of God's "free and sovereign
mercy in the conversion of a great multitude of souls in [such] a short
space of time," they compared it to "the miracle of Gideon's fleece." Incorporating the revival in America into the general history of the church
upon earth, Watts and Guyse considered this event not as a provincial
affair pertaining only to ecclesiastical life and experience in colonial New
England. For them the revival inaugurated an apocalyptic and eschatological moment in providential history: "such astonishing exercise" of
Christ's "power and mercy" in America unmistakably revealed that "he
begins to accomplish any [sic] of his promises concerning the latter days."
Loading the revival with such eschatological and apocalyptic significance,
the English ministers considered it a crucial trigger for the accomplishment of the rest of God's prophetic revelations, to be fulfilled at the end
of time and history. They were convinced that "this happy event" in New
England shows "how easy it will be for our blessed Lord to make a full
accomplishment of all his predictions concerning his kingdom, and to
spread his dominion from sea to sea, through all the nations of the
world."[78] The English ministers were thus the first to capture the full redemptive significance of the revival in America, and thus to integrate it
within salvation history. Perceiving the awakening as a sure sign of the
imminent fulfillment of God's revelations in the "latter days," they be-

---

[76] Edwards, in "Benjamin Colman's Abridgment," pp. 118–27.

[77] Stein, introduction, in *AW*, p. 20.

[78] Isaac Watts and John Guyse, "Preface to the First Edition (London, 1737)" of Edwards's *Faithful Narrative*, in *GA*, pp. 130–32.

lieved it would give rise to eschatological expectations and millennial visions in their own time. Edwards, as we shall see, would come to similar conclusions only several years later, during the Great Awakening.

In his *Faithful Narrative* (1737), Edwards was much more modest in his understanding of the revival, believing that its main concern was personal conversion. He therefore made no attempt to place the revival within a wider historical and eschatological and apocalyptic context. Instead, he resorted time and again to the "converting influence of God's Spirit" during the awakening in his town, presenting with much detail some specific cases of the morphology of conversion.[79] Redemption being related mainly to conversion, and thus concerning the condition of spiritual welfare, there is no discussion of history in the *Faithful Narrative*, nor any attempt to probe the general issue of God's redemptive plan. Even in his private notes in the *Miscellanies* written during this period, Edwards did not yet establish a coherent connection between grace and time. So far, he had spoken in general terms of God's work of redemption and his grand scheme in history, but without elaborating in specific historical terms what exactly the form and content of this great design were, nor demonstrating their manifestations in history.

In 1737, therefore, even in face of the "little revival," Edwards did not identify the historical event with God's redemptive design in history. The association he made between God's work of redemption and conversion appears in his public writings, such as the *Faithful Narrative*, and his private notes in the *Miscellanies* of that period. But this should not prevent us from seeing that the "remarkable religious" affair in which "the Spirit of God" so "extraordinarily"[80] manifested itself in his town eventually had a lasting impact on the formation of Edwards's philosophy of history. For as a direct consequence of this revival he began to ponder in earnest the historical issue of "the advancement of Christ's kingdom in the world" and his "mind ha[d] been much entertained and delighted with the scripture promises and prophecies, which related to the future glorious advancement of Christ's kingdom upon earth."[81] According to Alan Heimert, the "revivals of the 1730s encouraged Edwards's inquiries into the 'History of the Advancement of Christ's Kingdom,' and his attention to its progress in the contemporary world.' "[82] Furthermore, as Stephen Stein shows, in "no period was Edwards's public discretion on apoc-

---

[79] Edwards, *Faithful Narrative*, p. 179. For detailed relation of some cases of conversion, see pp. 191–205 in this work.

[80] "Benjamin Colman's Abridgment," pp. 115–16.

[81] Edwards, *Personal Narrative*, p. 800. According to Alan Heimert, Edwards wrote these words after the revival of 1734–35. See Heimert, *Religion and the American Mind*, p. 61.

[82] Heimert, *Religion and the American Mind*, p. 61.

alyptic issues more evident than at the time of the surprising conversion in Northampton during the winter of 1734–35." Yet, despite his increased involvement at the time with apocalyptic thought in the *Notes on the Apocalypse*, Edwards was reluctant to interpret the "little revival" in millennial terms, and he ascribed "no millennial significance"[83] to it.

The Work of Redemption and God's Self-Glorification

As suddenly as it came, so the revival declined in the summer of 1735. "The revival reached its peak in the early spring of 1735, after about three months of intense excitement." Soon it came into a full stop. "The spell was broken, the emotional climate changed at once . . . the limit of endurable ecstasies had been reached."[84] Edwards gazed with gloomy eyes at the decline of the revival and the withdrawal of the Spirit of God: "after that great work," he sadly noted, "there has been a very lamentable decay of religious affections, and the engagements of people's spirit in religion."[85] The glorious work "that went so swiftly and wonderfully while God appeared in mighty and irresistible power to carry it on," Edwards lamented in 1737, "has seemed to be very much at stop in these towns for a long time . . . God's Spirit has been withdrawn more and more" from New England.[86] Not only Edwards was saddened, for "it was clear to all that God had withdrawn his spirit. The heavenly shower was over."[87] Edwards, however, was not ready to give up his conviction that the revival was the "remarkable pourings out of the Spirit of God," or "a very extraordinary dispensation of Providence."[88] The whole affair left an indelible mark on him. Evidence can be found in his *Miscellanies* of that period that he tried again and again to modify his own previous conceptions regarding the relationship between redemption and history. Clearly, the revival phenomenon in his town had taught him an important lesson about the power of the Spirit of God in transforming not only the private spiritual welfare of individuals but also the structure of society as a whole. Therefore, redemptive activity could not be ascribed exclusively to the private dimension of the soul in conversion, or solely to the existential condition of human beings; it suggested many consequences concerning history.

[83] Stein, introduction, in *AW*, pp. 19–20.

[84] Winslow, *Jonathan Edwards*, pp. 164–65.

[85] Edwards, "To the Rev. Thomas Prince of Boston," December 12, 1743, in *LPW*, p. 116.

[86] Edwards, "To the Reverend Benjamin Colman," May 19, 1737, in *LPW*, p. 67.

[87] Winslow, *Jonathan Edwards*, p. 165.

[88] "Benjamin Colman's Abridgment," pp. 120–21.

During "the next few years" after the revival Edwards "struggled unremittingly to retrieve the halcyon days when Northampton was 'a city set on a hill.' "[89] This he did not only in the public realm, where he continually rebuked his people for the sad departure of the Spirit of God from their town, but also in his private study. The *Miscellanies* written immediately following the revival show that Edwards immersed himself in his private notes in the effort to incorporate the New England awakening in the context of providential history. Unwilling to see the awakening as an isolated and marginal phenomenon related only to certain ecclesiastical and religious conditions in provincial New England, Edwards tried to make sense of the rise and decline of the "little revival" and to capture its redemptive implications for the general history of the church upon earth.

Between 1735 and 1739, working alone in his study, Edwards transmuted his notes in the *Miscellanies* into a great laboratory where he renewed his effort to define God's end in creation and to grasp the relationship between divine activity and history. The same can be said about the development of his apocalyptic interpretation at this period. "With [Moses] Lowman's *Paraphrase and Notes* in hand, Edward reevaluated his earlier views on the Apocalypse and began a period of concentrated activity" in his *Notes on the Apocalypse*.[90] These were indeed Edwards's most productive years in terms of the shaping of his philosophy of history. This productivity in constructing his ideological premises regarding time and history cannot be understood without taking into account the painful experience of the decline of the revival, which induced in him an urgent desire to understand the reason for which God had created the world.

The sudden surge and fall of the "little revival" had left Edwards much bewildered regarding God's end in creation. To grasp these issues he turned in earnest to a serious exploration of God's aim in creation, this time attempting to explain it in terms of God's self-glorification and the display of the Deity's excellence in creation. He wrote in 1736 that the "Wisdom of God in the Work of Redemption" is evident in the fact that "God ordered all things for his own glory that however great & marvelous the exercises of his grace & love & condescension are to the creature, yet he alone may be exalted & that he may be all in all."[91] Note here the important shift from the creature to God's self-glorification. Faithful to his sense of God's absolute sovereignty in the created order, Edwards realized that redemption could not be properly conceived as an issue separate

[89] Goen, introduction, p. 47.

[90] Stein, introduction, in AW, p. 22. For the influence of Moses Lowman (1680–1752), the dissenting English scholar-divine, and his book *Paraphrase and Notes on the Revelation*, (1737), on Edwards's apocalyptic thought, see Stein, introduction, in AW, especially pp. 22, 55–59.

[91] Edwards, *Miscellany* no. 681 (c. 1736), in MISA, p. 242.

from God's display of his glory in creation. Since redemptive activity is inextricable from the disclosure of God's glory, the general issue of the work of redemption that he had been striving to understand since 1723, Edwards now associated it with God's self-glorification and less with the issue of human salvation. Compared with his previous concepts regarding God's great design, a real transformation had taken place. What is evident at this stage is the gradual identification of redemption with the glory of God. This reformulation is crucial to Edwards's later construction of the work of redemption as the great end of all God's works in creation.

Edwards continued to elaborate on this issue of redemption and the display of God's glory in a short *Miscellany* no. 699 (1736), called "END of the CREATION. GLORY OF GOD." As he now defined it, the "End of Creation" is the "Glory of God," since "God seeks the display of his own glory as a thing in it self excellent," hence "the display of the divine glory is that which is most excellent."[92] Incorporating his own concept of excellency, formulated in "The Mind" to combat the mechanical explanation of the nature of reality,[93] Edwards argued now that this term should be expanded to denote as well God's main goal in creation, namely, his self-glorification. The "wisdom of God in the work of redemption," therefore, engulfed all the universe since in creation God "ordered all things for his own glory" in order to manifest the "display of his own glory," or so that his "infinite goodness should be expressed" in "infinitely good & gracious deeds" in creation.[94] In 1736, then, the "end of creation" and the "glory of God" became inextricable from the structure of time.

> The grand design of Edwards's soteriology, however, manifests itself not in the glorification of individual believers but in the ever-advancing and ever-increasing process of God's self-glorification, which is God's ultimate end in creation.[95]

Edwards, as we have seen, constantly changed his mind regarding the issue of redemption and the nature of history. But in the end he found a solution to the mystery of time by combining his notion of God's work of redemption of 1723 and the concept of God's great design of 1731, with the notion of God's self-glorification as the ultimate end in creation. This move, which he made in 1736, constituted the main source for his later claim that the work of redemption is the "great end and drift of all God's works" and the ultimate reason for which he created the world.

---

[92] Edwards, *Miscellany* no. 699 (c. 1736), in *MISA*, p. 282.
[93] See Edwards, *The Mind*, especially pp. 332–38, 362–66, 380–82.
[94] Edwards, *Miscellany* no. 699 (c. 1736), p. 282.
[95] Morimoto, *Jonathan Edwards and the Catholic Vision of Salvation*, p. 156.

The Work of Redemption as the "Great End and Drift of all Gods Works"

During 1736 Edwards continued to explore the dialectic of God's transcendence and immanence in history. In the past he had constructed several theses regarding the relationship between grace and time, and now in 1736 he felt that he was able to link these separate threads of thought into a coherent teleology of time that would illuminate the association between God's redemptive activity in creation and the course of history. One of his early and daring attempts to do so figures in *Miscellany* no. 702 (1736), entitled "Work of Creation, Providence, Redemption." It is a long entry of 7,000 words, which suggests that Edwards had found an important solution to the problem of the wisdom of God in the work of redemption. Here his general, abstract notions about God's scheme in history give way to a specific formulation regarding the relationship between redemption and history, according to which the work of redemption signifies God's ultimate end in creation. To do this, as the entry shows, Edwards identifies creation with redemption, because the reason for which God created the world is the work of redemption:

> And that work of Gods providence, to which all other works of providence both in the material & immaterial part of the creation, are subservient is the work of redemption. All other works of providence may be looked upon as *appendages* to this great work, or *things* which God does to subserve that grand design. The work of redemption may be looked upon as the great end and drift of all Gods works & dispensations from the beginning & even the end of the work of creation it self.[96]

As Edwards came to think in 1736, the grand design of God in time and history is the work of redemption. The reason for this contention is that God's providence is indeed "superior to the work of creation." Edwards had developed this argument already in 1731, in *Miscellany* no. 547. Yet God's providence, as he argued now, is subordinated to the much wider work of redemption because it is upon this latter work that "all other works of providence" are dependent. Hence the work of redemption should be "called the end of the work of creation." Having had a liking for automatic machines, or engines, and borrowing mechanical philosophy's notion of the world as a huge machine, or automaton, Edwards compared the work of creation with an "engine," or a machine designated to accomplish the goal for which its maker invented it. For "the use and

---

[96] Edwards, *Miscellany* no. 702 (c. 1736), in *MISA*, p. 284.

improvement any artificer makes of an engine, or the work intends with
it is superior to his making the engine."[97] Since all parts in a machine are
subordinated to the purpose for which it was invented, so the creation of
the world should be seen as only one part of God's overall plan of redemption. This mechanization of God's redemptive activity, which testified to
mechanical philosophy's impact on his thought, is one of the most striking
characteristics of Edwards's philosophy of history. Later, as he strove to
enhance God's absolute sovereignty in time, the mechanization of God's
providence constituted a significant dimension in the *History of the Work
of Redemption* (1739), where Edwards declared that all the "changes and
revolutions" in history were "only the turning of the wheels of providence," as well as in other writings of that period.[98] Thus, in order to
emphasize God's sovereignty in history, Edwards tended more and more
in this period to identify providence with a machine, or a clock, saying
"the providence of God is like a wheel," or "a machine composed of
wheels."[99]

In Edwards's mechanization of God's work of redemption, the created
order does not stand for itself, autonomous of its maker, but is subordinated to its Creator's intention in making it. The notion of God's glorification, the end of creation as Edwards claimed in *Miscellany* no. 699,
became the view that the glory of God is most manifested in his providential design of the world. Hence, "God created the world to glorify himself
but it was principally that he might glorify him in his disposal of the
world or in the use he intended to make of it in his providence." Since
"Gods providential disposals of the material part of the world are all
subordinate to his providence towards the spiritual and intelligent part
of it," Edwards concluded that the work of redemption is that "great end
and drift of all Gods works and dispensations" from the beginning to
"the end of the work of creation." God's work of redemption, then, conceived in terms of his great design in creation, encompassed the entire
creation as well as the whole space of time and span of history. Further,
redemption is accorded an important cosmological dimension; it is immersed in time and history, from the creation of the world to its end, and
is not confined exclusively to the private dimension of conversion. As a
whole, then, "the work of creation in itself seems to be so done that it
should shadow forth the work of redemption"; or more specifically, "the

[97] Ibid. pp. 283–84. Edwards's use of technological metaphors may perhaps be understood in the broader context of the evolution of clocks into major cultural images during
the eighteenth century. See Otto Mayer, *Authority, Liberty & Automatic Machinery in Early
Modern Europe* (Baltimore: Johns Hopkins University Press, 1986).

[98] Edwards, *History of the Work of Redemption*, p. 128. See also Edwards's interpretation of Ezekiel's wheel (c. 1739), in *NOS*, pp. 373–77.

[99] Edwards, *Images of Divine Things*, 89 (1739), in *TW*, p. 86.

creation of the visible world" was done according to this "grand design [of] the work of redemption," and "all things" in heaven and earth, "especially in the state & circumstances of the world of mankind," are designated to "shadow forth the things that appertain to this work" of redemption.[100] With these concepts, Edwards discovered a reason for the sacred web of order evident in creation and also the teleology of order embedded in the structure of time. Given that the work of redemption is the sine qua non of the whole of creation, this work is the locus of the sacred dynamism inherent in time.

The extension of the work of redemption to make it the reason and goal of creation and identification of it with God's great design reveal the growth of Edwards's historical consciousness, and hence the development of his historical thought. Defined in cosmological terms, the work of redemption signified the heart of God's relationship to creation, since redemption is the essence of his activity in nature as well as of time. Evidently, this formulation of the order of redemption carries important implications concerning history. There cannot be any separation between redemption and history, for time in general and history in particular are subordinate to God's providential scheme and inseparable from his redemptive activity. Redemption and history are closely interwoven because "the work of redemption is gradually carried on in the world till the church shall be brought to the most perfect & glorious & happy state on earth." Having defined redemption in these historical terms, and declaring that the work of creation is subordinated to the work of redemption, Edwards solved the problem of "why God made the world by Jesus." The answer was that "the creation of the world was a work that was subordinated to the work of redemption," and "the work of redemption was properly the work of the Son." Several strains of thought that Edwards had developed in his theology of nature, especially regarding the laws of nature, were now incorporated to emphasize the cosmological dimension of redemption:

> The works of creation & the laws of nature and that course of nature that God established in creation is [sic] subordinate to the work of redemption, is confirmed by this that the laws & course of nature have often been interrupted to subserve to the designs of the great work of redemption to them and [lay] aside what by nature belonged to them by nature to serve them.[101]

The cosmological dimension of God's work of redemption shows that the whole cosmos is determined by God's redemptive activity: the coming of the "Creatour of heaven & earth himself" into

---

[100] Edwards, *Miscellany* no. 702 (c. 1736), pp. 283–84.
[101] Ibid., pp. 290–91.

this world his (as it were) leaving heaven quitting that glorious habitation &
coming down from it & dwelling in this lower world & even descending into
the lower parts of the earth to accomplish the work of redemption is a great
intimation that both the upper & the lower world heaven earth & hell have
their being in subordination to the work of redemption & from love to the
redeemed.

The entire creation as well as all historical events are necessarily subjected
to God's grand design in the affairs of redemption. In his enthusiasm over
his discovery that redemption is the sine qua non of the whole created
order, Edwards was even willing to withdraw some force from God's sovereignty, even to the point of subordinating God's power to the laws of
nature, in order to emphasize his main point that redemption is the sole
and ultimate goal of creation:

> The God of nature himself became himself subject in many respects to the laws
> of nature in order [sic] to redemption & that he might obtain the designed good
> for the redeemed in receiving nourishment in the womb of a woman & being
> brought forth thence (though not there conceived) in a natural way his living
> by meat & drink sleep &c—& which is much more he was subject to pain &
> death by virtue of the laws of nature.[102]

Since the work of redemption is the ultimate aim of the work of creation,
even God's absolute power can be limited in certain cases to further its
realization. Not only did God create space and time in order to proceed
with the work of redemption, he even laid some constraints upon himself,
subjecting some of his sovereignty to the laws of nature, in order to see
the fulfillment of the work.

To admit that God is subject to the laws of nature may amount to
heresy, in view of the fact that Edwards always emphasized God's absolute sovereignty in the created order. He was very careful therefore to
qualify this radical argument; except for sending Christ into the world in
the form of a human being, "the God of nature never so put himself out
of the way in any wise to use nature to accomplish any thing" in the
work of redemption and "never for any other purposes." On the contrary,
God's usual manner is to suspend certain natural laws for a moment so
that "the laws of nature have often been set aside that they might give
place to the designs of redemption." This was God's way in dividing "the
sea" in Exodus or in "causing the sun & moon to stand still in Joshuas
time." In other words, the "course of nature has been very often stop'd &
made to stand by" to further "the redemption of his people." All these
examples of course are radically different from the case in which God
makes himself succumb to the laws of nature. In this most exceptional

---

[102] Ibid., pp. 290–92.

act of sending Christ down to earth, God reveals that redemption was his ultimate goal and aim in the creation of the world. For God "became subject to nature as he assumed the nature of a creature & lived on earth a natural life & he yielded his own nature to be destroyed for the good of those that were to be redeemed."[103] Only in the extreme and urgent case of sending Christ to the world to proclaim the message of salvation and redemption, did God make himself for a moment subject to natural laws. This extraordinary manifestation, Edwards argued, proves beyond doubt that God's aim in creating the world was the work of redemption.

Edwards was very delightful with his conclusion that "all Gods work both of creation & providence, are subordinate to the work of redemption." Based on his searches in scripture, he composed twelve observations in further support of his contention. In Psalm 136, for example, he found a proof of "the eternity & and perpetuity [sic] of Gods mercy to his church" from "eternity," or before "giving being to the world," to the "eternity" which the saints will inherit after the "destruction" of the world "by the conflagration." In Corinthians 6:2, 3 he discovered another proof: "Because all things are subordinate to the work of redemption therefore both the beginning & the end of the world is by the Redeemer & he is appointed of the Father to be both the Creatour & the Judge of the world."[104] Such arguments served Edwards's proclamation of God's absolute sovereignty in time and history. More specifically, since the whole order of time is subordinated to God's design of redemption, which unfolds before the creation of the world and continues to do so after its end, history is a special dimension of sacred time situated within a theological teleology of redemptive structure.

Miscellany no. 702 (1736) signified a major turning point in Edwards's construction of time and history. Written after the decline of the revival in 1735, it testified to his struggle to understand not only what had gone wrong on this particular occasion, but also what is "God's wisdom in the work of redemption." It would take Edwards several more years to develop fully the findings of this *Miscellany* regarding God's designs of redemption and to connect these designs with the actual historical process. But he now felt he was on sure ground. In the next *Miscellanies* he continued to elaborate the points he had made in no. 702 regarding the work of redemption as the ultimate goal of God in creating the world. For example, since redemption is a decree of God since eternity, he devoted *Miscellany* no. 704 to the general issue of God's decrees and argued that "in the order of time" they "all are from eternity."[105] Being such a decree, the work of redemption must have begun well before the creation of the

[103] Ibid., pp. 291–92.
[104] Ibid., pp. 292, 295.
[105] Edwards, *Miscellany* no. 704 (c. 1736), in *MISA*, p. 314.

world, and therefore is not contingent on the passage of time or dependent on mere occurrences in history.

Yet, how can one learn about God's grand scheme in history if redemption is from eternity and has already begun before creation, and how one can understand the meaning of God's work of redemption if its full realization lies beyond history? The answer is to be found in Christian revelation, that is, in sacred prophecies. To this issue Edwards devoted *Miscellany* no. 752, written probably in 1738, where he claimed that Christian "revelation opens to us" an "account of the work of creation & this reveals to us the scheme of providence & what is Gods particular main design in the whole series of providences a design worthy of himself what great work that is that is his main work the main design of providence to which all events & revolutions of providence" are subordinated. Edwards was convinced that it is "most reasonable to suppose & natural to expect" that God "make known not only what manner of Being he is but also that he should lead mankind to an understanding of his works of creation & providence." This of course applies especially to the mystery of salvation history, where "men may know something of Gods scheme of providence." Divine revelation provides "a history of the series of events down from the creation" to the very end of the world when "the scheme of God shall be finished & his great design & great work consummated and all things brought to their last end & settled in their ultimate state to remain throughout eternity."[106] Thus established, divine revelation is inextricable from the process of history, for it unceasingly unveils the content and form of the work of redemption as the great design of God in creation and shows how it unfolds throughout the course of history. The entire process of history is a great revelatory, redemptive play, wherein divine revelation continuously foretells and proclaims the sacred progress of the work of redemption. What is evident here is the genesis of Edwards's historization of God's work of redemption.

Edwards's argument that the work of redemption is the end of creation and that God constantly reveals his providential scheme in history is of course opposed to Augustine's understanding of history. While Augustine stipulated that there is a great unbridgeable gap between grace and history, for Edwards the dimension of time is situated within the confines of divine grace, since God's work of redemption constitutes the reason for the creation of the world. Moreover, because redemption is the ultimate end of creation, and God "makes known" his "works of creation & providence," Edwards's God is not *Deus absconditus*, the hidden God, but rather *Deus revelatus*, the God who constantly reveals himself in his creation. This view also opposed Luther's deep sense of *Deus absconditus* and his empha-

---

[106] Edwards, *Miscellany* no. 752 (c. 1738), in *MISA*, pp. 401–2.

sis on *theologia crucis*. In contrast, Edwards developed his own *theologia gloriae* and stressed the notion of *Deus revelatus*. There is then an essential connection among Edwards's conversion, the formation of his theology of nature, which emphasized that God reveals himself in creation, and his construction of the order of time where he stressed that God could be known in history through his work of redemption. For Edwards believed that God appears in "those things by which he makes himself known, or by his *word* and *works*; i.e. in what he says, and in what he does," and it is God's intention "that his works should exhibit an image of himself their author . . . what manner of being he is, and afford a proper representation of his divine excellencies."[107] Proceeding from the subjective sense of redemption in terms of personal salvation to the ultimate purpose for which God created the world, Edwards proposed to explain God's work of redemption as part of the fabric of creation. Faithful to his sense of God's absolute sovereignty, he claimed that the work of redemption constituted the essential dynamism behind the sacred order inherent in the structure of the universe. In his own words: the work of redemption constituted "the great end and drift of all Gods works & dispensations from the beginning & even the end of the work of creation it self."[108]

More and more during the second half of the 1730s Edwards devoted himself to arguing that redemption is indeed the ultimate goal of creation. In *Miscellany* no. 760 he reiterated his views of *Miscellany* no. 702 and further advanced the contention that providence is more than the work of creation. The proof is in the form and content of the scriptures: "As providence is a far greater work than the work of creation & its end so the history" of the scriptures "is much more taken up in works of providence, than in the work of creation." The creation of the world comprised only a small portion of the Bible while the main bulk describes the unfolding of God's providence toward his church in time and history. Edwards concluded therefore that "creation was but a shadow" of the "history" of the scriptures, "which gives an account of the work of providence." The reason for this is that "all Gods works of providence are to be reduced to his providence towards" Christ and his church.[109] Edwards developed this argument further in *Miscellany* no. 762, saying that Christ's crucifixion was "foreordained" by "God in his decree & ordered in his providence" to be "the greatest of all his decreed events" upon which "all other decreed events depend . . . as their main foundation being the main thing in that greatest work" of God—"the work of redemption" which is "the end of all other works."[110] Redemption thus

[107] Edwards, *Concerning the End for which God Created the World*, pp. 424, 422.
[108] Edwards, *Miscellany* no. 702, p. 284.
[109] Edwards, *Miscellany* no. 760 (c. 1738), in *MISA*, p. 406.
[110] Edwards, *Miscellany* no. 762 (c. 1738), in *MISA*, pp. 407–9.

becomes not only the goal for which God created the world, but the main theme of history. In 1738, as can be seen in *Miscellany* no. 807, he reiterated these views, to declare that the "Work of Redemption" is the "Greatest of Gods work."[111]

In 1739 Edwards was confident enough to present his concepts regarding the nature of time and meaning of history to the public in a series of sermons under the title the *History of the Work of Redemption*, a title reflecting his long engagement with the problem of God's work of redemption. Similarly, the choice of the stage upon which to proclaim his ideology of history was not accidental. Contrary to his construction of the essential nature of reality, where Edwards knew that the natural audience for his theology of nature was the enlightened scientific community in England and Europe, for spreading his views regarding time and history he felt that the most obvious audience was close to home. Thus, the preaching of these sermons may be seen in the context of the decline of the "little revival" in New England, for Edwards felt obliged to announce his views about time and history to his congregation, the very people with whom he had experienced the most spectacular success of the awakening as well as its dismal decline. Given this shared religious experience, these were indeed the people most suited to hear from him about the mystery of God's redemptive activity in history.

Edwards's series of thirty sermons on the *History of the Work of Redemption* constitutes the fullest systematic exposition of his philosophy of history, and his most ambitious attempt to produce a universal ecclesiastical history, based on his redemptive mode of historical thought. The people who listened to these sermons must have recognized immediately how profoundly the revival in Northampton had shaped Edwards's ideology of history. For as he preached to his congregation, "from the fall of man to this day wherein we live the Work of Redemption in its effects has mainly been carried on by remarkable pourings out of the spirit of God" as manifested "by remarkable pourings out of the Spirit at special seasons of mercy,"[112] or, more specifically and historically, by "glorious revivals of religion."[113] The close association between revival and the effusion of the Spirit thus constituted the heart of God's work of redemption and the locus of the historical process itself. Redemptive seasons of grace determine the whole course of sacred, ecclesiastical history. In this way God's sovereignty in history is asserted and established through a definable historical phenomenon.

---

[111] Ibid.
[112] Edwards, *History of the Work of Redemption*, p. 143.
[113] Ibid., p. 457.

Six

Edwards's Philosophy of History:
The History of the Work of Redemption

'Tis an evidence that the work of redemption is the great thing, the
grand event of things that God had ultimately in view in his
creation of all the things that he has made in heaven & earth.
  (Edwards, *A History of the Work of Redemption*, 1739)

It may here be observed that from the fall of man to this day
wherein we live the Work of Redemption in its effects has mainly
been carried on by remarkable pourings out of the Spirit of God . . .
[and] the way in which the greatest things have been done toward
carrying on this work has always been by remarkable pourings out
of the Spirit at special seasons of mercy.
  (Edwards, *A History of the Work of Redemption*, 1739)

THE FIRST publication in 1774 of Edwards's series of sermons on the
History of the Work of Redemption was contemptuously reviewed within
a year in the *Monthly Review* (1775). The writer called it "a long, la-
boured, dull, confused rhapsody"; it is "pious nonsense" out of the pen
of a "poor departed enthusiast."[1] Almost 200 years later, Perry Miller,
who had an important part in reviving the study of Edwards's work,
called the *History of the Work of Redemption* "a pioneer work in American historiography," granted that "history is what the mind must perceive
in a fashion dictated by the mind itself rather than by date and documents." Miller understood the singularity of this work in terms of inaugurating a new mode of historical thought in America and felt that Edwards
should be considered as the first American to produce a systematic and
genuine philosophy of history. In formulating his ideas in these sermons,
Miller argued, Edwards "wrote the first truly historical interpretation in
American history," and had he completed the revision of his series of
sermons on the *History of the Work of Redemption* as he intended to do
before he died, "he would then also have furnished America with the
first glimmerings of historical method which, even though lacking the

---

[1] *The Monthly Review; or, Literary Journal*, LII, January to June, 1775, pp. 117–20, as
quoted in Gay, *A Loss of Mastery*, pp. 116–17.

scholarship to support it, would still have been, in the reckoning of today, an immense enrichment of the intellectual heritage of the nation."[2]

Other historians have not shared Miller's enthusiasm for the genius of Edwards's philosophy of history or for the uniqueness of his historical method. Ola E. Winslow, who has written what is probably the best biography of Edwards so far, cast doubt on his plan of the 1750s to transform the series of 1739 sermons into "a great work" wherein the "history" of God's work of redemption "will be carried on with regard to all three worlds, heaven, earth and hell."[3] Luckily, wrote Winslow, this "Gargantuan undertaking was destined to be left as a mere project. Doubtless better so. Who could write such a book? Hardly Jonathan Edwards."[4] This attitude probably determined Winslow's decision not to include any selection from *A History of the Work of Redemption* in her popular and influential anthology of Edwards's basic writings.[5]

A similar negative approach to Edwards's historical interpretation has appeared in other modern studies. Peter Gay, who discussed the body of historical works produced by Puritan historians in New England from William Bradford to Jonathan Edwards, argued that the "ultimate failure of Puritan historiography" occurred in the early eighteenth century, when it became obvious that these New England historians were no longer masters of the world around them, but rather victims of it.[6] With the profound changes that took place in the early eighteenth century—the transformation from the religious vision of a theocratic universe ruled by God's providence to the Newtonian mechanical theory of a clockwork universe directed by natural laws, the rise of deism, and the ideas of the Enlightenment and secularism—the Puritan rhetoric of history in New England came to an end with the gradual exclusion of God from the process of history. For Gay, Edwards was the epitome of this Puritan failure. More specifically, in the case of Edwards "we are bound to speak of tragedy," because of his "spiritual isolation" as well as his "physical isolation" from current intellectual trends in Europe, most notably the ideas of the scientific revolution and the Enlightenment. Thus, in contrast to Miller, Gay declared that Edwards, far "from being the first modern American," was in fact "the last medieval American—at least among the intellectuals."[7]

These conflicting assessments of Edwards's philosophy of history as presented in his sermons on the *History of the Work of Redemption* un-

---

[2] Miller, *Jonathan Edwards*, pp. 309, 311, 314.
[3] Edwards, "To the Trustees of the College of New Jersey," October 19, 1757, pp. 728–29.
[4] Winslow, *Jonathan Edwards, 1703–1758*, pp. 309–10.
[5] Winslow, ed., *Jonathan Edwards: Basic Writings*.
[6] Gay, *A Loss of Mastery*, p. 25.
[7] Ibid., pp. 24–25, 104, 114, 116.

derwent much change over time as scholars increasingly began to rehabilitate Edwards's historical thought in the larger context of his theological
and philosophical enterprise.[8] In an important study, Sang H. Lee placed
Edwards's vision of history within the context of his philosophical theology. For Edwards, "the creation is viewed as God's external exercise of
God's own dispositional essence, an exercise that brings about the extension or repetition in time and space of God's internal fullness." Therefore,
the whole space of history signified for him "a return to the eternal as
well as a movement to a goal yet to be achieved." In this theological
context "God is not only *in* history" in terms of "accomplishing the work
of redemption," but "seeks to redeem and sanctify history itself" by his
"own self-extension through history." The understanding in such terms
of the divine agency's overarching redemptive motive within history is
based on "the absolute sovereign will of the redeeming grace of God."
Within this wider philosophical context where God is the sole author of
history, to Edwards the essence of "the activity of divine providence takes
the specific form of the work of redemption," and history therefore "is
the arena within which God's will can and indeed must be accomplished."[9] God, then, has created the realm of history as a special dimension of time designed for the "exercise of His own dispositional essence"
in time, thus exhibiting his historical scheme of redemption.

The most systematic attempt to place Edwards's redemptive discourse
within the larger context of his theology and philosophy was made by

[8] For works dealing with Edwards's *History of the Work of Redemption* in particular and
his philosophy of history in general, see Heimert, *Religion and the American Mind*, and "The
Great Awakening as a Watershed," in *Religion in American History*, ed. John M. Mulder
and John F. Wilson (Englewood Cliffs, N.J.: Prentice-Hall, 1978), pp. 127–44; C. C. Goen,
"Jonathan Edwards: A New Departure in Eschatology," *Church History* 28 (1959): 25–40;
Ernest Lee Tuveson, *Redeemer Nation* (Chicago: University of Chicago Press, 1968); Sacvan
Bercovitch, *The Puritan Origins of the American Self* (New Haven: Yale University Press,
1975), and *The American Jeremiads* (Madison: University of Wisconsin Press, 1978); Ursula
Brumm, *American Thought and Religious Typology* (New Brunswick: Rutgers University
Press, 1970); James W. Davidson, *The Logic of Millennial Thought* (New Haven: Yale University Press, 1977); Mason Lowance, *The Language of Canaan* (Cambridge, Mass.: Harvard University Press, 1980); John F. Wilson, "Jonathan Edwards as Historian," *Church
History* 46 (1977): 5–18, "History, Redemption and the Millennium," in *JEAE*, pp. 131–
41, and introduction, in *HWR*, pp. 1–109; Stephen J. Stein, "A Notebook on the Apocalypse
by Jonathan Edwards," *William and Mary Quarterly* 29 (1972): 623–34, and introduction,
in *AW*, pp. 1–93; Lee, *The Philosophical Theology of Jonathan Edwards*; Stephen M. Clark,
"Jonathan Edwards: The History of Redemption" (Ph.D. diss., Drew University, 1986); William J. Scheick, "The Grand Design: Jonathan Edwards' *History of the Work of Redemption*," in *Critical Essays on Jonathan Edwards*, ed. William J. Scheick, pp. 177–88; Crawford, *Seasons of Grace*; and Conforti, *Jonathan Edwards, Religious Tradition, & American
Culture*. Conforti's study contains a good summary of the fate of Edwards's *History of the
Work of Redemption* in American religious tradition and culture.
[9] Lee, *The Philosophical Theology of Jonathan Edwards*, pp. 211, 214, 216.

John F. Wilson, who writes that Edwards's "notion of the Work of Redemption" is "fundamental to the relationship between God and creation," hence this concept "is primarily theological" and ought to be examined in that context. In such a setting, Wilson continues, the redemptive theme should be "seen in relation to the whole creation as the means to comprehend the relationship of the world to God." Tracing the evolution of this concept in Edwards's universe of thought, Wilson demonstrated the importance of this subject in Edwards's philosophical theology and showed that he returned to it "throughout his life, but especially in the early years of his maturity, at Northampton" during the 1730s. Having defined the *History of the Work of Redemption* as primarily a theological endeavor, Wilson argued that for Edwards "creation is a stage, the purpose of which is to permit the drama of redemption to be played out, [and] the outcome of the drama (and thus the reason for creation) is God's self-glorification." This larger context may explain why the long series of sermons on the work of redemption was "so central" to Edwards and why "he always intended it to be a summary of theological statement." In sum, Edwards's *Work of Redemption* should be read less as an historical work proper and more as a theological exposition. Accordingly, Wilson deemphasizes "the importance conventionally given to the term *history* in the title, arguing instead that the work is primarily theological and that Edwards's use of the term is in that context."[10]

Although modern studies have greatly expanded the understanding of Edwards's theological and philosophical enterprise in his sermons on the work of redemption, what is missing from these various interpretations is the ideological and philosophical context of Enlightenment narratives of history, without which it would be hard if not impossible to fully appreciate this work. More specifically, Edwards's long preoccupation with constructing the order of time cannot be understood without taking into consideration, in part, the serious threats that the Christian theological teleology of history had faced with the emergence of new modes of historical thought in the early eighteenth century, such as the growing validity and legitimacy attached to historical time, the increasing importance given to *historia humana*, and the new role accorded to human agency in the historical process. Enlightenment historical narratives gave rise to a new concept according to which the realm of history ceased to be a theater in which the drama of human life was directed and controlled by divine agency. Instead, the process of history came increasingly to be seen as based on the outcome of human actions and deeds rather than as the work of God's will. In part against such threats to the traditional Christian

---

[10] Wilson, introduction, in *HWR*, pp. 2, 31–32. See also Wilson, "Appendix B: Jonathan Edwards' Notebooks for *A History of the Work of Redemption*," in *HWR*, p. 556.

worldview, Edwards composed the *History of the Work of Redemption*. Instead of conceiving history from an anthropocentric point of view, as the direct result of human action and as a manifestation of immanent human progress, he constructed it solely from the perspective of God and his redemptive activity in creation. Taking God as the sole author of history, Edwards composed a history as it lies exclusively in the mind of the omniscient God. Based upon his theistic metaphysics, he argued that history has been constructed by divine providence as a special dimension of sacred, redemptive time designed solely for the accomplishment of God's plan of redemption, and therefore it should be understood from the perspective of its maker and author. History in such a system is a grand redemptive space of time designated from eternity by divine providence for God's self-glorification as made evident in his work of redemption; hence human beings' existence is totally dependent on God's power and will.

Edwards grappled for many years with the issue of the relationship between grace and time, or the dialectic of God's transcendence and immanence. Only in 1739 did he finally find the answer. All history is the story of God's work of redemption; human actions should be considered only as they manifest this divine activity. Theocentric history, therefore, or a history written exclusively from the perspective of God's redemptive plan, describing the power of divine agency and the progress of redemptive activity in time, and not a history based on anthropocentric considerations, was the underlying theme of Edwards's *History of the Work of Redemption*.

One of Edwards's main aims was to undermine the role of human autonomy and freedom in influencing the course of history. God is thus reenthroned as the true Lord of history and human action is accorded the secondary role of being directly affected and influenced by the mighty manifestations of God's redemptive activity. Indeed, this is a history which, like the world of the scripture stories,

> is not satisfied with claiming to be a historically true reality—it insists that it is the only real world ... destined for autocracy. All other scenes, issues, and ordinances have no right to appear independently of it, and it is promised that all of them, the history of all mankind, will be given their due place within its frame, will be subordinated to it.[11]

Edwards's *History of the Work of Redemption* is a universal history, because everything "else that happens in the world can only be conceived as an element in this sequence; into it everything that is known about the

---

[11] Erich Auerbach, *Mimesis: The Representation of Reality in Western Literature*, trans. Willard R. Trask (Princeton: Princeton University Press, 1953 [1946]), pp. 14–15.

world . . . must be fitted as an ingredient of the divine plan."[12] In such reasoning history is the theater of God, because his transcendent ends determine the drama of human history upon earth. Yet history is not merely the theater of God's judgments, for God constantly and progressively exhibits in history, through his word and work, the divine plan of redemption for fallen humanity.

Sacred History and *Historia Humana*

Along with the struggle, research, and intuition that enabled scientists to begin to unravel the secrets of the natural world, the historical narratives of the early Enlightenment led to a transformation in constructing the field of history and the legitimacy and validity of historical time. Generally speaking, Enlightenment narratives signified "a turning away from dogma and traditional conventions, a critical reappraisal of established authority in the fields of religion, politics, philosophy, and the arts." Thus the "human situation and man's liberty, the place of man in society . . . c[a]me to condition the guiding lines of thought."[13] This transformation lies at the beginning of the modern age: "Individuals increasingly came to define themselves as active subjects. They no longer tended to see their place in life as part of some natural, inevitable, and eternal plan. Their own enterprise and ability mattered; they possessed the opportunity (a key word) to determine their place through their own voluntary actions in this life and in this world."[14]

More specifically, the work of Enlightenment historians inaugurated "the conquest of the historical world."[15] Aiming to reveal the historical conditions of human life in the *saeculum*, writers established history more and more as an independent field of inquiry separated from religious and theological considerations, and stressed the moral values and instructive knowledge to be acquired in studying the past. Thus the study of history became an essential feature of the Enlightenment: the "eighteenth century was in fact the age of consuming interest in history." Especially in England during the Augustan era, "the value of history as a form of instructive knowledge was repeatedly affirmed."[16] As David Hume proclaimed: "this

---

[12] Ibid., pp. 15–16.

[13] Helmut O. Pappe, "Enlightenment," in *Dictionary of the History of Ideas*, 4 vols. (New York: Charles Scribner's Sons, 1973), II, p. 90.

[14] Isaac Kramnick, *Republicanism & Bourgeois Radicalism: Political Ideology in Late Eighteenth-Century England and America* (Ithaca: Cornell University Press, 1990), p. 8.

[15] Cassirer, *The Philosophy of the Enlightenment*, pp. 197–233.

[16] J.A.I. Champion, *The Pillars of Priestcraft Shaken: The Church of England and Its Enemies, 1660–1730* (Cambridge: Cambridge University Press, 1992), p. 25.

is the historical Age."[17] Edwards knew Hume's historical works as well as those of Henry St. John, Lord Bolingbroke, who wrote in his *Letters on the Study and Use of History* (1735): "We ought always to keep in mind, that history is philosophy teaching by examples how to conduct ourselves in all the situations of private and public life." For he "who studies history as he would study philosophy . . . will soon form to himself a general system of ethics and politics on the surest foundations, on the trial of these principles and rules in all ages, and on the confirmation of them by universal experience."[18]

Historical, earthly experience, then, instead of theological and teleological speculations regarding the unfolding mystery of divine activity, was gradually being established as the foundation for human conduct. Conceived increasingly as serving mainly didactic purposes and prudential instruction, history was accorded a prominent role as the locus of human life and experience: "History is the ancient author: experience is the modern language," declared Bolingbroke, "so history is conversant about the past, and by knowing the things that have been, we become better able to judge of the things that are."[19] Or, according to Edward Gibbon, history "is, indeed, little more than the register of the crimes, follies, and misfortunes of mankind."[20] The traditional centrality accorded to God's word and the importance of divine revelation for human existence were displaced by worldly historical experience. The field of history was slowly liberated from dependence on transcendental religious truths, and historical time gained a validity and legitimacy of its own. "In place of a static conception of divine, immutable order, a new sociological perspective takes over: society and culture are regarded as product of history, i.e. of man's free and creative will."[21] Closely related to these transformations were the growing privatization of religious life and experience and the emergence of the public sphere: "the spiritual institution was finally relegated to the private sphere, while the autonomous political institutions achieved the monopoly of publicity."[22] The privatization of religious belief, some of whose more prominent manifestations emerged in the Protes-

---

[17] Gay, *The Enlightenment: The Science of Freedom*, p. 369.

[18] Henry St. John, Lord Bolingbroke, *Letters on the Study and Use of History* (1735), in *The Works of . . . Henry St. John, Lord Viscount Bolingbroke*, 8 vols. (London, 1809), III, pp. 349–50.

[19] Ibid., pp. 355–56.

[20] Edward Gibbon, *Decline and Fall of the Roman Empire*, 1776–88, ch. 3, 340:20, as quoted in the *Concise Oxford Dictionary of Quotations* (Oxford: Oxford University Press, 1997), p. 150.

[21] Pappe, "Enlightenment," p. 92.

[22] Voegelin, *From Enlightenment to Revolution*, p. 20. For the shifting locus of order from the medieval divine cosmos to the secular sovereign state during the seventeenth century, see Stephen L. Collins, *From Divine Cosmos to Sovereign State: An Intellectual History*

tant evangelical awakening, as we have seen, also facilitated what Jürgen Habermas has termed the rise of the "public sphere" in the early eighteenth century, or the establishment of "the sphere of public authority" as "a sphere of freedom."[23]

It is not surprising that during "the eighteenth century the clear cut theological philosophy of history degenerated into an amiable and gentlemanly 'philosophy teaching by example',"[24] or, conversely, "history became in G. E. Lessing's phrase 'the education of the human race'."[25] As the realm of history became more and more the main medium for understanding and interpreting the nature of human experience in time, so it was less and less considered as the theater of God's judgments, or as the theater of the work of redemption. The "Enlightenment interested men in the secular past," not in the Christian mystery of salvation.[26] The transcendental universalism embodied in the Christian theological teleology of history was replaced by a human universalism; "the *corpus mysticum Christi* has given way to the *corpus mysticum humanitatis*."[27] Thus, for David Hume the chief use of history "is only to discover the constant and universal principles of human nature, by showing men in all varieties of circumstances and situations, and furnishing us with materials from which we may form our observations and become acquainted with the regular springs of human actions and behaviour."[28] Likewise, William Warburton (1698–1779), bishop of Gloucester, argued that "the knowledge of human nature" is "the noblest qualifications for the historian."[29] More serious, though, were the Enlightenment historians' denouncements of the Christian interpretation of history. Hume, for example, denounced ecclesiastical historians' interpretation of history: "The Monks, who were

of Consciousness and the Idea of Order in Renaissance England (New York: Oxford University Press, 1989); and Gauchet, *The Disenchantment of the World*.

[23] Jürgen Habermas, *The Structural Transformation of the Public Sphere: An Inquiry into a Category of Bourgeois Society* (Cambridge, Mass.: MIT Press, 1994), pp. 18, 4.

[24] Carl L. Becker, *The Heavenly City of the Eighteenth-Century Philosophers* (New Haven: Yale University Press, 1932), p. 18.

[25] Donald R. Kelley, introduction, in *Versions of History from Antiquity to the Enlightenment*, ed. Donald R. Kelley, p. 440. See also Paul Avis, *The Foundations of Modern Historical Thought* (London: Croom Helm, 1986).

[26] Owen Chadwick, *The Secularization of the European Mind in the 19th Century* (Cambridge: Cambridge University Press, 1995 [1973]), p. 189.

[27] Voegelin, *From Enlightenment to Revolution*, p. 10.

[28] David Hume, *Enquiry Concerning Human Understanding* (1748), in *Enquiries Concerning Human Understanding and Concerning the Principles of Morals*, ed. L. A. Selby-Bigge (Oxford: Clarendon, 1975), p. 83. See also David Wootton, "David Hume, 'The Historian'," in *The Cambridge Companion to Hume*, ed. David F. Borton (Cambridge: Cambridge University Press, 1993), pp. 281–312.

[29] Philip Hicks, *Neoclassical History and English Culture*, p. 142.

the only annalists" during medieval period, "lived remote from public affairs, considered the civil transactions as entirely subordinate to the ecclesiastical, and besides partaking of the ignorance and barbarity . . . were strongly infected with credulity, with the love of wonder, and with propensity to imposture; vices almost inseparable from their profession, and manner of life."[30] The gradual liberation of the historical realm from its traditional subjection to the Christian historical interpretation of history as the drama of human salvation, and the growing establishment of human autonomy within history, was one of the most daring programs of the Enlightenment. What was involved was not only the detachment of grace from time, redemption from history, or divine agency from temporal events, but ultimately the "abandonment of a [whole] world-picture"— the Christian historical worldview.[31]

With the gradual liberation of the field of history from theological considerations, the role of the biblical narrative as the main source for interpreting historical events and as the locus of historical consciousness was much modified: "The full force of the change in outlook and argument concerning the narrative biblical texts came in the eighteenth century . . . the narrative became distinguished from a separable subject matter— whether historical, ideal, or both at once—which was now taken to be its true meaning."[32] The symbolic power of the biblical stories was eroded and they could no longer furnish a sacred framework for interpreting secular history. "The Bible remained authority, but increasingly it was interpreted so as to conform to secular history and science, rather than determining the agenda of these disciplines."[33] This was a most decisive change. "In this epoch of full-grown history men have not acquiesced in the given conditions of their lives. Taking little for granted they have sought to know the ground they stand on, and the road they travel, and the reason why."[34] Instead of the Christian envisioning of world and history as formed by the sequence told by the biblical overarching narrative of salvation history, during the eighteenth century, as Hans Frei wrote, "It is no exaggeration to say that all across the theological spectrum the great reversal had taken place; interpretation was a matter of fitting the biblical story into another world with another story rather than incorporating that world into the biblical story."[35]

[30] Hume, *The History of England from the Invasion of Julius Caesar to the Revolution in 1688*, 6 vols. (Indianapolis: Liberty Classics, 1983), I, p. 25.

[31] Chadwick, *The Secularization of the European Mind in the 19th Century*, p. 193. See also Louis Dupré's important study, *Passage to Modernity*.

[32] Frei, *The Eclipse of Biblical Narrative*, p. 51.

[33] Harrison, *"Religion" and the Religions in the English Enlightenment*, p. 129.

[34] Lord Acton, *Lectures on Modern History* (London: Fontana, 1960 [1906]), p. 20.

[35] Frei, *The Eclipse of Biblical Narrative*, p. 130.

Eventually, the sacred stories of the Bible lost their attraction and hold on the historical imagination, as well as their integrity, because of the development of the historical-critical method and the rise of biblical hermeneutics during the eighteenth century. Religious faith and practices similarly underwent a crucial transformation: "In much the same way that the world became the object of scientific inquiry in the sixteenth and seventeenth centuries through a process of desacralisation, so too, religious practices . . . were demystified by the imposition of *natural laws*. As the physical world ceased to be a theatre in which the drama of creation was constantly re-directed by divine intervention, human expressions of religious faith came increasingly to be seen as outcomes of natural processes rather than the work of God or of Satan and his legions."[36] The same applied to history: with the disenchantment of the historical process, the secular interpretation of history gained momentum and informed new modes of historical consciousness. In fact, the development of historical consciousness during the eighteenth century may be regarded as one of the most important characteristics of modern thought: "Historical-mindedness is so much a preconception of modern thought that we can identify a particular thing only by pointing to the various things it successively was before it became that particular thing which it will presently cease to be."[37]

The Enlightenment justification for the moral, instructive, and edifying uses of studying the past was based on the transition from the prerogatives of faith to the claims of reason, or the epistemological separation of reason and revelation. "As in the realm of science, where attention had become focussed upon secondary causes, so too, in the sphere of history, theological explanations were regarded as incomplete."[38] Conceived increasingly as a realm independent of God's providential scheme, history no longer derived its meaning from the drama of fall and salvation. "The center of universality is shifted from the sacred to the profane level, and this shift implies the turning of the tables: that the construction of history will, in the future, not be subordinated to the spiritual drama of humanity, but that Christianity will be understood as an event in history."[39] Accordingly, Enlightenment historians stressed "the need for a closer analysis of historical sequences,"[40] tending to arrange events in the order of their occurrence independently of theological concerns about prophecy, prediction, and expectations, or in relation to the question of when the world would end. For example, in his *History of England* (1754–61), Hume

---

[36] Harrison, *"Religion" and the Religions in the English Enlightenment*, p. 5.

[37] Becker, *The Heavenly City of the Eighteenth-Century Philosophers*, p. 19.

[38] Harrison, *"Religion" and the Religions in the English Enlightenment*, p. 101.

[39] Voegelin, *From Enlightenment to Revolution*, p. 7.

[40] Pappe, "Enlightenment," p. 94.

declared that the historian's main task is to "take a general survey of the age, so far as regards manners, finances, arms, commerce, arts and sciences. The chief use of history is that it affords materials for disquisition of this nature."[41]

Enlightenment historians' construction of historical time was naturally marked by attempts to "liberate history writing from its subservience to theology" and to free it from the religious view which conceived of "the course of human history as the realization of a divine plan."[42] This process of "de-divinization of the world" shows that traditional Christian symbols were "no longer revelatory of the immersion of the finite world in the transcendent."[43] Thus, together with science, by inaugurating new modes and means for understanding the nature of reality, history became a model for scientific inquiry: "Just as mathematics becomes the prototype of exact knowledge, so history now becomes the methodological model from which the eighteenth century acquires new understanding for the general task and the specific structure of the abstract sciences."[44]

It was within this ideological context that the idea of progress became established as a key to the philosophy of history. "The belief in progress, the idea that human history forms a movement, more or less continuous, towards a desirable future, began to take shape late in the seventeenth century."[45] Instead of the religious vision of salvation and redemption, which would materialize only beyond history, the notion of immanent human advance was based on the belief that utopian visions of the pursuit of human freedom and happiness could be fulfilled within history. For the "belief in progress implies the assumption that a pattern of change exists in the history of mankind, that this pattern is known, that it consists of irreversible changes in one general direction only, and that this direction is towards improvement from 'a less to a more desirable state of affairs'."[46] No longer considered as the narrative of a God-given providential plan, the historical realm was defined as the means for the realization of the possibilities inherent in the nature of human beings. "For the men of the Enlightenment the idea of world-history was particularly congenial. It fitted in with their notion of progress, their view of mankind, advancing steadily from primitive barbarism to reason and virtue and civilization."[47]

---

[41] Hume cited by Pollard, *The Idea of Progress*, p. 34.

[42] Gay, *The Enlightenment: The Science of Freedom*, pp. 372–73.

[43] Voegelin, *From Enlightenment to Revolution*, p. 21.

[44] Cassirer, *The Philosophy of the Enlightenment*, pp. 200–201.

[45] Morris Ginsberg, "Progress in the Modern Era," in *Dictionary of the History of Ideas*, III, p. 633.

[46] Pollard, *The Idea of Progress*, p. 9.

[47] G. Barraclough, "Universal History" (1962), as quoted in Pollard, *The Idea of Progress*, p. 33.

This Enlightenment notion of human progress in history was inseparable from the conception of secular history. Secularization at that stage
meant "the attitude in which history, including the Christian religious
phenomena, is conceived as an innerworldly chain of human events,
while, at the same time, there is retained the Christian belief in a universal,
meaningful order of human history."[48] Indeed, Carl L. Becker said that
although "the eighteenth century was preeminently the age of reason,"
the "*Philosophers*" in fact "were nearer the Middle Age, less emancipated
from the preconceptions of medieval Christian thought, than they quite
realized or we have commonly supposed."[49] Yet this should not hinder us
from seeing the revolutionary ramifications of the Enlightenment historical imagination for traditional Christian thought, namely, its emphasis on
immanent human progress in secular time and its stress on the possibility
of the "redemption" of the human race in history. For the gradual liberation of history from the biblical historical narrative and the Christian
philosophy of history, and the emergence of an "autonomous temporal
framework" of history, signified the growing legitimacy accorded to the
historical process and to historical time.[50] Human history, accorded legitimacy and validity, was seen more and more as a special space of time in
which human beings could achieve freedom and autonomy; instead of the
Christian vertical expectations regarding the end of time as situated beyond the confines of history, "there [was] an inversion in the horizon of
expectations" for the fulfillment of human destiny within history.[51]

The significance of Edwards's construction of time and history may be
understood in this wider historical and ideological context. In fact, we
cannot judge—even grasp—Edwards's evangelical historiography without studying the environment that fostered it. In the face of the Enlightenment concept of history Edwards construed history as a special dimension
of sacred time formed from eternity by God's providence for the execution
of his plan of redemption for fallen humanity. Since God is the author of
history, the whole process is directed solely by the divine power and will.
To demonstrate this contention, the relationship between redemption and
history was redefined by making the latter totally dependent on the former. In place of the increasing emphasis on human autonomy in determining history, Edwards sought for the reenthronement of God as the Lord
of history and thus for the reenchantment of the historical process. This
enabled him to proclaim history as a dimension of sacred, redemptive
time structured by divine providence to exhibit God's plan of redemption,

---

[48] Voegelin, *From Enlightenment to Revolution*, p. 7.
[49] Becker, *The Heavenly City of the Eighteenth-Century Philosophers*, p. 29.
[50] Frei, *The Eclipse of Biblical Narrative*, pp. 1–5.
[51] Koselleck, "Modernity and the Plans of Historicity," in *Futures Past*, pp. 5–7.

identified with the "exercise of God's own dispositional essence," or "God's self-glorification."

Edwards's history is theocentric; the locus of history is God's redemptive activity in time and not human actions, which by definition are only a by-product of the divine agency. Written from the perspective of an omniscient God, Edwards's evangelical historiography deals with the "rise and continued progress of the dispensation of grace towards fallen mankind."[52] He admitted that "Scripture history" sometimes lacked the richness and diversity of "profane history," yet the former is better because it provides the whole framework of God's work of redemption: "Scripture don't contain a proper history of the whole" human experience, "yet there is contained the whole chain of great events by which this affair" or the work of redemption "is carried on from the foundation soon after the fall of man to the finishing of it at the end of the world."[53] Scripture history

> alone gives us an account of the first original of all things, and this history alone deduces things down in a wonderful series from that original, giving an idea of the grand scheme of divine providence as tending to its great end. And together with doctrines and prophecies contained in the same sacred Bible, gives a view of the whole series of the great events of divine providence, from the first original to the last end and consummation of all things, giving an excellent and glorious account of the wise and holy designs of the governor of the world in all.[54]

Given the superiority of sacred over profane history, because it "gives us a view of the grand design and glorious scheme" of divine "providence, from the beginning to the end of the world," Edwards asks rhetorically:

> Shall we prize a history that gives us a clear account of some great earthly prince or mighty warrior, as of Alexander the great or Julius Caesar; or the duke of Marlborough, and shall we not prize the history that God has given us of the glorious kingdom of his son, Jesus Christ, the prince and savior of the world, and the wars and other great transactions of that king of kings and lord of armies, the lord mighty battle, the history of the things he has wrought for the redemption of his chosen people.[55]

Edwards indeed borrowed the Enlightenment notion of progress, but instead of assigning it a prominent role in history, he stressed that human advance should be seen from God's perspective, namely, in terms of the

---

[52] Edwards, *History of the Work of Redemption*, p. 285.
[53] Ibid., pp. 242–43.
[54] Ibid., p. 284.
[55] Ibid., pp. 290–91.

work of redemption, which began before creation and will come to fulfillment only after the end of the world. "Things in their series and course
in providence," he argued in 1739, are based on "a progress toward a
certain final issue of things" from the creation to the end of the world.[56]
Since history comprises only a small part of God's overall plan of redemption, progress can be properly ascribed only to divine activity in time and
not to any ends to be pursued by human beings within history.

The sense of God's absolute sovereignty thus led Edwards to construct
a singular sacred history based not on human autonomy, but solely on
God's redemptive activity. He is faithful to the biblical, historical narrative,
in which "the religious doctrine," as Erich Auerbach demonstrated, "raises
the claim to absolute authority." For the biblical stories "are not, like Hom-
er's, simply narrated 'reality.' Doctrine and promise are incarnate in them
and inseparable from them." Thus, Edwards's *History of the Work of Redemption* is structured on the basis of the Old Testament, which

> presents universal history: it begins with the beginning of time, with the creation
> of the world, and will end with the Last Days, the fulfilling of the Covenant,
> with which the world would come to an end. Everything else that happens in
> the world can only be conceived as an element in this sequence; into it every-
> thing that is known about the world . . . must be fitted as an ingredient of the
> divine plan.[57]

The History of the Work of Redemption

Between the months of May and August 1739, Edwards preached a series
of thirty sermons on the *History of the Work of Redemption* in his Northampton parish. This was a rare occasion; it would be hard to find many
cases where a devoted pastor used his pulpit over several months to present such a long, systematic exposition of a philosophy of salvation history.
One can only imagine the atmosphere in the church where the congregation gathered to hear their minister expounding the mystery of sacred
history from creation to the end of the world. The people who listened to
Edwards were not young students eager to immerse themselves in abstract
theological and philosophical issues, but ordinary people of all ages and
sections of society who had never been trained to deal with such complicated ideological questions. Yet they all understood that the immediate
background of these sermons was the "little revival" that had taken place
in their town, and that by preaching these sermons "Edwards hoped to

---

[56] Edwards, *Notes on Scripture*, 389 (1739), pp. 374–75.
[57] Auerbach, *Mimesis*, pp. 15–16.

spark another revival" in their congregation.[58] Indeed, for several years they were accustomed to their pastor's many attempts to revive the happy days when "God dwel[t] and manifest[ed] his glory" in their town.[59]

For Edwards, however, the situation was different. Four years after the revival, he was finally moved to meet the challenge of explaining to his congregation the significance of that saving, historical event, and the meaning of this effusion of the Spirit of God. Basing himself on previous attempts in his *Miscellanies* and the *Notes on the Apocalypse* to explore the nature of time and the meaning of history, and as an outcome of his growing interest in apocalyptic issues during and after the revival of 1734–35,[60] Edwards was now more than ready for the task. He was increasingly convinced that the revival in Northampton was far from being a mere provincial event, but rather illustrated in very clear terms the entire course of sacred providential history. He came to the conclusion that this event exemplified above all the content and form of the historical scheme by which God realizes his plan of redemption and his grand design in history—namely, through a remarkable effusion of the Spirit and its immediate effect in the form of revival and awakening. It is not surprising, then, that in his sermons on the work of redemption Edwards for the first time conceived the essential association between the outpouring of the Spirit and the force of revival in changing human beings' condition, and made it the mark of his redemptive mode of historical thought. He pleaded with his audience to look upon history not as the story of human actions, but from the point of view of God's work of redemption, and to understand it as a special field of time designed from eternity for the manifestation of divine, redemptive activity.

The singularity of these sermons lies not only in the content but also in the form, or the place where Edwards expressed his maturing philosophy of history. Previous Protestant and Puritan ecclesiastical historians in England and New England formulated their interpretations of salvation history in their private studies, intending their work to be read mainly by educated people. Further, they commonly based their philosophy of history on an apocalyptic mode of historical thought, regarding the Apocalypse as the main guide for understanding the mystery of time and history. Edwards, on the contrary, expounded his ideology of history before his whole congregation. Confident of his findings in the 1730s *Miscellanies*, he was convinced that he had finally found the answer to the dialectic relationship between God's transcendence and immanence, and he felt an urgent need to communicate his views in order to raise his congregation's

---

[58] Stein, introduction, in *AW*, p. 22.
[59] "Benjamin Coleman's Abridgment, November 1736," p. 119.
[60] Stein, introduction, in *AW*, p. 19.

spirit after the sad decline of the revival. Edwards did not use Revelation as the sole basis of his historical interpretation. Instead, he asserted that since the work of redemption is the sine qua non of all God's works in creation, historical understanding should be viewed from the perspective of divine activity in time. Convinced that the scope of this activity was not limited to the operation of saving grace in the soul, or that it related solely to the mechanism of upholding and maintaining the structure of the physical world, he extended the content and form of God's work of redemption by claiming it to be the ultimate reason of creation itself. Hence, time and history should be defined by the theme of God's redemptive activity, or, as we will see later, principally in terms of a series of effusions of the Spirit and its historical manifestations in the shape of a succession of revivals and awakenings stretching from creation to the end of the world.

This insight, evidently, Edwards was more than eager to share with his congregation in the belief that it might comfort them after the withdrawal of the Spirit of God from their town. For such an historical explanation might show them that what had happened in New England in 1734–35, far from being an isolated local event, symbolized the whole rhythm of God's redemptive activity from the beginning to the end of the world. In preaching the sermons on the *History of the Work of Redemption*, therefore, Edwards strove to capture the significance of the New England revival of 1734–35 in the wide context of sacred, ecclesiastical history. By doing so, he constructed a singular philosophy of history, making "the phenomenon of the revival the key element in the drama of redemption," and conceiving "of revivals as the engines that drive redemption history."[61] The church at Northampton, therefore, ought to see itself as wonderfully blessed in being a place where God's Spirit appeared and dwelt for a moment, showing that the church was situated within the main course of sacred providential history. The New England revival was thus placed within a well-defined sacred, redemptive context and assigned a singular role in the unfolding plan of God's work of redemption in history.

To further support his congregation's spirit by showing them "the constancy and perpetuity of God's mercy and faithfulness towards" his church, as evidenced in God's "protecting her against all assaults of her enemies, and carrying her safely through all the changes of the world,"[62] Edwards carefully chose the biblical text that was the basis for his exposition of God's work of redemption: *"For the moth shall eat them up like a garment, and the worm shall eat them like wool: but my righteousness shall be for ever, and my salvation from generation to generation"* (Isaiah

---

[61] Crawford, *Seasons of Grace*, p. 132.
[62] Edwards, *History of the Work of Redemption*, p. 113.

51:8). The text not only talks about the fate of God's enemies, but makes it plain that God's righteousness and salvation are everlasting. Edwards attached great importance to this prophetic passage—"This verse," he declared, "is a proof of the indestructibility of the Church"[63]—and he inscribed it at the beginning of every sermon in the *History of the Work of Redemption* series. Indeed, as John F. Wilson remarks, this passage was chosen in order to contrast "God's everlasting righteousness and resolute intention to achieve salvation for his people with the fragility and transitoriness of earthly goods."[64]

Since the pursuit of salvation takes place within the historical process, redemption is firmly situated within the dimension of history and becomes inextricable from it. God's "righteousness" means his "faithfulness in fulfilling his covenant promises to his church," or his "bestowing the benefits of the covenant of grace" upon his people; for "God's righteousness or covenant of mercy is the root of which his salvation is the fruit." Salvation therefore constitutes an essential part of history because it is "the sum of all those works of God by which the benefits that are by the covenant of grace are procured and bestowed." In more historical terms, the "work of salvation itself towards the church shall continue to be wrought" until "the end of the world," namely, the "deliverance and salvation for the church from all her enemies."[65] Edwards used these words in the preface of the first sermon. To every succeeding sermon, immediately below the motto from Isaiah, he attached a "Doctrine" summing up his main thesis regarding the essential connection between redemption and history: "The Work of Redemption is a work that God carries on from the fall of man to the end of the world."[66] The people who had experienced the operation of saving grace during the revival of the 1730s could hardly have missed the point Edwards was trying to make here: in spite of the decline of the revival, God's work of redemption is a continuous process appearing in every generation. Never alien or indifferent to the course of history, God's redemptive activity is constantly and strongly manifested within the confines of history, constituting the whole locus of, as well as the dynamism inherent in, the historical process.

Following his exegesis of Isaiah 51:8 in the first sermon, Edwards went on to define systematically the theological and philosophical premises of his philosophy of history. This is the most important section of the series

---

[63] Wilson, introduction, p. 37.

[64] Ibid., p. 38.

[65] Edwards, *History of the Work of Redemption*, pp. 113–16.

[66] The "Doctrine" does not appear, for example, in sermon 3 because this sermon was a direct continuation of sermon 2. Most probably, the third sermon was delivered on the Sunday afternoon after Edwards had preached sermon 2 on Sunday morning. See Wilson's comment in *HWR*, 141, note 2.

of sermons because here he established the ideological and theological context for his redemptive mode of historical thought. One can see here how strongly Edwards's thinking about time and history during the 1720s and 1730s informed his sermons on the work of redemption. Many separate threads of thought developed in the *Miscellanies* were now linked into a coherent ideology. Edwards's main goal was not merely to console his people after the withdrawal of the Spirit, but to demonstrate to them that history is nothing else than the manifestation of God's redemptive activity, and thus to place the revival they knew within the wider context of God's work of redemption. It was not political, social, or religious transformations that signified the essence of the historical process but God and his redemptive activity.

The composition of the sermons on the *History of the Work of Redemption* signaled a major moment in Edwards's intellectual life, representing his fullest and most systematic articulation of a philosophy of history. There is of course a link between the *Miscellanies*, especially those written after 1735, and the sermons. The "little revival" of the 1730s forced him to focus more seriously and systematically on the issue of redemption and history; the "revivals of the 1730s encouraged Edwards's inquiries into the 'History of the Advancement of Christ's Kingdom,' and his attention to its progress in the contemporary world."[67] The "little revival" thus had a lasting impact on the formation of Edwards's philosophy of salvation history. Again, the differences between Edwards's and St. Augustine's historical contexts are revealing. Augustine composed the *City of God* at the time of the fall of Rome and the Vandals' siege of Carthage. In Edwards's case the cause leading him most directly to articulate his philosophy of history was a religious phenomenon reinforcing the association of conversion, redemption, and history.

Edwards in effect incorporated the insights he developed in his *Miscellanies*, especially those written during the 1730s, and made them the main source for his interpretation of history in the work of redemption. This is most evident in the first sermon, which lays down the ideological and theological groundwork for the whole series. It contains almost verbatim citations from *Miscellany* no. 547 (1731), where Edwards first developed the vision of God's "great design, to which divine providence subordinates all the successive changes that come to pass in the state of affairs of mankind," and his belief that there is "some design that God is pursuing, and scheme that he is Carrying on, in the various changes and revolutions that from age to age happen in the world."[68] In 1736, in *Miscellany* no. 702, he defined this general and abstract notion of God's providence,

---

[67] Heimert, *Religion and the American Mind*, p. 61.
[68] Edwards, *Miscellany* no. 547, p. 93.

arguing that the work of redemption is God's "great design" in time and history, hence the "grand design [of] the work of redemption may be looked upon as the great end and drift of all Gods works & dispensations from the beginning & even the end of the work of creation it self."[69] He inserted sections from this *Miscellany* almost verbatim into first sermon on the work of redemption, defining the whole order of time as subordinated to and controlled by God's great design, and correlating the end of creation with God's work of redemption.

The Redemptive Mode of Historical Thought

In the first sermon on the *History of the Work of Redemption* Edwards systematically set out the ideological and theological context of his redemptive mode of historical thought. His voice in this sermon, as in the whole series, is the confident one of a theologian and philosopher who believed he had found the solution to the secret of divine activity in time. He was more sure than ever of the truth of his conclusions regarding the dynamism inherent in God's plan of redemption and the main historical agent by which the divine agency manifested its redemptive activity. Before presenting them, however, he found it necessary to explicate the relation between grace and time by showing that God was the true author of history, and that providence has structured history from eternity as a dimension of sacred time for the exercise of God's redemptive activity and his self-glorification. The realm of history is a grand theater made for the exercise of God's excellency.

History, argued Edwards, began with "the fall" and the "corruption of nature" and stretches until "the end of the world," "so these two are the limits of the generations of men on the earth; the fall of man, the beginning, and the end of the world—the Day of Judgment—its end." Basing himself on his *Miscellany* no. 702, he argued that the boundaries of history are the same as "the limits of God's work of redemption," or "those progressive works of God by which that redemption is brought about and accomplished, though not as to the fruits of it, for they . . . shall be to all eternity." Since redemption is the ultimate mark of salvation history— "For salvation is the sum of all those works of God by which the benefits that are by the covenant of grace are procured and bestowed"—history is conceived in terms of the annals of God's work of redemption and is concerned with "all generations beginning with the generations of men on earth and not ending till these generations end at the end of the

---

[69] Edwards, *Miscellany* no. 702, p. 284.

world."[70] In this sense the "work of salvation and the Work of Redemption" signify "the same thing." There is no separation between grace and time, redemption and history, since the locus of the historical process is the power of divine activity. On the other hand, God's work of redemption indeed takes place in history, yet its final realization will not materialize within the historical dimension but in the eternal time that will follow after the end of the world. Although the work of redemption takes place in history, its "fruits" will be revealed only after the end of the world and "shall be to all eternity."[71]

Incorporating the ideas in *Miscellany* no. 702 (1736) that God's work of redemption is concerned not only with the issue of personal conversion and individual salvation but with the whole fabric of the universe, and hence encompasses the entire historical process, the first sermon carefully distinguishes between two different meanings of the work of redemption. First, in the "more limited sense," it means "the purchase of salvation," or "a purchase of deliverance." In this narrow sense, God's redemption is associated exclusively with Christ's gospel of salvation—"it was begun and finished with Christ's humiliation, or it was wrought while Christ was upon earth." In this more limited meaning, redemption denotes the historical revelation of Christ upon earth, beginning with "Christ's incarnation and carried on through Christ's life and finished with his death."[72]

Yet the work of redemption should be understood in a larger sense which comprises "the whole dispensation" of divine activity in time and space, or "all that God works or accomplishes tending to this end, not only the purchasing of redemption but also all God's works that were properly preparatory to the purchase, or as applying the purchase and accomplishing the success of it." A shift has occurred here from the Christocentric to the theocentric sense of the work of redemption, from Christ's gospel of salvation to God's grand redemptive design and the overall goal of the divine agency in creation. In this larger sense, the work of redemption does not concern only Christ's message of salvation but also, and moreover, the whole of God's and the Holy Spirit's "dispensation" in time, which began well before the "world was created, yea from all eternity" and the beginning of history and will be concluded only after its consummation. The entire universe, then, has become subordinated to and inextricable from God's redemptory activity. Edwards's main purpose in making the distinction was to expand the scope of redemption from Christ's promise of personal salvation to history as a whole. The work of redemption concerns "not only what Christ the mediator has done, but also what the Father and the Holy Ghost have done as united

---

[70] Edwards, *History of the Work of Redemption*, pp. 115–16.
[71] Ibid., p. 116.
[72] Ibid., p. 117.

or confederated in this design of redeeming sinful men; or in one word, all that is wrought in executing of the eternal covenant of redemption."[73] In this reasoning, the temporality of the historical process is determined essentially by the higher dimension of eternal time in which the everlasting covenant of redemption will finally be realized. In other words, being subjected to and regulated by divine agency, historical time is deprived of its own validity and legitimacy, and should be seen as dependent on God's redemptive plan in history. Transcendental goal and aim thus determine the temporal and contingent reality of the historical process.

In order to further illuminate the unity of the three persons of the Trinity—Father, Son, and Holy Ghost—in the work of redemption, and to demonstrate that redemption in its wider sense is related not only to the narrow historical time frame but to the wider dimension of eternity, Edwards incorporated the mechanistic explanation of God's great design in history, which he had developed earlier, in *Miscellany* no. 547 (1731). The work of redemption, he argued,

> 'tis all but one work, one design. The various dispensations and works that belong to it are but the several part of one scheme. 'Tis but one design that is done to which all the offices of Christ do directly tend, and in which all the persons of the Trinity do conspire and all the various dispensations that belong to it are united, as several wheels in one machine, to answer one end and produce one effect.[74]

The main reason behind such mechanization of the work of redemption is to further enhance God's sovereignty in the entire creation. Having already introduced this theme in *Miscellany* no. 702, when he identified God's great design with the work of redemption, Edwards now incorporated it into his sermons in 1739. With all three persons of the Trinity united in the accomplishment of redemption, God's redemptive activity acquires a much wider frame of time within which Christ's gospel of salvation constitutes only one part of the larger whole.

In explaining to his congregation the content and form of God's work of redemption, Edwards's mechanization of God's providence reached its highest level. He meant to establish God's absolute sovereignty in time and history, and thus he claimed that all the "changes and revolutions" that take place in history are "only the turning of the wheels of providence."[75] The same thrust is apparent in other writings of 1739. Very

---

[73] Ibid., pp. 116–18. For the distinction in Edwards's thought between individual eschatology and general eschatology, see Morimoto, *Jonathan Edwards and the Catholic Vision of Salvation*, pp. 142–47.

[74] Edwards, *History of the Work of Redemption*, p. 118.

[75] Ibid., p. 128. See also Edwards's interpretation of Ezekiel's wheel (c. 1739) in *Notes on Scripture*, 389, pp. 373–90.

often at this period he tended to associate God's providence with a machine, or a clock, writing "the providence of God is like a wheel," or "a machine composed of wheels."[76] He identified God's providence with the vision of the wheels in Ezekiel, arguing that divine

> providence is most aptly represented by the revolution or course of these wheels. Things in their series and course in providence, they do as it were go round like a wheel in its motion on the earth. That which goes round like a wheel goes from certain point or direction, till it gradually returns to it again. So is the course of things in providence.

This mechanistic vision of the operation of divine providence applies to both the natural and the moral world. "So the annual changes that appear in the natural world are as it were by the revolution of a wheel," and so "it is in the course of things in God's providence over the intelligent and moral world." And faithful to his typology of nature, Edwards said further that what "comes to pass in the natural world is . . . typical of what comes to pass in the moral and intelligent world."[77]

With the whole structure of the universe brought into this grand theological and teleological redemptive context, God's sovereignty within time is established and his lordship over history affirmed. For the work of redemption is not a matter of history alone, but also of time: "many things" in the scheme of God's work of redemption, "were done before the world was created, yea from all eternity." Thus, while Christ's gospel of salvation is inseparable from the historical dimension of time, namely, the period from the fall to the end of the world, the work of redemption encompasses the wider frame of eternal time, before the creation and after the end of the world. For "there were things done at the creation of the world in order to that work" of redemption "before man fell." Edwards used these distinctions to demonstrate to his congregation that redemption is the ultimate cause for which God created the world, and that it constitutes the essence of the historical process. To emphasize this, he reiterated the views of *Miscellany* no. 702, declaring that "the world itself seems to have been created in order" to effect that work of redemption, for the "work of creation was in order to God's works of providence."[78]

The direct source for Edwards's formulations regarding the relationship between grace and creation can be found in *Miscellany* no. 702 (1736), where he claimed for the first time that "the work of redemption is "the great end and drift of all Gods works & dispensations from the

---

[76] Edwards, *Images of Divine Things*, 89 (1739), p. 86.

[77] Edwards, *Notes on Scripture*, 389 (1739), pp. 373–74.

[78] Edwards, *History of the Work of Redemption*, p. 118. In *Miscellany* no. 702 (1736) this argument was defined in a different way: "the work of creation in itself seems to be so done that it should shadow forth the work of redemption." See p. 284.

beginning & even the end of the work of creation it self."[79] He continued to elaborate on this theme in 1739, arguing "if it be inquired which of these two kind of works is the greatest, the works of creation or God's works of providence, I answer providence because God's works of providence are the end of God's works of creation." Here the works of providence should be understood as the work of redemption, because all the works of creation were made for the sake of redemption. For example, "creating heaven was in order to the Work of redemption; it was to be an habitation for the redeemed and the Redeemer, Matt. 25:34." And "the lower world," or the earth, was designed "to be the stage of this wonderful Work [of redemption]."[80] Before the universe existed and before history began, divine providence had already determined to create the world as the great theater for the execution of the drama of salvation. A grand teleological theological structure of redemptive order pervades the whole fabric of the universe, and this overall design lies at the root of creation and determines its course. No separation can be allowed between grace and nature, nor can there be any alienation of redemption from history, since the work of redemption is the sine qua non of creation. Created order is placed totally under God's power and will, and history is no more than a special dimension of time constructed to promote a divine plan conceived well before the creation of the world and reaching realization only after its end.

Designed by divine providence "to be the stage" of the "wonderful Work" of redemption, history is a play written and directed by God. That drama necessarily involves judgment and destruction, since the divine wrath awaits those who do not belong to the church. They are doomed to destruction on the last day of judgment. Redemption *from* history, and not redemption *in* history, or in the world, is Edwards's understanding of the culmination of the redemptive process. History and nature will come to an end with the last judgment. Thus, as the fall should be interpreted in the literal sense, so too the end of the world—"at Christ's Second Coming to judge the world," he will "destroy heaven and earth, in a literal sense."[81] For on the eschatological day of judgment, after Christ and his church "shall enter" into "the highest heaven . . . this world shall be set on fire, and be turned into a great furnace, wherein all the enemies of Christ and his church shall be tormented forever and ever."[82]

The climax of the redemptive process, then, will put an end to the world. The "greatest fruits" of the work of redemption "are eternal

[79] Ibid.
[80] Edwards, *History of the Work of Redemption*, pp. 118–19.
[81] Edwards, *Notes on Scripture*, 389 (1739), p. 378.
[82] Edwards, *History of the Work of Redemption*, pp. 506, 505.

fruits" and will be revealed only "after the end of the world."[83] This judgmental eschatology may be compared with that of Calvin, who believed
that the "cosmos will be purified but not destroyed," and therefore he
was "waiting for future renewal and incorruption"[84] of the world:
"Therefore, if, at the present time, we see much confusion in the world,
let that faith encourage us and revive us, the faith that Christ shall one
day come and restore all things to their former condition [in integrum]."[85]
Calvin said that "God was reclaiming not only the cosmos and human
nature but history as well." The culmination of God's plan of salvation
and redemption, therefore, would be revealed in the "renewing" of the
"whole of creation and history." He therefore thought of the last judgment "as the final restoration of the order of the world."[86] As against
Calvin's eschatology of hope and renewal of the world, Edwards does
not admit the concept of renovation of the world. For him the material,
terrestrial world is condemned to eternal destruction. "Things in their
series and course in providence," he claimed, manifest "a progress towards a certain final issue, and every revolution brings nearer to that
issue"; namely, "Christ's second coming to judge the world and destroy
heaven and earth, in a literal sense."[87]

The history of the work of redemption, therefore, connects two crucial
epochs: the creation of the world, or the period which set the stage for
redemption, and the end, the point of termination which signifies the final
act in salvation history. The climax of the redemptive process is the end
of history, when God will judge the world and bring about its destruction.
No redemption is possible *within* history, only *beyond* it. These different
eschatological visions led to radically different conceptions regarding the
fate of the world for Calvin and Edwards. Edwards preserved the Augustinian vision of the goal of history as situated beyond history itself,
believing that the final stage of history would be manifested in a violent
eschatological event, putting an end to the world and to history itself.

Edwards's judgmental eschatology, in opposition to Calvin's eschatology of renewal, restoration, and hope, may throw some more light on his
notion of divine agency in history. Enclosed within an overall redemptive,
cosmological plan, history constitutes only one part of divine activity in
time. Within the larger time frame before creation and after the end of
the world, history is assigned the role of a stage upon which God executes

---

[83] Ibid., p. 119.

[84] Susan E. Schreiner, *The Theater of His Glory: Nature and the Natural Order in the
Thought of John Calvin* (Durham, N.C.: Labyrinth, 1991), p. 98.

[85] Calvin, *Commentary on Acts*, as quoted in Schreiner, *The Theater of His Glory*, p.
109.

[86] Schreiner, *The Theater of His Glory*, pp. 108–9.

[87] Edwards, *Notes on Scripture*, 389 (1739), pp. 375, 378.

his plan of redemption. Yet, "the greatest fruits" of this work would be revealed only "after the end of the world," and "will remain to all eternity after that." Being situated within the historical time dimension, the work of redemption itself does not belong to the time dimension of eternity: "The Work of Redemption is not an eternal work, that is, it is not a work always-a-doing and never accomplished. But the fruits of this work are eternal fruits. The work has an issue, but in the issue the end will be obtained, which end never will have an end."[88] On the other hand, since it is taking place within history, the work of redemption consists of many divine dispensations pertaining to the dimension of historical time as such:

> The various dispensations of God that are in this space do belong to the same work, tend to the same design, and have all one issue and therefore are all to be reckoned but as several parts of one work, as it were several successive motions of one machine to strike out, in the conclusion of one great event. (ibid.)

The inclusion of the redemptive process within history evidently leads to Edwards's reenchantment of the historical process. Whereas Augustine had detached redemption from history, believing God's redemptive activity was indifferent to the course of history, Edwards made history inextricable from redemption.

Being aware that these general formulations might be too abstract for his audience, Edwards tried to provide some specific examples of the manifestation of God's work of redemption in history. His illustrations show how essential the revival moment in his town was to the formation of his historical thought and how powerfully it informed his historical consciousness. The effect of the work of redemption is twofold: conversion and God's self-glorification. First, in regard to "the effect wrought on the souls of the redeemed," the work of redemption "is common to all ages from the fall of man" to the end of the world. In this sense it affects "the souls of the redeemed," that is, "with respect to the souls of particular persons in converting, justifying, sanctifying and glorifying of them" (p. 120). More specifically, in that capacity "the work of God" appears "in converting souls, opening blind eyes, and unstopping deaf [ears], and raising dead souls to life, and rescuing the miserable captured souls of men out of the hand of Satan." Redemption in this sense means accepting the gospel of Christ and joining his church upon earth. For "God has always, ever since the first erecting of the church of the redeemed after the fall, had such a church in the world" (ibid.). Yet, this spiritual, personal meaning is the narrow and limited one.

---

[88] Edwards, *History of the Work of Redemption*, p. 119. Subsequent pages appear parenthetically in the text.

Apart from its individualistic dimension, the work of redemption has a larger meaning in terms of the ultimate cause for which God created the world. Redemption should be examined "with respect to the grand design in general as it relates to the universal subject and the end of it," and understood in terms of how it "carried on from the fall" of man to the end of the world. Now the "Work of Redemption in that large sense" is clearly different from the narrow association between redemption and conversion, because it is carried on "by many successive works and dispensations of God, all tending to one great end and effect, all united as the several parts of a scheme, and altogether making up one great work" (p. 121). This larger meaning consists of God's "design of glorifying himself from eternity, to glorify each person in the Godhead" (p. 125). Edwards had already developed this argument in *Miscellanies* nos. 681 and 699 (1736). The wide sense of the work of redemption is related ultimately to God himself, or to divine activity in space and time of which conversion constitutes only a small part. The form and content of divine dispensations in this larger sense are obviously different from the private, personal work of conversion. Unlike conversion, which takes place in every generation, the realization of the wider goal of God's plan of redemption is determined "by successive works wrought in different ages, all parts of one whole or one great scheme whereby one work is brought about by various steps, one step in each age and another in another." It is this broader sense of the work of redemption in history, Edwards maintained "that I shall insist upon" in the series of sermons on the *History of the Work of Redemption*, "though not excluding the former," or conversion, "for one necessarily supposed the other" (p. 122). To deal only with the first and more limited sense of redemption would mean giving a long and tedious inventory of conversions in history; providing an overall exposition of the historical scheme of redemption called for a universal interpretation of salvation history dealing with God's grand design in time, as well as with the manifestations of the divine agency in the form of "successive work" of remarkable "providential events" in history (pp. 122, 175).

Edwards was ready to show his audience in more specific and concrete detail "the design of this great work or what things are designed to be done by it" in order "that the great works and dispensations of God that belong to this great affair of redemption may not appear like confusion to you." Since the work of redemption belongs to the dimension of historical time, five main goals are to be achieved in history by God's design. The first of these "is to put all God's enemies under his feet" so that "the goodness of God should finally appear triumphing over all evil." History in this sense may be most properly defined as the theater of God's judgment. This was the traditional Protestant and Puritan apocalyptic interpretation of history. But Edwards did not stop there. The second meaning of God's redemptive activity is "to restore all the ruins of the fall, so far as concerns the elect part of the world, by his Son" (pp. 122–25). Redemption means "the restitution of all things"—"Man's soul was ruined by the fall, the image of God was ruined, man's nature corrupted and destroyed, and man became dead in sin." The restitution implied here is associated with the restoration of "the soul of man in conversion and to restore life to him, and the image of God in conversion." The third goal is "to gather together in one all things in Christ in heaven and on earth," that is, "all the elect creatures." In consequence, God's fourth aim in the work of redemption is "to complete and perfect the glory of all the elect by Christ." Fifth, the last goal concerns God himself. In all the affairs of redemption "God designed to accomplish the glory of the blessed Trinity," because "God had a design of glorifying himself from eternity, to glorify each person in the Godhead" (pp. 124–25).

Conceived in such terms, history evidently has no particularistic center, in the form of a state or a nation, as previous ecclesiastical historians had portrayed it. God's absolute sovereignty and majesty is the locus of history, and the dynamism underlying the historical process is the universal power of the divine agency.

Revival as the Manifestation of Divine Agency in the Order of History

Edwards conceived of history exclusively from the perspective of God's plan of redemption in the order of time. Accordingly, as he wrote, his intention in preaching the sermons on the history of the work of redemption was to show "the scheme" of God's "government and the series of his dispensations towards his church and the world" as "he has ordered and disposed it from age to age" (p. 284). The history thus composed is written as it lies in the mind of the omniscient God. By interpreting history from the point of view of divine agency, Edwards established God as the Lord of history and argued that "all revolutions" in history "from the beginning of the world to the end of it, are but the various parts of some" divine redemptive "scheme" (p. 520). More specifically, it is God's work of redemption which determines the historical and existential condition of human life. Edwards then wished to strip the historical order of any independent validity and legitimacy, and to constitute history as a special dimension of redemptive time contingent on divine power. Since history is a grand plan designated for God's self-glorification, the fate of human beings is not separable from divine action in time: "Edwards was deeply committed to understanding the human saga as the production of a play that God had authored."[89] This view informed Edwards's "understanding both of God's historical agency and the general pattern of God's historical plotting."[90] Being the dimension of the contingent and the temporal, history is subject to and dependent on God. The responsibility for any progress in history thus rests solely in divine, redemptive activity. The clearest evidence for this contention is to be found in a series of remarkable effusions of the Spirit of God and their immediate effects in a succession of revivals and awakenings within human society throughout history.

This then is redemptive history. Like the ecclesiastical history to which Edwards was a heir, it deals primarily with the "rise and continued progress of the dispensation of grace towards fallen mankind,"[91] the outpouring of the Spirit of God in singular "dispensations of providence," and its immediate manifestations in the form of decisive periods of revivals, or "special seasons of mercy,"[92] throughout the history of the church. God indeed controls the historical process through a variety of divine dispensations, chief among them being the effusion of the Holy Spirit and its immediate effect in terms of a series of awakenings. Edwards believed that "God advances his work of redemption" most of all "through successive effusions of his Spirit."[93] When God sees that history is turning away from its predestined course, and is falling astray of his overall redemptive plan, he initiates "remarkable pourings out of the Spirit" to bring human society back to its appointed track. Not content with a general correlation between prophetic revelations and history, and dissatisfied with a simple causal relation between God and temporal, contingent events, as in the Protestant and Puritan apocalyptic interpretation of history, Edwards looked for feasible evidence of redemptive activity in history, trying to find a concrete agent upon which to establish God's will and power in the order of time. In 1739 he for the first time identified this agent with an effusion of the Holy Spirit and its results in series of revivals and awakenings:

> It may here be observed that from the fall of man to this day wherein we live the Work of Redemption in its effects has mainly been carried on by remarkable pourings out of the Spirit of God . . . [and] the way in which the greatest things have been done toward carrying on this work has always been by remarkable pourings out of the Spirit at special seasons of mercy.[94]

[89] Wilson, introduction, p. 73.

[90] Jenson, *America's Theologian*, p. 45.

[91] Edwards, *History of the Work of Redemption*, p. 285.

[92] Ibid., pp. 511, 143.

[93] Stein, introduction, in *AW*, p. 22.

[94] Edwards, *History of the Work of Redemption*, p. 143. Subsequent pages appear parenthetically in the text.

The whole thrust behind Edwards's sermons on the history of the work of redemption was to show his congregation the essential relationship between divine activity and revivals, and thus to present to them the historical scheme of God's work of redemption. This correlation between the operation of the Holy Spirit and its direct influence on the conditions of human life, he claimed, ought to be regarded as the ultimate manifestation of the historical agency of divine activity. The reason behind this argument is that the whole universe is imbued with a theological and teleological structure of sacred order. The world does not operate by chance, abstract laws of nature, nor is it blind to divine providence. On the contrary, the Holy Spirit constantly moves and guides the wheels of providence according to God's grand design of redemption. To illustrate this argument, Edwards resorted to his earlier mechanization of the work of redemption, first developed in *Miscellany* no. 547 (1731), saying that within a close-knit, theocentric universe the Spirit of God was accorded the dominant role of guiding the operation of the wheels of providence:

> The wheels of providence are not turned round by blind chance, but they are full of eyes round about, as Ezekiel represents; and they are guided by the Spirit of God, where the Spirit goes they go. And all God's works of providence through all ages: they meet in one at last as so many lines meeting in one center. (p. 519)

In this mechanistic image the Holy Spirit played a prominent role in the affair of redemption; the third person of the Trinity was entrusted with the power of directing the "stream of divine providence" and thus transforming the course of history (p. 517).

Having in 1736 defined the work of redemption as the main locus of divine activity in history, in 1739 Edwards elaborated further on the issue of divine agency in time. For the first time he made the connection between the operation of the Holy Spirit and revival. Remarkable outpourings of the Spirit of God at certain decisive turning points in history directly affect the emergence of religious revivals and awakenings, and these in turn transform the existential as well as the historical condition of human beings. This relationship between divine activity and fallen humanity, between the outpouring of the Spirit and "every remarkable new establishment of the state of his visible church" in the world, is the essence of the history of God's redemption (p. 266). Being inspired directly by the Holy Spirit, revivals inaugurate a special dimension of time during which divine providence dramatically changes the human condition, moving toward the accomplishment of God's overall plan of redemption: "So it has been in all remarkable pourings out of the Spirit of God that we have any particular account of in Scripture, and so it is foretold it will be at the great pourings out of the Spirit of God in the latter days" (p. 142).

Divine power, then, and not any sort of human agency, determines the progress of history. Throughout his sermons Edwards spared no effort to demonstrate the close connection between the effusion of the Spirit and revival, declaring that "it has been God's manner in every remarkable new establishment of the state of his visible church, to give a remarkable outpouring of his Spirit" (p. 266). Operating according to this singular relationship between the effusion of the Holy Spirit and revival, progress in the work of redemption is made according to some definable stages, or turning points, where God's Spirit causes a profound change in history in order to further his overall plan. In the face of degeneration, God's way has always been to revitalize history and relaunch his redemptive plan by an effusion of the Spirit. Decline and revival, degeneration and awakening—this is the historical structure and pattern of the redemptive process.

The effect wrought by the outpouring of God's Spirit is the main source of historical change. An understanding of history according to this shift between decline and revival shows that God's work of redemption is not based on unrestricted, linear progress but on the "pattern of ebb and flow, progress and decline," whereby "each movement carries the whole a step further."[95] This pattern determines the gradual progress of the work of redemption. For there is "not reason from God's Word to think any other than this work of God will be gradually wrought, though very swiftly, yet gradually" and "will not be accomplished at once." The reason behind this gradual process is that redemption "will be accomplished by means, by preaching the gospel, and the use of the ordinary means of grace, and so it shall be gradually brought to pass." No sudden revolutionary change is envisaged, no instantaneous eschatological salvation, but a gradual progress determining the work of redemption. In such an economy of salvation, "God's Spirit shall be poured out, first to raise up instruments, and then these instruments shall be improved and succeeded." Scriptural history is the best proof: "The Scriptures hold forth as though there should be several successive great and glorious events by which this glorious work shall be accomplished."[96]

The ultimate agent of change in the historical scheme of redemption is the power of God's Spirit and not earthly power invested in worldly rulers. "This great work shall be accomplished, not by the authority of princes, nor by the wisdom of learned men, but by God's Holy Spirit." For there is no comparison, Edwards assured his congregation, between the power of the Spirit and the historical work and deed "of some great earthly prince or mighty warrior, as of Alexander the Great or Julius Caesar, or the duke

---

[95] Stephen M. Clark, "Jonathan Edwards: The History of the Work of Redemption," *Westminster Theological Journal* 56 (1994): 47.

[96] Edwards, *History of the Work of Redemption*, pp. 458–59.

of Marlborough."[97] Edwards's refusal to accord earthly rulers a role in providential history is opposed, for example, to John Foxe's adoration of Queen Elizabeth as a "godly queen," Milton's and Marvell's glorification of Cromwell as "God's Englishman," or Cotton Mather's description of John Winthrop as "Nehemias Americanus," the father of a new Israel.[98] Nothing of this respect for the power of human rulers figured in Edwards's redemptive mode of historical thought. He reserved his admiration for the power of the Spirit. At the same time, he assigned the most important role in the history of the work of redemption to ordinary, common people: "in pouring out his Spirit chiefly on the common people, and bestowing his greatest and highest favors upon them," God is "admitting them nearer to himself than the great, the honorable, the rich and the learned."[99] These are the people whom the Holy Spirit affects most in terms of revivals. Thus, "God, by pouring out his Spirit, shall furnish men to be glorious instruments of carrying on his work."[100]

Edwards's insistence that revivals, taking place among common, ordinary people, manifest the core of divine agency in time, reveals an important "democratic" element in his historical imagination.[101] Instead of maintaining that certain famous rulers are invested by divine providence with a great role in salvation history, he claimed that revivals by their very nature arise among ordinary people. Such "democratization" of the work of redemption, whereby the effusion of the Spirit determines the life and experience of common people without any hierarchy of intermediate levels of ecclesiastical, political, or social authority, is compatible with Edwards's understanding of the encompassing character of the work of the Spirit. The pouring out of the Spirit and its immediate result in revival

[97] Ibid., p. 291.

[98] For Foxe's glorification of Elizabeth's role in salvation history, see John Foxe, *Acts and Monuments*, ed. G. Townsend and G. R. Cattley, 8 vols. (London, 1837–41), III, p. 601; I, p. 94; William Haller, *Foxe's Book of Martyrs and the Elect Nation* (London, 1963), pp. 224–25. For Milton's and Marvell's admiration of Cromwell as "God's Englishman," see John D. Hunt, *Andrew Marvell: His Life and Writings* (London: Paul Elek, 1978), pp. 123–24; Christopher Hill, *God's Englishman: Oliver Cromwell and the English Revolution* (Harmondsworth, Middlesex: Penguin, 1973), pp. 191, 267; John M. Wallace, *Destiny His Choice: The Loyalism of Andrew Marvell* (Cambridge: Cambridge University Press, 1968), pp. 30–38, 45–48, 54–58. Cotton Mather's views of Winthrop as "Nehemias Americanus" appeared in his book, *Magnalia Christi Americana, or, The Ecclesiastical History of New England*, ed. Thomas Robbins, 2 vols. (Hartford, 1853), I, pp. 118–31. See also Bercovitch, *The Puritan Origins of the American Self*.

[99] Edwards, *The Distinguishing Marks of a Work of the Spirit of God*, 1741, in GA, p. 295.

[100] Edwards, *History of the Work of Redemption*, p. 460.

[101] For an analysis of the democratic dimension in the history of Christianity in America, see Nathan O. Hatch, *The Democratization of American Christianity* (New Haven: Yale University Press, 1989).

applies to fallen humanity as a whole. Not through some chosen, worldly rulers, but in the heart of the common people God carries out his redemptive plan, effecting the revitalization of history by returning it to its predestined course, after many and frequent backslidings.

According to this structure, surges of unprecedented divine grace, as manifested in a series of decisive awakenings, were usually followed by decline, degeneration, sin, and despair. But, says Edwards, "whatever failed or declined, God still carried on this work from age to age, this building was still advancing higher and higher."[102] In the face of corruption and idolatry, God has always "kept the lamp alive." This, declared Edwards, has been God's usual manner throughout history: "Several times after exceeding great degeneracy, and things seemed to come to extremity, and religion seemed to be come to its last gasp, then God granted blessed revivals by remarkable outpouring of his Spirit."[103] This redemptive pattern shows that each "decline was followed by a new wave that rose to unprecedented heights. Surges of grace were followed by a curse of sin and despair."[104] The immediate result of such an understanding of the historical process was to strip secular, historical time of its validity and to reject the notion that human power and autonomy are responsible for progress in history. Instead, history is a place of trial where the Holy Spirit works constantly to awaken human souls to receive the gospel of salvation and redemption, transforming the condition of human beings from alienation to reconciliation with God.

The succession of ebb and flow, progress and decline, of revivals in history shows that God watches the affairs of fallen humanity closely and, through the outpouring of his Spirit, constantly revives it by modifying the human condition to further his plan of redemption. This pattern refers not only to the past, but also to the present and future. For example, before the overthrow of "Satan's kingdom" at the end of history "it will be a very dark time with respect to the interest of religion." This gloomy situation, said Edwards, is very common in the course of redemptive history:

> It has been so before those glorious revivals of religion that have been hitherto. So it was when Christ came, it was an exceeding degenerate time among the Jews, and so it was a very dark time before the Reformation. And not only, but it seems to be foretold in Scripture that it shall be a time of but little religion when Christ shall come to set up his kingdom in the world.[105]

---

[102] Edwards, *History of the Work of Redemption*, p. 229.

[103] Ibid., p. 233.

[104] Sidney Rooy, *The Theology of Mission in the Puritan Tradition* (Grand Rapids: Eerdmans, 1965), p. 296.

[105] Edwards, *History of the Work of Redemption*, pp. 456–57. Subsequent pages appear parenthetically in the text.

The effusion of the Spirit is thus the chief means of revitalizing history, transforming a state of despair into a joyful time in terms of the fate of the Christian church in the world, until the appointed time for the transformation of the world into the kingdom of God and his Son.

The association in Edwards's thought between the power of the Spirit and revival exemplifies the singularity of his mode of historical thought. Unlike previous ecclesiastical historians, who dealt with earthly affairs such as the rise and fall of empires, nations, states, and institutions, for Edwards the ultimate agent of change is "glorious revivals of religion" caused by the outpouring of the Spirit (p. 457). His redemptive history, therefore, has no sacred particularistic center in the form of a chosen state, an elect nation, or a godly ruler, as with earlier ecclesiastical historians. The final act in the drama of salvation—the defeat of Satan and Antichrist—will take place only at the moment when God's "Spirit shall be gloriously poured out for the wonderful revival and propagation of religion" (p. 460). The whole history of the work of redemption exhibits the "wisdom of God":

> This wisdom appears in his creating of the world, creating it for such an excellent use, and to accomplish so glorious work; and in bringing so great good out of such great evil, making the fall of man and ruin of mankind, in itself so deplorable, an occasion of accomplishing such a glorious work as redemption and of bringing his elect to a state of such unspeakable happiness. (pp. 524–25)

Edwards's mode of historical thought is based on divine grace and its determining influence on occurrences in history. It deals with a series of divine dispensations and their immediate results in a succession of revivals throughout the history of the church. The characteristic dynamism of this process consists in the close relationship between divine agency and the phenomenon of awakenings. Indeed, as Edwards came to believe, this is the pattern of history from beginning to an end: "So it has been in all remarkable pourings out of the Spirit of God that we have any particular account of in Scripture, and so it is foretold it will be at the great pouring out of the Spirit of God in the latter days" when God's "Spirit shall be gloriously poured out for the wonderful revival and propagation of religion" (pp. 142, 460). Evidently, in such a theological teleology, historical events acquire meaning only in so far as they represent the "great works and dispensations of God that belong to this great affair of redemption" (p. 122). On the other hand, redemption is not alienated from history. God is intimately associated with historical occurrences by taking an active side in the struggle waged on earth against Christ and his church. For "one great thing that God intended by the Work of Redemption" is to appear "gloriously above all evil and triumphing over all his enemies" (p. 124).

The radicalism of such a philosophy of salvation history is striking in the context of Protestant and Puritan historiography. In their attempts to provide theological, ecclesiastical, and historical justification for the break from the Church of Rome, Protestant historians—such as Philip Melanchthon, Robert Barnes, and Matthias Flacius in Germany, and John Bale and John Foxe in England—constructed an ecclesiastical history based primarily upon the historical and theological struggles that the Protestant churches in Germany and England waged against the Church of Rome.[106] These interpretations of salvation history were primarily occupied with the historical and theological justifications of each particular nation's role in the providential drama, describing and defining the history of their churches as institutions. Their ecclesiastical histories dealt mainly with the battle against the Church of Rome, with the rise of the true church as a sacred entity, situated within a political, social, and ecclesiastical context, and not specifically with revivals and dispensations. Similarly, the main purpose of New England Puritan historians was to justify the Puritan migration to, and experience in, New England in light of the true church's struggle against Satan and Antichrist in the Old World and its flight into the wilderness of America. Puritan historians in New England, like John Cotton, Increase Mather, and Cotton Mather, justified the migration to America in terms of the flight of the "woman of the wilderness," or the true church, into the wilderness of America as a sacred institution and not particularly in terms of revivals and awakenings.[107]

In contrast to these constructions of ecclesiastical history, Edwards's interpretation deals primarily with the effusion of the Spirit of God and with the ebb and flow of a series of revivals and dispensations throughout history. Thus, while other church historians had striven to construct a particularistic center in history for establishing a proof of God's redemptive activity, mostly in terms of the prominent role attached to each one's nation in the drama of salvation and redemption, Edwards had no such particularistic, nationalist center, but only God himself. Writing history as it appeared in the mind of the omniscient God and from the sole perspective of divine agency, Edwards composed a universal history in the true sense of the term, where earthly affairs are contingent on God's redemptive activity and acquire their meaning only in so far as they relate to the actions of divine agency in time. He did not develop any notion of God's "elect nation," as in Protestant England, nor did he discover any glorious Puritan "errand into the wilderness."[108] Since divine agency is

---

[106] Zakai, "Reformation, History and Eschatology in English Protestantism," pp. 300–318.

[107] Zakai, *Exile and Kingdom*, pp. 143–206.

[108] According to McDermott, "Edwards emerges as the prophet not of American's manifest destiny but of the traditional New England jeremiad." See McDermott, *One Holy and Happy Society*, pp. 5–6.

universal by nature, and its power described in terms of revivals and awakening, the redemptive mode of historical thought does not entail any nationalization of salvation history.

The Theological and Teleological Structure Inherent in the Redemptive Process

The redemptive mode of historical thought determined not only the content of Edwards's concept of the work of redemption, but also its form or structure. The sermons are organized according to a well-defined scheme. The history of redemption is depicted as based on a series of decisive turning points in which an outpouring of the Spirit leads to an impressive revival that profoundly changes the condition of life and historical experience. These two—effusion of the Spirit and revival—are the agents in the advance of God's historical plan of redemption and constitute the main theme of Edwards's work of redemption. There are many varieties of divine dispensations or various dispensations of providence, but none can be compared to the outpouring of the Spirit of God at certain decisive historical moments.

Having established the ideological and theological context of his work in the first sermon, Edwards went on in the second to explain "the various stages" of the work of redemption "from the fall of man to the end of the world,"[109] wishing "to cast that act of salvation into its larger historical context."[110] He divided the history of God's work of redemption into three main periods: the first, which extends from "the fall of man till the incarnation of Christ," signified "those things that were preparatory to Christ's coming and working out redemption." The second is "the time from Christ's incarnation till his resurrection," showing the "procuring or purchasing redemption." Finally, the third comprises "the space of time from the resurrection of Christ to the end of the world [which] is all taken up in bringing about the accomplishing the great effect or success of that purchase."[111] In this theological and eschatological scheme, God set the wheels of providence moving in order to advance his redemptory plan, and the "changes and revolutions in the world of mankind were all only the turning of the wheels of providence," tending especially to further "God's great works toward his church" (ibid.).

In each period Edwards identified some occasions for the extraordinary effusion of the Holy Spirit. In all, there were a few such historical mo-

---

[109] Edwards, *History of the Work of Redemption*, p. 127.
[110] Clark, "Jonathan Edwards," 46.
[111] Edwards, *History of the Work of Redemption*, p. 128. Subsequent pages appear parenthetically in the text.

ments, all of them taking place at decisive turning points in the annals of
the Christian church, thus signifying the essence of progress in history.
The first was during the time of Enoch; the second, during Israel's sojourn
in the wilderness of Sinai and the settlement of Canaan; the third, during
the time of Ezra after the return of the Jews from exile and captivity in
Babylon; the fourth, at the time of the establishment of the Christian
church in the world after Christ's resurrection. The final outpouring of
the Spirit would take place at the end of history with the transformation
of the world into the kingdom of God. To these one may add the effusion
of the Spirit during the Protestant Reformation, although Edwards did
not attach as much importance to this as to the others. What is common
to all these periods is that God poured out his Spirit in an exceptional
way only when the welfare of his church was gravely threatened, or when
a desperate state of sin and degeneration prevailed among his chosen, or
during a sad decline of interest in religion in the world as a whole. Further,
God singled out a certain locus in history, his chosen people, or his church,
and spared no effort to advance their cause by his redemptive activity.
When afflictions subjugated his chosen people, and when decadence appeared among them, he poured out his Spirit and changed their desperate
condition. God thus constantly seeks to revive and rehabilitate history in
order to further his overall plan of redemption. The work of redemption
is threefold: through the effusion of the Spirit God awakens his chosen
ones; revival transforms the welfare of the church in the world; and the
two together change history according to God's redemptive plan.

During the first period, the "church was under various dispensations
of providence and in various circumstances," chief among them the creation of "Adam and Eve," which typified "the first fruits of Christ's redemption" (pp. 128, 238). Indeed, before Christ's first coming "God
wrought many lesser salvations and deliverances for his church," yet these
were all but "images and forerunners of the great salvation Christ was to
work out when he came" (p. 129). Most eminent among these dispensations of providence was "the first remarkable pouring out of the Spirit
through Christ that ever was" during "the days of [Enoch]" (p. 141). The
first period, then, signifies the "great building," or the increase of the
gospel and the erecting of the church in the world, which "is the subject"
of the sermons on the work of redemption. Progress in history is determined by divine agency, which initiates changes in human life in order to
overcome the alienation between God and his fallen creatures. This progress is not linear, but depends on the rise and fall, progress and decline, of
revivals in the history of the church. There is an essential affinity between
conversion and God's work of redemption. Edwards put forward this
theme already in 1731, but now he placed it within the more general
context of his philosophy of salvation history:

And here by the way I would observe that the increase of Gospel light and the carrying on the Work of Redemption . . . from the first erecting of the church to the end of the world, is very much after the same manner as the carrying on of the same work and the same light in a particular soul from the time of its conversion till its perfected and crowned in glory. (p. 144)

The redemptory process is thus founded on the association between conversion and history. In this sense the drama of the history of salvation and redemption can be seen as the work of conversion writ large. As conversion "in a particular soul has its ups and down" while "the kingdom of God is building up in the soul," so "it is with respect to the great affair" of the work of redemption "in general as it relates to the universal subject of it." This association between the personal and the general scope of redemption is based on the argument that in both cases the divine goal is "the perfect restoring of the ruins of the fall." Hence, the "translation of Enoch was the first instance that ever was of restoring the ruins of the soul" in the history of God's work of redemption (pp. 144–45).

The effusion of the Holy Spirit during the time of Enoch signified a "providential event," or "a great advancement of the Work of Redemption" (pp. 175, 177). The same pattern applies to other major turning points in salvation history. The second outpouring, followed by another great revival, took place during Israel's sojourn in the wilderness of Sinai. In this period God caused "a remarkable pouring out of his spirit on the younger generation in the wilderness." Situated between Egypt and the Promised Land, the "dreadful wilderness" was a place of trial whose immediate "effect upon" the children of Israel "was to awaken them, convince and humble them, and fit them for great mercy." By "awakening providences," God showed his mercy toward the second generation of the Israelites in Sinai. More specifically, because "this younger generation were eminent for piety," and "showed a laudable and fervent zeal for God," their reward was that "wonderful blessings follow them," such as God giving them "the possession of Canaan." With the "men of former wicked generation being dead," God "sanctified this younger generation to himself" and "solemnly renewed his covenant with them." More particularly, this "renovation of the covenant" was accompanied by "remarkable pouring out of the Spirit, causing general reformation."[112] Indeed, argued Edwards, it is "questionable whether there ever was a time of so great a flourishing of religion in the Israelitish church as in that generation." Since "Moses' and Joshua's times" signified a decisive moment in the history of the work of redemption, at this period God made

---

[112] Ibid., pp. 189–92. Edwards developed this point first in his *Notes on Scripture* 282 (1738), pp. 238–41.

"the whole course of nature to be subservient to the affairs of redemption so that everything should yield [to] the purposes of that work and give place to the welfare of God's redeemed people."[113] Here he reiterates the views he advanced in *Miscellany* no. 702 (1736), where he first claimed that the "works of creation & the laws of nature and that course of nature that God established in creation is subordinate to the work of redemption" because "the laws & course of nature have often been interrupted to subserve to the designs of the great work of redemption."[114]

The glorious day of the "Israelitish church," however, soon degenerates; people forsake the true God and "fall into idolatry." But, as Edwards assured his congregation, this should be seen in light of the general pattern inherent in the redemptive process of history, namely, the model of progress and decline in the life of the church: "And time after time, when religion seemed to be almost gone and it was come to the last extremity, then God granted a revival and sent some angel or prophets to raise up some eminent persons to be an instrument of their reformation."[115] In face of the decline of the Israelitish church, God decided to revive the spirit of Israel and to show it his redemptive plan. So by "remarkable dispensation of providence" God began "a constant succession of prophets in Samuel's time that was to last for many ages." This was "the first thing of this nature that ever was done in the world," whose "main business" was "to foreshow Christ and his redemption." The prophets were "forerunners to prepare the way" for Christ's coming. (pp. 202–3, 238). As is evident in all these manifestations of divine activity, God closely watches occurrences in history in order to advance his plan. Eventually, in spite of many efforts to revive the work of redemption among the people of Israel, after Solomon "the Jewish church gradually declined more and more till Christ came." Yet "whatever failed or declined," Edwards assured his congregation, "God still carried on this work from age to age," and the building of his church in the world was "still advancing higher and higher," as made evident later with Christ's first coming. "For so wonderful were things ordered by the infinitely wise governor of the world, that whatever happened was order for good to this general design and made a means of promoting it" (p. 229).

The time had now come, Edwards told his audience, when the "declining of the glory of this legal dispensation made way for the introduction of the more glorious dispensation of the gospel"—"the evangelical dispensation." In this redemptive scheme "the glory of the Jewish dispensa-

---

[113] Edwards, *History of the Work of Redemption*, p. 193.

[114] Edwards, *Miscellany* no. 702, p. 290.

[115] Edwards, *History of the Work of Redemption*, p. 195. Subsequent pages appear parenthetically in the text.

tion must be gradually diminished to prepare the way for the spiritual glory of the gospel" (pp. 230–31). The replacement of the Jewish dispensation by the evangelical dispensation fits the pattern of redemptive ebb and flow. Even in the face of corruption and decadence, "God kept the lamp alive." After "exceeding great degeneracy" and when "religion seemed to be come to its last gasp, then God granted blessed revivals by remarkable outpouring of his Spirit" (p. 233). This constant revitalization of history is an essential mark of redemptive activity.

The end of the Jewish dispensation signified a turning point in the history of redemption; it marked the end of the first period in salvation history (from the fall to the incarnation of Christ), and the beginning of the second (from Christ's incarnation to the resurrection). In addition, it signified the end of Jewish scriptural history and the last time that the work of redemption was described in an historical work. So far the unfolding of the redemptive process had been recorded in the scriptures, but with Christ's first coming the prominent role was given to prophecy. Although "we have no account of the great part of this period in Scripture history, yet the events of this period" from Christ's incarnation to the resurrection "are more subject of Scripture prophecy." Believing that the text gives meaning to historical events, and not the other way around, Edwards based the history of the work of redemption on two main sources, or bodies of text: scripture history and scripture prophecy:

> There are two ways of the Scripture giving an account of the events by which the Work of Redemption is carried on: one by history and another is by prophecy. . . . Though the Scripture don't contain a proper history of the whole, yet there is contained the whole chain of great events by which this affair has been carried on from the foundation soon after the fall of man to the finishing of it at the end of the world either in history or prophecy. (p. 242)

To follow the history of God's work of redemption in the second period one needs to look at both scripture history and scripture prophecy, as well as at events "preserved in profane history." The latter, "the great revolutions that were among the nations of the earth" in the period before Christ's first coming, such as the fall of the Babylonian empire, the Persian empire, and so forth, as written in profane history, happened in order "for the kingdom of Christ" to come (pp. 244–45). All "those great shakings and revolutions of the nations of the world," foretold by the prophets at various times, such as Daniel's vision of the four beasts, "were all to prepare the way for Christ's coming" and to proclaim to the whole world that "the time of great messiah drew nigh" (pp. 246–47).

Before Christ's coming into the world, God once again attempted to revive the Jewish people. Whereas the Babylonian captivity signified a further decline of the Jewish dispensation, the return to Israel of the exiles at the end of this captivity marked an outpouring of God's Spirit. Once again, divine providence stretched out its hand to uphold God's chosen people. This time it was with "the pouring out of the Spirit of God that accompanied the ministry of Ezra the priest, after the captivity" in Babylon. This manifestation of the Holy Spirit "was followed with a great and general reformation" wherein the people of Israel "with great zeal and earnestness and reverence, gathered themselves together to hear the word of God read by Ezra," thus testifying to "their solemn renewing their covenant with God." This is the usual manner of God toward his church in the world:

> 'Tis observable that it has been God's manner in every remarkable new establishment of the state of his visible church, to give a remarkable outpouring of his Spirit; so it was on the first establishment of the church of the Jews at their first coming into Canaan under Joshua, as has been observed. And so it was now in this second settlement of his church in the same land in the time of Ezra. And so it was in the first establishment of the Christian church after Christ's resurrection.

More specifically, during the time of Ezra "this pouring out of the Spirit was a final cure of that nation of that particular sin," namely, "intermarrying with the Gentiles" (pp. 265–66).

The first three instances of the effusion of the Spirit occurred during the first epoch in the history of the work of redemption, the time from the fall to the incarnation of Christ. The fourth instance took place during the third period, which extends from the resurrection to the end of the world. The second period, from Christ's incarnation to the resurrection, is not marked by any isolated effusion. That epoch was "the most remarkable article of time that ever was or even will be," because during this time "the purchase of redemption was made" (pp. 294–95). The "birth of John the Baptist and the Incarnation of Christ" signified "the return of the Spirit" and the abolishment of the Jewish dispensation, but it was not followed by an extraordinary revival (p. 300). This would come only during the next period in salvation history.

Faithful to his understanding that the work of redemption is carried out mainly by the effusion of the Spirit, Edwards next attempted to illustrate this contention in regard to the third major period, from Christ's resurrection to the end of the world. During this time Christ, aided by the Holy Spirit, caused the "conversion" of millions to his gospel of salvation: "For Christ by his death having purchased the Holy Spirit, and having ascended and received that Spirit, he poured it forth abundantly for the conversion of thousands and millions of souls" (p. 375). Evidence for the pouring out of the Spirit during this period can be found in the "glorious success of the gospel among the Jews after Christ's ascension," which "began at Pentecost." "So wonderful was this pouring out" of the Holy Spirit "and so remarkable and swift the effect of it, that we read of three thousands that were converted to the Christian faith in one day." Soon after that "the Spirit of God was, nextly, wonderfully poured out on the Samaritans, which were not Jews by nation." This was followed by "the most remarkable pouring out of the Spirit" in "the city of Ephesus." And so began the long process of carrying the gospel to the Gentiles, and "the gospel sun that had lately risen on the Jews, now rose and began to enlighten the heathen world" (pp. 376–81). Later on in 1741, during the Great Awakening, Edwards declared in his commencement address at Yale, entitled *The Distinguishing Marks of a Work of the Spirit of God*, that the "apostolical age, or the age in which the apostles lived and preached the Gospel was an age of the greatest outpouring of the Spirit of God that ever was."[116]

The next important effusion of the Spirit was during the Protestant Reformation, when "God began gloriously to revive his church again and advance the kingdom of his Son." This redemptive act too came after a gloomy period in the history of the church, or "after such a dismal night of darkness" following the "rise of Antichrist," namely, the pope and the papacy.[117] There was then "a glorious outpouring of the Spirit of God that accompanied the first Reformation, not only to convert multitudes in so short a time from popery to the true religion, but to turn many to God and true godliness" (p. 438). This revival was accompanied by a great increase of learning "which is owing very much to the art of printing" (pp. 439–40). But soon this revival declined too and "now"—Edwards's own time—"there is an exceeding great decay of vital piety" (p. 438). The main reason for this unfortunate situation is the war that Satan ceaselessly wages against the true church, especially by infecting the world with "corrupted opinions." "Satan has opposed the light of the gospel that shone forth in the Reformation with many corrupted opinions, which he has brought and propagated in the world" (p. 430). Chief among the instruments used by Satan and his minions in their battle against the Christian faith are the "deists," who "wholly cast off the Christian religion, and are professed infidels. They ben't like the heretics, Arians and Socinians, and others, that own the Scriptures to be the word of God, and hold the Christian religion to be the true religion." The deists

deny the whole Christian religion. Indeed, they own the being of God but deny that Christ was the son of God, and say he was mere cheat, and so they say all the prophets and apostles were. And they deny the whole Scripture; they deny

---

[116] Edwards, *The Distinguishing Marks of a Work of the Spirit of God*, p. 226.
[117] Edwards, *History of the Work of Redemption*, p. 423. Subsequent pages appear parenthetically in the text.

that any of it is the word of God. They deny any revealed religion, or any word of God at all, and say that God has given mankind no other light to walk by but his own reason. (p. 432)

Edwards's attack on deism may be further explained by his dislike of the severe limitations the deists placed on the notion of God's absolute sovereignty: "Deists believed God bound by definition to act in an orderly, moral, and rational manner. His purpose was man's good."[118] All of Edwards's theological enterprise was to refute such anthropocentric considerations regarding the essence of divine activity in creation. The deists were the main target in Edwards's attack on the heresies of his own time. Their radical and dangerous ideas seemed to him to undermine gravely traditional Christian belief. The classic exposition of deism is John Toland's *Christianity not Mysterious* (1696), which argues against divine revelation and the supernatural. Samuel Clarke, in his *Demonstration of the Being and Attributes of God* (1704–5), defined four classes of deists, who taken together reveal the danger inherent in their views: for the first, God is only the Creator, with no further interest in the world; the second group admit a divine providence, but only in the material, not in the moral and spiritual, order; the third believe in certain moral attributes of God, but not a future life; and the fourth accept all the truths of natural religion, including belief in a life to come, but reject revelation. Such varieties of radical opinion may explain why Edwards assigned such a prominent role to deism in his attack on the heresies of his period, and why he was so apprehensive that deism would infect the whole English nation: "our nation . . . which is the principal nation of the Reformation, is very much overrun" by deism.[119]

It was in particular England, as well the British colonies in the New World, that Edwards blamed for the shortcomings and errors of his own time. Deism was only one part of a whole variety of "corrupt opinions and pernicious foolish errors" evident in this nation. Contaminated by dangerous new ideas stemming from the scientific revolution and the Enlightenment, what was evident in the British world was nothing but apostasy:

---

[118] Henry F. May, *The Enlightenment in America* (New York: Oxford University Press, 1976), p. 21.

[119] Edwards, *History of the Work of Redemption*, p. 432. For the deists' role in English and European thought, see Peter Gay, *Deism: An Anthology* (Princeton: D. Van Nostrand, 1968); Leslie Stephen, *History of English Thought in the Eighteenth Century*, 2 vols. (New York: Harcourt, 1962 [1876]); Fredrick C. Beiser, *The Sovereignty of Reason: The Defense of Rationality in the Early English Enlightenment* (Princeton: Princeton University Press, 1996), pp. 220–65; Harrison, *"Religion" and the Religions in the English Enlightenment*, pp. 85–98; and Brooke, *Science and Religion*, pp. 167–71.

In this kingdom those principles on which the power of godliness chiefly depends are in a great measure exploded, and Arianism and Socinianism and Arminianism and deism are the things that prevail and carry almost all before them. And particularly, history gives no account of any age wherein there was so great an apostasy of those that had been brought up under the light of the gospel to infidelity, never such a casting off the Christian religion and all revealed religion, never any age wherein was so much scoffing and ridiculing the gospel of Christ by those that have been brought up under gospel light, nor anything like it as there is at this day.[120]

In this dark time of decline there were, however, some signs of revival. In face of the war Satan was waging against the church, various instances of the "success" of the gospel appeared all over the world, such as in the "empire of Muscovy" or the "propagation" of the "gospel among the heathen here in America."[121] Edwards dwelt especially on America, trying to show his congregation the progress of the Protestant faith on the continent. He adopted Cotton Mather's and other New England historians' view that the "American continent" was under the dark dominion of "the devil," who for some hundreds of years kept this land to himself "out of the reach of the light of the gospel."[122] But the discovery of America, and especially the bringing of the light of the gospel to it by the Puritans as well as by other Protestant churches, "is one thing by which divine providence is preparing the way for the glorious future times of the church when Satan's kingdom shall be overthrown."[123] Among the many testimonies to the success of the gospel in his own time, Edwards cited the "remarkable revival of the power and practice of religion in Saxony in Germany" under the German pietist August Hermann Francke (1663–1727), and, most important, the "remarkable pouring out of the Spirit of God" in New England in 1734–35.[124] Initiated by divine providence, this revival

---

[120] Edwards, *History of the Work of Redemption*, p. 438. For a long time Edwards continued to express his deep dissatisfaction with the decline of religion in England. For an earlier example of his great disappointment in England's negative role in providential history, see the sermon of 1729, *Sin and Wickedness Bring Calamity and Misery on a People*, in *SDK*, pp. 497–505.

[121] Edwards, *History of the Work of Redemption*, pp. 432–33.

[122] Ibid., pp. 432–34. Compare *Miscellany* no. 815 (1739), in *MISA*, pp. 525–26. According to Cotton Mather, the Puritan emigration to New England was meant to cast "Light in Darkness" which prevailed in America. See Mather, general introduction, *Magnalia Christi Americana*, in Miller and Johnson, eds., *The Puritans: A Sourcebook of Their Writings*, 2 vols. (New York: Harper Torchbooks, 1963), I, p. 167.

[123] Edwards, *History of the Work of Redemption*, p. 434.

[124] Ibid., p. 436. On Edwards's impression of the revival in Germany, see also Edwards, "To Sec. Josiah Willard," June 1, 1740, in *LPW*, p. 83.

in Northampton, like similar contemporary revivals in Europe, took place to further the universal goal of God's work of redemption, namely, to prepare the way "for the glorious future times of the church when Satan's kingdom shall be overthrown not only throughout the Roman empire but throughout the whole habitable globe, on every side and in all continents."[125] No special eschatological quality was accorded to Puritan New England in Edwards's thought, nor was it invested with any singular apocalyptic mission in salvation history. Nationalization of the work of redemption is neither possible nor warranted.

In his endeavor to show that his own time signified a great decline in religion, Edwards argued that one main reason for this was "the increase in learning," the eminent role assigned to the ideas of the scientific revolution and the Enlightenment. He himself believed that "learning and knowledge should greatly increase before" the end of the world, developing this optimistic forecast already in part in *Miscellany* no. 350 (1729), where he proposed a close relationship between the "increase of learning" and divine "revelation."[126] To his great dismay, however, he learned from his own time and experience that although "learning is at a great height at this day in the world," the "world by their learning and wisdom don't know God." Instead of being guided by the light of divine revelation, learned people were going astray: "They seem to wander in the dark, are miserably deluded, stumble and fall in matter of religion as in midnight darkness." The advance of learning thus proved to be an obstacle to the growth of Christian faith and knowledge. No easy connection exists, as Edwards sadly came to realize, between the progress of divine revelation and the advancement of human learning. To the contrary:

> Learned men, and dreadfully divided in their opinions, run into all corrupt opinions and pernicious foolish errors. They scorn to submit their reason to divine revelation, to believe anything that is above their comprehension, and so being wise in their eyes, they become fools and ever vain in their imagination.[127]

Thus Edwards's early optimism regarding the progress of revelation and the advance of learning proved wrong; it only opened a Pandora's box.

The detailed description of the decline in religion in his own time served Edwards in his attempt to support his leading argument that a remarkable outpouring of the Spirit ensues only after a great decay in faith. "So it was when Christ came, it was an exceeding degenerate time among the Jews, and so it was a very dark time before the Reformation." The same

---

[125] Edwards, *History of the Work of Redemption*, pp. 434–35.

[126] Edwards, *Miscellany* no. 350 (c. 1729), p. 424.

[127] Edwards, *History of the Work of Redemption*, p. 441. Subsequent pages appear parenthetically in the text.

applied to the final epoch in the history of redemption: "it shall be a time of but little religion when Christ shall come to set up his kingdom in the world" (p. 457). His lamentations about the desperate situation of religion were partly intended to explain to his congregation that, in accordance with God's usual manner in the execution of his redemptive plan in history, they could confidently expect to see an outstanding effusion of the Spirit that would initiate yet another remarkable revival. He thus nominated his own age as the ripest time for another effusion of the Spirit: "when the appointed time comes for that glorious outpouring of God's Spirit," then God will show "men the insufficiency of [human wisdom]," and only he "himself by his own immediate influence enlighten men's mind." The most characteristic feature of the future divine dispensation would indeed be that

> God will improve this great increase of learning as an handmaid to religion, a means of a glorious advancement of the kingdom of his Son, when human learning shall be subservient to understanding the Scriptures and a clear explaining and glorious defending the doctrine of Christianity. (p. 441)

With these eschatological expectations and apocalyptic visions in mind regarding the place of his own time in providential history, Edwards went on to present the final stage of history, the space of time "from the present time till Antichrist is fallen and Satan's kingdom on earth destroyed" (p. 456). To interpret the final epoch in salvation history he employed his own historical scheme of redemption, arguing that the end of time would usher in a remarkable effusion of the Spirit which would be followed by a revival. No great social, political, or ecclesiastical revolutions would occur at the final stage in the history of redemption, but a most extraordinary outpouring of the Spirit would produce a major revival leading directly to the overthrow of the kingdom of Satan and Antichrist. Spiritual means rather than earthly power would determine the climax of salvation history.

By placing his own time at the final stage of salvation history, Edwards was aware of the danger that his eschatological interpretation might pave the way for unwarranted apocalyptic visions and dangerous eschatological expectations. The last period in God's work of redemption, he again promised, would be characterized by an effusion of the Spirit, not by a social or political upheaval: "It has been so before those glorious revivals of religion that have been hitherto" in the past, and so it will be when "that glorious work of God's Spirit begins by which Satan's kingdom is to be overthrown" (pp. 456–57). Yet, since this period is situated in the future, "we have nothing to guide us but the prophecies of Scripture" (p. 456). For when "Scripture history fails" to illuminate the future of the work of redemption, "there prophecy takes place; so that the account is still carried on, and the chain is not broken till we come to the very last

link of it in the consummation of all things."[128] Incorporating the distinctions he had made in earlier sermons in the series between scripture history and scripture prophecy, he claimed that the first could guide us only
"from the fall of man to the destruction of Jerusalem by the Romans."
But from that moment "to the present we had prophecy together with the
accomplishment of it in providence, as related in human histories. But
henceforward we have only Scripture prophecy to guide us,"[129] or the
book of Revelation.

For understanding the final act in the history of redemption, Edwards
relied on the revelations in the Apocalypse, chief among them the prophecy dealing with "that glorious work of God's Spirit by which Satan's
kingdom is to be overthrown."[130] On this point Edwards incorporated
into his general historical scheme of redemption the apocalyptic interpretation of Moses Lowman in *Paraphrase and Notes on the Revelation*
(1737),[131] specifically Lowman's reckoning of the period of the pouring
out of the sixth and seventh vials of the Apocalypse. "The present generation," Edwards thought, was under the "sixth vial," and therefore only
a few "events remained to be fulfilled before" the end of the world.[132]
Edwards particularly used Lowman's interpretation of the sixth and seventh vials to reinforce his main contention regarding the historical scheme
of God's work of redemption; namely, that the end of history would come
with an effusion of the Spirit: God's "Spirit shall be gloriously poured out
for the wonderful revival and propagation of religion."[133] The identification of the last two vials with an effusion of the Spirit at the end of history
thus enabled him to demonstrate the ultimate power of divine agency in
time from the beginning to the end of history; only by that means would
God finally overcome his arch enemies, Satan and Antichrist.

As in previous epochs during which the outpouring of the Spirit came
after a gloomy period, so now with the approach of the end of the world,
we "have all reason from Scripture to conclude that just before this work
of God begins it will be a very dark time in respect of the interest of
religion in the world." Such was always the case before "glorious revivals

---

[128] Stein, introduction, p. 23. The quotation is taken from Edwards's *A History of the
Work of Redemption*, in *The Works of President Edwards*, 4 vols. (New York, 1843), I, p.
368.

[129] Edwards, *History of the Work of Redemption*, in *HWR*, p. 456.

[130] Ibid.

[131] Stein, introduction, pp. 22–23, 55–59; Wilson, introduction, in *HWR*, pp. 422–23,
note 3, and p. 457, note 8. See also Edwards, *History of the Work of Redemption*, pp. 456–
57.

[132] Stein, introduction, p. 23.

[133] Edwards, *History of the Work of Redemption*, p. 460. Subsequent pages appear parenthetically in the text.

of religion." The same applies to the end of time, since "it seemed to be foretold in Scripture that it shall be a time of but little religion when Christ shall come to set up his kingdom in the world." Edwards had no illusions regarding the sad state of religion in his time: "It is now a very dark time with respect to the interest of religion," he lamented, a situation that called for the imminent "glorious work of God." In this eschatological scenario, however, he was prudent and did not presume to reckon whether "the times shall be any darker still, or how much darker before the beginning of this glorious work of God" at the end of time (p. 458).

Edwards asked his congregation not to expect a sudden great divine act or a miraculous revelation in the final stage of history. As in the past, God's work of redemption should be understood as taking place slowly and gradually, and not based upon an abrupt social or political upheaval: "There is not reason from God's word to think any other than this great work of God will be gradually wrought, though very swiftly, yet gradually." Edwards took special care to calm any unjustified enthusiasm, or splendid eschatological expectations, which might arise in view of the approach of the final stage in salvation history. Accordingly, as "the children of Israel were gradually brought out of the Babylonian captivity," and as "the heathen Roman empire was destroyed by a gradual though a very swift prevailing of the gospel," so even now with the coming of the final act in history "some great parts of Satan's visible kingdom shall have a very sudden fall, yet all will not be accomplished at once, as by some great miracle, as the resurrection of the dead at the end of the world will be all at once" (p. 459). Edwards knew of course that he was walking on very thin ice when describing the final period in salvation history. He could have found abundant examples of unfounded enthusiasm among religious millenarians during the early years of the Reformation in Germany as well as during the Puritan revolution in England. Therefore, he advised his congregation that even in the final act of salvation history, the work of redemption

> will be accomplished by means, by the preaching of the Gospel, and the use of the ordinary means of grace, and so shall be gradually brought to pass. Some shall be converted and be the means of other conversion; God's Spirit shall be poured out, first to raise up instruments, and then those instruments shall be improved and succeeded.

Also, "the Scripture hold forth" that "there should be several successive great and glorious events by which this glorious work shall be accomplished" (p. 459).

Having moderated his congregation's expectations regarding the character of this epoch in God's work of redemption, Edwards went on to explain the final act in the history of the drama of salvation and redemption. At the end of history, "[God's] Spirit shall be gloriously poured out for the wonderful revival and propagation of religion. This great work shall be accomplished, not by the authority of princes, nor by the wisdom of learned men, but by God's Holy Spirit." The consequence will be "to bring great multitudes to forsake that vice and profaneness that now so abundantly prevailed, and shall cause that vital religion that is now so despised and laughed at in the world to revive." This will be followed by a "work of conversion," which shall go on "in a wonderful manner." Further, "God by the pouring out his Holy Spirit, shall furnish men to be glorious instruments of carrying on his work; shall fill them with knowledge and wisdom and a fervent zeal for the promoting the kingdom of Christ and the salvation of souls and propagating the gospel in the world" (pp. 460–61).

It is in this spiritual manner that the "pouring out of the spirit of God" will effect "the overthrow of Satan's visible kingdom" in the world and "the destruction of Antichrist" (p. 462). Since only scriptural prophecy could foretell the events leading to the end of history, Edwards's description of the effusion of the Sprit in this period had to depend on the prophecies in the book of Revelation. More specifically, in adopting Lowman's apocalyptic interpretation of the vials, he determined that his own time corresponded to that time of the sixth vial of the Apocalypse.[134] Identifying the prophecies of Revelation with the outpouring of the Spirit, he argued that the sixth seal signified a remarkable effusion that would bring about the downfall of Satan and his minions, such as the "two mighty kingdoms of Antichrist and Mohammed," as well as "all the heresies, and superstitions, and corrupted opinions there are in the world."[135] After this battle is won, the "seventh vial shall be poured out" and will bring an end to all heresies "and infidelity and superstition," such as "Socinianism and Arianism and Quakerism and Arminianism." Then "Deism" as well shall be "crushed and driven away and vanish to nothing" (pp. 464–67). With the pouring out of the Holy Spirit during the time of the seventh vial the "kingdom of Antichrist shall be utterly overthrown." Finally, "Jewish infidelity shall be . . . overthrown" when "the thick veil that blinds their eyes shall be removed." Then, with the "national conversion of the Jews" shall "all Israel be saved" (pp. 468–69).

After the defeat of Satan and Antichrist, and the calling of the Jews, the stage is ready for the coming of the millennium. When the "visible kingdom of Satan shall be overthrown," then "the kingdom of Christ" will be "set up on the ruins of it everywhere, throughout the whole habitable

---

[134] Stein, introduction, p. 22.

[135] Edwards, *History of the Work of Redemption*, p. 463. Subsequent pages appear parenthetically in the text.

globe." And only then "the kingdom of Christ shall in the most strict and literal sense extend to all nations and the whole earth" (p. 473). This epoch will be characterized by "a state of peace and prosperity" since "this is most properly the time of the kingdom of heaven upon earth." Moreover, it signifies the time of "the principal fulfillment of the prophecies of the Old Testament that speak of the glorious time of the gospel that shall be in the latter days." The millennium will be "a time of great light and knowledge," as well as "a time of great holiness" wherein "religion shall be in every respect uppermost in the world." Further, during this period "shall all the world be united in peace and love in one amiable society," and an "excellent order in the church discipline and government [shall] be settled." Finally, the millennium will be a period "of great temporal [prosperity]." Following the Apocalypse, Edwards reckoned that the "duration" of this flourishing state of the church on earth would be "a thousand years"(pp. 479–86).

In terms of Protestant and Puritan apocalyptic interpretation, Edwards was introducing here a new meaning of the millennium. Instead of a tangible thousand-year period of Christ's rule with his saints upon earth, his millennium is conceived in spiritual terms and is thus deprived of the literal establishment of Christ's kingdom in the world. Edwards's millennium is devoid of the eschatological meaning and apocalyptic dimension described in scripture. For example, Milton in his eschatological expectations and millennial visions was convinced that "thy kingdom is now at hand, and thou standing at the dore. Come forth out of thy Royall Chambers, O prince of all the kings of the earth, put on the visible roabes of thy imperial Majesty, take up that unlimited Scepter which thy Almighty Father has Bequeath'd thee."[136] No millennial visions regarding Christ's majestic personal rule with his saints, no belief in the establishment of the kingdom of Christ for a thousand years upon the earth, appeared in Edwards's thought. For he believed that the kingdom of Christ, like the "Kingdom of God," does not "consist in what is outward and visible; it shall not be like the kingdoms of earthly kings," but would be manifested by a "remarkable pouring out of the Spirit."[137] Indeed, as he wrote in *Miscellany* no. 827 (c. 1740), entitled "Millennium," it is "a greater privilege to the church on earth to have" during the millennium "Christ, her head and Redeemer, in heaven at the right hand of God, than for him to be in this lower world." In fact, he believed that for Christ "to come down to this earth to dwell here, would be a second humiliation, a descending from an higher glory to a lower." Hence his emphasis on the spiritual

---

[136] Milton, *Animadversions*, as cited in William Haller, *The Rise of Puritanism* (Philadelphia: University of Pennsylvania Press, 1972), p. 357.
[137] Edwards, *The Distinguishing Marks of a Work of the Spirit of God*, p. 235.

meaning of the millennium: "Christ's reigning on earth by his Spirit is more glorious and happy for his church than his human presence would be."[138]

Edwards's concept of the millennium thus differed radically from those of previous Protestant and Puritan exegetes. He deemphasized Christ's millennial rule. He did not look for the personal return of Christ in his majesty to inaugurate the millennium, as the New England divine John Cotton did, nor did he envision any millennial reign of Christ and his saints upon the earth.[139] Further, in contrast to the overt millennial expectations among Protestants and Puritans in England and New England during the seventeenth century, he refused to identify the millennium with any violent social and political transformation that would usher in the transformation of the world into the kingdom of God and his Son Christ.[140] Characterized by "a state of peace and rest,"[141] which would come after the effusion of the Spirit and a revival, Edwards's millennium lacks Christ's personal thousand-year rule with his saints on earth. He dwelt more on the power of the Spirit than on millenarian expectations of earthly dominion. Faithful to his belief that the course of history is regulated by spiritual, redemptive means, he did not believe that the onset of the millennium would be signaled by a cataclysmic cosmic event. In contrast to the Protestant and Puritan apocalyptic mode of historical thought, which stressed belief in a tangible thousand-year period of Christ's rule, thus attributing great importance to this epoch, Edwards did not hold the millennium to be the climax of providential history. For him "the millennium was not the ultimate goal of the entire work of redemption, but only an earnest of the heavenly state which is the fullness of the kingdom."[142]

With the world turning from alienation to reconciliation with its Creator, and the church triumphant, the stage is ready for the last judgment. At this period, "the whole church shall be perfectly and forever delivered from this present evil world, forever forsake this cursed ground," while "the world shall be set on fire, and be turned into a great furnace, wherein

---

[138] Edwards, *Miscellany* no. 827 (1739), in *MISA*, pp. 537–38.

[139] For John Cotton's eschatology, see Bozeman, *To Live Ancient Lives*, pp. 237–62; Zakai, *Exile and Kingdom*, pp. 167–72, 178–90; and Stout, *The New England Soul*, pp. 19–20, 48–49.

[140] For radical millennial and eschatological visions in England and New England during the seventeenth century, see Christopher Hill, *The World Turned Upside Down: Radical Ideas During the English Revolution* (New York: Viking, 1978); and Philip F. Gura, *Glimpse of Zion's Glory: Puritan Radicalism in New England, 1620–1660* (Middletown, Conn.: Wesleyan University Press, 1984).

[141] McDermott, *One Holy and Happy Society*, p. 51.

[142] Stein, introduction, p. 24.

all the enemies of Christ and his church shall be tormented forever and ever."[143] Divine providence "begins its revolution at the creation, and finishes at Christ's second coming to judge the world and destroy heaven and earth, in a literal sense."[144] At that eschatological moment "the church be seen flocking together in the air to the place where Christ shall have fixed his throne."[145] With this final act, "the whole Work of Redemption is finished." The church, which like a ship endured "all the storms and tempests through the many ages of the world," shall finally "enter the harbor" of "the highest heavens, in complete and everlasting glory," and be transformed "into eternity after time shall be no more."[146]

This grand historical scheme of God's work of redemption makes clear that Edwards's philosophy of history, like his theology of nature and construction of space, was not related exclusively to his particular colonial experience, but transcended his own life in provincial British North America. Perry Miller has argued that the *History of the Work of Redemption* "embodies Edwards's time and place; it is the history of Northampton writ large. It is a cosmic rationalization of the communal revival."[147] Yet, although the social and ecclesiastical context of Puritan New England may indeed have contributed to the formation of Edwards's mode of historical thought, it does not carry the sole responsibility for its content and form. Edwards's universe of thought was much broader than the setting of his life in New England. His theological and philosophical enterprise should be seen, therefore, in light of his endeavor to find a meaningful response to the emergence of new modes of thought in Europe during the early modern period that gravely threatened, according to his thinking, traditional Christian life and belief. Within this ideological context, which determined the intellectual issues Edwards grappled with, as well as the philosophical and theological solutions he formulated, his construction of the order of time and nature of history may be examined and understood.

---

[143] Edwards, *History of the Work of Redemption*, pp. 498–505.
[144] Edwards, *Notes on Scripture*, 389 (1739), p. 378.
[145] Edwards, *History of the Work of Redemption*, pp. 498–505.
[146] Ibid., p. 508.
[147] Miller, *Jonathan Edwards*, p. 315.

Seven

"Chariots of Salvation": The Apocalypse and Eschatology of the Great Awakening

We have all reason from Scripture to conclude that just before this work of God begins it will be a very dark time with respect to the interest of religion in the world. It has been so before those glorious revivals of religion that have been hitherto. So it was when Christ came, it was an exceeding degenerate time among the Jews, and so it was a very dark time before the Reformation. And not only, but it seems to be foretold in Scripture that it shall be a time of but little religion when Christ shall come to set up his kingdom in the world.
 (Edwards, *History of the Work of Redemption*, 1739)

God seems now to be hastily gathering in his elect in all parts of the land; and probably the bigger part of adult persons that ever shall be saved, will be brought in now in a little time, and that will be as it was on that great outpouring of the Spirit upon the Jews in the apostles' days, the election will obtain, and the rest will be blinded."
 (Edwards, *Sinners in the Hands of an Angry God*, 1741)

'Tis not unlikely that this work of God's Spirit, that is so extraordinary and wonderful, is the dawning, or at least a prelude, of that glorious work of God, so often foretold in Scripture, which in the progress and issue of it, shall renew the world of mankind.
 (Edwards, *Some Thoughts Concerning the Revival*, 1742)

A FEW PHILOSOPHERS of history can boast that the views they develop in their private studies are actually materialized in history during their lifetime, and that the passage of time has testified to their historical prognosis. Edwards is among them, for in his interpretation of history he foresaw the Great Awakening of 1740–43. Believing God to be the sole author and Lord of history, and maintaining that divine activity is not blind to the process of history or alienated from the fate of the human beings within it, he argued that God works continuously throughout history to advance his work of redemption, which constitutes "the end and drift of all Gods works & dispensations from the beginning & even the end of the work of creation it self."[1] He therefore calculated that redemptive activity would culminate in another and final remarkable dispensation, whereby the "Spirit shall be gloriously poured out for the wonderful revival and propagation of religion."[2] So it was in the past, "and so it is foretold it will be at the great pourings out of the Spirit of God in the latter days."[3] This will be "the last and greatest outpouring of the Spirit,"[4] the penultimate event in salvation history preceding the millennium and the transformation of the world into the kingdom of God. Being the final effusion of the Spirit, it would inaugurate "the glory of the approaching happy state of the church" and its "most glorious and perfect state" on "earth."[5] As the final "great work" of the Spirit, such a glorious act "shall be accomplished, not by the authority of princes, nor by the wisdom of learned men, but by God's Holy Spirit." Rather than a magisterial reformation imposed from above, the final remarkable revival in history would take place when the Holy Spirit "shall bring great multitudes" to be "glorious instruments of carrying on" the work of redemption.[6]

This prognosis was put to the test almost immediately. Indeed, within a year after the 1739 sermons on the *History of the Work of Redemption*, the Great Awakening erupted in New England. Historical events therefore testified to and affirmed Edwards's prediction: once again God was advancing his work of redemption through the close and essential convergence between divine dispensation and revival. Here was the main source for the great enthusiasm with which Edwards greeted the Awakening and his unremitting zeal in defending it.

In 1739 Edwards argued that the work of redemption is carried out "by many successive works and dispensations of God," which inaugurate remarkable periods of revivals, or "special seasons of mercy."[7] On the basis of this theological teleology of history he now interpreted the Great Awakening, claiming that it heralded, along with other revivals taking place in the Protestant world during that time,[8] in Germany and Scotland, "the commencement of that last and greatest outpouring of the Spirit of God, that is to be in the latter ages of the world."[9] Being the penultimate

---

[1] Edwards, *Miscellany* no. 702, p. 284.

[2] Edwards, *History of the Work of Redemption*, p. 460.

[3] Ibid., p. 142.

[4] Edwards, *The Distinguishing Marks of a Work of the Spirit of God*, 1741, p. 230.

[5] Ibid., pp. 280–81.

[6] Edwards, *History of the Work of Redemption*, p. 460.

[7] Ibid., pp. 121, 511, 143.

[8] See, for example, Edwards's letter "To The Reverend William McCulloch," May 12, 1743, in *LPW*, p. 106, and in the same volume the letter "To the Reverend James Robe," May, 12, 1743, pp. 108–10.

[9] Edwards, *Distinguishing Marks*, p. 230.

stage in providential history, the revival signified a special realized, fulfilled time—*kairos*—an epoch in salvation history in which the eternal
judges and transforms the temporal. Hence his fervent belief that the New
England revival initiated a decisive apocalyptic and eschatological moment in salvation history as a whole: "Now [that] Christ is come down
from heaven into this land, in a remarkable and wonderful work of his
Spirit, it becomes" necessary for "all his professed disciples to acknowledge him, and give him honor."[10] God's present dispensation thus transformed the realm of history into a grand apocalypse—a special space of
time within which the Deity revealed the advance of his redemptive plan.
Likewise, believing the Awakening to open a new period in the realization
of sacred, prophetic revelations, Edwards conceived of it as an eschatological event proclaiming the final epoch in the drama of salvation and redemption: the New England revival, as part of the Protestant evangelical
awakening, "is the dawning, or at least a prelude, to that glorious work
of God," which "shall renew the world of mankind."[11] Edwards's apocalyptic visions and eschatological expectations now reached a zenith: "Neither earth or hell can hinder" God's "work that is going in the country,"
he proclaimed. And since "Christ gloriously triumphs at this day," all
should "give glory to him who thus rides forth in the chariots of his salvation."[12] The Awakening signaled the penultimate stage in God's historical
scheme of redemption; it was the realization of a divine plan that constituted the core of history, as well as its goal. In an age in which Enlightenment historians had made many efforts to exclude theistic considerations
from the realm of history, Edwards dwelt on God's close and intimate
relationship with it.

It is well known that Edwards hailed the Great Awakening from the
very beginning, working enthusiastically to advance the cause and defending it zealously against all adversaries. What is less known, however,
is how this undertaking was grounded essentially in the premises of the
redemptive mode of historical thought he had developed in his 1739 sermons, or to what an extent his philosophy of history determined his rhetoric during the Great Awakening. Having already constructed a theological
teleology of history, Edwards was in a position to assess the Awakening's
historical significance, and to evaluate its content and form within the
general context of his interpretation of salvation history. In contrast therefore to his reluctance to speculate about the meaning of the "little revival"
of 1734–35, he wasted no time in placing the Great Awakening within

[10] Ibid., p. 270.

[11] Edwards, *Some Thoughts Concerning the Present Revival of Religion in New England*,
1742, p. 353.

[12] Edwards, "To the Rev. Joseph Bellamy," January 21, 1741–42, in *LPW*, p. 99.

the broad context of God's historical scheme of redemption, turning to the past to provide the revival with historical justifications. The result was the construction of a singular rhetoric of history, an eschatology and apocalypse of the Great Awakening. The apocalyptic view of the Awakening sees it as a great revelatory sign in God's overall plan of redemption; its eschatology denotes the belief that this event marked a decisive stage in the realization of prophetic revelations regarding the end of time and history, such as Christ's second coming, the near approach of the millennium, and the transformation of the world into the kingdom of God.

Edwards's determined defense of the revival shows an important transformation in his mind. He increasingly turned to history to vindicate the revival and justify it in historical terms, apart from theological ones. Behind his rhetoric of history, or his apocalypse and eschatology of the Great Awakening, lies the redemptive mode of historical thought that brought him to see the contemporary revival as the penultimate event in salvation history. Hence his strong belief that the revival had opened a new space of experience and a new horizon of expectations in providential history for his fellow colonists. By urging people in New England to understand their actions and deeds within the general context of God's work of redemption, Edwards forged in them a new historical consciousness. His interpretation of the Awakening thus rescued it from its narrow colonial setting and conferred upon it great significance in sacred church history. His rhetoric of history thus served to impose order and meaning on historical contingency. The revival was not a mere provincial New England affair; rather, it signified a decisive event in the general annals of God's redemptive acts in history, inaugurating a new set of actions and expectations on the part of its participants. Edwards's historical interpretation imbued temporal contingency with divine meaning. Although his turning to history was slow and gradual during the revival, it nonetheless shows the increasing importance he attached to history in his attempt to place the New England moment in the wider context of salvation history. Without taking into account Edwards's distinct philosophical theology of history, it is difficult to understand his actions during the Awakening or the historical justification he provided for it.

An examination of Edwards's philosophy of history is essential to grasping the meaning he conferred upon the Great Awakening and the significance he attached to his own actions at the time. This is true more specifically with regard to certain works that appeared during the revival, such as *Sinners in the Hands of an Angry God* (1741), *The Distinguishing Marks of a Work of the Spirit of God* (1741), and *Some Thoughts Concerning the Present Revival of Religion in New England* (1742). They reveal a growing trend in Edwards to turn to the past in order to find historical justification and background for the present dispensation, and thus to place it in the center of salvation history. With the Awakening, historical considerations became inseparable from theological ones in Edwards's mind. Although he was first and foremost a theologian and a philosopher, the sheer magnitude of the revival led him increasingly to turn to history in order to explain this extraordinary New England moment. He defended it not only in theological terms, but also in historical ones, attempting to uncover the sacred historical context in which its participants ought to assess and understand it.

Understanding history from the point of view of an omniscient God, Edwards now believed, in contrast to his views on the "little revival," that the main goal of divine dispensation in the Awakening was not only the conversion and salvation of the fallen American colonists, but the redemption of history as a whole. The spiritual regeneration of local individuals was thus inextricable from the issue of redeeming time itself. This development stood behind much of Edwards's rhetoric of history during the Awakening, leading him to envision the New England revival in glorious terms, as "the glory of the approaching happy state of the church" on earth.[13]

Rhetoric and History in the Great Awakening

The Great Awakening set all New England aflame and deeply troubled the foundations of religious life and beliefs there. If Edwards was the charismatic leader of that great moment of *kairos*, which inaugurated the revival tradition in America, not the least cause of this was his success in endowing it with a significant meaning in salvation history. The revival demanded its own interpretation. It needed a person who could explain its historical significance and provide it with the broadest historical background. Edwards met the necessary qualifications. Having already developed a coherent philosophy of history, he was the best prepared of his contemporaries to assume this task of expounding the revival's historical meaning.

After the decline of the "little revival" of 1734–35, Edwards worked hard "to retrieve the halcyon days when Northampton was 'a city set on a hill.'"[14] Hence his enthusiastic welcome of George Whitefield's tour of New England in the fall of 1740, in the hope that the forthcoming trip of the "Grand Itinerant" to New England would "revive the flame again, even in the darkest times."[15] News of Whitefield's triumphant journey

---

[13] Edwards, *Distinguishing Marks*, p. 280.
[14] Goen, introduction, in *GA*, p. 47.
[15] Edwards, "To the Rev. George Whitefield," February 12, 1739/40, in *LPW*, p. 80.

through the southern and middle colonies in British America (1738–40), traveled fast and was widely covered in New England newspapers.[16] At Northampton Edwards read these reports with much eagerness, and learned about Whitefield's great oratorical skills and fervent spirit. He saw that, thanks to dramatic preaching and performance, Whitefield attracted people by the hundreds and thousands wherever he went, and a huge number of conversions followed. Edwards realized to his great satisfaction that this "Pedlar in Divinity"[17] was rekindling the fires of awakening from Georgia to New York. Later, during the fall of 1740, the revival was extended to Maine. These achievements led the "Grand Itinerant" himself to boast that through his activities God "intends to put the whole world a Flame."[18] In Whitefield's success Edwards saw a clear sign of "God's presence and the lively influence of his Spirit,"[19] and believed that the "smile of providence" was vividly present again in the land.[20] He expressed his great desire that God "would more and more pour out his Spirit upon us, and no more depart from us."[21]

Edwards's historical prognosis in his 1739 sermons was validated and fully affirmed with the onset of the Great Awakening; once again, through a remarkable divine dispensation, God's redemptive activity was being realized in history. In the good news that followed Whitefield's success he saw that the revelation of God's work of redemption was again beginning to unfold, and his apocalyptic visions and eschatological expectations rose high: "I hope this is the dawning of a day of God's mighty power and glorious grace to the world of mankind."[22] Defined in these terms, the Awakening reveals not only the power of the Spirit in achieving conversions but also the fulfillment of prophetic revelations concerning the end of history. This prognosis proved indispensable to the historical justification Edwards offered for the revival.

Edwards spared no time or effort to advance the Great Awakening. Beginning in 1740, he marshaled his intellectual energies to promote the cause, demanding that all "those that make mention of the Lord" should be "awakened and encouraged to call upon God, and not keep silence, nor give him any rest, till he establish and till he make Jerusalem a praise in the earth."[23] For his own part, Edwards enlisted himself fully in the cause

[16] On the coverage of Whitefield's grand tour of the American colonies in New England newspapers, see Stout, *The Divine Dramatist*, pp. 113–16.

[17] Lambert, "*Pedlar in Divinity.*"

[18] Stout, *The Divine Dramatist*, p. 117.

[19] Edwards, "To the Rev. Eleazar Wheelock," October 9, 1740, in *LPW*, p. 85.

[20] Edwards, "To the Rev. George Whitefield," February 12, 1739/40, in *LPW*, p. 81.

[21] Edwards, "To the Rev. George Whitefield," December 14, 1740, in *LPW*, p. 87.

[22] Edwards, "To the Rev. George Whitefield," February 12, 1939/40, p. 80.

[23] Edwards, "To the Rev. Eleazar Wheelock," p. 85.

of the revival, writing letters, sermons, and tracts, as well as frequently visiting various churches in New England to spread the revival gospel.

Historical justification of the Great Awakening, including giving it a wider background, became one of Edwards's main strategies in promoting the revival. From the beginning he declared that the present dispensation of the Spirit of God should be seen in historical terms within God's scheme of redemption: as the "apostolical age" was "an age of the greatest outpouring of the Spirit of God that ever was," and later "the [Protestant] Reformation" a time "of great pouring out of the Spirit to revive religion in the world," so indeed was the case with the current revival; it is "in general, from the Spirit of God."[24] Trying to capture the magnitude and significance of the Great Awakening in salvation history, Edwards made himself its most ardent champion in New England and the British world as a whole.

Edwards's historization of God's work of redemption during the revival influenced his rhetoric of history. During the "little revival" he had not as yet fully developed his redemptive mode of historical thought, so that he tended to portray it in terms of a local, provincial affair, almost entirely devoid of any sacred historical context. Its main goal, he believed, was conversion. Thus without any coherent philosophy of history at hand to assist him in interpreting this revival in broad historical terms, he was much puzzled, admitting frankly, "I forbear to make reflections, or to guess what God is about to do" with this event.[25]

During the Great Awakening, however, having forged the premises of his philosophy of history in the *History of the Work of Redemption*, Edwards was prepared to situate the revival in the context of God's historical scheme of redemption, contending that it constituted yet another crucial stage in God's work and envisioning its importance in salvation history. Being certain of the content and form of divine agency in the order of time, he had no hesitation in defining the Awakening as the penultimate event in sacred history: "Christ is come down from heaven into this land," he boldly proclaimed in 1741, in the form of "a remarkable and wonderful work of his Spirit."[26] Basing himself on such strong apocalyptic and eschatological conviction, he was fully persuaded that "what is now seen in America, and especially in New England, may prove the dawn of that glorious day," or the beginning of the final remarkable effusion of the Spirit. Having grasped the clue to God's redemptive activity in time, he wrote that "the very uncommon and wonderful circumstances and events of this work, seem to me strongly to argue that God intends it as the

[24] Edwards, *Distinguishing Marks*, pp. 226, 245, 260.
[25] Edwards, "Unpublished Letter of May 30, 1735," in *GA*, p. 109.
[26] Edwards, *Distinguishing Marks*, p. 270.

beginning or forerunner of something vastly great."[27] In 1735 Edwards was uncertain about God's intention in the "little revival." Five years later he had no difficulty in recognizing the present revival in his rhetoric of history as an apocalyptic and eschatological event, and as the penultimate stage in the drama of salvation and redemption.

Edwards thus acquired a new role during the Great Awakening, apart from that of theologian and philosopher. Attempting to provide historical justification for the revival, he refashioned himself more and more as an historian, one who constantly sought to unveil the sacred historical background for this New England moment. Upon this enterprise, in part, rests his great fame in the revival tradition in America.[28] In consciously assuming the task of siting the revival within ecclesiastical history, Edwards resembled other figures in the history of the church who wrote their narratives in response to some decisive historical changes in order to explain the changing circumstances of the Christian church in the world. Eusebius took upon himself the task of composing his *Ecclesiastical History* to supply the historical justification for the triumph of Christianity in the Roman Empire. Augustine wrote the *City of God* to defend Christianity against its many adversaries after the fall of Rome. Foxe composed his *Acts and Monuments*, commonly called "Book of Martyrs," in order to forge a new Protestant vision of England.

Such was also the case with Edwards. In fact, he had devised his major narrative of history before the beginning of the Great Awakening. Yet the philosophy of history he developed in 1739 enabled him to capture the full magnitude of the Awakening in providential history, as well as his special role within it. The new historical reality required him to transform himself from a mere narrator and recorder of redemptive activity as in 1739, into an actor in the divine drama engulfing the whole of New England. In this role Edwards made himself not only the theologian but also the historian of the revival. The formation of his apocalyptic and eschatological interpretation of the event was a gradual process, beginning in 1740 and reaching a climax in 1743,[29] as can be seen in works such as *Sinners in the Hands of an Angry God* (1741), *The Distinguishing Marks of a Work of the Spirit of God* (1741), and *Some Thoughts Concerning the Revival* (1742). Taken as a whole, these works reflect the development of Edwards's historical consciousness regarding the Great Awakening.

---

[27] Edwards, *Some Thoughts*, p. 358.

[28] See Conforti, *Jonathan Edwards, Religious Tradition, & American Culture*, pp. 47–49.

[29] In 1743 Edwards still argued: "We live in a day wherein God is doing marvelous things; in that respect we are distinguished from former generations." Hence, he continues, "I cannot think otherwise, than that what has now been doing, is the forerunner of something vastly greater, more pure, and more extensive." See Edwards, "To the Rev. William McCulloch of Cambuslang, Scotland," May 12, 1743, in *LPW*, p. 106.

The Eschatology of *Sinners in the Hands of an Angry God*

From the beginning of the Great Awakening in 1740, Edwards believed it to be "the dawning of a day of God's mighty power and glorious grace to the world of mankind."[30] It represented another "remarkable and wonderful dispensation of God's mercy"[31] in history. Edwards therefore gathered his powers to advance the cause and assist God "till he establish and till he make Jerusalem a praise in the earth."[32] Understood in these apocalyptic and eschatological terms, the present dispensation denoted a time of ultimate necessity, especially on the part of sinners and unconverted people; their conversion was a prerequisite for accomplishing the work of redemption. With the drama of salvation and redemption reaching a culmination, the private, existential dimension of conversion became inextricable from the general, external dimension of salvation history. Here lies the close association in Edwards's imagination between historical occurrences and the fate of human beings.

A profound sense of historical urgency demanding repentance runs through Edwards's most famous sermon, *Sinners in the Hands of an Angry God*, preached at Enfield on July 18, 1741, at the peak of the Great Awakening.[33] Historical interpretation is only implicit in this sermon, situated in the background, yet constituting an important source for the apocalyptic scenario it presents and establishing the basis for the vision of the sinners' awful fate before God's wrath. Indeed, the notion of impending judgment lurks behind the stage upon which the drama of the sinners in the hands of an angry God is taking place. For Edwards believed strongly that the time had come for God to unleash his wrath on those opposing

---

[30] Edwards, "To the Rev. George Whitefield," p. 80.

[31] Edwards, *Sinners in the Hands of an Angry God*, in *SJE*, p. 64.

[32] Edwards, "To the Rev. Eleazar Wheelock," October 9, 1740, in *LPW*, p. 85.

[33] The bibliography on this sermon is vast. A few of the more important discussions are: Edwin H. Cady, "The Artistry of Jonathan Edwards," *New England Quarterly* 22 (March 1949): 61–72; J. A. Leo Lemay, "Rhetorical Strategies in Sinners in the Hands of an Angry God and Narrative of the Late Massacres in Lancaster County," in *Benjamin Franklin, Jonathan Edwards, and the Representation of American Culture*, ed. Barbara B. Oberg and Harry S. Stout (New York: Oxford University Press, 1993), pp. 186–203; Wilson H. Kimnach, "The Brazen Trumpet: Jonathan Edwards's Conception of the Sermon," in *Jonathan Edwards: His Life and Influence*, ed. Charles Angoff (Rutherford, N.J.: Fairleigh Dickinson University Press, 1975), pp. 29–44; Ross J. Pudaloff, " 'Sinners in the Hands of an Angry God': The Socio-Economic and Intellectual Matrices for Edwards' Sermon," *Mosaic* 16 (Summer 1983): 45–64; Edward J. Gallagher, " 'Sinners in the Hands of an Angry God': Some Unfinished Business," *New England Quarterly* 73 (June 2000): 202–21; and Christopher Lukasik, "Feeling the Force of Certainty: The Divine Science, Newtonianism, and Jonathan Edwards's 'Sinners in the Hands of an Angry God'," *New England Quarterly* 73 (June 2000): 222–45.

the work of redemption. Historical transformation was thus leading to an existential choice on the part of human beings. The sermon is thus permeated with a powerful sense of time and a vision of history: "The wrath of almighty God is now undoubtedly hanging over great part of this congregation." In this eschatological moment inaugurated by the Great Awakening, Edwards pleaded with his audience: "let everyone fly out of Sodom."[34] The current divine dispensation revealed the culmination of salvation history and determined human beings' fate within it: their existential condition is inextricable from the unfolding revelation of God's work of redemption.

No single work in American religious history caused such great fear and trembling and none captured the imagination of so many generations as this sermon. The reason why this so-called spider sermon has enjoyed such notoriety is not hard to find. Through a long series of horrifying images and terrible visions regarding the miserable condition of sinners, Edwards depicted their existential state as dangling over "the pit of hell." The "wrath of God burns against them, their damnation don't slumber, the pit is prepared, the fire is made ready, the furnace is now hot, ready to receive them, the flames do now rage and glow . . . and the pit hath opened her mouth under them." He compared the life of an unconverted person with that of a small, helpless spider hanging with all the power of his weak muscles to a tiny cord over a consuming fire while God is ready to unleash his terrible wrath. Since their condition is based on the arbitrary, sovereign will of an angry God, sinners are constantly under the threat of "the fierceness" of God's "wrath." Thus, they have no alternative but to await "the dreadful pit of the glowing flames of the wrath of God," or "hell's wide gaping mouth open." Their awful fate is totally dependent on the arbitrary, fearsome will of an angry God: "The God that holds you over the pit of hell, much as one holds a spider, or some loathsome insect," Edwards exhorted the congregation in Enfield, "abhors you, and is dreadfully provoked; his wrath towards you burns like fire; he looks upon you as worthy of nothing else, but to be cast into the fire."[35]

Small wonder that this sermon is probably the most famous in the whole corpus of Jonathan Edwards's works. The personal tone only enhanced the great emotional power of the sermon: "O sinner! Consider the fearful danger you are in: 'tis a great furnace of wrath, a wide and bottomless pit, full of the fire of wrath, that you are held over in the hand of that God . . . you hang by a slender thread, with the flames of divine

---

[34] Edwards, *Sinners*, p. 65.
[35] Ibid., pp. 57, 51, 52, 55, 57.

wrath flashing about it, and ready every moment to singe it."[36] When it was first preached, this "most Terrible sermon," reported one listener at the Enfield church, caused "a great moaning & crying out through ye whole House."[37] The passage of time did not diminish the great emotional impact of this work. On the contrary, since the sermon was first delivered at Enfield, it "deserves to be the hallmark it has become in American religious history."[38] Even today, this sermon causes students of American history to feel a certain empathy with the awe and terror that seized its first listeners.

Yet if the emotional impact of the sermon is generally recognized, not so its ideological context. Strangely enough, the eschatological dimension and the apocalyptic context of *Sinners in the Hands of an Angry God* have not yet received due attention. The main theme, the imminent approach of God's judgment on those who refuse to receive his gospel of salvation, can only be understood within Edwards's philosophy and theology of history. His chief goal in this sermon was to establish an unbreakable link between the unfolding apocalypse of divine judgment and the human existential condition. In "a day wherein Christ has flung the door of mercy wide open, and stands in the door calling and crying with a loud voice to poor sinners . . . How awful is it to be left behind in such a day!" and not be included in "the Kingdom of God." Those that "are not to this day born again" and are "aliens from the commonwealth of Israel" are "going down to hell" and should be counted as "the children of the devil."[39]

Apocalyptic visions and eschatological expectations pervade Edwards's *Sinners in the Hands of an Angry God*. He believed that during the "great moment of the pouring out of the Spirit," when the Deity presents the climax of the work of redemption upon the stage of history and when "God seems now to be hastily gathering his elect,"[40] the destiny of human beings is inextricable from the course of salvation history. At the time "when God manifests himself in such a great work for his church, there is no such thing as being neuters; there is a necessity of being either for or against the king that then gloriously appears."[41] Salvation is inseparable from a true knowledge of divine activity in history, and vice versa.

For a long time this sermon was commonly referred to as a "hellfire" sermon. Yet, as every candid reader would admit, "it is actually focused on this life rather than the afterlife in hell. As such, it is more aptly called an eschatological sermon—one depicting the inevitability—and the tem-

---

[36] Ibid., p. 58.
[37] Stephen Williams as cited by Ola E. Winslow, *Jonathan Edwards*, p. 192.
[38] Winslow, *Jonathan Edwards*, p. 193.
[39] Edwards, *Sinners*, pp. 63–64.
[40] Ibid., p. 64.
[41] Edwards, *Some Thoughts*, p. 349.

poral unpredictability—of death and judgment."[42] The eschatological dimension does not apply solely to the human existential condition, but to the historical process as a whole. In fact, it is this special sense of time, the eschatology of God's work of redemption as it begins to unfold, that conferred on the sermon its awe-inspiring character. In a time of great divine dispensation, each individual faces an urgent existential choice regarding the welfare of his spiritual life. His or her portion in the drama of salvation cannot be separated from God's overall historical scheme of redemption, since the necessity of conversion is determined by the sheer magnitude of God's dispensation. Edwards therefore does not deal only with individual conversion; he does not merely describe the terrible fate of sinners facing God's wrath. The human condition and the fate of the individual cannot be separated from the historical process in which they are set: Christ "stands in the door calling and crying with a loud voice to poor sinners" to be "born again" and thus "fly out of Sodom."[43] Engulfed within these apocalyptic and eschatological occurrences, the fate of the individual cannot be separated from the historical moment in which his or her life is set.

Edwards's historical consciousness led to the composition of this eschatological sermon and determined its form and content. Dreadful forecasts of the individual's ultimate fate abound. Threats of "the vengeance of God on the wicked" and the terrible judgment about to fall on sinners and unbelievers fill the text, as well as visions of the imminent "destruction" promised to "every unconverted man" who "properly belonged to hell" while alive on earth (p. 51). What is most evident in this sermon is God's unmitigated wrath against those who frustrate the accomplishment of the work of redemption: "Those that are not to this day born again" are "alien from the commonwealth of Israel" and can expect nothing in the impending "day of wrath" (p. 63). These imaginings may be understood in the context of the retribution promised to sinners who reject the historical scheme of redemption: "Divine justice" indeed always calls "aloud for an infinite punishment" (p. 51). But during the present remarkable dispensation, the fate of those who do not undergo conversion, and thus refuse to respond to God's call for mercy and salvation, is the most frightening because they obstruct the course of salvation history. In a time of great historical urgency, as in the current revival where Christ "stands in the door" (p. 63), there is no other alternative but to advance the cause of redemption or to join Satan and his minions: "every unconverted man properly belongs to hell; that is his place; from thence he is" (p. 51). Or, in other words, at "a time when God manifests himself in such a great

[42] Wilson H. Kinmach et al., introduction, in *SJE*, pp. xvii–xviii, xxx–xxxi.
[43] Edwards, *Sinners*, pp. 63, 65. Subsequent pages appear parenthetically in the text.

work for his church, there is no such thing as being neuters; there is a necessity of being either for or against the king that then gloriously appears."[44] Since salvation history is reaching a climax, God's terrible anger against those "miserable creatures that he is now tormenting" in hell is surfacing on earth: "Yea, God is a great deal more angry with great numbers that are on earth, yea, doubtless with many that are now in this congregation." The apocalypse and eschatology of the Great Awakening brought "the fierceness" of God's "wrath" into the confines of history.[45]

An extraordinary historical situation demands the use of exceptional means on the part of God, as Edwards declared two months later in his commencement address at Yale in September 1741: "It may be reasonably expected that the extraordinary manner of the work then, will bear some proportion to the very extraordinary events."[46] As he had said in *Sinners in the Hands of an Angry God*, this included, among others, bringing images of God-inflicted torment from the hidden space of hell into broad daylight on earth, to serve as a warning to sinners. In this way Edwards infused history with great eschatological meaning. Formerly limited to the afterlife or the underworld, the dreadful visions of God's judgment now appeared in all their sound and fury upon the stage of history:

> The wrath of God burns against them, their damnation don't slumber, the pit is prepared, the fire is made ready, the furnace is now hot, ready to receive them, the flames do now rage and glow. The glittering sword is whet, and held over them, and the pit hath opened her mouth under them.[47]

"Unconverted men" therefore "walk over the pit of hell" while alive.[48] As opponents of God at the time of his great dispensation, their sufferings resemble those of hell; therefore, hell is their portion in this life as well as in the afterlife. So far God had reserved his most fearful punishments for hell, hidden away from the sight of living people. But with the culmination of the drama of salvation and redemption, he presents "the fierceness of his wrath" within history itself:

> O sinner! Consider the fearful danger you are in: 'tis great furnace of wrath, a wide and bottomless pit, full of the fire of wrath, that you are held over in the hand of that God, whose wrath is provoked and incensed as much against you as against many of the damned in hell.[49]

[44] Edwards, *Some Thoughts*, p. 349.
[45] Edwards, *Sinners*, p. 51.
[46] Edwards, *Distinguishing Marks*, p. 230.
[47] Edwards, *Sinners*, p. 51.
[48] Ibid., p. 53.
[49] Ibid., pp. 58–59. Edwards developed the notion of this hanging figure earlier in his sermon "The Free and Voluntary Suffering and Death of Christ," April 1736. See M. Z. Lesser, introduction, in *SDL*, pp. 21–22.

With such vivid and fearful images, Edwards fixed the awful presence of hell in his listeners' consciousness. This is why *Sinners in the Hands of an Angry God* has been called "one of the most affecting sermons ever preached in the English language."[50] He seemed to release Dante's *Inferno* from the underworld and place it within the historical process, an awful vision to warn all who could not see the great urgency and necessity demanded of them by God in advancing his work of redemption. History, in other words, would be an inferno for those who did not understand the eschatology of the Great Awakening.

In this sermon one can see the growth of Edwards's historical consciousness. Since the revival was transforming history into the dimension of realized eschatology, human fate had to be understood as inextricable from God's work of redemption unfolding within history. The salvation of individuals necessarily converges with the redemption of history. The individual's existential condition is posited in a radical dichotomy, between the gates of heaven and hell, while history is conceived as a redemptive journey from "Sodom" to Jerusalem. Situated between judgment and redemption, destruction and salvation, the fate of human beings is intertwined with the sacred historical framework within which their lives are set. Hence the urgency of the conversion demanded of sinners during the revival. In his sermon *God Glorified in the Work of Redemption* (1731), Edwards had declared conversion "a more glorious work of power than mere creation, or raising a dead body to life," and thus claimed that "the work of conversion, is a far greater, and more glorious effect, than mere being and life."[51] Ten years later, in 1741, that spiritual experience was integrated into the larger historical scheme of God's work of redemption. As Edwards's historical consciousness developed, conversion became inextricable from the redemption of history itself, which constituted the core of divine activity in time. The dimension of history thus became essential to the realization of the work of redemption.

The Awakening inaugurated a new stage in the drama of salvation, making conversion an essential part of providential history. The close association he made between history and conversion during the revival reinforced Edwards's argument that the present dispensation offered an existential choice to the unconverted: "now you have an extraordinary opportunity, a day wherein Christ has flung the door of mercy wide open, and stands in the door calling and crying with a loud voice the poor sinners." Crucial historical circumstances determine urgent personal choices. Sinners especially ought to "wake thoroughly out of sleep," or be "born

---

[50] Kinmach et al., introduction, in *SJE*, p. xxx.
[51] Edwards, *God Glorified in the Work of Redemption*, in *SJE*, p. 72.

again," and thus be included within "the commonwealth of Israel."[52] On "a day wherein many are flocking to him, and pressing into the kingdom of God," he warned, how "awful is it to be left behind." The revival thus marked a time of special urgency because it constituted a crucial stage in the history of God's work of redemption, as evidenced in the present "season of the pouring out of God's Spirit" in New England. To emphasize this point further, Edwards turned to past history:

> God seems now to be hastily gathering in his elect in all parts of the land; and probably the bigger part of adult persons that ever shall be saved, will be brought in now in a little time, and that will be as it was on that great outpouring of the Spirit upon the Jews in the apostles' days, the election will obtain, and the rest will be blinded.[53]

Theological considerations, to quote William James, deal "with personal destinies and keeping thus in contact with the only absolute realities which we know, must necessarily play an eternal part in human history."[54] Edwards's main hope in establishing the historical context of the revival was that understanding the sacred historical moment might induce sinners to grasp their destiny in salvation history.

The above comparison between "apostles' days" and the New England revival exemplifies Edwards's growing endeavor to justify the Awakening in historical terms. This analogy, as we will see, constituted a leading strategy in his attempt to furnish historical justification for the revival in other works as well, such as *The Distinguishing Marks* (1741) and *Some Thoughts* (1742). Edwards did not hesitate to compare the New England revival with God's great dispensation during the time of the apostles. The remarkable divine dispensation not only required conversion but fully illuminated the whole progress of salvation history. Hence, as in primitive times, the present dispensation revealed God's decree of salvation and damnation: in the remarkable effusion of the Spirit "the election will obtain, and the rest will be blinded." If "this should be the case with you," Edwards warned his audience, "you will eternally curse this day."[55] He was to dwell at length on this historical comparison, as well as on others, such as likening the Awakening to the Protestant Reformation.

Striving to further advance the cause of the revival, Edwards chose another powerful eschatological vision from scripture. Arguing for the necessity of conversion, he referred his audience to the well-known eschatological passage in Matthew 3:10, where John the Baptist proclaimed that

---

[52] Edwards, *Sinners*, pp. 63–64.
[53] Ibid.
[54] James, *The Varieties of Religious Experience*, p. 503.
[55] Edwards, *Sinners*, p. 64.

the time had come and the kingdom of heaven was at hand. In his belief that the Awakening inaugurated an eschatological moment in salvation history, Edwards cited St. John: "the ax is in extraordinary manner laid at the root of the trees, that every tree that brings forth no good fruit, may be hewn down, and cast into fire."[56] Toward the end of the sermon, he made it plain how the personal and the historical dimension converged so closely in his mind: "Therefore let everyone that is out of Christ, now awake and fly from the wrath to come. The wrath of almighty God is now undoubtedly hanging over a great part of his congregation: let everyone fly out of Sodom."[57] Without conversion there is no redemption, and without redemption there is no history. Sodom denotes a moment of great proportion in salvation history, a time of imminent divine judgment and destruction, but at the same time a moment of possible hope and deliverance. Only by escaping this sinful city could God's people embark on the road to the New Jerusalem, and thus continue to advance God's plan of redemption. The urgency of redeeming the soul cannot be separated from the issue of redeeming time, or the redemption of history as a whole. Behind the personal issue lies always the historical one, or the special historical moment in which human life is set.

Edwards believed that the Great Awakening inaugurated another *kairos* in salvation history, a time in which the eternal judges and transforms the temporal. This was the source of his comparison between the remarkable effusion of the Spirit in New England and that during the age of the apostles. In such moments, the course of history determines human fate. This at least is how the people who listened to Edwards at Enfield understood his message. Edwards's sermon had a tremendous impact on its audience. "The people of Enfield on that day were treated to nothing short of a spiritual revolution."[58] In the words of one of those who listened to Edwards: "before the sermon was done—there was a great moaning & crying out through ye whole House—What Shall I do to be Sav[ed]—oh I am going to Hell—Oh what shall I do for Christ, &c. &c."[59] The force of Edwards's words was based in part on the connection he made between the personal and the historical dimensions, bringing the terrible sufferings of hell to the surface of history. Not only in the afterlife, but also in this world, sinners are about to face their portion of hell.

Within this broad theological and ideological context Edwards's *Sinners in the Hands of an Angry God* acquires its full meaning. We can indeed study the language of this "horror sermon," but this alone will

---

[56] Ibid.
[57] Ibid., pp. 65–66.
[58] Kimnach et al., introduction, p. xxxi.
[59] Winslow, *Jonathan Edwards*, p. 192.

not offer us full understanding. For, as we will see, this is not an isolated text in Edwards's revival corpus, and its rhetoric of hellfire cannot be separated from his overall teleological theology of history. In fact, with this sermon Edwards launched the historicization of the New England revival, whose full manifestation appeared in the *Distinguishing Marks* and *Some Thoughts*. In the time of the pouring out of the Spirit of God, the experience of conversion becomes a necessary condition for salvation, and those who fail to undergo such spiritual experience belong to Satan and his minions: "The *devil* stands ready to fall upon them and seize them as his own" and the "old serpent is gaping at them."[60] Hence, the horrors facing sinners at the hands of an angry God are inextricable from the apocalyptic drama engulfing New England during the Awakening.

The frightening visions and horrifying symbols contained in this sermon, therefore, should not prevent us from seeing its importance as an historical text, a text that tells us much about Edwards's historical consciousness as well as about the special time he believed he was living in: "We live in a day wherein God is doing marvelous things," he wrote in 1743, "in that respect we are distinguished from former generations." Thus, he continues, "I cannot think otherwise, than that what has now been doing, is the forerunner of something vastly greater, more pure, and more extensive."[61]

Sinners in the Hands of an Angry God shows the growing importance Edwards attached to historical thought, and how historical reasoning became an integral part of his justification of the revival. He indeed dwelled at length on the existential condition of sinners, yet behind their dreadful portion stood a singular interpretation of history. Those who frustrate the historical work of redemption cannot but expect God's terrible wrath. With the advance of the Awakening Edwards turned more and more to history to explain the revival's significance within the annals of holiness and salvation. The New England revival demanded an historical justification, which Edwards was more than equipped to supply. The historical turn in his mind became more and more apparent as the revival spread in New England, becoming more explicit in his Yale commencement address, *The Distinguishing Marks of a Work of the Spirit of God* (1741), and reaching a climax with *Some Thoughts Concerning the Present Revival of Religion in New England* (1742). Taken together, these show how strongly Edwards's philosophy of history determined the meaning he attached to the Great Awakening, as well as the historical significance he accorded to his own actions at the time.

---

[60] Edwards, *Sinners*, p. 52.
[61] Edwards, "To the Rev. William McCulloch of Cambuslang, Scotland," May 12, 1743, in *LPW*, p. 106.

"The Glory of the Approaching Happy State of the Church":
The Distinguishing Marks

Two months after preaching at Enfield, on September 10, 1741, Edwards stood before the faculty and students of Yale College who gathered, "along with an auspicious company of 'ministers and other gentlemen,' to hear the commencement address." The present occasion was much weightier and more dignified than the one at Enfield, and Edwards must have calculated his message very carefully. Simply put, his goal in *The Distinguishing Marks of a Work of the Spirit of God* was "disarming those who would discredit the revival on the basis of its epiphenomena."[62] To tackle this view, he pleaded with his audience that the revival should not "be judged by any effects on the bodies of men; such as tears, trembling, groans, loud outcries, agonies of bodies, or the failing of bodily strength."[63] These are only peripheral and marginal manifestations, which have always accompanied a remarkable effusion of the Spirit, attested throughout salvation history, as during the Protestant Reformation or the Puritan Revolution.[64] Yet, behind the extravagant and bizarre behavior of some people lay something more profound that should be understood in terms of God's general historical scheme of redemption, or more particularly according to the extraordinary manner of the power of the Spirit.

Seeking to mitigate the rising doubts and the criticism levied against the revival because of the increasingly odd behavior and unrestrained enthusiasm of some converts, Edwards told his audience that "at the commencement of that last and the greatest outpouring of the Spirit of God, that is to be in the latter ages of the world, the manner of the work will be very extraordinary, and such as never has yet been seen."[65] The historical scheme of the work of redemption, as Edwards developed it in his 1739 sermons, determined the sheer magnitude of the revival, and the extravagant actions of some participants should be judged in light of its being the final great effusion of the Spirit. The "extraordinary" aspect of the effusion of the Spirit, or indeed historical necessity, would account for the enthusiasm that always tended to accompany important revivals. Apart from offering scriptural evidence that the revival was an authentic work of God, Edwards further developed his rhetoric of history, defining the historical source of the revival within the general framework of God's work of redemption. Placing the present dispensation within this broadest

---

[62] Goen, introduction, pp. 52–53.
[63] Edwards, *Distinguishing Marks*, p. 230.
[64] Ibid., pp. 245–46.
[65] Ibid., p. 230.

context was his main strategy in countering the many objections levied against it. Historical considerations became an essential part of his defense of the Awakening.

Having assigned the Holy Spirit the leading role in the rise and spread of revivals, Edwards now drew a comparison between the New England revival and the effusion of the Spirit in the age of the apostles. Already in his *Sinners in the Hands of an Angry God* he had made the analogy between the present dispensation and the "outpouring of the Spirit upon the Jews in the apostles' days."[66] But now he made this argument the cornerstone of his speech at Yale before the honorable company. In the Enfield sermon the historical comparison was mentioned only in passing, but now it came to the foreground. Critics of the Awakening, Edwards said, should take notice that the power of the Spirit evident in the present dispensation resembled the great dispensation "in the age in which the apostles lived and preached the Gospel." As in primitive times, the New England revival again displayed the remarkable power of the Spirit in transforming human life and existence, and thus eventually the course of history itself. Believing that the close connection between the effusion of the Spirit and revival was the ultimate manifestation of God's redemptive plan in history, Edwards did not hesitate to draw his audience's attention to the close affinity between the power and magnitude of the New England revival and the effusion of the Spirit during the apostolic period:

> The apostolic age, or the age in which the apostles lived and preached the Gospel, was an age of the greatest outpouring of the Spirit of God that ever was; and that both as to the extraordinary influences and gifts of the Spirit, in inspiration and miracles, and also as to his ordinary operations, in convincing, converting, enlightening and sanctifying the souls.[67]

This was not a negligible comment from the pen of an enthusiast, but a calculated statement from a philosopher of history. Reiterating the view he developed in 1739, that the end of history would manifest "the greatest outpouring of the Spirit of God," Edwards declared: "we have reason from Scripture prophecy to suppose, that at the commencement of that last and greatest outpouring of the Spirit of God, that is to be in the latter ages of the world, the manner of the work will be very extraordinary, and such as never has yet been seen" (p. 230).

Responding to critics of the revival who were alarmed by the enthusiasm apparent in the strange actions of some of its adherents, Edwards claimed it is "not reasonable to determine that a work is not the work of God's Spirit, because of the extraordinary degree in which the minds of persons

---

[66] Edwards, *Sinners*, p. 64.

[67] Edwards, *Distinguishing Marks*, p. 226. Subsequent pages appear parenthetically in the text.

are influenced and wrought upon." Against the claims that the New England revival was not evidence of the Spirit because of being "very unusual and extraordinary" in its character, Edwards reminded his audience that if the work of the Spirit in the Awakening is "very unusual, then it always was so, and was so in the apostles' days." In fact, in those early times

> never were there seen before such mighty and wonderful effects of the Spirit of God, in such sudden changes, and such great engagedness and zeal in such multitudes, such a great and sudden alteration in towns, cities and countries; such a swift progress, and vast extent of the work. (pp. 228–30)

Undoubtedly this description of the age of the apostles was based upon Edwards's own experience during the revival; it was a history of the New England Awakening writ large. Never indeed had the revival been placed in such broad historical context. Its resemblance, in terms of the power and scope of the Spirit, to the divine dispensation during the age of the apostles, transformed it from a mere provincial affair into a moment of great proportion in salvation history. By offering this broad historical justification, Edwards sought to assist adherents of the revival, and at the same time to calm the opposition of its foes.

As the remarkable dispensation of the Spirit in the past led to the establishment of the visible church during the time of the apostles, so now the present revival illuminated "the glory of the approaching happy state of the church" on earth (p. 280). The Awakening thus marked another important stage in providential history. This was the framework within which Edwards pleaded with his audience to consider the revival, and hence the strange actions of some of its most zealous participants. If the work of "the Spirit of God" is "very unusual" in the present revival, "then it always was so, and was so in the apostles' days." Elaborating on the close relationship between the means and effects of the effusion of the Spirit, Edwards went on:

> It may be reasonably expected that the extraordinary manner of the work then, will bear some proportion to the very extraordinary events, and that glorious changes in the state of the world, God will be about to bring to pass by it. (p. 230)

An extraordinary historical situation demands the use of exceptional means on the part of the Spirit, and an extraordinary effusion of the Spirit determines its reception on the part of human actors. Hence, the present revival ought not "to be judged by any effects on the bodies of men." Given the great historical urgency evidenced in the revival, the culmination of the work of redemption determined these unusual behaviors. To make this point Edwards repeated the fearful images he had developed in *Sinners in the Hands of an Angry God*, claiming that if "we consider human nature, we need not wonder" about these radical changes in human behavior. If "a person saw himself hanging over a great pit, full of fierce and glowing flames, by a thread he knew to be very weak, and not sufficient to bear his weight," it is only natural that "he be ready to cry out in such circumstances . . . How much more those that see themselves in this manner hanging over an infinitely more dreadful pit, or held over it in the hands of God, who at the same time they see to be exceedingly provoked?" (pp. 231–32). To God's extraordinary manner during the revival should be ascribed the inordinate response on the part of the people. Historical considerations therefore became essential to the understanding of the Great Awakening.

If the extraordinary manner of the Spirit, Edwards assured his listeners, led to the great "noise and stir" caused by the revival all over New England, then the rising opposition to it should also be understood in the general context of salvation history. He elaborated on the analogy between the Great Awakening and the time of Christ's first coming: "And we find that when Christ's kingdom came, by that remarkable pouring out of the Spirit in the apostles' days, it occasioned a great stir and ado everywhere." God's dispensation led to much strife and contention: "What mighty opposition was there in Jerusalem, on occasion of that great effusion of the Spirit that was there?" The same applied to the growing controversy surrounding the Great Awakening. The strong opposition the revival incurred in New England was used by Edwards as another proof of his contention that it bore the mark of the power of the Spirit. The more the opposition raged against the revival, the more the revival resembled the influence of the Spirit in primitive times, where the controversy "filled the world with noise, and gave occasion to some to say of the apostles, that they had turned the world upside down" (p. 235). Historical comparison became a leading means in Edwards's defense of the Awakening; to show it as a work of God, resting on solid historical foundations, he resorted more and more to the past.

Edwards first developed his comparison between the Great Awakening and the apostolic age in *Sinners in the Hands of an Angry God*. In the Yale address he was ready to expand this comparison to include the Protestant Reformation and the Puritan Revolution. The "remarkable pouring out of the Spirit, and revival of religion" in New England clearly resembled "the time of the Reformation." This was especially true with regard to "the Word of God as the principal means of carrying on God's work." As Luther returned its preeminence to God's word—*sola scriptura*—and established it as the locus of religious faith and experience, so, argued Edwards, was the case with the New England revival, "when persons affected in hearing the Word preached." For "all that is visible to the eye is unintelligible and vain, without the Word of God to instruct and guide the mind." Like the Reformation, therefore, the Great Awakening's goal was "propagating the church" in the world (pp. 239–40).

The historical example of the Protestant Reformation helped Edwards soothe opponents of the Awakening who were quick to find "the fall away into gross errors or scandalous practices" by many of its practitioners. Yet this, claimed Edwards, cannot serve as an argument that "the work in general is not the work of the Spirit of God." For "such things are always expected in a time of an important reformation of religion. If we look into church history, we shall find no instance of great revival of religion, but what has been attended with many" errors. This was the case "in the apostles' days" and of course during "the Reformation from popery," where many "fell away into grossest and most absurd errors, and abominable practices." It is almost a rule, continued Edwards, that "in times of great outpouring of the Spirit to revive religion in the world," a number of those in favor of the revival "have fallen off into whimsical and extravagant errors, and gross enthusiasm," and so forth. Such was the case not only during the age of the apostles and the Protestant Reformation but also in the time of the Puritan Revolution in England, or "in the days of king Charles I, the Interregnum, and Oliver Cromwell," and of course "in the beginning of New England, in her purest day, when vital piety flourished" (pp. 244–46). Later Edwards used this argument in his most ambitious attempt to defend the revival, *Some Thoughts Concerning the Revival*, where he contended that the "weakness of human nature has always appeared in times of great revival of religion."[68] More and more, then, Edwards's justification and defense of the revival was based on historical reasons and considerations.

As the Great Awakening rapidly spread throughout New England, Edwards increasingly tended to identify this event with the anticipated final effusion of the Spirit before the coming of the millennium and the transformation of the world into the kingdom of God. He therefore pleaded with his audience to reconsider the meaning of the revival in light of "the commencement of that last and greatest outpouring of the Spirit of God, that is to be in the latter ages of the world" wherein "the manner of the work will be very extraordinary." Those who listened to him could readily grasp the point he was trying to make, namely, that "the extraordinary manner of the work" will "bear some proportion to the very extraordinary events, and that glorious changes in the state of the world, God will be about to bring to pass by it."[69] The Awakening evidently belonged to the exceptional outpouring of the Spirit anticipated in the final stage of

[68] Edwards, *Some Thoughts*, pp. 318–19.

[69] Edwards, *Distinguishing Marks*, p. 230. Subsequent pages appear parenthetically in the text.

history, and should be considered by all, especially its opponents, in this
eschatological context:

> Since the great God has come down from heaven, and manifested himself in so
> wonderful a manner in this land, it is in vain for any of us to expect any other,
> than to be greatly affected by it in our spiritual state and circumstances, respect-
> ing the favor of God, one way or the other. (p. 276)

Attempting to illustrate the Awakening's singular historical moment,
Edwards compared it to the "little revival" in Northampton. The revival
of the 1740s "is undoubtedly, in general, from the Spirit of God." Its
sheer magnitude determines its place as the penultimate epoch in salvation
history. Compared to the revival of 1734–35, the "work of God that has
been carried" in New England "this year, has been much purer than that
which was wrought there six years before." Even "those that laughed
before" at the revival of 1734–35, "weep now" (pp. 260, 270). The Great
Awakening signals a most crucial epoch in salvation history: "Now [that]
Christ is come down from heaven into this land, in a remarkable and
wonderful work of his Spirit, it becomes all his professed disciples to acknowledge him, and give him honor." With such high eschatological expectations, Edwards did not hesitate to compare the revival of the 1740s
with the time before Christ's first coming: "And certainly, that low state
that the visible church of God has lately been sunk into, is very parallel
with the state of the Jewish church when Christ came" (pp. 270–71).
Edwards first developed this point in 1739, but now made it essential to
his defense of the Great Awakening. In such a context, evidently, the New
England revival appeared to herald, along with other current revivals in
the Protestant world, Christ's second coming, inaugurating a great apocalyptic and eschatological moment that would reveal "the glory of the approaching happy state of the church," its "most glorious and perfect
state" on "earth" (pp. 280–81). What was only implicit in *Sinners in the
Hands of an Angry God* was made most explicit in front of the dignified
audience at Yale, namely, Edwards's apocalypse and eschatology of the
Great Awakening. In the Yale address, then, Edwards released the New
England revival from its local setting and invested it with a glorious role
in salvation history. The fullest articulation of his historical understanding
of the revival would be provided a year later.

The "Glorious Work of God" which "Shall Renew the World of Mankind": *Some Thoughts Concerning the Revival*

"The Great Awakening of 1740 was at first hailed by its partisans . . . as
a supernatural work." Soon, however, "opponents of the Awakening were
starting their attack," claiming that "far from being a supernatural work,

the outburst was criminally excited by artificial stimulation."[70] The many "monstrous evils" that pervaded the revival proved to the anti-revival party that this event had nothing to do with God's word or with his Spirit, but was founded on unjustified enthusiasm.[71] "Visions and trances appeared, and some persons began to claim immediate inspiration for occasionally bizarre behavior. This, of course, was 'enthusiasm,' always an awful threat to orthodox Protestants and Puritans. Plainly, the revival was in danger of getting out of control."[72] Chief among the attackers was Charles Chauncy, the captain of the "anti-revival forces," who served as co-pastor of the First Church of Boston.[73] In his sermon *Enthusiasm Described and Caution'd Against* (1742), Chauncy launched the first onslaught against the revival, denouncing overt enthusiasm and calling for a return to sane and rational religion: "Make trial of your spiritual pretences by this rule: If you can submit to it, and will order your conduct by it, well: otherwise you only cheat yourselves, while you think yourselves to be *spiritual* men, or *prophets*: You are nothing but Enthusiasts."[74]

Chauncy, like many other opponents of the Great Awakening, rejected Edwards's contention that the Spirit of God had brought about the revival. Instead, as he wrote in another tract, *Seasonable Thoughts on the States of Religion in New England* (1743)—a compendium of horror stories about the worst emotional extravagances of the Awakening—what had taken place was not at all a "work of God." Against "the most flaming zeal" and unrestrained enthusiasm exhibited in the phenomenon of the present revival, Chauncy raised the voice of reason: "The plain Truth is, an *enlightened Mind*, and not *raised affections*, ought always to be the Guide of those who called themselves Men; and this, in the Affairs of Religion, as well as other Things."[75]

It was in this context that Edwards again assumed the task of defending the Great Awakening as a true sign of the work of God and as an authentic manifestation of the power of the Spirit. Once again he offered his apocalyptic and eschatological interpretation of the revival. The Awakening, he declared, "is undoubtedly, in the general, from the Spirit of God."[76] Con-

---

[70] Heimert and Miller, introduction, in *The Great Awakening: Documents Illustrating the Crisis and Its Consequences*, pp. xxxviii–xxxix.

[71] Winslow, *Jonathan Edwards, 1703–1758*, p. 194.

[72] Goen, introduction, p. 51.

[73] Ibid., p. 62.

[74] Charles Chauncy, *Enthusiasm Described and Caution'd Against* (Boston, 1742), in *The Great Awakening*, ed. Alan Heimert and Perry Miller, p. 230.

[75] Charles Chauncy, *Seasonable Thought on the State of Religion in New England* (Boston, 1743), in *The Great Awakening*, ed. Alan Heimert and Perry Miller, pp. 298–302. On the controversy between Edwards and Chauncy with regard to the Great Awakening, see Amy S. Lang, " 'A Flood of Errors': Chauncy and Edwards in the Great Awakening," in *JEAE*, pp. 160–76.

[76] Edwards, *Distinguishing Marks*, p. 260.

vinced that revival is the mark of divine agency in time, he even wrote to a friend: "If this ben't the work of God, I have all my religion to learn over again, and know not what use to make of the Bible."[77] For neither "earth nor hell can hinder" God's "work that is going on in the country." Since "Christ gloriously triumphs at this day," he demanded that all should "give glory to him who thus rides forth in the chariots of his salvation."[78]

Edwards's series of sermons on the work of redemption was published first in Scotland in 1774, and a reprint of the Scottish edition appeared in America only in 1782,[79] long after the Great Awakening of 1740–43. This work thus could not have had a direct public impact during the revival itself. But as regards Edwards himself, the ideas expressed in these sermons reinforced his historical consciousness regarding the meaning of the revival in the general context of God's work of redemption. This development can be seen in his most ambitious attempt to vindicate the Awakening, *Some Thoughts Concerning the Present Revival of Religion in New England*. Here Edwards strove to refute the "error of those who have had ill thoughts of the great religious operation on the mind of men, that has been carried on of late in New England."[80] Apart from theological justifications, he further proposed his historical analysis of the Great Awakening. "*Some Thoughts*," C. C. Goen writes, "carried forward" Edwards's "*heilsgeschichtliches* reading of human events in terms of historical progress toward a goal defined by the providence of God."[81] He thus further advanced his historical analysis of the eighteenth-century Protestant evangelical awakening in Europe and the Great Awakening in America, speculating on its eschatological and apocalyptic meaning:

> 'Tis not unlikely that this work of God's Spirit, that is so extraordinary and wonderful, is the dawning, or at least a prelude, of that glorious work of God, so often foretold in Scripture, which in the progress and issue of it, shall renew the world of mankind.[82]

Those who had listened to Edwards's sermons on the *History of the Work of Redemption* in 1739, where he tried to calm any enthusiasm regarding the end of the world, could now see that he had abandoned these cautious views and that his eschatological and apocalyptic imagination was running high.

In *Some Thoughts* Edwards defended the revival against the growing opposition of many skeptical and critical voices. He attacked the errors

[77] Edwards, "To Deacon Moses Lyman," August 31, 1741, in *LPW*, p. 97.

[78] Edwards, "To the Rev. Joseph Bellamy," p. 98.

[79] Conforti, *Jonathan Edwards, Religious Tradition, & American Culture*, p. 48; Wilson, introduction, pp. 21, 26.

[80] Edwards, *Some Thoughts*, p. 293.

[81] Goen, introduction, p. 71.

[82] Edwards, *Some Thoughts*, p. 353.

of those who "make their rule to judge of this work" from the perspective of "history, or former observations," instead of grounding it solely on "the Holy Scriptures." The main fault with these critics lay in their claim that "if there be anything new and extraordinary in the circumstances of this work that was not observed in former times, that is a rule with them to reject this work as not the work of God." Such an explanation, however, which denies the possibility of any great and sudden transformation in the course of salvation history, is totally wrong and unwarranted, because it "limits God where he has not limited himself" in the affairs of redemption. Against those who found no historical evidence for the outburst of the Great Awakening in the annals of the Christian church, Edwards reiterated the view regarding God's scheme of redemption that he had developed in his sermons on the *History of the Work of Redemption*:

> for whosoever has well weighed the wonderful and mysterious methods of divine wisdom, in carrying on the work of the new creation, or in the progress of the work of redemption . . . may easily observe that it has all along been God's manner to open new scenes, and to bring forth to view things new and wonderful . . . to the astonishment of heaven and earth, not only in the revelations he makes of his mind and will, but also in the works of his hands.

Edwards found evidence for this proposition in a comparison between the old and the new creation, which he first made in his Boston lecture in 1731. "As the old creation was carried on through six days, and appeared all complete, settled in the state of rest on the seventh: so the new creation, which is immensely the greatest and most glorious work, is carried on in a gradual progress, from the fall of man to the consummation of all things, at the end of the world."[83]

In response to the criticism levied against the Awakening, Edwards admitted that a "great deal of noise and tumult, confusion and uproar, and darkness mixed with light, and evil with good, is always to be expected in the beginning of something very extraordinary, and very glorious" in the "state of the church of God." The reason for such a phenomenon is the "weakness of human nature," which "has always appeared in times of great revival of religion."[84] The Great Awakening is no exception to this rule. Yet this should not hinder us from seeing the glorious power of God's hand in that event. Edwards therefore reiterated the belief first uttered in his Yale address in 1741, that "the extraordinary manner of the work then, will bear some proportion to the very extraordinary events."[85] Hence, if "we consider the errors that attend" the present revival, "they are not strange, upon the supposition of its being, as to the substance of

---

[83] Ibid., pp. 306–7.
[84] Ibid., pp. 318–19.
[85] Edwards, *Distinguishing Marks*, p. 230.

it, a work of God." For if "God intends this great revival of religion to
be the dawning, or a forerunner of an happy state of his church on earth,
it may be an instance of the divine wisdom, in the beginning of it, to suffer
many irregularities and errors in conduct." Given the inherent weakness
of human nature, so radical a transformation in the history of God's work
of redemption entails that the Deity would "permit a great deal of error,
and suffer the infirmity of his people much to appear, in the beginning of
a glorious work of his grace." Human errors and misbehavior are only
natural in such a decisive historical moment when God is about to radically change the course of history. The extraordinary means of the work
at hand produces extraordinary effects: "For as the work is much greater
than any other outpouring of the Spirit that ever has been in New England, so no wonder that the Devil is more alarmed and enraged, and
exerts himself more vigorously against it."[86] Therefore, to denounce the
present revival means rejecting the "whole tenure of the Gospel" and "all
the notion of religion that the Scripture gives us."[87] Faithful to his views
on the historical scheme of redemption, Edwards had no difficulty claiming the present dispensation to be "a great and wonderful event, a strange
revolution, an unexpected, surprising overturning of things, suddenly
brought to pass; such as never has been seen in New England, and scarce
ever has been heard of in any land."[88]

In confronting the growing reaction against the Awakening, Edwards
had no doubt that the Great Awakening "is the work of God," and "that
it is a very great and wonderful, and exceeding glorious work of God."[89]
To further demonstrate his point he used ideas first announced in the 1731
Boston lecture *God Glorified in the Work of Redemption*,[90] where he
claimed conversion to be a more glorious work than creation, as well
as his conclusion in *Miscellany* no. 547 (1731), regarding the work of
redemption as the great end and reason of creation. Thus, in 1742 he said
again that the "work of redemption" is "the great end of all other works
of God, and of which the work of creation was but a shadow." Since the
ultimate mark of divine agency in history is revival, which concerns in
part the work of conversion, Edwards declared: "I am bold to say, that
the work of God in the conversion of one soul . . . is a more glorious
work of God than the creation of the whole material world." The many
conversions of souls during the revival led him to claim that the Awakening "is very glorious" work because it is "vastly beyond any former out-

[86] Edwards, *Some Thoughts*, pp. 323–25.
[87] Ibid., p. 331.
[88] Ibid., p. 344.
[89] Ibid., p. 343.
[90] *Miscellany* no. 547, pp. 93–95.

pouring of the Spirit that ever was known in New England," as well as "in other British colonies in America."[91] In his ardor, Edwards abandoned the cautious tone of his 1739 sermons with respect to enthusiasm, contending that the Great Awakening, along with other contemporary revivals in the Protestant world, marked the dawn of the coming of the New Jerusalem, which signified a prelude to the millennium: "The New Jerusalem . . . has begun to come down from heaven, and perhaps never were more of the prelibations of heaven's glory given upon earth."[92]

Edwards had no doubt that "so great and wonderful work of God's Spirit is a work wherein God's hand is remarkably lifted up, and wherein he displays his majesty."[93] In 1739 he had argued that a remarkable effusion of the Spirit would precede the millennium and the transformation of the world into the kingdom of God. At that future time God's "Spirit shall be gloriously poured out for the wonderful revival and propagation of religion." This "great work," he continued, "shall be accomplished, not by the authority of princes, nor by the wisdom of learned men, but by God's Holy Spirit." But in 1739 he was not sure when and where it would take place: "We know not where this pouring out of the Spirit shall begin, or whether at many places at once." All he was certain of was that this future dispensation "shall soon bring great multitudes" to return to "vital religion" through the "work of conversion."[94] Since this prognosis of "multitudes" was realized in the Great Awakening, Edwards said, "these times are times of remarkable pouring out of the Spirit."[95] He therefore abandoned the cautious tone of 1739 and speculated that "this work of God's Spirit" is "the dawning, or at least a prelude, of that glorious work of God, so often foretold in Scripture, which in the progress and issue of it, shall renew the world of mankind."[96]

This often quoted passage from *Some Thoughts* has been taken as evidence that Edwards claimed the millennium would probably dawn in America.[97] Yet, according to Edwards's own historical scheme of redemption, this was not the case.[98] The millennium, in his historical reasoning, will come only after another and final remarkable effusion of the Spirit, to be accompanied by a great revival. This final revival will bring about,

[91] Ibid., pp. 344–45.
[92] Ibid., p. 346.
[93] Ibid., p. 352.
[94] Edwards, *History of the Work of Redemption*, p. 460.
[95] Edwards, *Some Thoughts*, p. 350.
[96] Ibid., p. 353.
[97] See, for example, Goen, introduction, in *GA*, p. 84.
[98] The first to develop this important revisionist argument, based on a close examination of Edwards's concept of the millennium, is McDermott in *One Holy and Happy Society*, pp. 50–60.

among other things, a great "work of conversion," the abolishment of "heresies, and infidelity and superstition," the "utterly overturn" of the "kingdom of Antichrist," and "the national conversion of the Jews."[99] Only after these transformations and struggles, leading to "the church's glory and triumph" in the world, will the period of the millennium begin; the "millennium is the sabbatism of the church," a time denoting "the happy state of the church and the world."[100] In other words, following his historical scheme, Edwards expected another remarkable revival before the millennium. As to the millennial age itself, the "Edwardsean millennium was to be a period of absolute stability and peace for the vast majority of its duration."[101]

Thus understood, Edwards's apocalypse and eschatology of the Great Awakening does not refer directly to the dawning of the millennium in America but to another remarkable effusion of the Spirit preceding the millennial period. This, for example, is why he was so disturbed to learn about the "slanderously reports" in Chaunchy's *Seasonable Thoughts* (1743), according to which, Edwards wrote, "I have often said the millennium was already begun, and that it began at Northampton" or in New England as a whole.[102] In his historical thought, the Awakening was not the dawn of the millennium but the beginning of the penultimate stage in salvation history—the "renewal of the world"—which will precede the millennial age. Edwards had no doubt that the New England revival marked another remarkable effusion of the Spirit that "shall renew the world of mankind," an essential precondition for the dawn of the millennium, but as for the beginning of the millennium itself, he believed it would come only "after the year 2000."[103]

This is also the context of Edwards's radical claim "that this work of God's Spirit" leading to the renewal of the "world of mankind" will "begin in America," and his belief that this land was the chosen one "where the first fruits of that glorious day" of the church would be fulfilled.[104] In 1739 he was not sure "where this [final] pouring out of the Spirit shall begin, or whether at many places at once."[105] But in 1742, in light of the Great Awakening, he was confident that the final effusion of the Spirit would take place in America. What is implied here, however, is not that America is the place where the millennium would begin, but

---

[99] Edwards, *History of the Work of Redemption*, pp. 461, 467–69.
[100] Edwards, *Note on the Apocalypse* 77, pp. 177–78.
[101] McDermott, *One Holy and Happy Society*, p. 59.
[102] Edwards, "To the Rev. William McCulloch," March 5, 1743/4, in *LPW*, pp. 135–36.
[103] Stein, introduction, in *AW*, p. 57.
[104] Edwards, *Some Thoughts*, pp. 353–54.
[105] Edwards, *History of the Work of Redemption*, p. 460.

rather that the final revival preceding the millennial age in God's historical scheme of redemption would probably commence on that continent. The New World may open a new chapter in the history of redemption, but not announce the millennium itself: "This new world is probably now discovered, that the new and most glorious state of God's church on earth might commence there; that God might in it begin a new world in a spiritual respect, when he creates the new heaven and new earth."[106] Had Edwards thought that the Great Awakening would inaugurate the dawn of the millennium he would have said so. But he thought the New England revival signified only the beginning of the final remarkable effusion of the Spirit preceding the millennium.

This notion can be further perceived in the comparison that Edwards made between the effusions of the Spirit during the Protestant Reformation and the New England revival: it is "worthy to be noted that America was discovered about the time of the Reformation, or but little before: which Reformation was the first thing that God did toward the glorious renovation of the world" after the "great antichristian apostasy."[107] Edwards's millennium would commence only after that "renovation" of the creation, which includes among others the "utterly overturn" of the "kingdom of Antichrist."[108] Yet, even if the millennium is not defined as taking place in America, this cannot diminish the important role accorded to New England in salvation history. For given the impressive revival there, Edwards indeed thought it was the place where the final effusion of the Spirit would first be manifested: "if we consider the circumstances of the settlement of New England, it must needs appear the most likely of all American colonies, to be the place where this work shall principally take its rise."[109] Such a scenario, "especially in New England, may prove the dawn of that glorious day: and the very uncommon and wonderful circumstances and events of this work, seem to me strongly to argue that God intends it as the beginning or forerunner of something vastly great."[110] New England indeed was accorded a special role but only because it was the geographical area first introducing to the world "that happy day of God's power and salvation," the "appointed season of the application of the redemption of Christ."[111]

With *Some Thoughts* Edwards's apocalyptic and eschatological interpretation of the Great Awakening reached its full articulation. He no

---

[106] Edwards, *Some Thoughts*, p. 354.
[107] Ibid., pp. 355–56.
[108] Edwards, *History of the Work of Redemption*, pp. 467–69.
[109] Edwards, *Some Thoughts*, p. 358.
[110] Ibid.
[111] Ibid.

longer hesitated to identify the time and space where the "last and greatest outpouring of the Spirit of God, that is to be in the latter ages of the world"[112] and to declare that now the Lord "comes forth in that last and greatest outpouring of his Spirit, to introduce that happy day of God's power and salvation" when he "is setting his king on his holy hill of Zion."[113]

After proclaiming in his sermons of 1739 the historical "narrative of the glorious work of God," Edwards applied it to the revival of the 1740s. In the end, however, his great expectations proved unfounded. God's "season of grace" turned to be rather "a season of remarkable darkness, and hiding of God's face, and buffetings of Satan."[114] As Edwards knew from the premises of his own historical scheme of redemption, based on the ebb and flow, rise and decline, of awakenings throughout history, eventually the revival of the 1740s had to come to an end: "the Spirit of God began to withdraw" from New England and "this great work" of the revival, he lamented, "has been on the decline." The Devil again took the "advantage" now and many were "led far away from God and their duty."[115]

Although in the end the revival petered out, this did not shake Edwards's mode of historical thought, or inspire doubt about the validity and relevance of his philosophy for salvation history. He was convinced that "God will revive his work [of redemption] again before long; and that it will not wholly cease till it has subdued the whole earth,"[116] and that "the beginning of that glorious work of God's Spirit, which in the progress and issue of it, will overthrow Antichrist, and introduce the glory of the latter-days, is not far off."[117] So, however distressing the decline of the revival, it remained compatible with Edwards's overall concept of God's historical scheme of redemption. For he was certain that

> from the fall of man to this day wherein we live the Work of Redemption in its effects has mainly been carried on by remarkable pourings out of the Spirit of God . . . [and] the way in which the greatest things have been done toward carrying on this work has always been by remarkable pourings out of the Spirit at special seasons of mercy.[118]

[112] Edwards, *Distinguishing Marks*, p. 230.

[113] Edwards, *Some Thoughts*, pp. 358, 370.

[114] Edwards, "To the Rev. William McCulloch of Cambuslang, Scotland," May 12, 1743, in *LPW*, p. 106.

[115] Edwards, "To William McCulloch," March 5, 1743/4, in *LPW*, p. 134.

[116] Edwards, "To the Rev. William McCulloch," May 12, 1743, p. 106.

[117] Edwards, "Humble Attempt," in *AW*, p. 421.

[118] Edwards, *History of the Work of Redemption*, p. 143.

This general rule of God's historical scheme of redemption applies not only to past events but also to the future. Edwards did not survive to see himself vindicated in another revival. However, had he lived longer he would not have been surprised to hear about the Second Great Awakening at the end of the eighteenth century and early in the nineteenth, as well as the many later revivals that have taken place in America.

Ethics

Eight

Edwards and the Enlightenment Debate on Moral Philosophy

Hutcheson denies that post-lapsarian is inherently sinful and that all apparent morality can be reduced to a more or less complicated function of this sinfulness . . . and that man's moral institutions can be understood to arise from the prescriptions of an avenging God, whom his creatures follow in terror and hope.

(Knod Haakonssen, *Natural Law and Moral Philosophy*, 1996)

Mr. Hutcheson has taught us, by the most convincing arguments, that morality is nothing in the abstract nature of things, but is entirely relative to the sentiment of mental taste of each particular being.

(David Hume, *Philosophical Essays Concerning Human Understanding*, 1748)

God wont leave the world of mankind to themselves without taking any care to govern & order their state so as that this part of the world may be regulated decently & beautifully . . . he will take care that the world of mankind will be regulated with respect to its moral state & so will maintain a good MORAL GOVERNMENT over the world of mankind.

(Edwards, *Miscellany* no. 864, c. 1740)

I want . . . to demonstrate the palpable inconsistency and absurdity . . . particularly [of] that grand objection, in which the modern writers have so much gloried, and so long triumphed, with so great a degree of insult towards the most excellent divines and, in effect, against the gospel of Jesus Christ, viz. that the Calvinistic notions of God's moral government are contrary to the common sense of mankind.

(Edwards, "To The Reverend John Erskine," July 7, 1752)

My discourse on virtue [*The Nature of True Virtue*] is principally designed against that notion of virtue maintained by My Lord Shaftesbury, [Francis] Hutcheson, and [George] Turnbull; which seems to be most in vogue at this day . . . which notion is calculated to show that all mankind are naturally disposed to virtue, and are without any native depravity."

(Edwards, "To the Reverend Thomas Foxcroft,"
February 11, 1757)

EDWARDS'S LIFE of the mind may be characterized as a long and consistent struggle against the rise of new modes of thought in early modern history that threatened traditional Christian belief: during the 1720s, he developed his natural theology, attempting to define the essential nature of reality against the mechanical, scientific philosophy of nature; during the 1730s, he constructed a general ecclesiastical history in response to the Enlightenment narratives of history; the premises of such an evangelical historiography, based on revival and awakening as the main means of divine agency in time, he immediately applied to the Great Awakening. And during the 1750s, in the final decade of his life, he embarked on another ambitious enterprise—a philosophical and theological critique of the Enlightenment project in the realm of ethics and morals, aiming to show that "virtue must chiefly consist in love to God," who is "the head of the universal system of existence; the foundation and fountain of all being."[1]

After events in his church led to his dismissal in 1750, Edwards went into exile in 1751 in the frontier settlement of Stockbridge in western Massachusetts, becoming a minister of the small congregation and a missionary to the Housatonic Indians there. The hard life of the mission outpost did not hinder him from continuing his intellectual activity against new ideas coming out of Europe. More specifically, he assumed the task of providing an alternative to Enlightenment conceptions of ethics and morals. The outcome of this theological and philosophical enterprise may be seen in Edwards's ethical writings: *Freedom of the Will* (1754), the two dissertations, *Concerning the End for which God Created the World* and *The Nature of True Virtue* (written in 1755), and *Original Sin* (1758). Taken as a whole, these works represent Edwards's aim to establish "God's Moral Government of the world,"[2] and to demonstrate that the Deity is the sole source of ethics and morals. For Edwards believed that "nothing is of the nature of true virtue . . . in which God is not the first & the last."[3]

In Edwards's mind ethics and morals could not be separated from divine activity in time since in these spheres the Deity constantly advances his historical work of redemption for fallen humanity. In accordance with his theistic metaphysics, he believed that God "will take care that the world of mankind will be regulated with respect to its moral state & so will maintain a good MORAL GOVERNMENT over the world of mankind."[4] Hence, "it is chiefly by the exercise of moral government that God dis-

---

[1] Edwards, *The Nature of True Virtue*, in *EW*, pp. 550–51.
[2] Edwards, *Miscellany* no. 864 (c. 1740).
[3] Edwards, *Miscellany* no. 1208.
[4] Edwards, *Miscellany* no. 864, (c. 1740).

plays his moral perfections which are in a peculiar manner the glory of the divine nature."[5] Thus, as was the case previously in the realm of nature and history, Edwards strove to assert God's "absolute and universal dominion"[6] in the sphere of ethics and to show that the Deity is the true foundation of all morals.

God's moral government is inextricable from the issue of time and history in Edwards's thought since it leads fallen humanity to progress from alienation to reconciliation with God. The personal state is closely associated with saving grace, and thus with the time dimension of salvation history, or God's work of redemption.

> at the end of the world all mankind together shall stand before the judgment seat of the supream universal Lawgiver & Judge to be judged by him or to have all things visibly set to rights, & justice made visibly to take place with respect to all the persons actions & affairs in the moral world by the supream infinitely wise & holy & just head of it.[7]

As with conversion, where the spiritual experience of saving grace signifies God's indwelling in time, so in the realm of morals and ethics the Deity works toward rescuing corrupted humanity from its "native depravity." Here lies the connection in Edwards's moral thought between saving grace and the nature of true virtue; virtue mediates between the moral welfare of the individual and the eschatological future of salvation. Since morality is inseparable from the grand teleology of order inherent in creation, God advances the work of redemption in the realm of ethics as well as in conversion and history as a whole.

Edwards's ethical writings cannot be considered outside his state of exile and displacement in Stockbridge in 1751 after his dismissal from Northampton. After the decline of the Great Awakening, and as a direct consequence of his zealous preaching on the nature of true faith and conversion, Edwards faced a gloomy situation in his church. "A great difficulty has arisen between me and my people, relating to qualifications for communion at the Lord's table," he sadly noted in a letter to a friend in 1749.[8] His announcement that he intended to discontinue his grandfather's practice of admitting to communion those in good standing unless they could provide evidence of a work of grace in their lives provoked an open rupture. Edwards knew very well that the outcome of this controversy "will issue in separation between me and my people."[9] Following

---

[5] Edwards, *Miscellany* no. 1127 (c. 1750).
[6] Edwards, *Concerning the End for which God Created the World*, p. 424.
[7] Edwards, *Miscellany* no. 1007 (c. 1742).
[8] Edwards, "To the Reverend John Erskine," May 20, 1749, in *LPW*, p. 271.
[9] Ibid.

the Awakening, his new ideas regarding the nature of true religion and the centrality of conversion experience were not acceptable in his church and led to banishment from his beloved town. Exile was now his portion. Yet, as he learned, despite the gloomy prospects of a hard life in the frontier settlement, exile had its own merits and advantages.

Exile is an important theme in Western culture, and of course in the history of Christianity. St. John, the author of the book of Revelation, wrote his prophetic eschatological narrative after being exiled to Patmos. His book, announcing the coming of the kingdom of God, the millennium, and the New Jerusalem, exercised an enormous influence on the Christian sense of time and history for over two millennia. The Marian exiles, a group of English Protestants who escaped to continental Europe during the reign of Queen Mary (1553–58), promulgated the idea that England was God's elect nation, providing an important source of English patriotism.

The same can be said about Edwards. He wrote some of his best-known works in Stockbridge, attempting to provide an apology for Christian belief concerning ethics and morals in a world turning away from traditional Christian thought. Thus, from exile he launched his attack on the Enlightenment moral philosophers who excluded theistic considerations from ethics and morals. Exile was the place to engage seriously and systematically with the Enlightenment debate on moral philosophy. Life in the small settlement on the frontier and preaching to the Indians did not demand as much work and obligations as the many ecclesiastical duties he had performed in Northampton. Exile thus afforded time, leisure, and a quiet place where he might grapple with pressing ideological and theological issues that had been long on his mind. As can be seen in the Stockbridge writings, he devoted more and more time and energy to ethical and moral issues, attempting to hold the tide against the Enlightenment project in the realm of ethics and morals. More specifically, he wished to refute the rejection of "our modern freethinkers"[10] regarding Christian belief in God's justice "in the eternal damnation of sinners."[11]

Already in *Charity and Its Fruits; Or, Christian Love as Manifested in Heart and Life* (1738), Edwards attempted to deal with the Christian moral life against the Enlightenment's concept of moral theory, asserting that only from "love to God springs love to man"; hence, without "love to God there can be no true honor," or virtue.[12] Later, during the 1740s, as can be seen in the many *Miscellanies* written during that period, he began to explore seriously the issue of "God's Moral Government of the

[10] Edwards, "To the Reverend John Erskine," July 7, 1752, in *LPW*, p. 491.
[11] Edwards, *Concerning the End for which God Created the World*, p. 536.
[12] Edwards, *Charity and Its Fruits*, pp. 137, 142.

world." As had been in his endeavors in the realms of nature and history, so now in the sphere of ethics he declared that "God wont leave the world of mankind to themselves without taking any care to govern & order their state"; or more specifically, God "will take care that the world of mankind will be regulated with respect to its moral state & so will maintain a good MORAL GOVERNMENT over the world of mankind." The Deity is not "an indifferent spectatour" to human affairs; therefore, God "must maintain a moral government over mankind."[13] The full systematic discussion and elaboration of these issues was left to the 1750s.

But it was in exile during the 1750s that Edwards embarked on a new ambitious project: providing the public with major treatises aiming to reassert Christian teaching regarding God's moral government. "I hope now," he wrote in 1752, shortly after settling in Stockbridge,

> in a short time to be at leisure to resume my design of writing something on the Arminian controversy . . . [but] first to write something upon . . . free will and moral agency . . . strictly examining the modern notions of those things . . . [and] endeavoring also to bring the late, great objections and outcries against the Calvinist divinity from these topics, to the test of the strictest reasoning.[14]

Here Edwards outlined in general the major works he would be engaged in writing during his exile: *Freedom of the Will*, *The Nature of True Virtue*, and *Original Sin*. In these treatises, more specifically, he rejected "that notion of virtue maintained by My Lord Shaftesbury, [Francis] Hutcheson, and [George] Turnbull; which seems to be most in vogue at this day," and according to which "all mankind are naturally disposed to virtue, and are without any native depravity."[15] During the 1750s Edwards therefore transformed his abode in the frontier settlement into a kind of laboratory where he developed his ideas on the true nature of ethics and morals, thus providing an apology for the relevance of Christian ethical teaching in a world tending more and more to exclude theistic considerations not only from nature and history, but also from ethics and morals. The unhappy personal state of exile thus did not hinder him from deepening his involvement and dialogue with the ideological and theological controversies of his time surrounding the true source and foundation of ethics and morals, the Enlightenment debate on moral philosophy.

Edwards's ethical writings of the 1750 brought to a conclusion his lifelong attempt to construct the whole world around him in accordance with his religious persuasions. Four decades after the young man had begun in earnest and great enthusiasm to redefine the world around him in space

---

[13] Edwards, *Miscellany* no. 864 (c. 1740).
[14] Edwards, "To The Reverend John Erskine," July 7, 1752, p. 491.
[15] Edwards, "To the Reverend Thomas Foxcroft," February 11, 1757, in *LPW*, p. 696.

and time, nature and history, according to the new religious self he had acquired during his conversion moment, now in exile in a frontier settlement and in the final decade of his life, Edwards dedicated his thought and energy to the issue of ethics and morals in an attempt to refute the claim made by "modern writers" that "the Calvinistic notions of God's moral government are contrary to the common sense of mankind."[16]

The Enlightenment Disenchantment of the World of Ethics and Morals

During the early eighteenth century, theories of morals appeared which stood in contrast to traditional Christian teaching. Enlightenment writers such as the Scottish philosopher Francis Hutcheson and the philosopher and historian David Hume argued that it is possible to have knowledge of good and evil without, and prior to, knowledge of God. The main assumption behind this conception of ethics was the belief that human beings can know from within themselves, without reliance on traditional sources of religious authority, what God intends and expects of them as moral creatures. Edwards owned and read many works of Enlightenment moral theorists,[17] such as Hutcheson's *An Inquiry into the Original of Our Ideas of Beauty and Virtue* (1725) and *An Essay on the Nature and Conduct of the Passions and Affections with Illustration on the Moral Sense* (1728),[18] and Hume's *An Enquiry Concerning Human Understanding* (1748), *A Treatise on Human Nature* (1739), and *Enquiry Concerning the Principles of Morals* (1751). In these works he could see that the new theories of morals were leading to the detachment of the moral system from God. "I am glad," Edwards wrote in regard to Hume's works on moral philosophy, to have the opportunity "to read such corrupt books; especially when written by men of considerable genius; that I may have an idea of the notions that prevail in our nation."[19] Accordingly, in his ethical writings, such as *Charity and Its Fruits* (1738), and more im-

[16] Edwards, "To The Reverend John Erskine," July 7, 1752, p. 491.
[17] Edwards read many works by British moral philosophers, including, more specifically, Hutcheson and Hume. See "Jonathan Edwards' Reading 'Catalogue' with Notes and Index," ed. L. Brian Sullivan, Works of Jonathan Edwards Office, Yale Divinity School, New Haven, Conn.; Fiering, *Jonathan Edwards's Moral Thought and Its British Context*; and Paul Ramsey, "Appendix II: Jonathan Edwards on Moral Sense, and the Sentimentalists," in *EW*, pp. 689–705.
[18] See Francis Hutcheson, *An Inquiry Concerning Beauty, Order, Harmony, Design*, ed. Peter Kivy (The Hague: Martin Nijhoff, 1973); *Francis Hutcheson: Philosophical Writings*, ed. R. S. Donwie (London: J. M. Dent, 1994); and *Francis Hutcheson: On Human Nature*, ed. Thomas Mautner (Cambridge: Cambridge University Press, 1995).
[19] Edwards, "To the Reverend John Erskine," December 11, 1755, in *LPW*, p. 679.

portant in *Concerning the End for which God Created the World* (1755), *The Nature of True Virtue* (1755), and *Original Sin* (1758), Edwards attacked the Enlightenment view of ethics and morals, claiming it is "evident that true virtue must chiefly consist in love to God,"[20] or that "all true *virtue*" is based on "love of Being, and the qualities and acts which arise from it."[21]

Edwards's long involvement with ethics and morals may be understood in the wider ideological context of early modern history and the Enlightenment project, or its new science of morals. The first half of the eighteenth century witnessed a growing and continuous attempt on the part of moderate, or rational, Enlightenment British thinkers to establish new concepts of moral theory.[22] Chief among these is the theory of a "moral sense," the *sensus communis* of classical thought, hence the name "British school of moral sense." In claiming that the moral sense is the faculty by which we distinguish between moral right and wrong, the theory formulates a distinctive conception of moral judgment. The name "*moral sense*," wrote one of its main proponents, Francis Hutcheson, signifies "an *internal sense*," or "that determination to [approve] affections, actions, or characters of rational agent, which we call *virtuous*."[23] God, he continues, "the author of nature," furnished us with the moral sense, or "strong affections to be the spring of each virtuous action, and made virtue a lovely form, that we might easily distinguish it from contrary, and be made happy by the pursuit of it."[24] In this sense, the Deity "has given us a *moral sense*" to guide our actions and conduct.[25] Since this faculty is exercised through feelings or sentiments, it counts as a sense. The moral sense is "superior sense, natural . . . to men . . . determining them to be pleased with actions, characters, affections."[26] Our observation of an instance of virtuous action, then, occasions a feeling of pleasure or satisfaction, which enables us to distinguish that action as virtuous. Conversely, our observation of an instance of vicious action occasions a

---

[20] Edwards, *Concerning the End for which God Created the World*, p. 550.

[21] Edwards, *The Nature of True Virtue*, p. 548.

[22] Henry F. May divided the Enlightenment in Europe into four categories, the first of which is the Moderate, or Rational, Enlightenment, which preached "balance, order and religious compromise, and was dominant in England from the time of Newton and Locke until about the middle of the eighteenth century." See May, *The Enlightenment in America*, p. xvi. The theory of moral sense was developed by people who belonged to the Moderate, or Rational, Enlightenment.

[23] Hutcheson, *An Inquiry Concerning Beauty, Order, Harmony, Design* (1725), ed. Peter Kivy, pp. 24–25.

[24] Ibid., p. 25.

[25] Hutcheson, *An Inquiry concerning the Original of our Ideas of Virtue or Moral Good*, in *Francis Hutcheson: Philosophical Writings*, ed. R. S. Donwie, p. 75.

[26] Hutcheson, *An Inquiry Concerning Beauty, Order, Harmony, Design*, p. 26.

feeling of pain or uneasiness, which enables us to distinguish that action as vicious.

The moral sense theory arose within a larger intellectual development in the early modern period. Locke's *Essay Concerning Human Understanding* (1689) led to a new theory of knowledge that rejected external authority as the guarantor of truths. The new scientific ideas paved the way for the belief that speculations about the will of God were no longer prerequisites for doing physics. Likewise, the moralizing tendency in British thought of the eighteenth century can be attributed in part to the decline of theology and the reduced authority of religious sanctions. With the increasing insufficiency of theological ethics, where sanctions were the chief interest, moral philosophers attempted to find a substitute for religion as the basis of society and human conduct, thus emancipating ethics from the theological tradition of their time. By the first half of the eighteenth century two schools existed among British moral philosophers: the intellectual, represented by Ralph Cudworth and Samuel Clarke, and the sentimental. Unmetaphysical in character, both systems rejected the legislative theory of God's relation to moral law, argued for the independence of morality from God, and emphasized that God's mere will does not constitute the distinction between right and wrong. But while the intellectualists stressed reason as the faculty that perceives moral distinctions, the sensationalists argued for the faculty of feeling. Virtue was understood as real and natural. Although both schools claimed that virtue is natural, for the intellectual school virtue is natural because it conforms to the intelligible nature and essence of the things of the world, and can be discerned primarily by reason; for the sentimental school, on the other hand, virtue is natural because it conforms to the human condition, reveals uncorrupted human nature, and should be perceived by feeling. In this wider context, where God's relationship to the world underwent a radical transformation, the possibility emerged of accounting for morality without an appeal to a divine authority. In line with the new epistemological theory, the most promising direction for the search for a moral basis appeared to be in human nature itself.

The theory of moral sense was first developed by Francis Hutcheson, in his *Inquiry into the Original of Our Ideas of Beauty and Virtue* (1725), and was followed with some modification by David Hume. By the word "sense" they meant feeling: the moral sense is the capacity to experience feelings of approval and disapproval, and as such it stands against the view that moral distinctions are perceived by reason. In other words, the theory of a moral sense is to be understood within the context of an empiricist epistemology and in opposition to rational theories of ethics.

The term "moral sense" was first suggested by Anthony Ashley Cooper, third Earl of Shaftesbury, in *An Inquiry Concerning Virtue* (1699) and in

Characteristics of Men, Manners, Opinions, Times (1711). In these works he appeals to psychological experience as a foundation for morals. He thus attributes to a moral sense our ability "*to be capable of* Virtue, and *to have a Sense of* Right *and* Wrong,"[27] or to distinguish between good and evil, virtue and vice, claiming that this sense, along with our common affection for virtue, accounts for the possibility of morality. In contrast to Hobbes, who offers a radically egoistic view of human nature, Shaftesbury argues that we have social impulses that are expressed in our sense of benevolence, beauty, and justice, and these are not reducible to self-interest. He held that "morality must be deduced from the nature of man as it is," and that "the human system or constitution is a complex compound of natural affection and a self-conscious faculty of reason and reflection, in which moral judgment and action have their origin."[28] Shaftesbury thus developed a system of non-intellectualist ethics based on the contention that there is "a form of moral appreciation and judgement that is affectional and sensory in its nature rather than intellectual."[29] Yet it was Francis Hutcheson, Shaftesbury's principal follower, a professor of moral theology at Glasgow, who constructed an explicit theory of a moral sense, or a new moral philosophy.

Hutcheson's primary aim was to refute the egoistic interpretation of ethics, recently revived by Bernard Mandeville in *The Fable of the Bees; Or Private Vices, Public Benefits* (1705–29), where Shaftesbury's claim concerning the innate goodness of human beings is rejected. In defending the ancient view of man as an essentially social being, Hutcheson attacked "the notorious self-love theorists old and new, Epicurus, Hobbes, and Mandeville."[30] His first move was to fit the moral sense into Locke's theory of knowledge, arguing that its proponents account for our knowledge of moral right and wrong as Lockean reflexive perception. Second, to refute Mandeville's interpretation of ethics as cynical egoism, Hutcheson claims that human beings have disinterested motives, namely, they can act for the good of others and not merely for their own advantage: since "no love to rational Agents can proceed from Self Interest, every action must be disinterested, as far as it flows from Love to rational Agents."[31]

---

[27] Shaftesbury [Anthony Ashley Cooper], *An Inquiry Concerning Virtue or Merit* (1699), in L. A. Selby-Bigge, ed. *British Moralists: Selection from Writers Principally of the Eighteenth Century*, 2 vols. (Oxford: Clarendon, 1897), I, pp. 23, 33.

[28] Rivers, *Reason, Grace, and Sentiment*, II, p. 154.

[29] Norman Fiering, *Moral Philosophy at Seventeenth-Century Harvard* (Chapel Hill: University of North Carolina Press, 1981), p. 180.

[30] Rivers, *Reason, Grace, and Sentiment*, p. 159.

[31] Hutcheson, *An Inquiry Concerning the Original of Our Ideas of Virtue or Moral Good*, 2nd ed., 1726, in L. A. Selby-Bigge, ed., *British Moralists: Selection from Writers Principally of the Eighteenth Century*, I, p. 87.

This disinterested motive, which he terms "Benevolence, or Love"—the quality of being concerned about others for their own sake—constitutes "the universal Foundation" of the "Moral Sense."[32] Here lies the innate, God-given moral sense in human beings. Being divinely implanted at all times and places, this sense is universal and constitutes the natural (that is, God-given) goodness of mankind. The "Author of Nature," he thus declares, "has given us a Moral Sense, to direct our Actions, and to give us still nobler Pleasure."[33] Accordingly, the "frame of our nature" endows us with moral sense "by which we perceive virtue or vice, in ourselves or others,"[34] and this sense is the source of moral obligation. Hutcheson asserts the existence of several "internal" senses, among them honor, sympathy, morality, and beauty, but discusses only the latter two at length.

This moral theory, which internalizes morality by claiming that virtuous behavior stemmed from inner impulses, is thus primarily concerned with qualities in persons, that is to say "virtue, which [Hutcheson] considered to be natural to man."[35] Virtue for him is the motive of benevolence approved by the moral sense, and vice is a motive that overcomes benevolence and is accordingly disapproved of by the moral sense. Since "Men have, by Nature, a moral Sense of Goodness in Action, . . . they are capable of disinterested Love" or benevolence.[36] Hutcheson's theory of moral sense constitutes the first explicit statement of utilitarian ethics: benevolence aims at the happiness of others; a wide benevolence is more to be approved than a narrow one, and a universal benevolence most of all. He thus developed the idea of a moral sense cognitivism, or the idea that "man is naturally supplied with a special moral sense." In such moral theory, then, "morals, in the sense of both sentiments and ideas, come naturally to man."[37]

The same endeavor to ground morality exclusively in the benevolence of human nature appears in Hume's moral philosophy. For him, as with Hutcheson, morality is an entirely human affair based on human nature and not on a divine will. Yet there are considerable differences between them. The English and Scottish moralists who belonged to the Shaftes-

[32] Hutcheson, *An Inquiry Concerning the Original of Our Ideas of Virtue or Moral Good*, pp. 99, 118.

[33] Ibid., p. 83.

[34] Hutcheson, *Essay on the Passions*, revised ed. (London, 1742), in Hutcheson, *Four Early Works on Motivation*, edited with an introduction by Paul McReynolds (Gainesville, Fla.: Scholars' Facsimiles & Reprints 1969), pp. 4–5.

[35] Haakonssen, *Natural Law and Moral Philosophy*, p. 66.

[36] Hutcheson, *An Inquiry Concerning the Original of Our Ideas of Virtue or Moral Good*, p. 134.

[37] Haakonssen, *Natural Law and Moral Philosophy*, p. 66.

burian tradition believed that although morality may be deduced from human nature, it is God who constituted that nature and hence the moral faculty is a divine implementation. Hutcheson's moral sense, for instance, depended on the existence of a superior being. However, while Hume agreed that "Mr. Hutcheson has taught us, by the most convincing arguments, that morality is nothing in the abstract nature of things, but is entirely relative to the sentiment of mental taste of each particular being,"[38] he himself "was the only eighteenth-century moralist" who argued for "an experimental theory of morals based solely on experience and observation of human behavior, society, and history, divorced from any attempt at religious explanation."[39] Believing that ethics and religion were separate subjects of inquiry, he attempted to provide an analysis of moral principles without connection to religion. Thus, while Hume saw himself as Hutcheson's follower in the ethics of sentiment, he did not adhere to Hutcheson's belief that moral sense depended on the existence of a superior being, or God. Instead, he defined "virtue as personal merit, or what is useful and agreeable to ourselves and to others."[40] Despite these differences, Hume, like Hutcheson, emphasized that the source of morals is feeling, not reason. Given that "the non-rational, innate source of moral [is] in sentiment," he claimed that moral "distinctions have their origins" in "impressions."[41] "Morality," he thus believed, "is more properly felt than judg'd," hence "to have the sense of virtue, is nothing but to *feel* a satisfaction of a particular kind from the contemplation of a character."[42] And again, "No action can be requir'd of us as our duty, unless there be implanted in human nature some actuating passion or motive, capable of producing the action."[43]

Like Hutcheson, who exerted a strong influence on him, Hume developed a theory of moral sense inherent in human nature. In *An Enquiry Concerning the Principles of Morals*, he indeed uses the word "sentiment," or "moral sentiment,"[44] more commonly than "sense," but the meaning is the same. For him "the general foundation of MORALS" is

[38] Hume, *Philosophical Essays Concerning Human Understanding* (1748), as quoted in Mautner, ed. *Francis Hutcheson: On Human Nature*, p. 152.

[39] Rivers, *Reason, Grace, and Sentiment*, II, p. 282.

[40] Ibid., p. 288.

[41] Ibid., pp. 290–91.

[42] David Hume, *A Treatise of Human Nature*, ed. L. A. Selby-Bigge (Oxford: Clarendon, 1928), pp. 470–71.

[43] Ibid., p. 518.

[44] David Hume, *An Enquiry Concerning the Principles of Morals* (1751), in *David Hume: Essays Moral, Political, and Literary*, ed. T. H. Green, 2 vols. (London: Longmans, 1882), II, p. 251.

derived from "SENTIMENT," or "by an immediate feeling and finer internal sense," and hence is based on "the particular fabric and constitution of the human species."[45] At the source of ethics, then, stands the "sentiment of benevolence"; this "sentiment can be no other than a feeling for the happiness of mankind, and a resentment for their misery."[46] Accordingly, Hume continues, "morality is determined by sentiment." From this he defines "virtue to be whatever mental action or quality gives to a spectator the pleasant sentiment of approbation; and vice the contrary."[47] As a species we possess a disposition—a moral sense, or sentiment—to feel approbation and disapprobation in response to the actions of others.

This Enlightenment debate on moral philosophy, especially its theory of innate moral sense, had serious implications for Christian ethics. When Hutcheson expressed his views in public, the Presbytery of Glasgow condemned him for expressing dangerous ideas opposed to Christian teaching, namely, that the standard of moral goodness is the promotion of the happiness of others, and that a knowledge of good and evil does not depend on a knowledge of God. Indeed, the "guiding assumption behind" the new moral theory "was the belief that God's intentions for man, His expectations of human beings as moral creatures, could be discovered independently of the traditional sources of religious authority, through a close investigation of human nature."[48] From the point of view of traditional Christian ethics, therefore, Hutcheson first denied that "post-lapsarian is inherently sinful and that all apparent morality can be reduced to a more or less complicated function of this sinfulness." Second, he denied that "man's moral institutions can be understood to arise from the prescriptions of an avenging God, whom his creatures follow in terror and hope."[49] Instead, his philosophy was based on a deep confidence in human nature. An even more serious challenge to orthodox Christianity was the absence of any theological foundations in Hume's moral philosophy, his refusal to search outside human nature for the origins of moral principles, and his tendency to follow the ancient classical moralists. "Hume made explicit his hostility to Christian ethics and allied himself with the classical moralists, especially Cicero."[50]

Hutcheson's and Hume's theory of moral sense thus gradually freed ethics from its traditional subservience to theology: "The *emancipation of ethics* at the beginnings of the modern age went hand in hand with

---

[45] Ibid., p. 170.

[46] Ibid., pp. 179, 259.

[47] Ibid., p. 261.

[48] Fiering, *Jonathan Edwards's Moral Thought and Its British Context*, pp. 6–7.

[49] Haakonssen, *Natural Law and Moral Philosophy*, p. 66.

[50] Rivers, *Reason, Grace, and Sentiment*, II, p. 298.

optimism, progress, and undeniable advancement of life. The loss of religious tradition may be painful—yet the moral foundations were still preserved."[51] But not for Edwards. Arguing against the secular moralists, the sentimentalists, he said that moral sense is "merely a variety of natural conscience" and hence cannot be the source of ethics and morals. In fact, much of what was claimed for the moral sense "was reducible to self-love . . . rather than virtue." Hence, "one cannot attribute to the natural man the pure inclinations of heart that constitute true virtue."[52] The source of true virtue is necessarily founded, as we are about to see, upon "spiritual and divine sense."[53]

Edwards and the British School of Moral Sense

The New England theologian Edwards would not accept a theory of morals or virtue based exclusively on human nature and hence independent of God, who exercises "absolute and universal dominion" over the created order. The Deity determines that "the whole universe, including all creatures animate and inanimate, in all its actings, proceedings, revolutions, and entire series of events, should proceed from a regard and with a view to God, as the supreme and last end of all."[54] In reaction to the school of moral sense, Edwards intended "to reconstruct for religious authority a moral role that was not already expropriated by the new moral philosophy."[55] In his scientific writings, composed during the early 1720s, Edwards had denounced the detachment of grace from nature, striving for the reenchantment of the world in the hope of demonstrating the infinite power of God's sovereignty in both the "order of nature" and the "order of time."[56] Likewise, in his historical philosophy he reacted against attempts to exclude theistic considerations from history. Now in the realm of ethics, he argued that the will of God is the sole source of morality and virtue. Against Hutcheson and others, who developed the idea of disinterested benevolence as the exclusive criterion for moral judgment, Edwards assessed moral matters by their "worth in the sight of God," and claimed that without "love to God there can be no true

---

[51] Gerhard Ebeling, "Theology and the Evidentness of the Ethical," *Journal for Theology and the Church*, II, p. 102, as quoted by Fiering, *Moral Philosophy at Seventeenth-Century Harvard*, p. 301.

[52] Fiering, *Jonathan Edwards's Moral Thought and Its British Context*, pp. 136–38.

[53] Edwards, *The Nature of True Virtue*, p. 622.

[54] Edwards, *Concerning the End for which God Created the World*, p. 424.

[55] Fiering, *Moral Philosophy at Seventeenth-Century Harvard*, p. 301.

[56] Edwards, *Miscellany* no. 704, p. 314; Edwards, *Freedom of the Will*, p. 177.

honor,"[57] or, again, that "nothing is of the nature of true virtue, in which God is not the *first* and the *last.*"[58]

Edwards devoted much time and energy to the refutation of the moral sense theory. In 1738 he preached a series of sermons, posthumously published in 1852 under the title *Charity and Its Fruits; Or, Christian Love as Manifested in Heart and Life.* Being well acquainted with Hutcheson's writings,[59] he attempted to present in these sermons "a finely woven systematic treatise on the Christian moral life."[60] In opposition to attempts by Enlightenment writers to base ethics and morals on secular and naturalistic foundations, Edwards declared that the gracious affections stand above and beyond the natural affections of which all are capable, and true virtue stands above and beyond the disinterested benevolence that marks the ultimate achievement of natural man. During the 1750s, he devoted more energy to these issues.

In his own day Edwards's theological standing rested significantly on his *Freedom of the Will,* which is both a defense of Calvinism and an assertion of God's absolute sovereignty. He attacks the Arminians' and deists' "grand article concerning *the freedom of the will requisite to moral agency,*"[61] the belief that absolute self-determination of will is necessary for human liberty and moral virtue, or that "such a Freedom without necessity is necessary to morality."[62] If the Arminian view is correct, God's providential and redemptive economy is contingent on the unpredictable actions of moral agents. God is not really almighty because the doctrine of free will places human actions and their results beyond his control. Such a condition contradicts the doctrine of divine foreknowledge and the premise that God, as absolute governor of the universe, orders events according to his sovereign wisdom and will. Edwards argued that since "every event" in the physical as well as the moral world "must be ordered by God," the "liberty of moral agents does not consist in self-determining power." He aimed to demonstrate that "God's moral government over mankind, his treating them as moral agents . . . is not inconsistent with a determining disposal of all events." Human beings must do as they will, in accordance with their fallen nature, and they have liberty only in the sense that nothing prevents them from doing what they will in accordance with their nature. Because "nothing in the state or acts of the will of man is contingent" but "every event of this kind is necessary," God's

[57] Edwards, *Charity and Its Fruits,* 1738, in *EW,* pp. 63, 137, 142.

[58] Edwards, *The Nature of True Virtue,* p. 560.

[59] Paul Ramsey, "Jonathan Edwards on Moral Sense, and the Sentimentalists," in *EW,* p. 703.

[60] Paul Ramsey, introduction, in *EW,* p. 2.

[61] Edwards, *Freedom of the Will,* p. 163.

[62] Edwards, *Miscellany* no. 1234.

foreknowledge eliminates the possibility of contingency in the world, for contingency is the antithesis of God's unlimited prescience. Given that "the power of volition" belongs only to "the man or the soul," there is no such thing as "freedom of the will."[63] That freedom is incompatible with the individual's necessary willing of what he or she can will in accordance with a nature of self already determined. In the end, Edwards saw the whole spectrum of moral endeavor solely in terms of his notion of the visible saints, whose character was "already determined."[64]

Edwards rejected the belief in the liberty and freedom of the will because such a doctrine stipulated that human beings "have a liberty of contingence, and self determination of will," and, therefore, they and only they should "be blamed or praised for what they do." For him such a belief in self-determination was fatal to true Christian doctrine and stood in opposition to human nature. Hence he declared: "I think the notion of liberty, consisting in contingent self-determination of the will, as necessary to the morality of men's dispositions and actions, almost inconceivably pernicious." For him belief in the freedom of the will fosters independence from the Deity, thus rejecting God's moral government of the world. Hence these "schemes of morality and religion, which are a kind of infidel schemes, [are] entirely diverse from the virtue and religion of the Bible." The belief that freedom of the will is "the ground of all moral good and evil," he said, glorifies the creature rather than the Creator. It tends to "prevent any proper exercise of faith in God and Christ, in the affair of our salvation, as it tends to prevent all dependence upon them." According to such doctrine, he continues, whereby "our own holiness is from ourselves as its determining cause," it is clear that "man is not dependent on God; but God is rather dependent on man in this affair: for he only acts consequently, in acts in which he depends on what he sees we determine and do first." Against this Edwards reiterated his strong belief in God's absolute sovereignty in the realms of ethics and morals, declaring that the "nature of true faith implies a disposition to give all the glory of our salvation to God and Christ."[65] The glory of human beings has nothing to do with their salvation, for salvation may be obtained only through the acknowledgment of God in creation.

The same effort to assert God's sovereignty characterizes *Original Sin*. This work played a part in the larger debates between the Enlightenment belief in the innate goodness of human beings and the emphasis placed by the Reformation on human depravity. For example, following Hutche-

[63] Edwards, *Freedom of the Will*, pp. 163, 431–33.

[64] John E. Smith, *Jonathan Edwards: Puritan, Preacher, Philosopher* (Notre Dame: University of Notre Dame Press, 1992), p. 78.

[65] Edwards, "To the Reverend John Erskine," August 3, 1757, in *LPW*, pp. 719–23.

son's moral theory, the Scot George Turnbull (1698–1748) denounced the
idea of sheer evil in human beings. Believing that "there is no reason to
think, there is any such thing as pure disinterested malice in the most
vicious mankind," since all vices are but corruptions of high and noble
affections, he asserted that "Man" is made "for eternal progress in moral
perfection and happiness, proportionally to his care and diligence to improve it."[66] Against the Enlightenment notion of human beings as fundamentally rational and benevolent, Edwards provided "a *general defense*
of that great important doctrine" of original sin. This doctrine proclaims
both the depravity of the human heart and the imputation of Adam's first
sin to his posterity: all Adam's posterity are "exposed, and justly so, to
the sorrow of this life, to temporal death, and eternal ruin, unless saved
by grace." The corruption of humankind, however, cannot be accounted
for by considering the sin of each individual separately. It is essential to
the human condition based on "the *arbitrary* constitution of the Creator"
in creation.[67]

In *The Nature of True Virtue* (1755), Edwards responded more directly
to contemporary "controversies and variety of opinions" about "the nature of true virtue."[68] This work, as he acknowledged, was "principally
designed against that notion of virtue maintained by My Lord Shaftesbury, [Francis] Hutcheson, and [George] Turnbull," according to which
"all mankind are naturally disposed to virtue, and are without any native
depravity."[69] In response to these Enlightenment ideas of ethics and morals, he further elaborated his views on the nature of true virtue, while
continuing his attack against the moral sense theory. His purpose was to
define the disposition that distinguished the godly, claiming that true "virtue most essentially consists in benevolence to Being in general." True
virtue is a kind of beauty. In moral beings, virtuous beauty pertains to a
disposition of heart and exercise of will, namely, "that consent, propensity
and union of heart to Being in general," or God, "which is immediately
exercised in good will." Hence, true virtue in creatures appears in the
degree to which their love coincides with God's love of his creation and
agrees with the end that he intended for it. In this regard, a true system
of morals and ethics is inseparable from religion because the former is
grounded on the latter; religion is the true foundation and only source of
all virtue. And given that "true virtue must chiefly consist in love to God,
the Being of beings," continues Edwards, "he that has true virtue, consisting in benevolence to Being in general [or God], and in that compla-

[66] George Turnbull, *Principles of Moral Philosophy* (London, 1740), pp. 298, 272.
[67] Edwards, *Original Sin*, pp. 102, 395, 403.
[68] Edwards, *The Nature of True Virtue*, p. 539.
[69] Edwards, "To the Reverend Thomas Foxcroft," p. 696.

cence in virtue, or moral beauty, and benevolence to virtuous being, must necessarily have a supreme love to God, both of benevolence and complacence." Against Hutcheson's and Hume's disunion between morals and religion, Edwards claimed that virtue is by necessity grounded in God since the Deity "is the head of the universal system of existence."[70] Hence, for him regeneration was inextricable from true virtue, and vice versa. No wonder that orthodox Christians in England, who strove to emphasize the superiority of Christian ethics, considered Edwards's *The Nature of True Virtue* as "the most elaborate, acute, and rational account of this interesting subject."[71]

Clearly, Edwards was fully aware of the grave ramifications of the Enlightenment theories of ethics and morals for Christian belief. As he sadly noted in 1757, "I wish that at this day, when every evangelical doctrine is run down, and such bold attempts are made to drive all out of doors, the press mayn't labor only with performances that are leveled against Christ, and the religion he taught."[72] No wonder that he found great fault with "some writers on morality" who indeed "don't wholly exclude a regard to the *Deity* out of their schemes of morality, but yet mention it so slightly." He suspected, and with reason, that these moral philosophers "esteem" God "less important" in the realm of morals and "insist on benevolence to the *created system* in such a manner as would naturally lead one to suppose they look upon that as by far the most important and essential thing in their scheme." In contrast, he claimed that if "true virtue consists partly in a respect to God, then doubtless it consists *chiefly* in it," for the Deity should be "the supreme object of our benevolence." Hence, "unless we will be atheists, we must allow that true virtue does primarily and most essentially consist in a supreme love to God." Those who oppose this assertion deny that "God maintains a moral kingdom in the world." Morality, then, cannot be separated from God: "a virtuous love in *created* beings, *one to another*, is dependent on, and derived from love to *God*." Moreover, the foundation of morality cannot be separated from the theological teleology of order inherent in the universe: "they are good moral agents whose temper of mind or propensity of heart is agreeable to the *end* for which God made moral agents." And since the "last end for which God has made moral agents must be the last end for which God has made all things: it being evident that the moral world is the end of the rest of the world; the inanimate and unintelligent world being made for the rational and moral world."[73]

---

[70] Edwards, *The Nature of True Virtue*, pp. 539–51.
[71] Rivers, *Reason, Grace, and Sentiment*, II, p. 194.
[72] Edwards, "To the Reverend Thomas Foxcroft," p. 695.
[73] Edwards, *The Nature of True Virtue*, pp. 552–60.

Edwards's attack on the moral sense theory may be understood in this overall theological and teleological context. The new "*schemes* of religion or moral philosophy," he claimed, based on the notion of "benevolence to *mankind*, and other virtues depending on it," are "fundamentally and essentially defective" because they "have not a supreme regard to God, and love to him," which is "the *foundations* of all other virtues." More specifically, the reason why "Hutcheson and Hume" mistook private affections for true virtue is because of their tendency "to leave the Divine Being out of their system, and to neglect him in their consideration." In contrast to the view of moral sense as the source of morality, Edwards argued that only "spiritual and divine sense" is that faculty by which "those that are truly virtuous and holy perceived the excellency of true virtue." Attempting to reconcile the divine prescience with the contingency of human actions, he stressed the possibility of reconciling virtue with necessity in the fact that God is at once the type of all perfection, and is under a necessity to be perfect. Hence, given that the "spiritual and divine sense" is "agreeable to the necessary nature of things" of the world, and because it is "the representation and image of the moral perfection and excellency of the Divine Being," it is clear that "moral sense" is "inferior" to it. Thus, Edwards concluded, "nothing is of the nature of true virtue, in which God is not the *first* and the *last*."[74] He thus distinguished between the true virtue of regenerated saints, whose actions are motivated by their supreme love to Being in General, or God, and the counterfeit virtue of sinners, who love only themselves and the world. Whatever is done to promote the glory of God is virtuous.

[74] Ibid., pp. 603–4, 610, 620–24, 560.

Epilogue

Edwards and American Protestant Tradition

In this kingdom [England] those principles on which the power of
godliness chiefly depends are in great measure exploded, and Arianism and Socinianism and Arminianism and deism are the things
that prevail and carry almost all before them. And particularly, history gives no account of any age wherein there was so great an apostasy of those that had been brought up under the light of the gospel
to infidelity, never such a casting off the Christian religion and all revealed religion, never any age wherein was so much scoffing at and
ridiculing the Gospel of Christ.

(Edwards, *History of the Work of Redemption*)

MUCH HAS BEEN written on the adaptability and replication of English
norms of thought and behavior in American colonial societies, the strong
mimetic impulse found among colonial elites, and the Anglicization of
colonial America and the rise of Anglo-American commercialism and consumer society.[1] Less attention, however, has been given to colonial *opposition* to intellectual developments and ideological transformations taking
place in European centers of learning and scholarship during the eighteenth century. Yet voices of resistance to and rejection of British and
European modes of thought had been raised in colonial British America
before the time of the American Revolution (1763–89), and these reveal
the complexities involved in the development of the transatlantic intellectual world. Edwards's life of the mind reveals the dialectic implied in the
ideological and intellectual negotiation and exchange between periphery
and center.[2] His lifelong philosophical and theological controversies with

[1] See, for example, Timothy H. Breen, "An Empire of Goods: The Anglicization of Colo-
nial America, 1690–1776," *Journal of British Studies* 25 (1986): 467–99; David G. Allen,
*In English Ways: The Movement of Societies and the Transferal of English Local Law and
Custom to Massachusetts Bay in the Seventeenth Century* (Chapel Hill: University of North
Carolina Press, 1981); Neil McKendrick, John Brewer, and J. H. Plum, eds., *The Birth of
Consumer Society: The Commercialization of Eighteenth-Century England* (Bloomington:
Indiana University Press, 1982); Lambert, *"Pedlar in Divinity"*; and Stout, *The Divine Dra-
matist.*

[2] An analysis of the relationship between center and periphery in regard to England and
her colonies in America can be found in the following works by Jack P. Greene: *Peripheries
and Center: Constitutional Development in the Extended Polities of the British Empire*

contemporary scientific, historical, and moral strains of thought show that not only adaptation and replication but also opposition to European intellectual traditions played a part in the creation of the Atlantic world. Moreover, his rejection of scientific ideas, his theories of ethics and morals, and his shaping of historical thought in the early modern period had a lasting influence on the formation of Protestant culture in America.

Edwards's universe of thought provides a good illustration of the process of ideological communication across the Atlantic. The relationship between the New England theologian and the transatlantic Protestant world has traditionally been interpreted mainly in terms of Edwards's role in the Great Awakening.[3] Indeed, Edwards's impact on Protestant religious culture is widely acknowledged. The language of the eighteenth-century transatlantic revival was "the language of covenant, conversion and New Birth."[4] Edwards contributed a great deal to it in terms of both form and content in his many writings pertaining to the revival. The role of "printed sermons, theological discussions, and polemic essays, particularly those written by or about Jonathan Edwards, or George Whitefield," was "highly significant in the creation" of the eighteenth century transatlantic evangelical movement.[5] Less attention, however, has been given to Edwards's interpretation of natural philosophy, history, and ethics in the wider context of early modern history and the transatlantic Protestant reaction to the emergence of new modes of thought during the scientific revolution and the Enlightenment. Edwards's works and their impact on many circles in the Protestant evangelical awakening should be examined in this context of early modern intellectual history.

Edwards was a leader in the Protestant evangelical awakening. Evidence can be found in the enthusiastic reception of his writings and their impact on many theologians in Europe. During the revivals of the 1730s and 1740s, Edwards not only rapidly emerged as a leader in New England but his various writings pertaining to the revivals were soon printed in Europe. An English edition of his *A Faithful Narrative of the Surprising*

---

and the United States, 1607–1788 (Athens: University of Georgia Press, 1986), *Imperative Behaviors & Identities: Essays in Early American Cultural History* (Charlottesville: University Press of Virginia, 1992), *Pursuit of Happiness: The Social Development of Early Modern British Colonies and the Formation of American Culture* (Chapel Hill: University of North Carolina Press, 1988), and "The Uneasy Connection," in *Essays on the American Revolution*, ed. Stephen Kurtz and James Hutson (Chapel Hill: University of North Carolina Press, 1973), pp. 32–80.

[3] See, for example, Crawford, *Seasons of Grace.*

[4] Susan O'Brien, "Eighteenth-Century Publishing Networks in the First Years of Transatlantic Evangelicalism," in *Evangelicalism: Comparative Studies of Popular Protestantism in North America, the British Isles, and Beyond, 1700–1990*, ed. Mark A. Noll, et al., p. 42.

[5] Ibid., p. 41.

Work of God (1737) appeared in London in 1737 and was soon reprinted in Edinburgh in 1737 and 1738. Its influence was felt also in the Welsh revival. A Scottish edition of *The Distinguishing Marks of the Work of the Spirit of God* (1741) appeared in 1743, and the sermon *Sinners in the Hands of an Angry God*, delivered on July 1741, was circulated in Glasgow in 1742. A Scottish edition of this sermon was published in 1745.[6] In England Wesley eagerly read the *Faithful Narrative* in October 1738, and this work as well as other writings, such as *Distinguishing Marks* and *A Treatise Concerning Religious Affections* (1746), exercised an enormous influence on the English Methodist movement, the "Wesleyan Revival."[7] Likewise, Edwards's *The Nature of True Virtue* (written in 1755, published in 1765) was regarded by orthodox Christians in England who opposed Enlightenment theories of morals and strove to emphasize the superiority of Christian ethics as "the most elaborate, acute, and rational account of this interesting subject."[8] Edwards's *A Faithful Narrative* appeared in 1738 in German, as did his *Life of David Brainerd* (1749). Apparently, "the relevance of Edwards's kingdom of God was more sharply perceived in Eastern Europe than in his own congregation."[9] Finally, Edwards's interpretation of salvation history, the *History of the Work of Redemption*, greatly influenced transatlantic evangelicalism: "Assessments of the significance of the revivals subsequent to the Great Awakening would ensconce in American and British evangelical culture Edwards's vision of the pivotal role of revivals in God's grand scheme for mankind."[10]

Thus, although he lived on the periphery of the eighteenth-century British empire, Edwards's thought and actions were an integral part of the transatlantic "republic of letters" and Protestant world. The Great Awakening, in which he enlisted all his power and zeal, was inextricable, as he always maintained, from the long series of revivals and awakenings in the Old and the New Worlds, constituting an important dimension of the transatlantic evangelical movement. Edwards was of course fully aware of the

[6] Crawford, *Seasons of Grace*, pp. 227, 99, 104, 161, 149; Lesser, introduction, in *SDL*, p. 3.

[7] Albert C. Outler, ed., *John Wesley* (New York: Oxford University Press, 1964), pp. 15–16. For the relationship between Edwards's and Wesley's interpretations of religious experience, see Taves, *Fits, Trances & Visions*, p. 50. The publication of Edwards's revival writings in England and Scotland, such as *Faithful Narrative*, *Distinguishing Marks*, and *Some Thoughts Concerning the Revival*, is discussed in Goen, introduction, in *GA*, pp. 1–90.

[8] Rivers, *Reason, Grace, and Sentiment*, vol. II: *Shaftesbury to Hume*, p. 194.

[9] Ward, *The Protestant Evangelical Awakening*, pp. 90–91, 275.

[10] Crawford, *Seasons of Grace*, p. 138. See also Conforti, *Jonathan Edwards, Religious Tradition & American Culture*, pp. 47–49.

international dimension and his role in it. Writing in 1745 to a friend in Scotland, he declared that the "Church of God, in all parts of the world, is but one; the distant members are closely united in one glorious head."[11]

It has been suggested that between the 1740s and 1770s England and her colonies were bound together in an "empire of goods," a phenomenon that reflected the long process of the Anglicization of colonial America.[12] Yet, along with this emphasis on "things," in recent years historians of religion have begun to explore the rich religious connections and correspondence between Britain and her colonies in America, which created the eighteenth-century "transatlantic community of saints."[13]

Viewed in this ideological and theological context, Edwards's thought shows clearly that the development of an American culture during the eighteenth century did not depend on a simple and linear transference of ideas from the core culture in Britain, nor on an easy accommodation of them in America; it was not, as Perry Miller puts it, simply a "movement of European culture into the vacant wilderness of America."[14] Rather, in some matters it was the rejection of certain well-established European intellectual traditions that helped the formation of a well-defined Protestant cultural space in America. Edwards's opposition to the Enlightenment concept of ethics and history is evidence not only of the growing readiness of people in the colonies to distance themselves from European intellectual traditions, but also of their growing confidence in their ability to forge new foundations for an American culture and identity. This process was to reach its height during the era of the American Revolution, when Americans rejected British authority. Yet its origins can be traced many years before the struggle for independence. When well before 1763 Edwards was convincing colonists to criticize certain modes of thought predominant in the British intellectual world and not to accept them automatically, the center had already begun to lose some of its power and attraction over the periphery. "We have our books, and our learning from" England, wrote Edwards, "and are upon many accounts exceedingly liable to be corrupted by them. This country is but a member of the body of which they are the head, and when the head is so sick, the mem-

---

[11] Edwards, "To a Correspondent in Scotland," November 1745, in *LPW*, p. 180.

[12] Breen, "An Empire of Goods," p. 471.

[13] Susan O'Brien, "A Transatlantic Community of Saints: The Great Awakening and the First Evangelical Network, 1735–1755," *American Historical Review* 91 (1986): 811–32, and "Eighteenth-Century Publishing Networks in the First Years of Transatlantic Evangelicalism," pp. 38–57; Crawford, *Seasons of Grace*; Noll et al., eds., *Evangelicalism*; Leigh E. Schmidt, *Holy Fairs: Scottish Communions and American Revivals in the Early Modern Period* (Princeton: Princeton University Press, 1989); Lambert, *"Pedlar in Divinity"*; and Stout, *The Divine Dramatist*.

[14] Miller, preface, in *Errand Into the Wilderness*, p. vii.

bers it is to be feared, will not long be in health."[15] Together with social, political, and economic changes in British America during the eighteenth century, a significant ideological process was also under way, whereby ideas coming out of the center in the Old World were met with strong opposition in the colonial periphery.

By denouncing modes of thought and belief that had developed at the heart of the British empire, Edwards asserted that the center was no longer a model to be emulated: "England, the principal kingdom of the Reformation," he observed, is overcome by "licentiousness in principles and opinions," such as "Arianism and Socinianism and Arminianism and deism." Nowhere in the world is there "so great apostasy of those that had been brought up under the light of the gospel to infidelity, never such a casting off the Christian religion and all revealed religion."[16]

Indeed, this New England divine and philosopher was "the most powerful enemy" of the "rational English Enlightenment."[17] His brilliance as a theologian and philosopher endowed Edwards's negative response to the new theories of ethics and history with an enormous influence on, for example, the first and second Great Awakenings. More specifically, his attack on the British school of moral sense was incorporated, adopted, and diffused by the New Divinity School, and in fact was its hallmark during the eighteenth and nineteenth centuries: "The advocacy" of Edwards's "theory of moral agency was undoubtedly the most important mark of the New Divinity"[18] and of Edwards's followers, such as Joseph Bellamy (1719–90), Samuel Hopkins (1721–1803), and Jonathan Edwards Jr. (1745–1801), who "sought to defend Calvinism from rationalist attack and to focus it upon experience of grace as the definitive religious event."[19] More specifically, the "innovations of the New Divinity reveal Edwards's most creative and important contributions to New England theology." In their continuation of Edwards's "intellectual efforts to balance piety and moralism,"[20] the New Divinity men were his most im-

---

[15] Edwards as cited in Perry Miller, "Jonathan Edwards's Sociology of the Great Awakening," *New England Quarterly* 21 (1948): 54–55.

[16] Edwards, *History of the Work of Redemption*, p. 438.

[17] Henry F. May, *The Enlightenment in America* (New York: Oxford University Press, 1976), pp. xii, 49.

[18] William Breitenbach, "The Consistent Calvinism of the New Divinity Movement," *William and Mary Quarterly* 41 (1984): 257.

[19] William K. B. Stoever, "The Calvinist Theological Tradition," in *Encyclopedia of the American Religious Experience*, ed. C. H. Lippy et al., 3 vols. (New York: Scribner, 1988), II, pp. 1047–48; James D. German, "The Social Utility of Wicked Self-Love: Calvinism, Capitalism, and Public Policy in Revolutionary New England," *Journal of American History* 82 (December 1995): 965–98.

[20] William Breitenbach, "Piety and Moralism: Edwards and the New Divinity," in *JEAE*, pp. 178, 195.

portant direct heirs, and part of the "most sustained, systematic, and creative intellectual tradition produced in this country—the New England theology."[21]

Likewise, Edwards's reaction to the new modes of historical thought that were bringing about the secularization of the Christian theological teleology of history by according human beings a decisive role in shaping the course of history led him to develop a singular evangelical historiography according to which revivals and awakenings, being the direct manifestation of the effusion of the Spirit of God, constitute the heart of the historical process. By placing revival at the center of salvation history, Edwards conditioned many generations of Protestants in America to see religious awakening as the essence of sacred, providential history. The publication of the *History of the Work of Redemption* in the 1770s, which is the best exposition of Edwards's philosophy of history, "helped to fuel the transference of religious convictions into the political realm," a transference that was important during the American Revolution and later crucial to the "revival of interest in eschatology" and the millennium "that occurred in the 1790s."[22] This book went through a "process of canonization during the Second Great Awakening, 1800–30, and added to [Edwards's] stature as the preeminent authority on revivalism." During the Second Great Awakening the work "proved to be popular both with lay readers and revivalistic preachers." Edwards's philosophy of history thus helped to create the revival tradition in America. "Indeed, the *History of the Work of Redemption* served to 'universalize' the revivals of the Second Great Awakening, situating them in a cosmic scheme of redemption and exciting interest in such evangelical causes as missionary work at home and abroad."[23]

Edwards was almost alone in the eighteenth century in rejecting the ideas of the universal moral sense and the essential goodness of the common man, or "the psychological optimism of the Shaftesbury-Hutcheson gospel of the innate goodness of man," which only "the two great wars of the twentieth century and the Holocaust have been able to shake into ruins."[24] In the English Enlightenment of the eighteenth century, Edwards's views, strongly opposed to the then dominant philosophy of Locke and Hume, in fact illustrate the expiring power of Calvinism. But in terms of the formation of American culture, his attack on the school of moral sense helped to create a well-defined American Protestant culture.

[21] Kuklick, "Jonathan Edwards and American Philosophy," in *JEAE*, p. 257.

[22] Wilson, introduction, in *HWR*, pp. 92–93. See also Bloch, *Visionary Republic*; and Weber, *Rhetoric and History in Revolutionary New England*.

[23] Conforti, *Jonathan Edwards, Religious Tradition & American Culture*, pp. 47–49.

[24] Fiering, *Jonathan Edwards's Moral Thought and Its British Context*, p. 148.

Timothy Dwight, president of Yale College, called Edwards "That moral Newton, and that second Paul," and Lyman Beecher declared that in his youth, he "had read Edwards's Sermons. There's nothing comes within a thousand miles of them now."[25] More specifically, Edwards's "theory of moral agency was undoubtedly the most important mark of the New Divinity."[26] Striving to ground religion exclusively in the experience of saving grace and to define that experience as the ultimate religious event, New England theologians closely followed Edwards in his defense of Calvinism against rationalist attacks by Enlightenment writers. Chief among them was Joseph Bellamy who, like Edwards, strove to see the "connection between regeneration and moral virtue." In the attempt to refute "the Enlightenment's attack on orthodoxy," Hutchesonian "ethics, rationalist morality, and natural religion turn up at every corner of Bellamy's arguments," where he denounces them, among others, as "epicurean and atheistical."[27]

At the end of the eighteenth century, over a hundred ministers in New England were preaching Edwards's version of Calvinism; "by 1790 self-proclaimed New Divinity pastors controlled New England churches in and west of the Connecticut River Valley" and "were scattered throughout Vermont and Maine and even New York and New Jersey." Jonathan Edwards Jr. was not far from the truth when he said in 1787 that "a majority of the ministers [in Connecticut] mean to embrace the system of my father and Dr. Bellamy."[28] Later, during the nineteenth century, the legacy of the New Divinity continued to be spread, among others, by Lyman Beecher (1775–1863), the father of Harriet Beecher Stowe and leader of the New England Second Great Awakening.[29]

By the middle of the eighteenth century, "both theological and economic developments transformed the implications of Calvinism for New Englend society."[30] Edwards's theology of morals and ethics and later his followers' great emphasis on the traditional values of Christian faith and belief did not hinder the rise of the spirit of capitalism in America. On the contrary, the theology of the New Divinity greatly facilitated the growth of the capitalist economy. One of the main reasons was that "Edwards and his followers paradoxically equated self-interest with human

[25] Henry F. May, "Jonathan Edwards and America," in *JEAE*, pp. 21–22.

[26] Breitenbach, "The Consistent Calvinism of the New Divinity Movement," p. 257.

[27] Mark Valeri, *Law & Providence in Joseph Bellamy's New England: The Origins of the New Divinity in Revolutionary America* (New York: Oxford University Press, 1994), pp. 48–49.

[28] Ibid., p. 4.

[29] See Mark A. Noll, "Jonathan Edwards and Nineteenth Century Theology," in *JEAE*, pp. 260–88.

[30] German, "The Social Utility of Wicked Self-Love," pp. 970–71.

depravity and identified self-interest as the source of most beneficial social, political, and economic behavior." Given that virtue involves self-
love, such a view indeed endorses self-interest. "Thus, the New Divinity
of Edwards and his followers taught New Englanders (and perhaps their
evangelical heirs to the present) that they needed both capitalism and
salvation."[31]

Edwards's influence on Protestant America was not confined to the
eighteenth and nineteenth centuries. His views about the corruption of
human nature and concomitantly about God as the true foundation of
virtue and morals were revived during the twentieth century by H. Richard Niebuhr, the influential theologian of the New Orthodoxy. In his attempt to understand contingent existence as the manifestation of divine
glory as sheer grace, and in order to proclaim *soli Deo gloria*, Niebuhr
"found Jonathan Edwards, more than any other precursor, to be his men-
tor."[32] Against Progressive-era scholars and critics such as Charles Beard
and Vernon L. Parrington, who argued during the first decades of the
twentieth century that Edwards "demeaned man in order to glorify God,"
Niebuhr claimed that Edwards's pessimistic view of human beings had
been confirmed in view of the "extent to which human brutality can go,
of the fury that can be unleashed when the human animal is attacked,"
and the "shuddering of man's inhumanity to man" during the horrors
of the twentieth century.[33] Modern history confirms Edwards's historical
prognosis: "Edwards' intense awareness of the precariousness of life's
poise, of the utter insecurity of men and of mankind which are at every
moment as ready to plunge into the abyss of disintegration, barbarism,
crime and the war of all against all, as to advance toward harmony and
integration."[34]

The same can be said about the legacy of Edwards's philosophy of history, or his evangelical historiography. In contrast to the Enlightenment
fashioning of secular, historical time and its growing emphasis on human
agency in determining history, Edwards claimed that earthly, mundane
events are intelligible only by reference to God's work of redemption. At

---

[31] Ibid.

[32] Hans W. Frei, "H. Richard Niebuhr," in *Theology and Narrative: Selected Essays*, ed.
George Hunsinger and William C. Placher (New York: Oxford University Press, 1993), p.
221.

[33] Niebuhr, "The Anachronism of Jonathan Edwards," pp. 481–82. This address was
originally delivered in Northampton, Mass., on March 9, 1958, to commemorate the bicentennial of the death of Jonathan Edwards. See also the various essays in *Edwards in Our
Time: Jonathan Edwards and the Shaping of American Religion*, ed. Sang Hyun Lee and
Allan C. Guelzo.

[34] Niebuhr, *The Kingdom of God in America*, pp. 137–8.

the heart of history, then, are revivals, whereby the Spirit of God constantly advances the work of redemption. These awakenings are the sole and exclusive domain of God's will and hence outside the reach of human agency. Edwards "made the phenomenon of the revival the key element in the drama of redemption. He conceived of revivals as the engine that drives redemption history."[35]

This philosophy of salvation exercised enormous influence in New England and Protestant America in general. Edwards, "who saw tantalizing signs of the approaching millennium in the Great Awakening," is considered "the putative father of American postmillennialism," or the belief that the coming of Jesus would occur only after the millennium.[36] During the early nineteenth century, one evangelist described Edwards's *History of the Work of Redemption* as "the most popular manual of Calvinist theology." One of the reasons for that assertion was that in his philosophy of history Edwards offered "an original contribution to evangelical historiography." Indeed, for antebellum evangelists Edwards's philosophy of salvation history provided the main source for understanding history as a "grand narrative propelled by a divine 'design and covenant of redemption.' " He emerged "as an authority not only on personal piety and individual conversion, but also on the 'morphology' of revivals and their millennial significance." In sum, as "the father of the great colonial revival," or the Great Awakening of the 1740s, "Edwards had laid the groundwork for the Second Great Awakening." His influence, according to one nineteenth-century evangelical, is evident in the fact that he persuaded "a generation that feared more than they knew about revivals of their utility and benefit."[37]

Likewise, Niebuhr argues that Edwards's philosophy of history influenced nineteenth-century evangelists' understanding of "the coming of the kingdom," leading them to believe that "the divine sovereignty was the fruition not only of divine goodness but of human badness in conflict with that unconquerable goodness."[38] Further, his theology of history, emphasizing that "effort to progress toward the coming of the kingdom by self-discipline" led not only to "the recognition of divine sovereignty" within the realm of history but "ushered in . . . a new awareness of the coming kingdom." Through his and others' efforts during the Awakening, "the coming of the kingdom" became "the dominant idea" in American Protestantism.[39] Niebuhr sees Edwards's theme of "God's redemption of

[35] Crawford, *Seasons of Grace*, p. 132.
[36] Moorhead, *World Without End*, pp. 5–6.
[37] Conforti, *Jonathan Edwards, Religious Tradition & American Culture*, pp. 48–49.
[38] Niebuhr, *The Kingdom of God in America*, p. 138.
[39] Ibid., pp. 135–38.

the world as at once the core of the Christian movement in America and the central meaning and significance of the culture."[40] In this context, the effect of Edwards's philosophy of salvation history "was to legitimate and foster popular expressions" of Protestant religious thought and experience, which encompassed "the Shakers as they developed Ann Lee's visions, Joseph Smith, Jr., and the Latter-day Saints, John Humphrey Noyes and his Perfectionists . . . and even the remarkable Mary Baker Eddy."[41]

In England Edwards might count as only one among the many Protestant evangelists in the first half of the eighteenth century who attempted to revitalize religious life and experience within a well-defined religious culture and tradition; in America, on the other hand, due to his brilliance as a theologian and philosopher and in the absence of a centralized religious establishment, he contributed much to forging the ideological foundations of a distinct Protestant culture in America. Yet, as I have attempted to show, the creation of such a religious tradition was not unrelated to the wider intellectual context of the early modern era. On the contrary, it was essentially a reaction to the Enlightenment's new science of ethics and history. Edwards's genius enabled him to forge, out of his criticism of the Enlightenment project, a novel tradition most adapted to the American mind. Its powerful influence on American culture and history has not diminished over time; its manifestations are still evident in many spheres of American life and thought at the turn of the second millennium.

Seeing Edwards's life of the mind and his influence on American Protestant culture in this broad perspective, it is no exaggeration to call him the "American Augustine." As the Doctor of the Church formulated out of his many controversies an interpretation of Christian thought and belief that exercised an enormous influence on the history of Christianity, so the New England theologian constructed out of his many struggles against various strains of early modern thought an interpretation that has had a lasting influence on Protestant life and culture in America. Following their conversion experience, both Augustine and Edwards took upon themselves, each in his own time and place and each in response to the theological and ideological problems he faced in his own time, the mission of defending the Christian faith against its adversaries and enemies within and without. Thus, they both dedicated their lives to a grand intellectual mission of constructing a defense of the Christian church. As a result, both were not only apologists of Christianity but philosophers of importance who undertook a whole reconstruction of the human condition in many spheres—in space and time, soul and ethics. They reserve for them-

---

[40] Wilson, introduction, in *HWR*, p. 95.
[41] Ibid., p. 94.

selves a prominent place in the history of philosophy and theology because of their ability to reconstruct Christian life and experience in the midst of historical transformations within the civilizations of their own time. As Augustine influenced the course of Christian thought and belief for many centuries, so Edwards in his own time contributed much to forging the ideological foundations of a distinct Protestant culture in America. In both cases, then, the self-imposed mission to respond to certain strains of thought led in the end to the creation of a corpus of works that provided a meaningful Christian world-picture in which later generations could find answers and solutions to the problems they were facing within a growing and changing world.

Index

Order of redemption, 215
Order of time, 17–18, 32, 37, 39, 132–
   133, 138–143, 146, 152, 174, 183–185,
   187, 191, 200, 202, 217, 247, 319. *See
   also* Time
Ordo naturae (Order of nature), 17, 32–
   33, 37, 57, 72–73, 85, 88, 90, 105–108,
   116, 119, 127, 133, 138–139, 319. *See
   also* Nature
Ordo salutis, 80

Paganism, 176
Pandora's Box, 264
Papacy, 261
Paradise, 71
Parrington, Vernon L., 332
Patmos, 310
Peirce, Charles S., 29
Pelagians, 15
Pentecost, 261
Persians, 11, 259
Pierpont, Rev. James, 37
Pierpont, Sarah, 37
Pietism, 41, 59, 120–127, 136
Pilgrimage, 25, 177
Pilgrims, 26, 56, 61
Pit of Hell, 280–289
Platonism, 113–119
Pope, Alexander, 121–122; "An Essay on
   Man," 122
Postmillennialism, 40, 333
Poverty of mechanical philosophy, 116–
   118
Princeton University. *See* College of New
   Jersey
Progress: Edwards's use of, 201–202, 233–
   234, 248, 250–256; Enlightenment con-
   cept of, 6, 196, 202, 224, 231–234, 318
Progressive Era, 332
Promised Land, 257
Prophecy, 95, 135, 168–169, 234–271
Protestant apocalyptic tradition, 19, 20,
   23, 161–163, 179, 235, 270, 274, 296,
   299
Protestant culture in America, 25, 325–333
Protestant Evangelical Awakening, 2–3, 38,
   41, 43, 120–127, 136–138, 162, 247–
   248, 325–327
Protestant historiography, 168–174, 179,
   188, 194, 254
Protestant Reformation, 58, 147, 154,
   168–172, 176, 178–179, 252, 256, 261–

262, 264, 267, 272, 278, 286, 289, 292–
   293, 301, 321, 329
Pufendorf, Samuel, 9; *An Introduction to
   the History of the Principal Kingdoms
   and States of Europe*, 8–9
Puritan apocalyptic tradition, 19, 161–
   163, 235, 270
Puritan historiography, 172–174, 180,
   222, 254
Puritan ideology of history, 168–174, 180,
   188, 194, 254
Puritanism, 88, 263
Puritan migration to America, 20, 162,
   173–174, 180, 254, 264; eschatology
   and apocalypse of, 162–163, 180, 254
Puritan morphology of conversion, 56, 62–
   63, 69–70
Puritan Revolution, 172–173, 267, 289,
   292–293

Quakers, 15, 268

Rapin-Thoyras, Paul de; *Historie d'Angleterre*, 8, 11, 142
Redeeming time, 150, 189, 198, 276, 287
Redemptive mode of historical thought, 1–
   24, 39, 55, 127, 132, 141–181, 239–247
Reenchantment: of the soul, 133–138; of
   the world, 17, 32, 37, 57, 85–127, 133–
   138, 140–191, 194, 232, 245
Renaissance, 143
Revelation, 72, 74, 93–95, 135–137, 142–
   144, 165, 168–169, 174, 218–220
Revelation, the Book of. See *Apocalypse*
Revival(s), 13, 18–19, 20–23, 38–40, 52,
   79–80, 122, 132, 136, 139, 152–163,
   174, 180–181, 184, 205, 217, 220, 247–
   271, 272–303, 308, 330, 333–334; and
   conversion, 78–80, 150–163, 205–210;
   as divine agency, 247–255; Edwards's defense of, 40–44; and effusion of the
   Spirit, 139, 152, 163, 247–271; in Europe, 20, 23, 41–42; millennial significance of, 40–44; in New England, 13,
   18–19, 20–23, 40–44, 205–210, 234–
   236, 245–255, 263–264, 272–303; and
   salvation history, 150–155, 157. *See also*
   Great Awakening; Little Revival; The Second Great Awakening
Revival tradition in America, 22, 40, 279
Revolution(s), 21, 56
Robespierre, Maximilien, 145, 147